T0360818

COLLAPSE III

First published in 2007 in an edition of 1000
comprising numbered copies 1–950
and 50 *hors-commerce* copies

Reissued Edition 2012

ISBN 978-0-9567750-5-4

Published by
Urbanomic Media Ltd.
The Old Lemonade Factory
Windsor Quarry
Falmouth
TR11 3EX
UK

Distributed by the MIT Press,
Cambridge, Massachusetts and London, England

All texts remain © of the respective authors.
Please address all queries to the editor at the above address.

www.urbanomic.com

COLLAPSE

Philosophical Research and Development

VOLUME III

Edited by

Robin Mackay

URBANOMIC

FALMOUTH

COLLAPSE III

November 2007

EDITOR: Robin Mackay

ASSOCIATE EDITOR: Dustin McWherter

Unless otherwise indicated, page references in this volume refer to the following English translations of the works of Gilles Deleuze:

– *Nietzsche and Philosophy*, trans. H. Tomlinson (London: Athlone, 1983).

– [with F. Guattari] *Anti-Oedipus - Capitalism and Schizophrenia*, trans. R. Hurley, M. Seem and H. R. Lane (Minneapolis: University of Minnesota Press, 1985).

– *Cinema 1: The Movement-Image*, trans. H. Tomlinson and B. Habberjam (London/NY: Continuum, 1986).

– *Spinoza: Practical Philosophy*, trans. R. Hurley (San Francisco: City Lights, 1988).

– [with F. Guattari] *A Thousand Plateaus*, trans. B. Massumi (London: Athlone, 1988).

– *Logic of Sense,* ed. C. Boundas, trans. M. Lester, C. Stivale (Columbia University Press, 1990).

– *Empiricism and Subjectivity: An Essay on Hume's Theory of Human Nature*, trans. C. V. Boundas (NY: Columbia University Press, 1991).

– *The Fold: Leibniz and the Baroque*, trans. T. Conley (London: Athlone, 1993).

– [with F. Guattari] *What is Philosophy?* trans. H. Tomlinson and G.Burchell (NY: Columbia University Press, 1994).

– *Negotiations* trans. M. Joughin (NY: Columbia University Press, 1995).

– *Essays Critical and Clinical* trans. D.W. Smith & M.A. Greco (NY/London: Verso, 1998)

– *Pure Immanence: Essays on A Life*. trans. A. Boyman (NY: Zone, 2001).

– [with C. Parnet] *Dialogues II*, trans. H. Tomlinson, B. Habberjam and E. R. Albert (London/NY: Continuum, 2002).

– *Desert Islands and Other Texts 1953-1975*, ed. D. Lapoujade, trans. M. Taormina (NY: Semiotext(e), 2004).

– *Two Regimes of Madness: Texts and Interviews 1975-1995*, ed. D. Lapoujade, trans. A. Hodges and M. Taormina (NY: Semiotext(e), 2006).

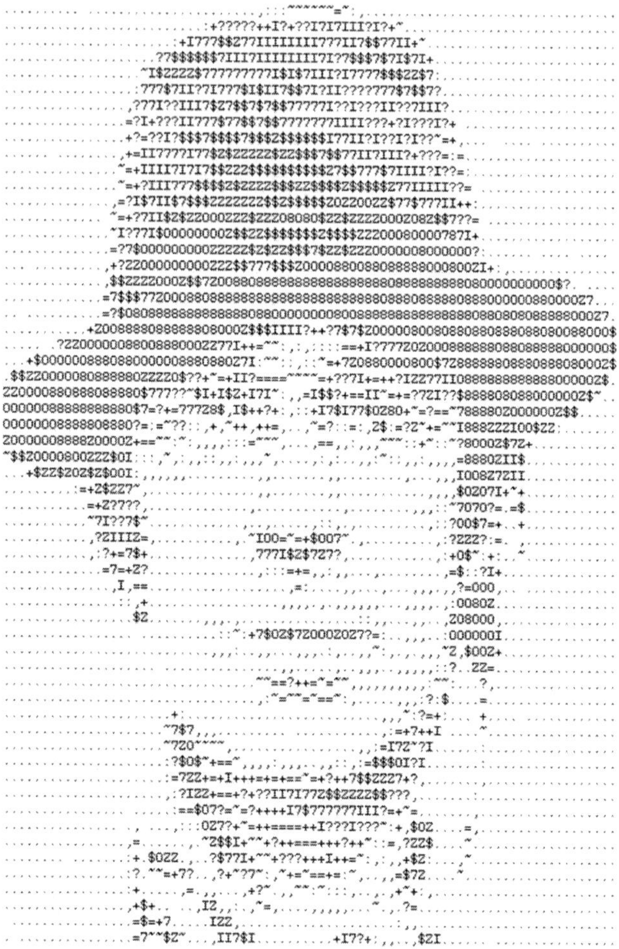

Computer Deleuze

Editorial Introduction

Robin Mackay

Welcome to our third volume, the greater part of which is devoted to the work of Gilles Deleuze.[1] Alongside a number of searching examinations of his work, it also features two previously untranslated texts by Deleuze himself. Although assembled under the working title 'Unknown Deleuze', the volume announces no scandalous revelation, no radical reinterpretation; rather, this title simply indicates a humble acknowledgement of the fact that, *philosophically speaking*, Deleuze remains something of an enigma.

It is not without trepidation that we devote almost an entire volume to one particular philosopher; even more so given the ever-accelerating trend of secondary commentary and the rash of titles claiming to apply Deleuze's thought to

---

1. In the second part of the volume we present a record of the conference 'Speculative Realism', which elaborates certain themes taken up in COLLAPSE Volume II. Since these themes were already introduced in that volume, we will remark here only that one should not anticipate a discursive statement of fully-formed philosophical positions, but rather a continuation – in the absence of the extended interviews featured in previous volumes – of COLLAPSE's commitment to the publication of 'live philosophy'. 'Speculative Realism' is a conversation between four philosophers who think outside partisan affiliations to particular thinkers or schools, and thus is genuinely exploratory. Its 'unfinished' aspect reflects its status as a document of contemporary philosophy in the making, in which new conceptual approaches are proposed, the borders between science and philosophy probed, and the history of thought mined for fresh insights.

areas as diverse as dance, feminism and geography. These latter might be taken as proof enough of the continuing fecundity of Deleuze's philosophy, but they belie the fact that it is still difficult to situate his work philosophically. Interdisciplinary appropriations too often compound this, turning 'Deleuzianism' into a game of recognition and thus merely succumbing to a new image of thought (*everyone knows* what a rhizome is …) Although doubtless such works can and do succeed in producing worthwhile and productive syntheses, it is difficult to assess their claim to represent Deleuze's thought without a renewed, properly philosophical effort to examine the latter. But should this even matter, given that Deleuze himself told us simply to use concepts 'like a toolbox'? Such a riposte typifies the most deleterious aspect of the 'success' currently enjoyed by Deleuze; for any precision tool must be mastered before it is 'put to work', and for this one must understand, in turn, its own workings and its interaction with the rest of the conceptual 'equipment' in hand.

The first of our texts by **GILLES DELEUZE** himself, a short interview from 1981, offers a review of the enduring concerns of his ambitious philosophical project. Despite its brevity, the exchange merits translation because it sees Deleuze, despite his antipathy to being asked 'general questions',[2] speaking on a general level about his philo-sophical work, even going so far as to make a distinction – heretical by the lights of *Capitalism and Schizophrenia* – between his own concerns and those of Félix Guattari in that work. In this exchange Deleuze recapitulates and reaffirms the major themes of his thought – a renewed

2. *Dialogues II*, 1.

philosophy of nature; the problem of the image of thought; the construction of a science of the problem, and of a new metaphysics; the battle against neurosis and the typology of multiplicities. The other contributors to our volume take up, in various ways, the question of the interconnection of these themes – how do they come to be integrated into *a* philosophy?

With a style that combines the resources of the conceptual, the poetic, the mythical and the etymological, **ARNAUD VILLANI** has constantly aspired in his work to do justice to the richness of Deleuze's thought, just as this thought itself, he argues, aims above all to do justice to the 'burl' of the real.[3] Gerard Manley Hopkins, who Villani cites here, is indeed an intriguing reference-point for Deleuze, with his language of 'inscapes' and 'instress', 'oftening' or repetition, and 'cleaves or folds' in the 'burl of being'; but it is Villani's aim, without annulling this poetic affinity, to distance Deleuze from any model that would have us rely on God's grace (Hopkins) – and equally, on the grace of the universal (Badiou)[4] – to take us from one 'cleave of being' to another.

For, as critics who attribute to Deleuze a politically suspect 'aestheticism' point out, it is in the practical sphere that an affirmation of 'life, in all its frightening complexity'[5] is not enough: this complexity must be negotiated, reduced, decided upon. Against charges that Deleuze falls short of this exigency, Villani emphasizes the importance of the moral and political in his work, arguing that the central

3. A. Villani, present volume, 52.

4. See E. Alliez, 'Badiou: The grace of the universal', *Polygraph*, vol. 17, 2005:267-73.

5. G. Deleuze, 'Questions', present volume, 42.

problem of a Deleuzian metaphysics is that of 'isolating the conditions of possibility for a complex act'.[6] Indeed, Villani suggests that philosophy itself begins precisely when we try to think experience without sublimating its infinite riches by investing them in back-worlds. Succeeding in this would mean that action, no longer having a special status to whose strictures the poetic and noetic would have to be submitted, would multiply their infinite riches: like the sensible and thought, it would remain true to the 'burl of being' rather than fearfully ceding to a vicarious relation to it. Ethical action would not betray the infinitude of experience but would affirm it in its every work.

Such complexity would not at all preclude action from being 'pointed', punctual;[7] only it would be a matter of an intense, implicated concentration rather than a decisive rupture: singular in the sense of the haecceity, the non-substitutable moment, rather than levelling all moments with a dis-qualified void. Here Villani pinpoints the most troubling consequence of the demand – increasingly made in respect of Deleuze's (and Guattari's) work – that a philosophy should prove its political mettle before even being considered as philosophy. This is a question of beginnings: in beginning with the infinitude of lived experience, Deleuze wished to see the 'drastical' rise to it; whereas in beginning with the demand for 'decision', we decide in advance against a truly philosophical – metaphysical – thought, thus impoverishing action and making political 'truth' the locus for an effect closer to the positive feedback of *hype*, drastically

---

6. Villani, present volume, 56.

7. *Ibid.*, 58.

disengaged from the real, than to a 'labyrinth of creation'[8] with a 'thread' always connecting it to the outside, keeping it open.[9]

Why would a 'pure metaphysician' see a theory of artistic creation as an essential component of his project? Precisely because 'complex action' finds at least one of its models in the artist's attempt to endow the work – through a series of selections or decisions 'concerning for example the relation of two neighbouring colours'[10] – with the infinite complexity of his experience. This is the process that ÉRIC ALLIEZ & JEAN-CLAUDE BONNE detail in *Matisse-Thought*,[11] where they advance a radical new thesis with regard to Matisse's development – namely, that the 'Fauve period' was not a wild anomaly but a period of rigorous experimentation which laid a methodological groundwork for everything that would follow. In the process, they demonstrate the pertinence of a Deleuzian 'metaphysics', in the rich sense explored by Villani, to an alternative conception of modern art and, indeed, modernity.

Rethinking Matisse's painting as a practice of the 'all-over', in which the force of local actions is always determined in relation to neighbouring forces within a virtual 'whole', Alliez and Bonne recall the importance for Matisse of 'a complete vision' of this 'whole'[12] – not a formal blueprint to be 'transferred' to the canvas but 'an idea which one

---

8. *Ibid.*, 56.

9. T. Duzer, present volume, 254.

10. Villani, present volume, 56.

11. E. Alliez & J-C. Bonne, *La Pensée-Matisse: portrait de l'artiste en hyperfauve* (Paris: Le Passage, 2005).

12. Cited in Alliez & Bonne, *Pensée-Matisse*, 75.

does not truly know except in so far as it develops with the growth of the painting'.[13] Their thesis is that the importance of Fauvism, for Matisse, lay in a 'strict quantitative ordering' by which it governed this processual development.

As 'the empirical exercise of sensibility [...] can grasp intensity only in the order of quality and extensity',[14] so the indissociability of quality and quantity indicates their mutual origin in intensity. The pursuit of the Idea in the processual unfolding of the work is not a quest for a particular contrast between 'a certain red and a certain green',[15] since these qualities mean nothing apart from their quantity; it seeks, rather, an actualisation (one of many cases of solution) in which the 'proportions of tones' (quantities of qualities) will act like a kind of lens, converging sensations in order to repeat or rehearse an Idea (*focus imaginarius*) in itself imperceptible since intensive.[16] The Idea of the whole does indeed come first, but its *expression* is assured only through a painstaking process of experimental *construction*.[17]

---

13. Alliez & Bonne, present volume, 209.

14. *Difference and Repetition*, 240.

15. Alliez & Bonne, present volume, 217-8.

16. *Ibid.*, 217; on the Idea as 'ideal focus' see *Difference and Repetition*, 169.

17. In a recent book, film-maker David Lynch adumbrates the characteristics of this constructivist-expressionist conception of the Idea as infinite heterogeneous multiplicity, and its actualization as intensive unfolding of differences: (1) *All at Once*: The Idea as event or encounter, as a singular moment or haecceity (the Idea is neither foundational or generic, but is always encountered within lived series). Why does touching the roof of a car heated by the sun 'cause' the appearance of 'the Red Room [...] the backwards thing [...] and then some of the dialogue'? (2) *Fragments:* The encountered Idea is already partially unfolded into a set of sensible fragments, only ever encountered in a state of 'degradation', but this degradation is in its very nature in so far as it appears. (3) *Expression:* The 'adventurous character of Ideas' implies a dialogue, a continuing conspiracy ('The Idea tells you to build this Red Room. So you think about it. Wait a minute, you say, the walls are red, but they're

Editorial Introduction

An early experience during Matisse's apprenticeship with Moreau shows how this problematic had exercised Matisse, from the very first attempt to copy a painting in the Louvre, Chardin's *The Pipe*: he was 'baffled' by 'an elusive blue [...] a blue that could look pink one day, green the next.' In a strange, inverted prefiguration of his mature method, Matisse 'even cut up his own preparatory oil sketch and stuck bits on to Chardin's canvas, where each separate section was a perfect match, but when he put them together, there was no longer any correspondence at all. "It is a truly magical painting," he said, adding that this was

---

not hard walls. Then you think some more [...] they're curtains. And they're not opaque, they're translucent. Then you put these curtains there, but the floor [...] it needs something [...]'). This pregnancy of the Idea, in the process of its expression-construction, suggests a new understanding of *anamnesis*: The retention of the singularity and the unpacking of its intensive differences 'incarnates' the Ideal event, so the work becomes the ground for repetition, rehearsal or recollection of what was inactual but was somehow encountered ('[...] you go back to the idea, and there was something on the floor, it was all there. So you do this thing on the floor, and you start to remember the idea more [...]') The successive posing of questions operates an 'enframing' of the Being-Idea-Problem constraining it to bring forth 'cases of solution' (*b*eings) to which the former remains irreducible but without which it would remain the object of a sterile and mute contemplation (whether phenomenological or 'Platonic'). In this sense, and *contra* Heidegger, science, when it experiments, is no different from art, their estrangement merely responding to a conventional partition of Problems-Ideas on the basis of the apparent duality of quality and quantity, itself testifying to an 'image of thought' that capitulates to the covering-over of intensity or difference-in-itself. (The theme of *mathesis universalis*) (4) *The whole must be made:* This estrangement is dissolved in a 'superior empiricism': Ideas as experienced intensive states, in pure memory, employed in the assessment of an attempted repetition ('when you veer off, you *know* it [...] this isn't like the idea said it was'), in ensuring a fidelity to the event through its mediate reconstruction (or retro-struction) through the manipulation of quantity and quality in an 'all-over' organisation ('The idea is the whole thing – if you stay true to the idea, it tells you everything you need to know [...] You try some things and you make mistakes, and you rearrange, add other stuff, and then it feels the way the idea felt.') (D. Lynch, *Catching the Big Fish: Meditation, Consciousness, and Creativity* (London: Tarcher/Penguin, 2007).

the only copy he had in the end to abandon.'[18] Matisse was to pursue the reverse-engineering of this 'magic', the life of the painting, throughout his career – and this, as Alliez and Bonne show, through a meticulous and rigorous thinking of the dynamic relations between the intensive and extensive, quality and quantity.

That Alliez and Bonne see this new conception of painting as implicitly prefiguring a new political formation only makes more urgent the completion of Villani's 'typology of complex action': for does politics, can politics, really proceed in such a fashion (even if 'the factors of decision and prediction are limited'): 'by experimentation, groping in the dark, injection, withdrawal, advances, retreats […]'?[19] In any case, their analyses, like Villani's, are invaluable in uncovering the connection between what we might have understood as Deleuze's metaphysics *stricto sensu* (the typology of multiplicities, the necessity of the virtual, difference), his ethics (denunciation of the priestly type, active and reactive forces), and his aesthetics (the notion of *intensity* as infinitely expressive force). Rendering back over to every instant of life what properly belongs to it, rather than sequestering it in an inaccessible site from which it will subject us, requires all of these resources.

As the coruscating conclusion to **QUENTIN MEILLAS-SOUX**'s contribution reminds us, it is not a question of 'full communication', which on the contrary represents a kind of extinction instinctively repugnant to the philosopher, personified in the conceptual incontinence of the

---

18. H. Spurling, *The Unknown Matisse: A Life of Henry Matisse*, (London: Hamish Hamilton, 1998; 2 Vols.) Vol.1, 85-6.

19. *A Thousand Plateaus*, 461.

'ideas men'.[20] Against all 'anarcho-delirious' worship of flux, Meillassoux reads Deleuze as a Bergsonian philosopher of *subtraction*.

The symphonic sweep of Meillassoux's text – from the *scherzo* of the opening conceit, which introduces an 'unknown Deleuze' in the guise of an obscure pre-Socratic, to the thunderous challenge with which it closes – is an index of the mercurial tenor of Deleuze's own work. Meillassoux's methodological proposal that we approach Deleuze through a mere fragment in order to 'reconstruct' his thought is not at all facetious: Better a modest, even reductive, model culled from a Deleuzian fragment, but understood 'from the inside' – through (re)construction rather than exegesis,[21] than an opaque interpretative quagmire where partially-understood terms become precious tokens too profound to be understood – much less rationally reconstructed – by the profane. But in fact, Meillassoux meticulously demonstrates how the quest for immanence, the theme of 'selection', the refusal of the reactive, and the logic of matter, are all comprised, concentrated, in the tiny fragment, a prismatic shard in which is revealed a distinct-obscure image of the whole of Deleuze's thought.

Pursuing Deleuzian immanence through Bergson's critique of Kant and his theory of pure perception, we meet again with Villani and Alliez and Bonne's analyses, in so far as the thing-in-itself is also a 'telephone to the beyond': a true metaphysics opposes Kantian critique with an affirmation that everything is before us just as it

---

20. Meillassoux, present volume, 105; See *What is Philosophy?*, 10.

21. See Meillassoux's own justification of the methodological approach, present volume 69-70.

appears, owing nothing to a synthesizing subject. But this immanence raises new problems: why is the 'burl of being' differentiated at all, what kind of interruption of matter is a living being? As Meillassoux demonstrates, pure immanence and individuation can only be reconciled by thinking the body as the locus of a drastic subtraction from the infinitude of matter, a primary selection that provides the terms for the selection of will. This double selection is a key notion in Meillassoux's thought, and here as elsewhere it informs a logic of the event as non-probabilisable and non-deterministic hazard. Events are the movements of 'atoms of void' across lines of flux, but, in line with Deleuze's upholding of Leibnizian continuism, rather than a cut in the fabric of being, here the void is revealed as a stitch in time, a virtual loop drawn out from the weft of the actual.

HASWELL & HECKER's performances of work created using composer Iannis Xenakis's digital UPIC system operate a molecular re-engineering of the body through sound, inducing synaesthaesia and an attunement to the microsonic. In their contribution to our volume they present some of the graphisms which are the basis of these trans-formational events, and their album of UPIC recordings *Blackest Ever Black*. In creating this new work for the UPIC, a computerised system that directly 'translates' drawings[22] into sound, Haswell and Hecker invite a renewal of Xenakis's musical thinking. As discussed in our accompa-nying text, within Xenakis's own *oeuvre* the UPIC allowed the application to the microphonic texturology of his *concrète*

---

22. Among the drawings used is one representing the microscopic structure of a new material developed by scientists as an optimally non-reflective black surface – hence the title *Blackest Ever Black*. (See http://www.newscientist.com/article/dn3356.html).

works the same analytical resources his orchestral works had brought to bear on macrocompositional problems. But the invention of the UPIC was also inspired by a will to induct a new generation into abstract spaces of sound which went beyond the confines of musical tradition.

Haswell and Hecker's work demonstrates that it would be wrong to reduce Xenakis's marshalling of synaesthesia to a wish to get 'through' the music, to step 'outside-time'. Although he will often seem to view the human ear as a lamentable constraint, a symptom of being a '"Two-faced" mortal',[23] Xenakis, like Deleuze, is ultimately a chronicler of our amphibious condition: the 'outside-time' structures he seeks are always subject to the vagaries of perception, and although our unconscious may be roamed by packs of molecular sound, sonic events are unavoidably always the product of an integration.[24] As in Deleuze, virtual and actual are not the object of a value-laden dualism, but are the inextricable conditions for the emergence of a real: without both of them, no music.

As well as clear Leibnizian-Deleuzian themes (sustained and stable tones as exceptional cases of glissandi; *petites-perceptions*;[25] infinities within infinities[26]), thinking through Xenakis also returns us to a theme that recurs throughout this volume: that of the 'contraction' of quantitative material phenomena into qualities. For Bergson,

---

23. (Parmenides) – Xenakis, *Formalized Music: Thought and Mathematics in Music*, trans. S. Kanach (NY: Pendragon, 1992), 203.

24. See Xenakis, *Formalized Music*, 8

25. Haswell & Hecker, present volume, 111-2.

26. Xenakis in B. A. Varga, *Conversations with Iannis Xenakis* (London: Faber, 1996), 205-6.

in liminal phenomena (*e.g.* the lower notes of the scale)[27] a 'detension'[28] comes into operation whereby we begin to break through the operation of contraction-memory and perceive matter itself, perceive the quantifiable series of intensities that science describes. Xenakis investigated this in the form of 'acoustic beats', where the interference patterns of waveforms create rhythmic pulses.[29] These phenomena reveal a continuum between tone and rhythm, a continuum suppressed by the stave's perpendicular separation of infrasonic statistical aggregates (notes) and macrotemporal arrangements (rhythmic placement). In rendering this same stratification transparent,[30] the UPIC engineers a 'transcendental encounter' with the selection we make from matter.[31] The time of music is a biological artefact, a two-dimensional sandbox made by 'folding' the vibratory continuum along a seam constituted by the limits of our auditory system ('Our brain does a kind of statistical analysis', 'Our ear is nothing but a periodicity-counter');[32] a crease in our relation to the physical vibratory continuum. In mimicking these foldings the UPIC gives us the means to probe them, to 'take the reverse path'[33] and to reinsert ourselves into the concrete continuum of sound, outside the traditional strictures of music, with its double-selection of preconstituted 'notes' and metric combinatorial space.

---

27. See Meillassoux, present volume, 79-80.

28. *Ibid.*, 80.

29. Xenakis in Varga, *Conversations,* 64.

30. See Haswell & Hecker, present volume, 119.

31. *Ibid.*, 86.

32. Xenakis in Varga, *Conversations,* 78, 91.

33. Meillassoux, present volume, 82.

Contraction is thereby revealed as a property, not of a synthesizing subject, but of the folds of matter – revealing to us the 'concrete scale of temporalities'[34] along with our own temporality or rhythm.

We do not truly know how the twenty-one year old student **GILLES DELEUZE** came to write the introduction to a republication, by a private press specializing in esoteric works, of Johann Malfatti de Montereggio's nineteenth-century esoteric work *Mathesis: Or Studies on the Anarchy and Hierarchy of Knowledge*.[35] During his early years (1944-8) at the Sorbonne, Deleuze participated in monthly salons organised by the wealthy banker Marcel Moré, a friend of Bataille's. In the leftist Catholic context of the soirées at Moré's apartment and the so-called *sessions de la Fortelle* hosted in mediaevalist Marie Madeleine Davy's grand *château* as 'cover' for Resistance activities, discussions of esoteric topics undoubtedly played a part in what must have been a heady atmosphere, mingling extra-academic intellectual exploration with furtive, morally-charged acts of resistance. Young lights of the Parisian intellectual scene including Deleuze and his close friend Michel Tournier were also, no doubt, respectful of mystically-inclined hostess Davy,[36] whose work suggested that the truth of mediaeval

---

34. *Ibid.*, 80.

35. We are endebted to Knox Peden, Thomas Duzer, David Reggio and Christian Kerslake for valuable information and discussion on Deleuze's text which has informed the following notes.

36. See F. Dosse *Gilles Deleuze et Félix Guattari: Biographie croisée* (Paris: La Découverte, 2007), 116; and J. Moncelon, *Marie Madeleine Davy ou le désert intérieur* (Paris: Les Cahiers d'Orient et d'Occident, 2006). Deleuze prefaces another of the early essays, 'From Christ to the Bourgeoisie' with a dedication to Davy, who also edited a series of books for Griffon d'Or, the publisher of *Mathesis* (see C. Kerslake, 'The Hermaphrodite and the Somnambulist: Deleuze and Jean Malfatti de Montereggio and

philosophy was to be discovered in a closely-guarded, esoteric, monastic thought that had remained faithful to the mystery of divine revelation.

But if it was through the patronage of Moré and Davy that Deleuze came to write the piece, this reveals little about his motivation in doing so, nor why he later requested its excision from his official bibliography. In any case, within this essay Deleuze is already operating a characteristic philosophical ventriloquism: To a large extent his reading of Malfatti is an opportunity to articulate his own preoccupations, themes which traverse all of his works of the 1940s. The real question is what Deleuze found in Malfatti that could be affined to his own project.[37] It seems that ultimately Deleuze sees in mathesis a kind of ethical

Occultism' in Culture Machine (2007), at http://culturemachine.tees.ac.uk/Cmach/Backissues/j008/InterZone/kerslake.htm, n. 2).

37. This is not to deny that Deleuze was interested in Malfatti's book, for certain key images present in Malfatti recur throughout later works – see Christian Kerslake's work ('The Hermaphrodite and the Somnambulist – *op.cit.* – and *Deleuze and the Unconscious*, London: Continuum, 2007, particularly Chapter 4), which suggests deeper connections between Deleuze and 'occult' thought, constructing a kind of counter-history to the official account of Deleuze's work by indicating a porous boundary between the canon and 'discredited' occult works. The methodological key to Kerslake's approach might be found in his argument that insisting on the 'obnoxious term "occultism"' itself represents a kind of implacable resistance to the all forms of priestly tradition – even esoteric tradition – in favour of an anti-establishment dedication to all that is obscure and repressed (Kerslake, 'The Hermaphrodite', n. 27). In that case, if it seems immoderate to us to undertake a wholesale reinterpretation of Deleuze's work on this basis, this apparent immoderacy itself answers to the performative exigency of an 'occultist' revolutionary stratagem. Kerslake's renewal of the link between the problem of resistance and the mysteries of the occult is pursued within an irreproachable scholarly framework, which perhaps only augments its seditious potential, even if in the short term it courts the risk of encouraging an interpretation of Deleuze as 'mystic'. What must ultimately be sought is a key to Deleuze's integration of these 'occult' elements, along with the 'official' history and practice of modern European philosophy, into one singular mode of thought. Kerslake's work is invaluable and pioneering in its painstaking recovery of long-forgotten resources that may be necessary for this task, and demonstrates, once again, just how many 'Unknown Deleuzes' there are.

imperative indexed to the refusal of transcendence, and a monism elaborated on the basis of lived experience. As always, then, in the background, it is Spinoza who silently presides over the work in progress.

Deleuze's philosophical voice emerges during a period where the rallying-cry of a philosophy which aims to sweep away the severity of interwar *epistemologie* was that of a 'return to the concrete'.[38] The moral disquiet aroused by the dark years of Occupation seemed to demand an unmediated examination of the moral and philosophical stakes of lived experience. For Sartre and his contemporaries an appropriation of Heidegger's work offered a powerful and convenient way to recuse the already-palling academic Brunschvicgian credo that the only way to rigorous philosophical questioning was through an apprenticeship in scientific thought: Instead, it opened up a much-needed *immediate* philosophical access to the politically-dramatic problem of freedom.

Nevertheless, Deleuze does not appear to have taken the easy path of simply neglecting or dismissing science on account of the monstrous engines of death it had recently produced. He does identify the need for the return to 'concrete life' as being an exigency posed at root by 'the principle of an anarchy',[39] that of the apparent irreconcilability of science and philosophy. But, far from seeking to collapse the entire field onto either of these mutually

38. David Reggio explores this aspect of Deleuze's work in 'Jean Malfatti de Montereggio: A Brief Introduction', at http://www.goldsmiths.ac.uk/history/news-events/malfatti.php; and 'The Deleuzian Legacy', *History of the Human Sciences* 20:1 (2007), 145-60.

39. Deleuze, 'Mathesis', present volume, 142.

incomprehending discourses, Deleuze describes both as being based upon an uninterrogated ground: that of objectivity (science) and that of the representations of a cognizing subject (philosophy). This dualism, of course, is 'essentially the Cartesian opposition between extended substance and thinking substance'. However, in his aspiration to a *mathesis universalis*, Descartes himself envisions 'a third order, irreducible to the other two [...] the unity, the hierarchy beyond all anarchic duality'.[40] Similarly, runs Deleuze's argument, Malfatti's book set out to rediscover this *mathesis universalis* in which (in ancient Indian civilisation) mathematics and metaphysics had enjoyed an original unity, and so to restore us to this unified plane.[41]

This notion that the knowledge handed down by our intellectual forefathers was subtended by a mysterious lore was indeed widespread into the nineteenth century, frequently paired with that of a unified science or *mathesis universalis*. In the 1946 edition of *Mathesis*, Ostrowski mentions fellow nineteenth-century thinkers Oken and Ampère as seeking the same 'universal synthesis' as Malfatti, and repeats Malfatti's own claims that this mathesis is descended from Plato and Proclus. Descartes, in outlining (in the *Regulae* and the *Géometrie*) his model for a universal science of discovery, similarly confides that he seeks only to *re*discover a hidden science which, going beyond the purely formal and deductive methods available to mathematics in his own day, would explain how the ancients were able to

---

40. Deleuze, 'Mathesis', present volume, 143.

41. 'Incognitum' (present volume 156-75) examines the first, numerological or arithmosophical study; For an account of the content of Malfatti's *Mathesis* in its anatomical, embryological and medicinal aspects, see C. Kerslake, 'The Hermaphrodite'.

achieve such prodigious feats of discovery.[42]

Deleuze superposes Malfatti's vision of *mathesis universalis* onto that of Descartes; but he also 'twists' Descartes himself. For Deleuze's understanding of mathesis as a third type of knowledge misunderstood by both science and philosophy owes less to Descartes's vision of an *ars inveniendi* that to the 'three kinds of primitive notions' invoked in the correspondence with Elizabeth,[43] where Descartes's response, when pressed on the nature of the union of mind and body, is that although following the thread of philosophical meditation leads us ineluctably to conclude the truth of dualism, in our pre-philosophical state, and in the greater part of our lives where philosophical meditation is pushed aside by everyday life, the reality of this union is

---

42. See M. Otte & M. Panza. *Analysis and Synthesis in Mathematics: History and Philosophy*, *Boston Studies in the Philosophy of Science* 196 (Boston: Kluwer, 1997). For an account of the importance of *mathesis universalis* in Descartes' mathematical thought, including a history of the notion itself, see C. Sasaki, *Descartes's Mathematical Thought, Boston Studies in the Philosophy of Science* 237. (Dordrecht: Kluwer, 2003). Importantly, according to Descartes a part of this *mathesis universalis* lies in the determination of the conditions of a problem (See *Regulae* Book II 'Concerning Problems') – and here, indeed, for Deleuze too one rediscovers the unity of science and philosophy: 'It is in this manner, it seems to me, that philosophy might be considered a science: the science of determining the conditions of a problem' (Deleuze, *Responses*, present volume, 41). However, as Deleuze remarks, Descartes's achievements here belong to the mathematical *stricto sensu*; he failed to apply his discoveries about the constitution of problems to the philosophical sphere ('Descartes the geometer goes further than Descartes the philosopher' – *Difference and Repetition* 323n. 21). Of course, it would be Bergson who would remedy this failure; but all too *philosophically*, so that Deleuze would need to re-inject a differential mathematics into the Bergsonian account of problems, via Riemann, Lautman *et al...*

43. In particular, Descartes's letter of 28 June 1643: R. Descartes *Oeuvres Philosophiques*, ed. F. Alquié (Paris: Garnier, 1973, 3 Vols) Vol III. 43-4 (R. Descartes *Philosophical Writings*, trans., ed. E. Anscombe & P.T.Geach, London: Thomas Nelson, 1970, 279).

quite present *to the senses*,[44] so that the common man perceives no dualism, but a perfect unity. The truth of dualism and the fact of union cannot be present together – we come to appreciate both points of view, suggests Descartes, only in alternating between long periods of unreflective life where union is known experientially 'by means of ordinary life and conversation',[45] and short bursts of meditation. In his 1972 edition of Descartes's *Oeuvres philosophiques*, Alquié will explicitly link Descartes's third mode of knowledge to 'what we call the pre-reflexive',[46] rendering pithily Descartes's contention thus: 'to be conceived of, the union must be lived' [*'pour concevoir l'union, il faut le vivre'*].[47] From the point of view of a philosophy of the mind and a science of pure extension, the union is contingent. And yet it is 'proved' by experience, before philosophical reflection even begins, and again when it ends.[48]

This torsion exerted on Descartes allows Deleuze – at the price of the relation to Malfatti's text becoming somewhat strained – to connect the problematic of *mathesis universalis* to the existentialist 'return to the concrete'. Attaining mathesis will not be a question of lost lore and mystical initiation, but of a transformative thinking of one's own individual existence and its relation to one's fellows, and to the universal.

Sartre was the foremost contemporary influence on Deleuze's philosophical thought. But if Deleuze's

---

44. *Ibid.*, 44 (279).

45. Descartes, *Oeuvres*, 45 (*Writings*, 280).

46. *Ibid.*, 45n2.

47. *Ibid.*, 45n1.

48. *Ibid.*, 47n1.

contemporaries whispered of him as a 'new Sartre'[49] it was more for his startling creative freedom of thought than for his fidelity to the *maître*'s word. In his early works, Deleuze takes up certain Sartrean themes only to critique and transform them, always on the basis of the argument inherited from *The Transcendence of the Ego* – one of Deleuze's earliest and most abiding philosophical influences – for a field of immanence pre-existing the subject.

In 'Mathesis' Deleuze takes up Sartre's critique, in *Being and Nothingness*, of Heidegger's notion of the 'crew' [*Mannschaft*] as model for thinking others [*l'autrui*].[50] For Heidegger, the other is no object; rather *Mitsein* is part of the very structure of *Dasein*, as a sort of primary 'ontological solidarity'. Sartre complains that Heidegger has only *described* the problem of others rather than *solving* it, and that his common existence, the primacy of the 'us', tends to level all distinctions, making of each individual a mere case of a generality. But Deleuze in turn felt that Sartre's model of a 'reciprocity of consciousnesses', each using their intentions and desires to paper over the crack in the world which is the other, also evaded the real problem of others: it imagines pure consciousnesses stealing the world from each other, undermining each others' centralisation, with the world being merely the empty field across which their combat rages. Sartre's progress over Heidegger lies in the fact that he recognizes the relational aspects of the subject to the other; but his error is to make the other its own *I*, an inverted image of myself.[51]

---

49. Dosse, 116.

50. J.-P. Sartre, *Being and Nothingness*, trans. H. E. Barnes (London: Methuen, 1986), 246-52.

51. See A. Beaulieu, *Gilles Deleuze et la phénomenology* (Paris: Sils Maria, 2004), 61-3.

In another 1946 paper, 'Description of a Woman', Deleuze condemns Sartre's conception of love, which, he argues, seems to be predicated upon a sexless and neutral world of 'pure souls', so that sexuality is conferred upon the beloved only by the lover. In moving toward the definition of an immanent, *a priori* structure of the other – and therefore a conception of desire without lack – Deleuze announces the 'great principle'[52] of his early work: 'Things haven't been hanging around waiting for me in order to exist'.[53] For 'I do not attach my little significations to things. The object does not *have* a signification, it *is* its signification:[54] The world is already a world of *concepts*, of things bonded with significations, before the subject even appears.[55] In concrete, pre-reflexive experience, it is not that 'I am tired', but that there is a 'tired world' in which the road, the sun, are all tired.[56] Equally, there is not an objective cube and the space which we impose upon it as form of appearance, nor even a fullness hollowed-out 'behind' our adumbrations of it, but the cube as concept.[57] Into this immanent world comes the other, as possibility of *another* world, and at once I become I, that is, I decompose these concepts,

---

52. G. Deleuze, 'Description of a Woman', trans. K. W. Faulkner, *Angelaki* 7:3 (2002: 17.

53. Deleuze, 'Mathesis', present volume, 148. *Cf.* 'Description of a Woman', 17, 20; Not only is Deleuze, therefore, no phenomenologist, he is also no 'correlationist'!

54. G. Deleuze, 'Statements and Profiles', trans. K. W. Faulkner, *Angelaki* 8:3 (2003): 17.

55. Hence 'concepts are the things themselves, but things in their free and wild state, beyond "anthropological predicates"' (*Difference and Repetition* xx-xxi, translation modified).

56. Deleuze, 'Description of a Woman', 17-8.

57. Deleuze, 'Mathesis', present volume, 148-9.

making part of them 'mine' and part the objective world's. Where before there was a world of concepts 'in the flesh', or 'phosphorescent objects',[58] now there is 'my world', a world that immediately appears 'mediocre'.[59] Expelled by the 'intimate phosphorescence' of pure immanence, each individual qua individual must face the other-as-possible-world in 'mediocrity', without any common measure, each taking on the problem of life on their own account: how is the universality of life to be thought, regained?[60]

The immediate political stakes of 'Mathesis', where this

58. All of this is developed most beautifully in Michel Tournier's novel *Friday* (trans. N. Denny, NY: Pantheon, 1985), a book that is absolutely crucial for understanding of the early Deleuze – It is clear that in the Sorbonne years, in advance of the 'rhizome Deleuze-Guattari', there was a 'rhizome Deleuze-Tournier'. In Tournier's novel, Robinson is disabused of the conception of the subject in the world as a 'spotlight' passing over various indifferent objects with its attention and intentions, realising that it is modelled upon the thought of *another* as a secondary structure of selection within a world that *must already be constituted* in order for that selection to take place. This first world, one of 'objects phosphorescent in themselves', is ruptured by some singular anomaly or inconsistency, and 'excretes' the subject. In 'Tournier and the World Without Others' (*Logic of Sense*, 341-59), Deleuze will explicitly name this a structuralist theory of the other (the other is a structure which particular others can come to occupy); but the importance of *Friday* lies in its demonstration that the 'structure' is neither ontological nor eternal – in certain circumstances it is liable to decompose, returning the world to its phosphorescent state through a series of intermediate disintegrations – from Robinson on the isle of Speranza to Robinson-Speranza. Tournier-Deleuze participate at once in the structuralist destitution of existentialism and in a virtual flattening of structure into a field of immanence – however knotted, the thread that binds us can always be unravelled and followed back to this virtual field.

59. See Deleuze, 'Statements and Profiles', 86-7: in this 1946 essay the 'crew' represents the possibility of reconciliation with the otherwise threatening and hostile 'alternative possible world' of the other: I 'team up with the other' to realize a world beyond what has now become 'my world' and thus mediocre. Although the threat of rivalry still subsists within 'the spirit of the crew', 'The Crew is the only way to escape from mediocrity'. *i.e.* from the contingency that appears as soon as one 'owns' the world as a subject. Meanwhile the task of philosophy is that of 'remov[ing] any pejorative sense from the word mediocrity'.

60. Deleuze, 'Mathesis', present volume, 144.

convoluted philosophical argumentation rejoins the urgent contemporary affirmation of the concrete, are made plain in Deleuze's citation of Ostrowski's preface.[61] The 'human problem', a practical problem which mathesis aims to solve, is that of the betrayal or affirmation of 'complicity'. Where Nazism, 'a unity founded on a cult of force', assembled its crew on the basis of a subjection to general principles and a biopolitical substitutability, we must found a conscious complicity on the basis of an initiatory experience of the universality of life, guided by the principles of mathesis. The 'human problem'[62] lies not in creating a crew whose members would be 'equal' and interchangeable, but in 'passing from a state of latent ignorant complicity to an affirmative complicity', affirming that 'the universality of life as an outside' is attested to in each apparently isolated individual, and indeed genetically conditions and constitutes him.[63] Far from mathesis being a transcendent mysticism, then, for Deleuze it describes a discourse on the condition of *a life*, relating it to the infinity of Life; a logic of 'the multiplicity of living beings which knows itself as such' and 'refers back to unity' through 'complicity'.

1953's *Empiricism and Subjectivity* seems a valuable 'missing link' between 'Mathesis' and *Difference and Repetition*, in that it marks the first appearance of a quasi-mathematical concept of integration in precisely the same context – the creation of the social in a model that refuses forced sociality in favour of the *positive realisation of complicity* ('The question is no longer about transcendence, but rather about integration';

61. *Ibid.*, 145-6.

62. *Ibid.*

63. *Ibid.*

Editorial Introduction

'The problem of society [...] is not a problem of limitation, but rather a problem of integration [...] to integrate sympathies' writes Deleuze, building on the thesis of the positivity of institutions outlined in 'Instincts and Institutions').[64] This in turn may point the way towards Deleuze's ultimate model of *mathesis universalis* in *Difference and Repetition*, that based upon differential calculus. If that work turns to mathematics *simpliciter*, this would seemingly tip the balance of the 'anarchy' in favour of science; but equally there seems to be a reciprocal movement whereby Deleuze 'esotericises' that very mathematics, by approaching it through routes he calls 'barbaric' and even explicitly 'esoteric'.[65]

In the 1946 essay, mathesis is neither mathematical nor mystical. Like Bergson's intuition, it relates to the individual's solitary path, once displaced from 'a world' to 'my world', towards a rediscovery of the immanence of the concrete and immediate – a way to recover from a 'fundamental lapse of memory' on the part of Being itself[66]

---

64. In *Desert Islands*,19-21.

65. *Difference and Repetition*, 170. Deleuze's other 'occult' influence, the Polish messianist Hoëne Wronski, was also a mathematician, and defined a quite properly mathematical 'supreme law' which, unifying all mathematical functions and thus all scientific knowledge, was to provide the only possible opening to a true *mathesis universalis*. For a general account see P. d'Arcy, Hoëné-Wronski, une philosophie de la création (Paris, 1970); For a mathematical exposition see C. Phili, 'La loi supréme de Hoëné Wronski: La rencontre de la philosophie et des mathématiques', in E. Ausejo, & M. Hormigón (eds) *Paradigms and Mathematics* (Madrid: Siglo XXI de España Editores, 1996). More important to Deleuze, however, is Wronski's defence of a true (non-finitistic) mathematics of the infinitesimal (See A. Guerraggio & M.Panza, 'Le Réflexions di Carnot e le Contre-Réflexions di Wronski sul calculo infinitesimale' in *Epistemologia* 8:1, 1985:3-32). For it is on this point that Deleuze will take his stand against the divergence of mathematics from philosophy, in advocating a return to 'barbaric' or 'esoteric' interpretations of the calculus.

66. 'Bergson, 1859-1941', in *Desert Islands and Other Texts*, 23.

through an understanding of the meaning of individuation (the 'natal'[67] rather than being-towards-death). Mathesis treats of the nature of life anterior to philosophical reflection and scientific objectivity, that is to say before the cleavage between the subject and object of thought: it returns us to 'things-in-themselves in their wild state', the world of *concepts fauves*.

In *Le désir de l'éternité*,[68] Alquié had founded human experience on an essential loss and nostalgia attendant upon our finitude, allowing as true philosophers only those who had the courage *not* to claim vainly to reestablish links with the infinite and the immortal (Spinoza, therefore, the ultimate enemy). Why, then, does Deleuze aver that he learnt the specificity of philosophy from Alquié?[69] Perhaps because he affirms Alquié's conception of philosophy as being linked with a fundamental encounter, whilst refusing the proposition that in this initiatory moment we meet the *inadequacy* of our finite thought: for Deleuze, to authentically encounter our 'mediocrity' or 'enfoldedness' is at the same time to discover the thread that can guide us back to infinite immanence: When we truly encounter that which can only be experienced from the point of view of our individuation, we also encounter a phosphorescent outside that no longer receives its status from elsewhere, and that is our true 'common measure'.[70] This, finally, is the meaning of

67. Deleuze, 'Mathesis', present volume, 152.

68. Paris: PUF, 1943.

69. 'The Method of Dramatization', in *Desert Islands*, 107.

70. Since Deleuze's Malfatti not only reverses the cogito – ('sum, ergo cogito') but also introducing sexuation and reproduction into it ('sum, ergo genero') – this text evidently belongs to the period when 'there was still a specifiable relation between sexuality and metaphysics' (Deleuze, 'Questions', present volume, 40). The notion of the sexual act as the highest point of pre-reflexive existence, when the individual,

mathesis for Deleuze; all that is 'mystical' about it is that each must live it on their own account – in Alquié's words, *pour concevoir l'union, il faut le vivre.* We must initiate ourselves into the immanence of conscious complicity[71] – not, like Descartes, 'by means of ordinary life and conversation', but perhaps like Bergson, through a concentrated effort to reach 'the immediate data', guided by symbols-concepts.

It is a paradox that a philosopher who spoke out in the strongest terms against the history of philosophy as an oppressive institution[72] should demand, for a full understanding of their work, a formidable labour, precisely, in the history of philosophy – and not even just in philosophy, since from the start Deleuze drew upon eclectic resources. A difficulty facing the would-be student of Deleuze's works is that, considering this breadth along with the complicated conceptual modulations to which he subjects his sources, Deleuze seems simultaneously to demand and to repel close scholarly scrutiny. JOHN SELLARS, however, has had the courage to begin this work, specifically in exploring Deleuze's (and Deleuze/Guattari's) use of ancient

---

the species, and nature itself are affirmed at once, is obliquely taken up in 1953's 'Instincts and Institutions' where the question of reflex, 'at the intersection of a double causality' leads to the question 'Useful for whom'? – See 'Instincts and Institutions', in *Desert Islands*, 20-1.

71. Marie Madeleine Davy dedicated much study to the concept of 'initiation' (Moncelon, 5). Other echoes of Davy's doctrine of a 'pure experience of the presence of the divine which cannot be transmitted' (Moncelon, 3) can be found in Deleuze's work. For Davy, 'The liberatory awakening is achieved in the desert, *i.e.* in the country of thirst, of the reading of signs and of the encounter. The true encounter takes place within, and becomes experience. An inexpressible experience whose essence is unknowable' (*Ibid.*, 2). For a less apophatic but undoubtedly related understanding of the 'inner desert' as initiation in Deleuze, see 'The Shame and the Glory: T.E.Lawrence' in *Essays Critical and Clinical*, 115-25.

72. See *Dialogues II*, 13.

29

sources. In thus calling Deleuze's bluff, he makes possible an intriguing glance behind the scenes, of a type that no amount of enthusiastic intra-Deleuzianism could yield.

In order to determine what transformations Deleuze exerts upon the supposedly Stoic theory of time advocated in *Logic of Sense*, Sellars compares Deleuze's exposition against that of the Stoic thinkers themselves. Now, Deleuze certainly never concealed the fact that he approached other philosophers, not with a view to representing them faithfully, but with a view to producing new 'monsters'. Accordingly, whatever cautions it may suggest to us regarding our reading of Deleuze, Sellars's article should not be read as a debunking 'exposé'. Rather, like Meillassoux's demonstration of the 'grafting' of Bergsonian onto Nietzschean selection, it exemplifies a 'stratigraphic' superposition in the 'ideal space' which, according to Deleuze, is characteristic of philosophy.[73] Explicitly-held doctrines are traced back into the problematics that spawned them, introducing a depth of field into the linear view of the history of philosophy. If, in the process, positions become attached to the 'wrong' names, it might well be said that this reveals the real, effective, process of doing philosophy: creative moments only arise out of such slippages and misalignments. That said, as a case study in Deleuze's 'ventriloquism' in the history of philosophy, Sellars's is certainly a cautionary tale: in the absence of research such as this, mere recitals or applications of theories such as 'the stoic theory of *Aiôn* and *Chronos*' will conspire against any possible estimation of the extent and nature of Deleuze's philosophical inventiveness.

---

73. *Dialogues II*, 16.

If Meillassoux proposed that we make the text 'not the *object*, but the *instrument* of the elucidation' of Deleuze's work,[74] **MEHRDAD IRAVANIAN**'s is an even more radical methodological proposal. Perhaps, in addition to drawing on his architectural practice, recalling the Islamic tradition according to which any 'text' that can be systematically extracted from the Koran belongs equally to the word of God,[75] Iravanian offers a development of Deleuze's thought in *The Fold* that owes absolutely nothing to external interpretative resources, but seeks an 'unknown Deleuze' through an approach at once graphic and truly 'literal', dealing with 'unread characters'.[76] This explication of Deleuze's book employs the text both as methodological programme and raw material for a transversal experiment in architectural ontology and impersonal memory.

THOMAS DUZER's text 'In Memoriam' of Deleuze offers a concentrated survey passing through the major themes of our volume, and indeed of Deleuze's *oeuvre*, working backwards from the philosopher's dramatic exit from our world, over a decade ago now. In particular, Duzer sets out vigorously to defend Deleuze against Badiou's *post-mortem* critique, quite correctly refusing to cede to the conception of Deleuze as 'virtuoso phenomenologist'.

We have already mentioned the diversity of sources Deleuze drew upon in assembling his singular philosophy. In particular, the eclectic table of references in *Difference and Repetition* has only just begun to be mined for insights

---

74. Meillassoux, present volume, 65

75. For instance, using the numerological system of ABJAD: See 'Incognitum's contribution to **COLLAPSE** Vol I (Sept. 2006), 189-210

76. Iravanian, present volume, 232.

into the development of his thought. **J.-H. ROSNY**'s enchantingly weird SF tale 'Another World' sheds some light on one of the now-obscure authors cited therein.

Rosny discovers two necessary tendencies at work in life and in thought, corresponding to the 'two deaths' unveiled by Meillassoux,[77] or to *Anti-Oedipus*'s two poles of paranoia ('a growing simplification [...] more and more abstract negative concepts [...] pseudo-void')[78] and schizophrenia ('the mind is lost in the infinity of forms and actions').[79] We might draw a parallel also between Rosny's faith in scientific thought and the instinct for beauty, and Xenakis's affirmation that universality is achieved 'not through emotions or tradition, but through the sciences,' guided by the artist's intuition.[80] Duzer characterizes the Deleuzian break from truth-as-master-category as consisting precisely in such *experimentation*,[81] and Rosny, as will be seen in this tale, was the champion, above all, of experimentation.

In trying to identify the philosophical specificity of Deleuze, one name arises most often. It seems as if, in order to give Deleuze the proper philosophical status he deserves, the same must be done for Bergson, who – at least in the Anglo-American philosophical community – languishes on the sidelines, still apparently harbouring 'something that cannot be assimilated' to 'an image of thought called philosophy.'[82] Along with Deleuze's attempts, already

---

77. Meillassoux, present volume, 102.

78. Rosny, *Les sciences et le pluralisme* (Paris: Alcan, 1922), 4.

79. *Ibid.*, 4

80. Xenakis in Varga, *Conversations,* 47.

81. Duzer, present volume, 249.

82. *Dialogues II*, 15, 13.

in his early works, to recreate a true ('phosphorescent') Bergsonianism *against* the contemporary heralding of phenomenology as the arrival of a true (that is, corrected) Bergsonianism, we should mark Meillassoux's identification of a *differential* between Bergson and Deleuze: What is important in the relation Bergson-Deleuze is their *divergence*, what Deleuze *selects* from Bergson. And the extent to which, in making his selection, he sets out to become 'more Bergsonian than Bergson'. One could say this also of the other philosophers Deleuze encounters – is he not also 'more Kantian than Kant' in his pursuit of a transcendental philosophy and an immanent critique beyond the inherited philosophical categories which Kant desperately tried to re-erect within them? 'More Sartrean than Sartre' in selecting the pre-reflexive immanence of *The Transcendence of the Ego* as the master's singular moment, and setting out to preserve and prolong it? A supreme 'Leibnizian' in preserving the monadological *mathesis* but affirming the primacy of divergent series …? Every philosopher is the site of warring endeavours; Deleuze extracts what he considers the most powerful, the most revolutionary lines, and extends them as far as they will go (for example, in his 'selective reading' of *chronos* and *aiôn*). We certainly need, for example, a *critical* examination of Bergson, with an eye to what is irretrievably obsolete in his thought – but, as Meillassoux shows, Deleuze himself already carries out this operation: and in fact the shaping of Deleuze's philosophical assemblage often occurs when lines of argument selected from one influence limit those from another.[83]

---

83. We have seen above that the rethinking of *l'autrui* was a founding moment in Deleuze's formation, as the 'possible worlds' of Leibnizian perspectivism cut across Sartre's oppositional model. We would also indicate the important critique

Of course, we should not be afraid to do the same with Deleuze himself; to read him selectively would indeed be an apt task for a post-Deleuzian era. But in order to get to the stage where we can do so, we have to understand – or even better, reconstruct – the various dimensions of Deleuze's philosophical thought, paying attention to their interrelations and interdependencies. Another 'differential' appears to be key to this task: Thomas Duzer's article confirms that an examination of Deleuze's work would today be unthinkable without reference to Alain Badiou's *The Clamor of Being*. And the service Badiou's remarkable and provocative book has done to Deleuze consists in making it impossible for 'Deleuzianism' to remain a comfortable orthodoxy sheltered from all criticism and unprepared to define and defend its key concepts rigorously. There can be no doubt that the controversy – at once ontological, political and aesthetic – between Badiou's still-evolving work and the legacy of Deleuze's, will be an enduring one. But what counts is to ensure that it serves to deepen our appreciation of the complexity of the work of both thinkers, rather than betraying it through mutual caricature and partisanship. This means preserving the chances, not of a reconciliation, but of a fruitful confrontation.[84]

---

of Bergson's critique of intensity (*Difference and Repetition* 239), on the basis of the Nietzschean requisites for a theory of force (See *Nietzsche and Philosophy*, 27 – Bergson's mistake was precisely to have 'invoked the rights of quality', confusing quality with the intensive and attributing to the former what belongs properly to the latter). The relevance to Alliez and Bonne's reading of Matisse should be obvious.

84. Note that both Villani – a key protagonist in the initial, hostile reaction to Badiou's book in French Deleuzian circles – and Meillassoux – a former pupil of Badiou's (although by no means a 'disciple', since he has clearly defined an original philosophical project of his own) both end up, along with Badiou (but in very different ways) defining Deleuze's primary philosophical orientation as *ascetic*, whether (for Meillassoux) 'subtractive', or (for Villani) 'drastical'.

So what indeed, for instance, 'made [Deleuze] choose the word "life" as Being's main theme'? This is, as Badiou says, 'a real question'.[85] But here as elsewhere, the *bons mots* that have entered into circulation as convenient slogans for 'summing up' Deleuze have served his philosophy badly. '[N]ever write a single sentence which is not immediately a vitalist affirmation' – rather than abusing this as a confirmation for whatever tendency we have decided in advance to advocate or denigrate in Deleuze, it must be subjected to the kind of close scrutiny exemplified by the contributions to this volume.

We wager that as this is done, it will become evident that Deleuze's vitalism, rather than being a simple 'given', constitutes a central *problem* in his work. As Duzer hints, even in his death Deleuze morally distanced himself from a vitalism that would uphold the sanctity of life at all costs. The 'life' Deleuze speaks of is expressed in stranger, more hidden varieties: it has as much, if not more, in common with the 'life of music'[86] whose forms Xenakis dissected; the life of colour as explored in Matisse-thought[87] (or, indeed, the 'exemplary life of the soil' of Dubuffet's *texturologies*, or 'one of Pollock's lines');[88] the life of knowledge as evoked in Malfatti's *Mathesis*,[89] or the vitalism-structuralism of Rosny's structures of beauty or his evocation of the 'life

---

85. A. Badiou, *Briefings on Existence: A Short Treatise on Transitory Ontology*, trans. N. Madarasz, NY: SUNY Press, 2006, 64.

86. Haswell & Hecker, present volume, 114.

87. Alliez, present volume, 212.

88. *Dialogues II* (Preface to English Edition), viii.

89. *Scientia vitae in vita scientiae* appears on the title page of the Malfatti volume – see present volume, 140, 143.

of science'[90] – and even (affording a glimpse of one of those common inherited problems of Badiou and Deleuze) the 'life of mathematics' spoken of by Cavaillès and Lautman,[91] than with a vulgarised Bergsonian *élan vital*. Only once we understand the common thread that runs through these 'forms of life' will it be opportune to ask (but perhaps then the question will not seem so simple) whether this 'vitalism' can be salvaged from a philosophically fatal analogy with the biological animal. In short, if Deleuze's thought is a 'Fauvism' then it is one which, like Matisse's, owes nothing to a Romantic conception of expression valorising spontaneity and anarchical liberation.

The contributors to this volume instead describe a life as the outcome of meticulous selections, a barricade against the infinitude of matter which nevertheless maintains a

90. 'Just as the syntheses, the orientations, the repetitions of the organism, have not resulted in uniformity (the living being is more and more differentiated), so the syntheses, the orientations, the repetitions of science do not have homogeneity as their outcome.' *Les sciences et le pluralisme*, 7.

91. It is surprising to see such a phrase in the work of such a reputedly 'severe' philosopher. For Cavaillès, it seems, this mathematical life was nurtured through a series of 'gestures' which transformed previous thoughts into the objects of a new thought, gestures which he set out to describe and classify. (See the 1939 discussion between Lautman and Cavaillès in 'La pensée mathématique', *Bulletin de la Société française de philosophie*, 40 (1939), 1-39; reprinted in Jean Cavaillès *Oeuvres Complètes de Philosophie des Sciences* (Paris:Hermann, 1994), 593-630.

Along with Brunschvicg's 'Mathematical Philosophy', French *epistémologie* was also animated, albeit unavowedly, by the Bergsonian theme of the primacy of the problematic (see E. During '"A History of Problems": Bergson and the French Epistemological Tradition', *Journal of the British Society for Phenomenology*, vol. 35 no. 1, January 2005). More fruitful, therefore, than betraying it by making it the object of an exclusive dialectical choice between philosophers of 'life' and those of 'the concept' (See Badiou, 'The Adventure of French Philosophy', *New Left Review* 35, Sept.-Oct. 2005), would be to explore as a singular formation this vigorous philosophical movement founded on the practice of interrogating science in its becoming rather than as stockpile of knowledge (for such an approach, see Frédéric Worms 'Between Critique and Metaphysics' in *Angelaki* 10:2 (Aug. 2005):39-57).

thread back to that infinitude. And a subject which – far from preceding and governing what is perceived, 'belongs wholly to matter'.[92] Given the equal importance for Deleuze of the problems of the withdrawal from flux, of actualization, and of construction, his metaphysics cannot be reduced to a quasi-religious valorization of the virtual. The virtual, the 'dream',[93] will always lack reality, which belongs to the 'inclusive disjunction of the actual and the virtual'[94] and their mutual interplay.[95]

Yes, Deleuze's thought unfolds within the element of philosophy, it is *a philosophy*[96] in the grandest and most speculative sense: a genetic structuralism, a transcendental empiricism, an abstract vitalism, an ethics as 'knowledge of life and life of knowledge';[97] but above all it develops the logic of multiplicities[98] required to describe – within a pure immanence, infinitely implicated, shaped by problem-ideas or nested series of differences – the constructive-expressive

---

92. Meillassoux, present volume, 75.

93. Villani, present volume, 50.

94. *Ibid.*, 51.

95. It seems equally mistaken to think the relation as one of irreversible emanation from virtual to actual, or of spiritual ascent from actual to virtual: Deleuze speaks of 'virtuals' and 'the actual particles by which they are *both emitted and absorbed*' ('The Actual and the Virtual', *Dialogues II*, 112; italics ours; *Cf.* the important concept of 'miraculation' in *Anti-Oedipus*, 12-3.

96. See Duzer, present volume, 250-1.

97. Deleuze, 'Mathesis', present volume, 147.

98. Whilst Badiou tells us simply that 'Deleuze despised logic' (A. Badiou, *Briefings on Existence: A Short Treatise on Transitory Ontology*, trans. N. Madarasz, NY: SUNY Press, 2006, 122). Deleuze displaces it into an empiricist *mathesis universalis*: 'logic does not interest us, either everything is logical or nothing is' ('Capitalism and Schizophrenia' in *Desert Islands*, 2004 *XX*) yet 'empiricism is fundamentally linked to a logic of multiplicities' (*Dialogues II*, 'Preface to English Edition', viii).

actualisation of a singularity through partial, local cut-outs integrated to make a whole, a new, singular and dynamic point of view, a life.

We do not claim to have presented in this volume a definitive and complete account, but instead a series of cut-outs, a kind of collage, or a transversal selection of elements, towards an 'all-over' portrait of Gilles Deleuze. As the contributors demonstrate – something that is often missed when theorists seek to make use of one or another of Deleuze's concepts – Deleuze is a philosopher whose thought is at its most powerful when concentrated, grasped as a whole, even if at those rare moments when we manage to do so – when 'all parts have found their definitive relations'[99] – we are all too aware that it will once again escape us. This, after all, is the measure of the complex action of a philosopher's thought, which must therefore be 'creatively limited'[100] in order to be prolonged. We intended to make possible some such moments of concentration, some such creative selections.

We would like to end by expressing our sincere gratitude to all of our contributors, who have given freely of their work and of their time, in what has once again been a truly collaborative process. The assembly of this volume has proved the most challenging yet, but, as we hope to have indicated in this brief survey, in the making it has become far more than the sum of its parts.

Robin Mackay

Falmouth, October 2007.

99. Alliez & Bonne, present volume, 218

100. *A Thousand Plateaus* 344-5; See present volume, 116.

Responses to a Series of Questions[1]

Gilles Deleuze

ARNAUD VILLANI: Are you a 'monster'?

GILLES DELEUZE: To be a monster is first of all to be composite. And it's true that I have written on apparently diverse subjects. But 'monster' has another meaning: something or someone whose extreme determinacy allows the indeterminate wholly to subsist (for example a monster à la Goya). In this sense, thought itself is a monster.

AV: *Physis* seems to play an important role in your work.

GD: You're right, I believe that I turn around a certain idea of Nature, but I have not yet arrived at considering this notion directly.

1. This exchange between Arnaud Villani and Gilles Deleuze took place in November 1981, and appeared in A. Villani, *La guêpe et l'orchidée* (Paris: Belin, 1999), 129-31.

AV: Can we call you a 'sophist' in a positive sense – has the *antilogos* returned, despite Plato's attack on the Sophists?

GD: No. For me the *antilogos* is connected less with the tricks of the Sophist than with Proust's 'involuntary'.

AV: Thought is 'spermatic' in your work. Is there a clear relation, in this sense, with sexuality?

GD: That was the case up until *Logic of Sense*, where there was still a specifiable relation between sexuality and metaphysics. Afterwards sexuality seemed to me rather to be a badly-founded abstraction.

AV: Could we trace your evolution in terms of syntheses?

GD: I see my evolution otherwise. You know the 'Letter to a Harsh Critic':[2] that's where I explain my evolution as I see it.

AV: Thought as provocation and adventure?

GD: In what I have written, I believe strongly in this problem of the image of thought and of a thought liberated from the image. It's already in *Difference and Repetition*, but also in *Proust and Signs*, and again in *A Thousand Plateaus*.

AV: You have an ability to find, despite everything and everyone, true problems.

---

2. *Negotiations*, 3-12.

40

GD: If that's true, it's because I believe in the necessity of constructing a concept of the problem. I tried to do so in *Difference and Repetition* and would like to take up this question again. But practically speaking, this approach has led me to ask, in each case, how a problem might be posed. It is in this manner, it seems to me, that philosophy might be considered a science: the science of determining the conditions of a problem.

AV: Is there a beginning of a rhizome Deleuze-Guattari-Foucault-Lyotard-Klossowski-etc.?

GD: That could have happened, but it didn't happen. In fact, there is just a rhizome between Félix and myself.

AV: The conclusion of *A Thousand Plateaus* consists in a topological model which is radically original in philosophy. Is it transposable into mathematics, biology?

GD: To my mind, the conclusion of *A Thousand Plateaus* is a table of categories (but an incomplete, insufficient one). Not in the style of Kant, but in the style of Whitehead. So that 'category' takes on a new, very special sense. I would like to work more on this point. You ask if a mathematical or biological transposition is possible. No doubt it is the other way around: I feel that I am Bergsonian – when Bergson says that modern science has not found its metaphysics, the metaphysics it needs. It is that metaphysics that interests me.

AV: Could it be said that a love of life, in all its frightening complexity, has informed your work all along?

GD: Yes. This is what disgusts me, in theory as in practice – every type of complaint in regard of life, every tragic culture, that is to say, neuroses. I really can't stand neuroses.

AV: Are you a non-metaphysical philosopher?

GD: No, I feel I am a pure metaphysician.

AV: In your view, can a century be Deleuzian, light? Or else are you a pessimist as to the possibility of our being delivered from identity and the power of traces?

GD: No, I'm not at all pessimistic since I don't believe in the irreversibility of situations. Take the current cata- strophic state of literature and thought. To me, that doesn't seem grave for the future.

AV: And after *A Thousand Plateaus*?

GD: I just finished a book on Francis Bacon, and have only two other projects: one on 'Thought and Cinema' and another which will be a large book on 'What is Philosophy' (taking up the problem of categories).

AV: The world is double, macrophysical (where the image of thought works well enough) and microphysical (and your model, years after the same revolution in science, in art, takes account of this in philosophy). Is there a polemical relation between these two points of view?

GD: The distinction between macro and micro is very important, but it belongs more to Félix than myself. For me, it's more the distinction between two types of multiplicities. This is what is essential for me: that one of these two types refers to micro-multiplicities is only a secondary consequence. For the problem of thought, just as for the sciences, the notion of multiplicity, as introduced by Riemann, seems to me more important than that of microphysics.

'I Feel I am a Pure Metaphysician': The Consequences of Deleuze's Affirmation

Arnaud Villani

I have often noted the remarkable extent to which, since 1981, this affirmation[1] has transformed the major axes of my interpretation of Deleuze. And for good reason: In an anti-metaphysical epoch wholly occupied, in Heidegger's wake, with 'overcoming metaphysics as one overcomes tears', here is a philosopher who dares to affirm his filiation with Bergson and Whitehead. It is important first of all not to doubt the sincerity of his remarks, and this against the tendency (Cressole, Badiou) that would attribute to Deleuze postures devised primarily with a view to the effects his words would have upon his students. Furthermore, it is important explicitly to draw out their consequences for his philosophy, and then for philosophy as a whole. This is what I propose to do here.

---

1. See present volume, 42.

To understand what is at stake in this formula, we must reprise the problem of the moral and the political. In *Précis de philosophie nue*,[2] I tried to develop the hypothesis of a sort of immanent eternity, an eternity of this earthly life, in so far as every second of a person's life, properly scrutinised, offers, both in sensibility (the senses, sensuality, the passions) and in thought, a kind of infinite opening. Sensoriality (affectivity) and thought are hypercomplex spaces, given over to the infinite. Nothing limits them, either in space or in time, and not only because they often unfold outside space and time. We could, in very classical terms, call the first sphere 'aesthetic', the second 'noetic'. It might be thought that this infinity (so keenly felt in the descriptions of Virginia Woolf, James Joyce, and in Roussel's *La vue*) owes to the fact that the given, offering something upon which to nourish and develop sensibility, passion and thought, never really constitutes an obstacle for them. It is not the *subject* of these domains, but rather their *object*. When we consider the practical sphere, on the other hand, the status of the external given is inverted. It becomes all-powerful, authoritarian, inflexible. Not without reason do we speak of 'brute fact'. And the whole problem of the practical sphere consists in circumventing this resistance, in coming to terms with it or accommodating it, or most often in vanquishing it as one does an enemy.

Therefore the practical sphere better deserves the name of 'drastical'. This is the name I will reserve for it, considering, apart from the sense of the verb *dran* in Greek (to act), that the complexity that characterises the first two spheres must, in the act and in the 'decision' that precedes

2. Nice: Éditions de la revue NU(e), 2005.

it, be *firmly, pitilessly restrained in order to become effective*. But is not such a restriction also to be found in sensibility (as was understood by Bergson, for whom the colour red was the 'summary' of trillions of vibrations per second), and even in thought, since all noetic activity is subject from the very beginning to the severe limitation of the terms in which it is developed? For to think without language is impossible; and words, by themselves, apart from their relations with others, are never susceptible to *infinite* modifications, nuances or distinctions.

Certainly, sensibility and thought must be entrusted to a language in order to become effective (*wirklich* – it is the spirit of this word which commands Hegel to eject from the dialectic the crazy riches of 'sense-certainty' and its appearances, incapable of being *spoken*). But the proof that these two domains harbour an open infinity is the eagerness exhibited by totalitarian systems in trying to check them. Whereas the practical consists essentially in a *choice*, in a *drastic reduction of complexity*, a gesture that could be likened to that of Procrustes, when he stretched or sliced travellers to make them fit his bed. To choose is to endow one's act with a meaning, by depriving it deliberately of that which one does not choose. Thus political choice, moral choice (Hercules before the roads of vice and virtue), the choice of a unique method in the domain of technique and science. The anguish of choice is the *angustiae*, the narrow defile through which we must pass.

I will provisionally make the following remark: If Deleuze is able to convince a neophyte from the word go of the considerable importance of his philosophy with regard to questions of art and to all that pertains to sensibility, affect, a 'new image of thought', his work poses redoubtable problems of interpretation when one considers its ethical and political leanings. Since up until now its most profound basis has not been interrogated, this difficulty has engendered lines of argument as erroneous as can be, interpretations which literally invert the Deleuzian philosophy and contradict its most frequently affirmed and reiterated postulates. All of which should be a first warning for us: we must not take lightly Deleuze's affirmation of a metaphysics. It concerns his whole philosophy. In other words, it invites us to rethink in a new light, in this great philosopher of freedom, the relations between sensibility, thought and action. And in particular, to consider the reasons why – as might also have been the case with Nietzsche's 'great politics' – the work of a very great philosopher for whom the infinite in thought and in the senses were always of the first importance, seems to end up with apparently fugitive arguments, or *prima facie* disappointing solutions, in the domains of the moral and the political.

Constructing a Model of Complex Action

Let it be understood: it is not a matter here of developing a gnoseology of complexity – although it could indeed be said that the latter is a feature of Deleuze's philosophy, in the use he makes of Bergson or Leibniz, and in the theory of *multiplicity*, *rhizome* or *chaosmos*. But for us, from now on, it will rather be a question of understanding the *severance* which, it is said, separates the sensible and intelligible spheres from that of action. Sensibility has no limits, thought can go to infinity, without even speaking of the relations of sensorial sensibility to the sensibility of sentiments, of the relations

48

of sensations between themselves, of relations between all thoughts, and finally of relations between the two spheres. But the *acts* which they permit (and which permit them) rest upon the *decision* (trenchant by definition) to refuse the infinite. Now, the metaphor for the act has remained unchanged since the 'epactic discourse' attributed to Socrates.[3] *Agô* for a horse-breeder, is 'to make the heads of cattle advance by driving them before oneself, to make them pass, one by one, from the dispersion of the pasture into the confinement [denumerable, and this is even probably the moment of the invention of numbers] of the enclosure'. *Agô*, which is found in our 'action', always has a drastic aspect. It abbreviates a natural complexity into a cultural simplicity.

For the choice to be a choice, it must restrict the field, it must effect a passage from a volume to a surface, from a surface to a line, from a line to a point. But let us admit that complexity can be compacted or abbreviated into a point without being lost (the thematic of naturing-nature) and that once the eye, the sluice, the threshold, is passed, it will redeploy itself by *spacing itself out*, by once again taking on volume. Let us admit then that choice will no longer be a matter of fleeing complexity or of making 'difference expire', and refuse to harden *airêsis* (the differing choice) into an unpardonable heresy, or the divergent political position into a one-way ticket to the scaffold or the gulag. Would this not then be a fine genealogy for the Deleuzian theory of *inclusive disjunction*?

---

3. The epactic model of discourse (as in Plato's *epaktikoi logoi*) insists upon an ascent to the absolute definition of concepts before discussion commences – hence the Platonic quest for the Idea. But the original sense of the Greek verb *épagô* is 'to drive a herd before one', in other words to make a diversity of dispersed animals pass into the unity of an assembled herd in the enclosure.

The model that I put forward borrows from Bergson, in pursuing his intuition. It is that of the *double cone*: The problem of action, whether political or moral, is visibly concentrated at the 'bottleneck' through which the content of the first cone passes into the second – the image of the hourglass. Now, precisely, choice is always a function of time. We might say that urgency is the mother of choice. Choice is 'pressing'. A space (to be defined) of complexity, one image of which might be the coexistence of virtuals or 'pure memory', coincides with another space through the uncircumventable tract of a temporal passage. The grains present themselves – a 'presentiment' of themselves – at the bottleneck. To succeed in endowing each grain with the 'spirit of complexity' represented by the whole to which it belongs – this could, as in the Battle of the Caudine Forks, free this spirit, make it once more occupy the whole space. In Husserl, this would be the problem of present attention, the thin line, the points between the trailing lines of retention and protention. In Deleuze, the problem would be at least as complex, with the special status of the 'and', the *aiôn* which 'leaps over' the present like a formal narrowing of time, or again, the suspension, in the evolution of cinema, of the 'sensori-motor' and intrigue, which are completely aligned with the impoverished model of action, in a 'neo-realism' capable of redeploying affects and percepts in all their proper richness.

In the virtual (in what Bergson calls 'dream') there is nothing but energy; no forces or forms. There is no opportunity to collapse the quantum wave function, to distribute it into assignable particles. But in dream, in narcotics, in surrealism, in the non-act, the *real* is lost. And here is precisely the occasion to redefine the latter more conceptually. The 'real' in Deleuze would be the *inclusive disjunction of the actual and the virtual, of intelligent sensibility and action.* For it is evident that the tendency to define the real in terms of action and 'fact' is the naïveté proper to traditional thinkers when they succumb to a kind of narrow thinking. The true problem (and thus philosophy) begins when one tries to think the relation of the ideative sphere, in all its richness, and the sphere of action, in its apparent poverty – if you like, the relation between qualitative multiplicity (free repartition in the whole field) and quantitative multiplicity (where, the elements being significantly reduced, they can be tracked 'by eye' and each individual located within the field) – the two senses of the radical **nem-.*[4] In a word, the relation of the heterogenising and the homogenising. How to make of action a multiplicative, potentialising, opening movement? How to do politics without totally quitting poetics? How to keep intelligence and sensibility in action?

As will have been understood, the opposition is not, to a great extent, between sciences and art, technique and philosophy, politics and poetics; but rather, in each domain, between that which opens and multiplies and that which closes and restrains. The theory of infinite sensibility – which I call *sursensibility* – analyses those moments where sensibility is married with other faculties and rises to power, producing the synergy of intelligence, memory and imagination. Kant sketched this possibility in the aesthetic idea, 'which prompts much thought.'[5] In *noetics,* contemporary thought makes up for lost time in seeking

---

4. See *A Thousand Plateaus,* 557n.51.

5. Kant, *Critique of Aesthetic Judgment.* trans. W.S.Pluhar, Indianapolis: Hackett, 1987), 182 (§49).

all possible means of developing a 'complex thought'. We must be attentive, however, to what philosophy already has to offer from this point of view, with the 'thinking of totality' or 'inseparate thought' of myth and of the first Greek thinkers; with the 'symbol' in the pre-Socratic and tragic thinkers; 'hyperbole' in Hölderlin; the 'choice of choice' in Kierkegaard; the 'interval' or 'dialectical passage' in Hegel and Bergson. For its part, contemporary episte-mological research continues to privilege complexity, with Atlan's 'self-organisation', Morin's 'ternary concept', the 'homeorhesis' of theories of flows, and Bertalanffy, von Neumann and Luhmann's 'systems theory'.[6]

If metaphysics can be called the science of the highest realities, the 'first' realities in all senses of the term, do we not have here the means of endowing this venerable 'science' with a reality which resists enclosing it in the corsets of general and special metaphysics? Wouldn't the first fact of metaphysics as first science be this difficulty of doing justice to complexity, to multiplicity, to singularity, to the 'density' which the poet Hopkins means to signify when he tries to give an account of the astonishing 'burl' of a divine real? If rite, myth and religion can translate the overflowing *feeling* which results from the first fact of the infinity of the 'real' (a sort of 'I believe', an adhesion to a type of 'faith', an unre-flective 'natural attitude'), *metaphysics* might be the decision *in thought* to reflect upon the possibility of *giving a full and*

6. See F. Fogelman Soulié & M. Milgram (eds), *Les Théories de la complexité: Autour de l'œuvre d'Henri Atlan (La Couleur des idées)* (Paris: Seuil, 1991) and H. Atlan, *Les étincelles de hasard* (2 Vols, Paris: Seuil, 2003); E. Morin, *La nature de la nature* (Paris: Seuil, 1977), J. de Rosnay, *Le macroscope* (Paris: Seuil, 1975), L. Bertalanffy *Théorie générale des systèmes* (Paris: Dunod, 2002), C. Baraldi, G. Corsi, E. Esposito (eds) *Luhmann in glossario* (Milan: Franco Angeli, 1996).

just account of this hyper-physical infinity. But then, could one imagine any problem which better articulates what is at stake here, than that of thinking the loss that accompanies certain modes of thinking, and all action in general? To pose this question in all consciousness, is to be a metaphysician. And I wager that Deleuze, in calling himself, and in feeling himself to be, a pure metaphysician, wanted first of all to bring this idea, this problem, to the fore.

THE METAPHYSICS OF COMPLEX ACTION

We begin with a commonsense remark: The epoch of gods (Gods) and of transcendent objects is not all that old. A few thousand years ago, there were only intensities. It is the *sacer*, denoting the fearful reception of intensity, that in *religio* is translated into the precondition to every manner of ritualising, phrasing, and transforming intensity into names and dogmas. Now, these intensities, even if they refer to hypermundane realities, are nevertheless themselves *of this world*. It is in this world that we experience them. What Hegel and Feuerbach after him saw, and rightly no doubt, as the projection of the 'part of the immutable' or of the 'figure of the ideal' in a 'wholly other' or an elsewhere, begins with that mysterious frontier between the internal and external where shamans little by little imposed the idea of the soul, capable of a 'delocalising' voyage. Metaphysics begins when the possibility is perceived of a distinction still more radical than that between internal and external, thought and action, the animate and the inanimate. Metaphysics, in its classical form, seems to be born when something comes to light of an absolute difference, a difference in nature, between the intensity which endures forever or preserves itself, and the intensity which ends by declining, diminishing, being abolished.

The tendency of metaphysics, and of a religion that has cut its links with paganism – that is to say, with a certain *natural* unity of intensity and non-intense space – consists in a most risky wager: concentrating all intensity into an unreachable and unexperiencable space, into a hyperbolic Beyond, which thus benefits from all the 'great words' that make us dream: Ideal, Absolute, Infinite, Eternal, Sublime, Immutable, All-Powerful, etc. Pondering this more closely, one finds here a thinking of the *razzia*: the plundering of all the riches of one place and their transference *en masse* into another, preferably hidden (*adêlon*). The Greeks and Romans understood each other quite well when it came to this art of razing whole towns, leaving nothing behind in their wake.

In other words: to have done with the intensity of this world and to repatriate the Infinite and the Too-much into 'heaven'. Religion and metaphysics will then be arranged so as to 'breath' and 'ventriloquise', each on its own account, the revelations of the Absolute in person (what Nietzsche calls 'the telephone to the beyond'), revelations which only the initiated can grasp and interpret. It will then remain only for them to trace thought and action – which remain (whether one likes it or not) in the intramundane – from these phrases emitted by the Absolute. So many metaphors and apophatic warnings are deployed from on high that it will be necessary to suggest this place devoted to '*to mê dunon*', that which never sets.

One might think that things have moved on and that we are now grown-ups, having attained 'majority' as Kant

hoped. If it is undesirable to put down these great con-
structions of the imagination, of thought and sensibility
– whose architectural equivalent indicates at least that the
'divine places', according to Jean-Luc Nancy's fine thought,
are valued for their 'volume' and not necessarily for their
content[7] – on the other hand it is more than time to return
to *intramundane intensity*. Which comes back to saying – and
this is exactly the meaning of the formula 'God is dead' and,
in its positive aspect, Nietzsche's cry 'long live *physis!*', that
it is from 'down here' that the riches of the sensible and of
the thought which is devoted to it, must come forth, as we
ourselves do. Our problem is no longer that of sacrificing
these riches by forcing them through the disfiguring defile
of a 'narrow gap', so as to find them again, supposedly
transfigured, there where there is in all probability neither
world nor sense to perceive them. We have not changed
the statement of the problem: 'How to save the richness
of the instant?' But we have modified its implications. An
immanent metaphysics does not save the world by throwing
it overboard, it examines the possibility of preserving the
immanent riches of sensibility and thought in synergy, in
an action which might perpetuate and *live up to* them. It
appears then that the first coherent gesture of a metaphysics
of complex action consists in developing a theory of art.
And this is what, incontestably, Nietzsche and Deleuze
succeeded in doing.

Hegel, who exploits the breach opened up by Kant
towards a metaphysics of immanence, but proves equally
unable to bring the project to fruition, proves most lucid

---

7. See J-L. Nancy, 'Of Divine Places' in *The Inoperative Community*, ed. P. Connor,
Minneapolis: University of Minnesota Press, 1991, 110-50.

when he opens the *Phenomenology of Spirit* with the central problem of *Sinnliche Gewissheit* ('*Sense-Certainty*'). We know his response, which consists in the immense detour through the *Phenomenology* itself to recuperate *in fine* this dazzling certitude of the sensible finally reconciled with Spirit. This response disappointed the great art-theorist Maldiney. He did not hesitate, in his *Regard, parole, espace*,[8] to denounce it as a 'false beginning' for phenomenology. For every artist, as we know, even if his work is particularly *pensive*, departs from this marvellous intuition to which, in a sense, his work pays homage. The only theorist, I would say, who permits us to see clearly in this debate, a debate whose essential importance it is time to consider, is Ehrenzweig. His idea of a 'labyrinth of creation' (exposited in *L'ordre caché de l'art*)[9] already constitutes a theory of complex action. He maintains convincingly that a series of decisions (concerning for example the relation of two neighbouring colours) can come, in the best of cases, to endow *action* (the ensemble of gestures which constitute the work) with as many riches as can be comprised in sensibility, imagination, memory and thought, as comprised in 'the experience' of the artist.

Recall also that Deleuze's *Logic of Sensation* shows how Bacon's creative act liberates the canvas from all that is opposed to the 'rising of the wave of sensation'. It is more than likely that a similar study of his *Proust and Signs* would see in the involuntary, conceived as 'the spider's strategy', a way of bringing forth intensities and liberating them within the act itself. It would not be difficult, once the problem of immanent metaphysics in Deleuze is seen as the *isolation of*

8. Lausanne: L'Age d'homme, 1994

9. Paris: Gallimard, 1982.

the conditions of possibility for a complex act, to find this problem in the theory of the concept, in disjunctive syntheses, or in the fold. All these assets could be summarised as part of the effort to allow the 'encounter' to deliver all its power, to go, as he says, 'to the limits of what it can do'.

A Typology of Complex Action

We seek an action which frees, unshackles, opens before the event (the flow which comes to encounter another flow) a smooth space, without 'frictions' to restrain it, which will permit it to *liberate the architectonic volume* which it comprises (this concern is manifest, for example, in Deleuze's *Kant's Critical Philosophy*). Such an action would be as complex as the intelligent sensibility that was its source – the 'drastic' would have the same status as the 'aesthetic' and the 'noetic'.

First of all – and without insisting on this, since Deleuze himself does not allude to it – one might, in the margins of this typology which alone can lead to a 'superior empiricism' (that is to say one *where action would not be condemned to an essential poverty*, but would 'overflow'), would suggest a new interpretation of *mimesis*. I mention this possibility because many of the questions I posed to Gilles Deleuze in 1981[10] turned around a Romantic reading of '*physis*'. As Aristotle, the inventor of the formula, knew, and as the Romantics rediscovered in the 'sentiment of (the power of) nature', *mimesis physeôs* never has anything to do with an 'imitation of the natural', but everything to do with a contagion of naturing forces. The 'intelligent sensibility' of the Romantic Friedrich, that of Monet or of Sisley, that of Macke or of

---

10. See present volume, 39.

Kandinsky during his non-figurative breakthrough in the period of the *Blaue Reiter*, leads, as if 'involuntarily', to the only pictorial gestures capable of rediscovering, at the end of action, the full complexity which initiated the attempt.

I could say the same of another action in which it would be difficult, in truth, to distinguish between the conception of action and action itself. I mean the *ruse*, that veritable constellation of intelligence which escorted Greek thought and *praxis* continually for six centuries. Detienne and Vernant's analyses[11] have brought to light the necessary qualities of mind and the essential grasp of the 'favourable time', the 'opportune moment' (*Kairos*). We must understand these requirements once more. To my eyes, they wholly coincide with the idea of *punctualisation*. The spirit must be acute (*agkhinoia*) and apt at conjecture (*eustochia*), but the situation must be analysed *in its widest context*. Hegel insists also on the ruse's acute, 'piquant' aspect: He employs the radical *ak- to designate its *fine point*.[12] Comprised in this image is the *bottleneck* of the hourglass of which we spoke at the outset: the nondenumerable overflowing of the temporal and spatial situation must be *concentrated* in the favourable instant, characterised, let us not forget, as *the instant which will never return*. For just one sole instant is capable of realising this *aleph*, this *maximum in minimo* of the theologians (namely the *Virgin's womb*), an immense space concentrated into a point and awaiting its redeployment. On this condition, action might recuperate all the tenor of

---

11. See M. Detienne & J-P. Vernant, *Les Ruses de l'intelligence: la mètis des Grecs* (Paris: Flammarion, 1974).

12. In the *First Philosophy of the Spirit* – See G.W.F. Hegel *System of Ethical Life and First Philosophy of Spirit*, ed. trans. H.S. Harris & T.M. Knox. (NY: SUNY Press, 1979).

sensible intuition and the reflection upon its components – an action which is complex in so far as it harbours what is effectively the counterpoint of the situation, marries itself to the fluctuation of things themselves, and, respecting the 'way of things' by furnishing their image in negative, permits not only the unscathed exit from a potentially deadly impasse, but even gives us the perfect example of a true 'act of knowledge'. 'To act in full knowledge of the facts', as Aristotle's 'prudence' would have it (that *phronêsis* analysed so ably by Aubenque)[13] – this expression might well find a more profound sense here.

If the imitation of naturing and the intelligence of the ruse might constitute the first types of complex action – both, let us note, relating to the force of 'nature' as all-over-flowing and undulating situation (Nietzsche's 'tempestuous sea' of the real) – they do not, however, tell us *how* sensible intelligence transforms itself into action. The moment of passage remains mysterious, and neither Hegel nor de Certeau managed to penetrate its secret. It would seem that Deleuze dedicated a large part of his work to inquiries concerning this passage. And if he said that I 'mediterranianised' him,[14] it is because he must have felt how this inquiry led back – for me, in any case – to Greek thought. Consider firstly to what extent he privileged in Spinoza *active* passions, in Nietzsche *active* forces. Examine the concept which he borrows, in fine Deleuzian fashion, from Spinoza: *expression*. It could be summed up by speaking of 'that which follows from the necessity of a nature'. Equally,

---

13. P. Aubenque *La prudence chez Aristote* (Paris: PUF, 2004).

14. See Deleuze's letter, reproduced in A. Villani, *La guêpe et l'orchidée* (Paris: Belin, 1999).

note the following: Not only does he distinguish, in the three syntheses, the immanent which opens, juxtaposes and potentialises, from the transcendent which, each time, ends in an *overnarrow* gesture, extracting substance, proscribing one of its possibilities, releasing responsibilities. He already produces a *theory of the act* which is entirely continuous with the increase in power of sensibility and intellection: this can be seen in Daphnis and Chloé's 'so this is love'; for when it happens, love is as much a new sensibility as a brusque comprehension of life and the opening of a field of infinite action. The immanent conjunctive synthesis is an *intelligent and sensible act.*

In general fashion – and this proves to what extent this problematic of action is central in Deleuze's work, even if it never appears in explicitly thematised form – everything comes back to the theory of difference. As Deleuze perfectly understood (but what *didn't* he understand?), difference 'alone' is pure chaos, for it cannot be referred to anything that would even allow it to be apprehended. A difference in potential is necessary to allow a sensation to be apprehended, but sensation is a *series of sensations*, thus a difference of differences of potential. Inversely, when articulated through the identical, difference is sequestered into an identitarian logic which makes it pass to a secondary plane – that is to say, annuls its singularity. There remains, then, just one other possibility, which Deleuze calls 'difference *and* repetition'. It is a question of producing an (infinite) series of differences of differences, of differences '*en bloc*', producing the movement of all these differences differing from themselves at every moment; in short, the rhizome, the bloc of memories or sensations, heterogeneous continuity, the fold. So that *the fold appears to us as the 'concept' of every complex action* in so far as it perpetuates the intelligent sensibility from which it originates and no longer leaves any visible scission between knowledge and action. The fold is an *act of sensible intelligence*. It is obviously on the basis of such reflections, germane to Deleuze's thought in its detail and as a whole, and only upon them, that we must try to elaborate with all the necessary finesse the Deleuzian/Guattarian concept of micropolitics. But this will be the object of another study.

CONCLUSION

Why are totalitarian ideologies forever the shameful impasses of History, those where humanity did not merely go astray, but in a sense saw its hideous limit appear in outline, like the skull-and-crossbones of a pirate crew preparing to board? Because, not content with developing a sub-sensibility (indifference to the other, sadistic hatred, insensibility to compassion, affected sentimentality, a passion for death and suffering) and a sad caricature of thought, they *dessicated, as do all tyrannies, the very root of action.*

The act contents itself with being the irreflective obedience to order-words, however inhuman they might be. As to the acts of those in charge, they are designed to suffocate all liberty to act, every active invention.

Inversely – and this may well sound like the very model of art according to Nietzsche (as I tried to show in the *Cahier de l'Herne* dedicated to that author)[15] – the act of creation does

---

15. A.Villani, 'Nietzsche et la musique' in C. Tacou & M. Crépon (eds.) *Cahier de l'Herne Nietzsche*, 2000.

not even achieve its highest complexity in the 'masterpiece'. The greatest creator is he who creates 'something with which to create' (I have called this, on the model of the Aristotelian 'thought of thought', a '*physis physeôs*', a 'production of production'). More generally, before dreaming of moving on to a 'post-Deleuzianism', as seems a fashionable wish, have we truly drawn all the possible usage from Deleuze's insistence upon the difference between *active* and *reactive* forces? In his work there is a profound reflection on action. For my part, I will continue to prefer a system where the aesthetic and noetic are as open, multiform and complex as they can be when one welcomes with rigour the requisites of an immanent metaphysics: that is to say a philosophy of the infinite, even if the 'drastic' must remain *pointillist*, precisely because a theory of their relations, whether in Deleuze or in Nietzsche, remains in part to be developed. For if, inversely, the drastic is affirmed, programmed, hammered home, whilst the other two spheres remain simplistic and narrow, superficial and embryonic, action will be nothing more than the effect of its own declaration or, as Deleuze feared, this series of 'order-words' which, alas, we are accustomed to call 'language'. What is more, who does not see that sensibility and thought taken seriously and *rising to power*, indicating their infinite nature, are themselves *already* actions? When Deleuze redeploys Plotinus and his theory of contemplation, this is what he wishes us to understand. There will be then only one object of metaphysics conceived as immanent: active (creative) sensibility, the act of intellection (and not solely intelligence *in act*); and an action, ultimately, which, far from immobilising the real, takes up arms with it, finally liberating its immense virtual forces.

Subtraction and Contraction: Deleuze, Immanence, and *Matter and Memory*.

Quentin Meillassoux

In memory of François Zourabichvili

We begin with a remark from Chapter 2 of *What is Philosophy?*, which discusses the plane of immanence. This book, of course, is by Deleuze and Guattari, but the text, in this case, clearly indicates a Deleuzian provenance:

> Spinoza was the philosopher who knew full well that immanence was only immanent to itself and therefore that it was a plane traversed by movements of the infinite, filled with intensive ordinates. He is therefore the prince of philosophers. Perhaps he is the only philosopher never to have compromised with transcendence and to have hunted it down everywhere.[1]

Further on, Deleuze writes:

> Spinoza is the vertigo of immanence from which so many philosophers try in vain to escape. Will we ever be mature

---

1. *What is Philosophy?*, 48.

enough for a Spinozist inspiration? It happened once with Bergson: the beginning of *Matter and Memory* marks out a place that slices through the chaos – both the infinite movement of a substance that continually propagates itself, and the image of thought that everywhere continually spreads a pure consciousness in principle (immanence is not immanent 'to' consciousness but the other way around).[2]

There are at least two ways to approach such a text. The first way – the most natural way – would be to try to understand by applying oneself to a more in-depth reading of Deleuze. This would necessitate, for example, an elucidation of what Deleuze means by 'plane of immanence' or 'chaos'. It would also mean resituating this text in the light of Deleuze's *Cinema* – and more especially in the light of the two commentaries in *The Movement-Image* dedicated to the first chapter of *Matter and Memory*.[3] But there is a second way of approaching this text, and it is this alternative that we shall pursue here. It might at first seem somewhat artificial, but we hope that its aim and its interest will rapidly become evident.[4]

In what, then, does this reading consist? No longer in trying to understand the text in question on the basis of a

2. *Ibid.*, 48-9. Translation modified.

3. *Cinema 1: The Movement-Image*, Chapters 1 (3-12) and 4 (58-72).

4. Although this article is concerned with the link between *Matter and Memory* and Deleuze's philosophy, we will make no further reference to the analyses in *Cinema* of Bergson's masterwork, and the reader may, quite rightly, be surprised at this. But our aim is to clarify, to grasp the intimate relation between these two thinkers, something which is not the same as undertaking an exegesis of those Deleuzian texts expressly dedicated to Bergson. Our path, as will be seen, is constructive, not exegetical. And although the convergence of these two perspectives – that of reconstruction and that of commentary – may naturally follow from our enterprise, this cannot be fully demonstrated within the current article.

certain reading of Deleuze, but in trying to understand – or to better understand – Deleuze, on the basis of a certain reading of the text. In other words, it consists of making this text, not the *object*, but the *instrument* of the elucidation.

To understand this point of view, let us place ourselves in the following imaginary situation: let us decide to read Deleuze as a pre-Socratic, of whose writings we possess only a few rare fragments, including the text in question, which we will call the 'Fragment of the Double Crown' since in it two philosophers are said to be princes. To these fragments, we must add a 'life' of Deleuze by Diogenes Laertius,[5] which teaches us little, apart from the fact that he was known as an original philosopher, rather than as a simple disciple of Spinoza or Bergson; and that his philosophy was known as a philosophy of immanence. This very term, in its banality, means nothing more precise to us than those terms such as 'water', 'air' or 'fire' which designate the first principle of this or that pre-Socratic. The project of we 'Deleuzian philologists', then, is as follows:to extrapolate, on the basis of this fragment of the crown, the meaning that the pre-Socratic Deleuze attached to the notion – crucial for him, mysterious for us – of immanence.

How shall we proceed?

If we hope to understand immanence on the basis of this one text alone, we must turn, not to Deleuze, but to Spinoza and to Bergson, whose works, unlike Deleuze's, have been passed down to us in their totality. For in this text, Deleuze tells us not what immanence *is*, but *where it is to be found* – pinpointing the place where 'complete'

---

5. One might think here of André Bernold's beautiful and amusing text 'Suidas' (*Philosophie* 47, Autumn 1995: 8-9).

immanence, immanence '*par excellence*', is situated. If we wish to understand this concept, it thus seems that we must turn firstly to Spinoza, the greater prince of immanence, and only secondly to Bergson, the lesser prince of immanence.

Imagine a particular school of thought, constituting itself around this interpretative strategy – 'The Major Crown School'. This school, in truth, is going to run into a certain difficulty. If we turn to Spinoza, we will end up encountering the following aporia: we know that according to Deleuze, immanence in some way 'saturates' Spinoza's philosophy. Everything in Spinoza, Deleuze tells us, breathes immanence. But to say that immanence is everywhere in Spinoza, is to render it as difficult to perceive as a diffuse light: if it is everywhere, then it is nowhere in particular. And this is why the attempt to understand Deleuzian immanence on the basis of Spinoza will not be greatly profitable for us.

In this case, let us take a second school of interpretation, that of the 'Minor Crown', whose heuristic principle will be as follows: what is most interesting in this fragment is what it tells us about Bergson, namely that immanence is something that *happened* – once, and once only – to Bergson. If for Spinoza's philosophy immanence is a state, for Bergson's it is an event. This princely immanence which came over Bergson, did so in one text only – *Matter and Memory* – but, quite clearly, what's more, only in one part of this text: it is suggested to us that the beginning of *Matter and Memory* constitutes a 'peak of immanence' in all of Bergson's thought. Now, this makes Bergson most precious in our quest to understand what Deleuze means by immanence; for it implies that in *Matter and Memory* is to be found that which is missing in Spinoza's philosophy, *viz.*, a *differential of immanence*. Now, as physicists are well aware, to isolate or to constitute a magnitude, it is essential to have at one's disposal a variation, a difference in magnitude: to isolate the action of a force, we must have access to a variation of speed. So we can say the following: to isolate Deleuzian immanence, we must have available a variation of immanence, in the shape of a withdrawal, a reflux, of immanence. Now, it is immanence, according to Deleuze, that would ebb away after the beginning of *Matter and Memory*.

We may assume this 'beginning' to designate the first chapter of *Matter and Memory* – that is to say the theory of images, and with it the theory of pure perception. This is what seems to be suggested by the strange expression in our text: 'consciousness in principle'. This expression, in fact, quite overtly refers to the theory of pure perception – to which we shall return – a theory which, Bergson tells us, is true in principle, but not in fact – that is to say, once one ceases to think perception as undiluted with memory. We can thus say the following: to understand Deleuzian immanence, we must ask what ebbs away, what is lost, after the first chapter – and in particular, after the theory of pure perception which is at the heart of it

However, this perspective meets with a problem: if something ebbs away, from Deleuze's point of view, from Bergson's point of view nothing seems to be lost. Obviously, Bergson never wrote anything like 'immanence came to me once, but only once – and then, nevermore!' … Like every philosopher, Bergson maintained that his argument lost nothing in its development, that it approached truth more closely as it progressed. The problem, in short, is as follows: how to seize this reflux, if we know nothing of the Deleuzian sense of immanence, and if Bergson himself makes no indication of any retreat in his argument? We must distinguish a norm, a scale of measurement internal to *Matter and Memory* – a norm in light of which we would be able to register a variation. The only solution is to maintain that it is possible to diagnose the existence of a reflux, if not from Bergson's point of view, at least from the point of view of the *aspiration to be* Bergsonian. Something must be lost from a point of view immanent to the text: and thus from the point of view of a Bergsonian, if not from that of Bergson himself. So we must examine the exigencies which Bergson imposes on himself in the preface to *Matter and Memory* – exigencies which, according to him, the theory of the first chapter satisfies – and then establish how what follows in the text, beginning with the introduction of memory, fails to respond to them with the same degree of radicality. These exigencies will stand as the conditions of immanence which the first chapter satisfies to a degree unequalled by the rest of the work.

We would then find ourselves before the following possibility: we have said that Bergson holds that the theory of pure perception, true in principle, is not so in fact – for this theory does not take into account the fact that every perception is mixed with memory. If we can manage to prove that the pure and simple truth of the theory of pure perception was a *sine qua non* condition for a wholly immanent philosophy, we could then ask ourselves how such a theory could be modified so that it would be true not merely in principle, *but also in fact*.

And in this way we might stand a chance of constructing a fictional theory – one which would be neither Bergson's or Deleuze's but which, drawn entirely from Bergson, would present instructive homologies with Deleuze's theory. In effect, we would have constructed an original philosophy of princely immanence which consequently would be similar to Deleuze's in many respects, and would aid us in understanding the latter.

Now, why attempt such a construction, when we have available to us Deleuze's entire philosophical *oeuvre*, and not just sparse fragments?

For at least two reasons:

1) The first is of a general order: it is always interesting to try to understand a philosopher without interpreting them in the strict sense, but by asking whether it is possible to reconstruct them: because as partial as such a reconstruction might be, it does assure us of truly understanding what we are talking about. Given also that our understanding of Deleuze is itself, let us admit, incomplete, we might anticipate through this indirect approach the possibility of better understanding that which resists interpretation.

2) The second reason is as follows. We would like to show that the fictional system we are to work out functions as a sort of reduced model which brings to light the essential link between many aspects of Deleuze's work. It cannot be denied that this reduced model will also seem a reductive one: it will build Deleuzian 'sim-concepts' without the power to recreate the subtlety of the originals. But this simulacra of Deleuzian philosophy will perhaps have the advantage of exhibiting something – even if only a little –

of the hidden structure of the Idea. It will display, in any case, a necessary chain of decisions of thought, capable of clarifying the coherence of their model.

1. THE ANTI-KANTIAN STAKES OF *MATTER AND MEMORY*

Let us try to show how the theory of pure perception, as unveiled in the first chapter, seems to respond in a more satisfying fashion than the rest of *Matter and Memory* to Bergson's own requirements, as laid out in his 'Preface to the Seventh Edition'.[6]

It does indeed seem, in light of this preface, that a fundamental objective of *Matter and Memory* was to render Kantian critique unnecessary, and thereby to deny the need for limiting the applicability of metaphysical knowledge. This is a project one might call immanentist, precisely in so far as it is metaphysical: because metaphysics, for Bergson, means here (that is to say, at the point where metaphysics is opposed to critique): the refusal of the existence of an enigmatic thing in itself, supposedly different from the phenomenon. On the contrary, it will be a question of grasping that being is nothing that transcends the appearance – that being is more, perhaps, but not essentially other, than the appearance. The theory of the image answers to this project.

Bergson writes: '[R]ealism and Idealism both go too far [...] [I]t is a mistake to reduce matter to the representation which we have of it, a mistake also to make of it a thing able to produce in us representations, but itself of

---

6. H. Bergson, *Matter and Memory*, trans. N.M. Paul and W. S. Palmer (NY: Zone, 1991), 9-16.

another nature than they.'[7] Matter must be considered as a set of images – and by this term, we must understand what common sense itself understands spontaneously when it conceives of matter: 'For common sense, the object exists in itself, and, on the other hand, the object is pictorial, as we perceive it: Image it is, but self-existing image.'[8] In thus maintaining that matter exists in itself just as we perceive it, Bergson explicitly undertakes to circumvent, and even to render unnecessary, Kant's Copernican revolution. Criticism is explicitly set up as the philosophical adversary that must be opposed, by neutralising the opposition to which it gives birth, that between realism and idealism – an opposition which, in turn, is indexed to the opposition between Descartes and Berkeley. Descartes 'put matter too far from us when he made it one with geometrical extension',[9] for this results in making incomprehensible the emergence within it of sensible qualities. So Berkeley was right to affirm that secondary qualities had as much objective reality as primary qualities – but his illusion was to believe that this makes it necessary to transport matter into the mind. For such a subjectivisation of matter means that it is incapable of accounting for the objective order of phenomena as ratified by the success of physics, constraining him to make such a mathematical order of phenomena the result of a divine, providential subjectivity.

Kantian critique is the consequence and result of this double impasse, since it undertakes to ratify the subjectivisation of the intuited object, whilst thinking the objective

7. *Ibid.*, 9. Translation modified.

8. *Ibid.*, 10.

9. *Ibid.*, 11.

order of phenomena as a condition for experience, and even for perception.

2. PURE PERCEPTION

How does the theory of pure perception, put forward in the first chapter, answer to Bergson's 'contra-critical' project? Let's briefly recount its essential features. The theory of pure perception is what we might call a *subtractive* theory of perception: it seeks to establish that there is less in perception than in matter – less in representation than in presentation. Returning now to images: images, Bergson tells us, act and react one upon another according to constant laws, which are laws of nature. In this ensemble of images, nothing new seems to happen except through the intermediary of certain special images, the foremost example of which is my body. For my body is an image which acts like other images, receiving and imparting movement, with this one difference: that it 'appears to choose, within certain limits, the manner in which it shall restore what it receives'. My body is thus a 'centre of action', not a producer of representations. Whence Bergson's double definition: '*I call* matter *the aggregate of images, and* perception of matter *these same images referred to the eventual action of one particular image, my body*.'[10]

What is the essential import of such a subtractive theory of perception? It appears to be as follows: if, to pass from matter to perception, we must add something, this adjunction would be properly unthinkable, and the mystery of representation would remain entirely intact. But this is

10. *Ibid.*, 22.

not at all the case if we pass from the first to the second term by way of a diminution, and if the representation of an image were held to be less than its simple presence. Now, if living beings constitute 'centres of indetermination' in the universe, then their simple presence must be understood to presuppose the suppression of all the parts of the object that are without interest for their functions. Bergson thus supposes that living beings allow those exterior actions to which they are indifferent, to traverse them; whilst other beings, isolated, become perceptions by virtue of this isolation itself.

Whence the relation, literally that of part to whole, that exists between conscious perception and matter. We 'might even say', writes Bergson, 'that the perception of any material point whatsoever is infinitely greater and more complete than ours.'[11] To perceive is to come to rest on the surface of images, it is to impose upon the latter a superficial becoming, far removed from the infinite profundity of material perception.

So, we perceive but a tiny part of the images which form our environment – and it is within this part that our choices operate. There are, therefore – and this point must be emphasised, since Bergson himself does not do so, and we will have need of it in what follows – there are therefore, it seems to us, *two* selections at work in the theory of perception: the 'selection of images', which gives its title to the first chapter, is both a selection made by the body, *before* the choice, and a selection proceeding from the choice made by the mind within the perceptive elements *already* selected by the body from the infinity of images. For if the mind is

11. *Ibid.*, 38.

free, it is free in so far as it chooses, selects certain actions, from amongst the multiplicity of possible actions which it perceives in the world itself; but mind cannot choose unless an *anterior* selection, itself *unfree*, is already in operation – *viz.,* the selection of images by bodies, a selection which, this time, constitutes the *terms* of the choice.

The body is like a continuous emission of an infinite matter whose particles constitute the terms of the choice offered to the mind. The body selects the terms, the mind chooses between the terms. There are thus three realities within perception: matter, body, mind. Communication, selection, action.

Alternatively, we could put things as follows: basically, what allows there to be bodies is finitude. Yes, the extraordinary gain of the body for Bergson is the finite; it is a massive interruption, carried out within the infinitude of communications. The body is like a windscreen for the mind against the infinite: whereas in every parcel of matter, however minute it might be, we can envisage an infinity of information, the body conquers finitude through the power of refusal. And right here is the emergence of the living being at the very heart of the inorganic: a barricade erected by a formidable power of *disinterest for that which communicates*. The living is not primarily the emergence of a power of interested choice, but the emergence of a massive disinterest in the real, to the profit of certain rare segments of the latter, which constitute the whole of perception. The body is that which discerns, in the infinity of imagistic communication, certain rare virtual actions capable of interesting action. It is only secondarily, in a second moment, when the body has made consciousness disinterested in almost

74

all images, that the free choice of the mind can come into effect. The selection we shall call 'first', that of the body, is the following: perception as set of possible actions. The selection we shall call 'second', that of the mind, is – let us note – far less impoverishing than that of the body: the mind chooses an option at the expense of a finite number of equally possible options, whereas the body selects a finite number of options, at the expense of an infinity of images which pass through it without trace.

We say, then, that perhaps the most remarkable characteristic of the Bergsonian theory of perception – and that which makes it an anti-Kantian theory of rare radicality – is that for Bergson, perception is not a *synthesis* but an *ascesis*. Perception does not, as in Kant, submit sensible matter to a subjective form, because the link, the connection, the form, belongs wholly to matter. Perception does not connect, it disconnects. It does not inform a content but incises an order. It does not enrich matter, but on the contrary impoverishes it.

4. MEMORY-CONTRACTION

Let's return to our initial project. The perspective we have adopted is as follows: to try to show that the theory of pure perception responds better than the rest of *Matter and Memory* to the requirements of anti-Kantian immanence. To uphold this thesis, therefore, would mean demonstrating how this requirement seems to be betrayed the moment that Bergson makes of such a theory – which refuses to see any essential difference between matter and perception – a theory that is true in principle but not in fact – and this because perception is in fact always mixed with memory.

Our task is to isolate the reason why the immanentist requirement must consist in maintaining that this theory is true not only in principle but also in fact – and to try to show how such a thesis might be defended.

So, the coincidence of perception with the object perceived thus holds, according to Bergson, in principle rather than in fact. And this because the ground of real and quasi-instantaneous intuition upon which our perception rests 'is a small matter compared with all that memory adds to it'.[12] But here Bergson brings in two types of memory.

This distinction, however, does not coincide with the famous distinction of Chapter 2 between the two memories, that is to say the distinction between the habit memory inherent to the motor mechanisms of bodies, and the memory-images of properly mental memory. The distinction which interests us, and which already appears in the first chapter, is deployed within the memory put into play by the mind itself. It opposes, within mental memory, the two forms which the latter takes in its mixture with perception. These two memories might be called recall-memory and contraction-memory.

Recall-memory constitutes a complex circuit with perception, by means of which what Bergson calls in Chapter 2 'attentive perception' becomes possible. It consists in the fact that every memory-image capable of interpreting our current perception intertwines so closely with it that we can no longer discern what is perception and what memory. The example Bergson gives is that of reading, which he says is like a veritable work of divination:

---

12. *Ibid.*, 66.

we do not simply passively perceive the signs on the page; for the mind, on the basis of various characteristic traits, fills the interval with memory-images projected onto the paper and substituted for the actual printed characters. The second type of memory which impregnates our perception is not that which impregnates the present with our memory of the past, but that which constitutes that present itself: contraction-memory. For however brief a perception might be, it always occupies a certain duration and thus necessitates an effort of memory which prolongs a plurality of moments one into the other. So that, as Bergson writes: 'memory in these two forms, covering as it does with a cloak of recollections a core of immediate perception, and also contracting a multiplicity of external moments into a single internal moment, constitutes the principal share of individual consciousness in perception, the subjective side of the knowledge of things'.[13]

The problem of the cognition of matter thus becomes the following: our perception seems (this was the decisive advance made in the first chapter) to join directly with matter in itself. In the object, we perceive the image in itself which it effectively is. Matter contains no depths, no hidden aspect. In this sense, Bergson's immanentism held fast to the fact that matter is given wholly as that which it is: no space being left for a thing in itself inaccessible to cognition, a hidden transcendence. And, what's more, the world was not immanent *to* consciousness, it was not a transcendence-in-immanence like Husserlian objectivity.

On the contrary, it was consciousness that slid over the surface of matter in itself, the latter being identical to

13. *Ibid.*, 34.

what common sense believes it is in grasping it. But in introducing memory, Bergson seems to distance himself strongly from such common sense. For from that point on, matter becomes what remains of perception once one has retracted that which memory, in its two forms, continually introduces into it.

Now, it appears to us that this correction irremediably compromises Bergson's immanentism, and this, not because of the introduction of memory-recall, but rather that of memory-contraction. Memory-recall, in fact, does not obliterate the possibility of an intuition of matter in itself. We can, by according sufficient attention to the perceived object, make it so that the stereotypes of the past will not cover over the singularity of the real thing. This is, for example, what we do when proof-reading a text: we force ourselves to read the words as they are written, and not as we know they are written. An effort of concentration thus suffices, in principle, to extirpate the veil that memory-recall throws over present perception, so as to liberate matter from the mechanisms of recognition. The immanentism of pure perception is thus unaffected by the addition of memory-recall. But the same is not true, we would suggest, of memory-contraction. To see why, we must first give a more precise account of what this second form of memory consists in, and above all, what the operation of extraction consists in, whereby this memory is removed from the perception with which it is supposedly mixed. The essential characteristics of this second form of memory are described in the fourth and last chapter of *Matter and Memory*.

Contracting memory originates in the Bergsonian theory of the rhythm of durations. Bergson will introduce this rhythm with a significant and still celebrated example: that of the vibration of light. In the space of a second, he writes, red light accomplishes 400 trillion vibrations – in other words an immense number of events, which it would take us no less than 25,000 years to enumerate, were each vibration to last long enough to impinge upon our consciousness. So we carry out an incredible contraction of material reality when we perceive in one moment what includes within itself an immense number of events. Now, it is this work of contraction that gives rise to qualities. According to Bergson, the heterogeneity of qualities is due to the contraction of homogeneous – and in virtue of this fact, quantifiable – vibrations, from which matter is composed.

Let's cite the crucial passage :

> May we not conceive that [...] the irreducibility of two perceived colours is due mainly to the narrow duration into which are contracted the billions of vibrations which they execute in one of our moments? If we could stretch out this duration, that is to say, live it at a slower rhythm, should we not, as the rhythm slowed down, see these colours pale and lengthen into successive impressions, still coloured, no doubt, but nearer and nearer to coincidence with pure vibrations? In cases where the rhythm of the movement is slow enough to tally with the habits of our consciousness – as in the case of the deep notes of the musical scale, for instance – do we not feel that the quality perceived analyses itself into repeated and successive vibrations, bound together by an internal continuity?[14]

In other words, what matter is in itself can be grasped again through a certain thought-experiment, whether or not

---

14. *Ibid.*, 203.

we admit the idea of a variability of rhythms of duration, of a degree of tension as Bergson calls it, which makes us comprise under the form of distinct qualities an immense number of events which, for matter, represent so many moments in which the qualities are strung out. The slower the rhythm is, the more distinct the material events, and the more diluted the qualities, once the latter become noticeably dispersed in the course of temporal succession. The notion of rhythm thus gives us to apprehend what we might call a 'concrete scale of temporalities'. We only live at one scale of matter – immensely vaster than that of the atom, and immensely less vast than that of galaxies. We thus occupy a scale of durations, a particular rhythm of the current of time, which renders us unconscious of all events below two millionths of a second, whereas such a duration is sufficient for luminous matter to produce millions of vibrations, that is to say millions of distinct events.

5. Critique of Memory-Contraction.

We will call 'detension'[15] the operation through which Bergson 'decontracts' the qualitative product of memory, so as to decant material perception from its mnemonic and subjective envelope – and this to rediscover matter such as it is in itself, rather than for us. Let us try to explain, then, what seems to us to pose a problem in this theory of detension, all the while attempting to give a Bergsonian dynamic to our dissatisfaction.

---

15. Obviously, in a different sense to that which Bergson gives to this term when he uses it in chapter 3 of *Creative Evolution* (trans. A. Mitchell, NY: Dover, 1998), to designate the engendering of space by duration, at the moment where the latter attains the limits of its creative *élan*.

We know how Bergson criticises the thesis according to which there would be only a difference of degree between perception and memory, that is to say the empiricist thesis according to which memory would be only an attenuated perception: if this was the case, he remarks, we would also have to maintain the inverse proposition – that is, that an intense memory could not be distinguished from a weak perception – an inversion which suffices to demonstrate the incoherence of the thesis. This being the case, we will express in a similar fashion our doubts concerning the operation of detension: if the slowing of the rhythm of duration is equivalent to dilution, or to a 'stringing-out', as Bergson says, of qualities, then we must also maintain the inverse, that *every experience of the dilution of colours or of the movement of sound towards the bass is equivalent to the experience of a slowing of time.* Or further, if one maintains that material duration makes colours paler and sonorities deeper, one must then also maintain that every perception of a pale colour or of a low sound makes us change in our rhythm of duration. But this is evidently not the case, since on the contrary we enjoy a capacity to traverse the palette of the painter or the scale of the piano without at all modifying our vital rhythm, since the low notes do not modify the rhythmic exigencies of the score or of the metronome. The rhythm of duration and the tonality of the scale are thus indifferent one to the other: not only because the lowest notes can be played in a more rapid rhythm than the highest, but also because time can pass quicker whilst I listen to a certain low sequence that I particularly like, whereas time might seem to drag listening to a high sequence that I do not enjoy.

On this basis, it seems that I cannot carry out a real

detension of perception, in order to disentangle matter in itself from subjective memory. Examining the question more closely, it might be said that the difficulty in disentangling perception from memory-contraction comes from the fact that the latter is supposed to constitute the very qualities of perception – which is not the case with memory-recall. Whereas in the case of the latter, I can make the concrete experiment of the dissociation of memory and perception – the experience of attentive reading – here this is no longer possible. In fact, I find myself face to face with the following aporetic alternative: either I try to intuit the result of detension directly – but in that case I would be led back to the experience of *my own* duration, and not that of material duration, the experience of colours which pale or of sounds which become lower. Or I return to science, distinguishing the vibratory and homogeneous nature of matter – but in this case I content myself with registering the result of an experiment, rather than thinking the supposedly continuous nature of homogeneous matter and of heterogeneous perception. In the latter case, therefore, I accede to the vibratory nature of matter, but only by way of a science which is discontinuous with my concrete perception of qualities.

In other words, memory-contraction seems to abolish the principal result of the theory of pure perception, namely that of the cognisability of the in-itself. For matter appears to us as that which has not been made the object of the work of contraction. But since this contraction has always already taken place, since its effect is supposed to reach the elementary components of perception, we cannot see any convincing way to take the *reverse path*, so as to rediscover matter in itself not yet affected by our subjective duration. In yet other words, the vice of contracting-memory seems to be that it plunges us once again, from a theory of perception-ascesis – a profoundly original moment of the Bergsonian conception, a moment also when his anti-criticism is at its most radical – into a theory of perception-synthesis, one which by virtue of this fact is subject to the Kantian separation of the for-us and the in-itself. For the force of the ascetic theory of perception consisted in the fact that the form of matter was posited in matter itself: synthesis was material, and consisted in the regulated relations that the images maintained one with another; representation added no sort of synthesis to matter. But everything changes with the contracting theory of memory; for now perception once again introduces a form into matter itself, a synthesis – specifically, a temporal compression – which is hailed as the genesis of immediate qualities. But if perception is synthetic, then we are truly condemned never to discover the nature of the matter so synthesised, since we are trapped within the limits of such a synthesis. This is result of the experiment we have made of our incapacity to intuit a detension which takes us outside the qualitative world proper to our intimate duration.

To better grasp the difficulty, we might invoke Kant's *Anticipations of Perception*. We know that, in the first *Critique*'s *Analytic of Principles*, Kant maintains that we can anticipate not only the form of the phenomena, but also, to a certain extent, its matter – and this by affirming that every reality admits of a degree, that is to say an intensive quantity, not divisible into units but into differentials. We know in fact that time is divisible to infinity, and that consequently between a degree x of a given quality, a degree supposed conscious, and the degree 0 of consciousness, are ranged an infinity of moments in time, which are the object of syntheses that are not yet conscious. Thus, the immediately apparent qualities of perception have in fact already been informed by consciousness. Perception is the sum – or, better, the integral – of differentials which alone can be identified with the thing in itself. But to rediscover this thing in itself such as it is, we must have at our disposal an operation of derivation that we would be sure would correspond to the exact inverse of the pre-conscious integration of perception. Now, it is this which we cannot determine with any certainty in any case. In this sense, Bergson appears to founder upon a difficulty which, apart from some obvious differences, recalls that which contributes to Salomon Maïmon's justification of his scepticism: for Maïmon, in his *Essay on Transcendental Philosophy*, having precisely identified the noumena with the differential of consciousness, and the phenomena with its integration by the productive imagination, proscribed himself from operating the reverse path through the understanding – the path that would go from the phenomena to the noumena. According to him, the noumena must remain unknown to us, because we could never be sure that the derivation proposed by the philosopher to rediscover the noumena would be the exact symmetrical counterpart of the integration within consciousness of such a noumena.[16]

In short, it seems to us that all the anti-Kantian and immanentist gains of perception-ascesis are put at risk by

---

16. For a more detailed examination of this aspect of the *Essay on Transcendental Philosophy* see J. Rivelaygue, *Leçons de métaphysique allemande*, vol.I (Paris: Grasset, 1990), 134-149.

Bergson's return to the circle of subjective synthesis. As soon as Bergson introduces the work of synthesis into subjectivity, he brings back the possibility of a thing in itself inaccessible to thought – and thus the possibility of a radical transcendence. The stakes of the discussion thus become as follows: can one envisage a theory of perception-ascesis which avoids passing via the synthetic moment of contraction? What would such a theory look like, and how might one try to justify it?

6. THE RETURN TO PURE PERCEPTION

How to think pure perception without contracting-memory? Let us return to the rationale which seemed to lead Bergson to introduce the idea of contraction. This rationale, if we reflect upon it, seems to be reducible to one fact: *viz.*, that the science of elementary matter decomposes minimal conscious durations into extraordinarily rapid events – specifically, the vibrations of light. It is such a vibratory reality of matter that the theory of contracting memory seeks to account for, by pinpointing the process by which this material state is transformed for us into distinct qualities. But is there anything in this fact that a theory of the image alone could not account for? It seems that the difficulty comes from the fact that an image – that of a perception or colour – is supposed to contain many other images – those of 'vibrathomogenes'. Now if an image was to present to us matter such as it is in itself, must not its prodigious vibration also appear to us? Since this is not the case, we must indeed admit that our grasping of the world introduces an operation which modifies it.

However, Bergson himself gives us the means to

respond easily to this objection: has he not told us that the theory of the image supposed that there were many more things in matter than in representation? Did he not found his immanentism on the fact that matter is *not other, but more* than representation? This being accepted, what prevents us from attributing to matter all the images that we can extract from it? For if matter is a set of picturesque images, there is nothing to stop us saying that it is also, in addition, a set of images in which qualities no longer have any place: nothing stops us from making of matter all the images which we might have at every scale of time, and indeed of space. This, let us repeat, was the very force of the subtractive theory of pure perception: the thing in itself is all the points of view it is possible to take on that thing: from the most intimate, those of its tiniest details, to the most remote. In that case, why not say the same of luminous matter, and hold that light is *all* the images that can be taken from it: the colours of the spectrum, as well as homogeneous vibrations? Nothing prevents us from according to the matter-image these two points of view: maintaining that it is heterogenous and homogeneous *as well*, both image-perception *and* experimental image, coloured image *and* vibratory image. This amounts simply to saying of matter that it is composed of radically distinct images according to its temporal and spatial scales. In other words, it amounts to according to matter all the rhythms of duration, and to making of human perception not the *contraction* of material quantity, but the *selection* of one of the rhythms of a matter-image which contains each and every one of them.

7. THE SUBTRACTIVE MODEL

From this point on, we can start to examine what the purely subtractive model drawn from *Matter and Memory* would consist in – a model of subtractions without contractions.

Here are the two postulates from which we begin:

1) Matter is composed of images. These images all communicate one with another, according to laws that we identify with the laws of nature. This communication we will name with the term *flux* – the flux by which images receive and transmit movement to images. Matter thus consists in a multiplicity at once qualitative and quantitative, picturesque and homogeneous.

We can then agree on the following terminology: we will call *heterogeneous* a multiplicity that is not simply qualitative, but at once qualitative and quantitative. If the homogeneous remains identifiable with quantity, the heterogeneous ceases to be identifiable with quality. The heterogeneous is more heterogeneous than quality, comprising not only the differences of qualities between themselves, but also the differences of quantities between themselves, and the difference of quality in general from quantity.

2) To these images, connected to each other by flows, we must add *interceptions*, cuts, which from the point of view of images mean nothing more than a local isolation – their becoming-superficial. Here, we distance ourselves, for reasons of clarity, from Bergson's theory taken strictly: rather than saying that the rarefaction of images in perception is due to the fact that the living being allows itself to be traversed by most images only to retain a few of

them, we say that this rarefaction is due to cuts, barrings, which only permit certain flows to penetrate into consciousness. The essential remains: perception is in every way still thought as a rarefaction of matter.

We can formulate these two postulates more precisely by including both in the following proposition: *there is becoming, and becoming is fluxes and their interceptions.* This statement allows us to say the following: a flux is not sufficient to constitute a becoming – for this, there must also be interception. Fluxes, certainly, transmit movement: but this movement is not a becoming, in the sense that, ruled by the laws of nature, it connects every image to every other image, according to a necessity which saturates the real in some way. Every thing being connected to every other according to laws, the cognition of an image is sufficient in principle for us to determine the present, past and future movement of all the others – and this to such a point that the very difference between the three dimensions of time is erased, to the profit of an immutable web of transmissions of movements. One is faced with an immobility made of movements, analogous to that of a powerful jet of water, in which the continuous movement of matter gives rise to a continuous immobility of form. Flows, left to themselves, are just such a pure mobility, immobilising themselves by the very fact that no obstacle obstructs their deployment: they are the bonds between all things ruled by fixed laws.

For there to be becoming, something must happen, and for something to happen, it is not enough that something comes to pass – on the contrary, it must be the case that something does not pass: there must be a disconnection. This is the only way to introduce a becoming into matter, without introducing anything other than matter: it is the only way for us to uphold Deleuze's 'magical formula: PLURALISM = MONISM',[17] without its leading us back to dualism. The monism of heterogeneous matter will accommodate within itself the pluralism of eventality, without for all that accommodating anything other than matter – that is, without introducing ontological duality.

Let us see how such an operation is possible. The condition of there being a becoming is that a change is produced which cannot be reduced to a material flux. This imposes the following thesis upon us: there must exist a becoming of interceptions themselves. It must be that the interceptions change. But how is such a change thinkable? In view of what we have said above, this can only happen in one way: *the interceptions of flux must move along the lines of flux.*

So we obtain schema 1:

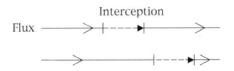

Schema 1: Interceptions of flux and flux of interceptions.

We can see here that a becoming is always two becomings – for there to be becoming, becoming must become twice: as flux of images, and as flux of interception of images. Becoming is thus composed of a double 'arrowing', which,

17. *A Thousand Plateaus*, 20.

however, introduces no ontological dualism. The first arrow is that of flux. Only the second arrow introduces becoming. Through this double arrowing, then, one can achieve *the grafting of the Bergsonian theme of the image onto the Stoic theme of incorporeals*, as mobilised by Deleuze in *Logic of Sense*.[18] We shall thus dub the temporal dimension of flux *Chronos*, and the temporal dimension of interceptions, *Aiôn*. What authorises us to adopt, not only the Stoic language, but also the Deleuzian terminology as it is put to work in *Logic of Sense*? Two things:

1) Firstly, we know that the division between *Aiôn* and *Chronos* in *Logic of Sense* distinguishes the temporality of deep causes, the temporality of corporeal mixtures, from that of incorporeal events. Now, it is indeed to this type of division that the preceding double arrowing corresponds: fluxes are indeed dynamic mixtures of matter, and the interceptions are indeed incorporeals, since they are nothing material. In addition, the becoming of interceptions is a becoming which rises to the surface from the depths of images, since the result of the interception is the becoming-superficial of matter: its reduction to its envelopment in perception. So that we can legitimately take up Deleuze's exclamation with regard to incorporeals: '*Everything now returns to the surface*'.[19]

2) Secondly, we can attribute to *Aiôn*, thus redefined as displacement of cuts, a property homologous to that of the Deleuzian *Aiôn*: namely *eventality*, understood as a unique Event in which all events communicate, 'the affirmation of all chance in a single moment', the 'unique cast for all

---

18. *Logic of Sense*, 'First Series of Paradoxes of Pure Becoming', 3-6.

19. *Ibid.*, 10.

dicethrows'.[20] In fact, in order to think the process whereby the interceptions are displaced, the temporality in which the interceptions change, we must exclude every form of material explanation.

If the displacement of a disconnection proceeds from material laws, it will be reduced to a flux like any other – and no becoming would exist. But if there is becoming, no physical law can account for it. Neither determinism, nor probability – the double explicative paradigm of material processes – can therefore be mobilised to account for the displacement of incorporeals. So if we wish to say something positive with regard to such a becoming of breaks, it falls to us to posit that this becoming certainly constitutes a chance occurrence, but one which is non-probabilisable, since it is the result of a unique throw of the dice, launched from all eternity upon the immutable table of fluxes.[21]

Let us attempt, then, to indicate more precisely the meaning of *Aiôn* so understood as the displacement of disconnections. Firstly, we must return to the being of disconnections. We said above that one thing at stake in the subtractive model was the avoidance of every form of dualism, or of differentiation between modes of being. Disconnected-being cannot therefore be anything other than flux-being. Now, in order to maintain this, it is not enough to say that disconnected-being is nothing: for to say this would be to lead ourselves back to a Epicurean–style dualism – that is to say, a dualism of matter and void.

---

20. *Ibid.*, 205.

21. On Deleuzian chance, understood as unique dice-throw and eternal return, see Alain Badiou's commentary in *Deleuze: The Clamor of Being* (trans. L. Burchill, Minneapolis: Minnesota University Press, 2000), 'Eternal return and chance', 67-78.

The 'ontological landscape' furnished by our model in fact resembles an 'inverse Epicureanism': not one of real atoms displacing each other in a hazardous fashion (precipitated by the *clinamen*) in an infinite void, but one of 'atoms of void' displacing each other in a hazardous fashion within the infinite plenitude of fluxes. It must therefore be that disconnection itself is ultimately reduced to the plenitude of heterogeneous flux. But how to think a break of flux, which is itself a flux, without annulling it as break? Very simply, by reducing the break to a *detour* of flux, accompanied at the same time by a *retardation effect* imposed upon this same flux. It suffices to multiply the detour to infinity to obtain a retardation itself as durable as desired. A break is a local accumulation to the nth power of detours of flux. We therefore find ourselves within a strictly continuist ontology, which produces 0 on the basis of an infinite summation of 1 – or which produces nothing on the basis of a infinite summation of the real.

In identifying break with detour, we assure ourselves that nothing exists apart from matter. But it remains true that, if there is becoming, we must maintain the distinction between *Chronos* and *Aiôn*. Why? Becoming, as we have said, depends on the becoming of breaks – and therefore on the becoming of detours. The becoming of a detour is its displacement on a line of flux. But how, or under what conditions, can such a displacement be thought? Under one simple condition: *we must have a past*. Now, *Chronos* tells us nothing about the past of a break. This can be seen quite easily in the following schema:

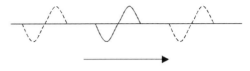

Schema 2: The wave.

If a detour had a material past, it would then be reduced to a *wave* – the wave whose displacement is shown in the schema. In the most general sense we understand by 'wave' a material movement whose past as well as its future can in principle be reconstructed, in a deterministic or probabilistic way. To be pregnant with its past, if one might so speak, as well as with its future – to detain one and the other, enveloped in its actual-being – this is what is proper to the wave. Now, the detour is not materially distinct from the wave – since it itself is made of matter only – but its displacement must be, since its temporality is hazardous. We must therefore sketch a *second line of the past*, alone capable of distinguishing these two indiscernibles, the wave and the interception. We therefore have the following schema:

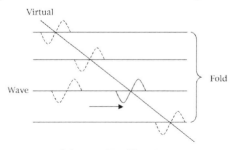

Schema 3: The Virtual.

This second line of the past, which is no longer that

93

of the wave, I name *the virtual*. We can fix the vocabulary, then: a detour possessing a material past will be said to be a wave; a detour proceeding from the line of the virtual will be said to be *a fold*. Without entering into detail, we can see clearly that the virtual thus characterised has many decisive points in common with the Deleuzian virtual:

– The virtual is not indeterminate, but entirely determined;

– The virtual is real – if not, there could be no becoming of the fold – the virtual is thus opposed to the actual, but not to the real;

– The virtual is not, like the possible, the phantasmatic double of the actual – identical to the actual but minus existence – rather, the virtual and the actual have no reason to resemble each other;

– Finally, the virtual is the ontological condition of authentic becoming, that is to say of the unforeseeable creation of novelty.[22]

But it will perhaps be argued that this introduction of the theme of the virtual into the interceptive model is of no interest. All we have done is to inject into our model the Bergsonian virtual, inherent to the conception of duration as unforeseeable creation; and by this fact, and for all that the virtual undoubtedly represents the essential Bergsonism heritage in Deleuze's thinking, the model proposed will only be as homologous with Deleuze as Bergson is. All of which is certainly correct. But what makes the introduction of the virtual into the subtractive model interesting is that

---

22. On these aspects of the virtual, see in particular: 'The Actual and the Virtual' in *Dialogues II*, 112-5; and A. Badiou, *Deleuze, op.cit.*: 'The Virtual', 43-64.

it means we have to modify, on an essential point, the Bergsonian notion of the virtual. The modification might be formulated thus: *we are led to think the virtual independently of the couplet quantity-quality*. Now, this couplet, in Bergson, constitutes a primordial polarity for the thinking of pure duration. In the *Essay on the Immediate Data of Consciousness*,[23] for example, pure duration is qualitative multiplicity, as opposed to an homogeneous and quantitative matter which by virtue of this has no duration. Whereas in *Matter and Memory*, as we have seen, quality and quantity are now thought in continuity with each other – but it is precisely memory's role to obtain quality via the contraction of quantity.

On the other hand, in the subtractive model, this polarity becomes inadequate for thinking the virtual, and this for the simple reason that the fluxes are already both wholly qualitative and wholly quantitative. More particularly, quality ceases to be in itself the mark of novelty. Which implies that the language of unforeseeable creation will not be primordially a language of quality, but a language of *folding* – of the fold's becoming-virtual: a language which would be, ultimately, a topology, or rather a *geology* of the virtual. Through this we do indeed engender an effect of homology with Deleuze: namely a Bergsonian heritage of the virtual, expressed in geological rather than qualitative terms:[24] to say that 'there is becoming' is to say that 'there are virtual folds', or that 'there is folding'.

---

23. Translated by F.L.Pogson as *Time and Free Will* (London: Allen & Unwin, 1950).

24. One thinks here of two texts of Deleuze's: *The Fold*; and, in *A Thousand Plateaus*, '10,000BC: The Geology of Morals' (39-74).

To progress further along the path of a reconstruction of Deleuzian thought via the beginning of *Matter and Memory*, we must now emphasise the following point: we began knowingly from a theory which is not exactly that of pure perception, but which is somewhat less rich. Because not only did we divide *Matter and Memory*, making the first chapter autonomous, but we also divided the theory of pure perception itself. Let us explain. In the theory of pure perception, Bergson gives himself an indeterminate centre of action, that is to say a free being: it is such a freedom that is at the origin of the selection, amongst images, of those alone which interest the living being. Now, the refusal of all dualism constrains us, for our part, not to accord existence to beings endowed with freedom. For we would then have two types of being, free beings and beings subject to material laws. If Deleuze sees an immanentism in pure perception, it is no doubt because he divines a monism beneath the apparent dualism of freedom and matter. To extract this monism, it must be shown that what Bergson calls freedom can be obtained as a particular case of subtractive becoming. In other words, it must be shown in what way the living being is a particular case of such a becoming.

Let us reformulate things more clearly. It must indeed be seen that in admitting of fluxes and interceptions, we have not yet admitted of any living being, nor *a fortiori* any free being. An interception, even a sum of interceptions, do not make a living being. For what is a living being, according to the Bergsonian inspiration? It is a *local rarefaction* of fluxes: because a living being is a body – that is to say, a *selection* – but a selection that we have named as *primary*: a selection anterior to all free choice, and one which offers us the terms from which a freedom might potentially be chosen. In other words, a living being is a *place* where fluxes can no longer pass through fully and indiscriminately. Consequently, we can advance the following definition of the living being: *a living being is a discontinuous loop of interceptions.* A loop, because it is necessary to assure a place for the rarefaction of fluxes; a discontinuous loop, because a living being cannot entirely cut itself off from the fluxes – otherwise it would no longer have any affective and/or perceptive relation with the surrounding world. I mean by 'rarefaction' any localised impoverishment of fluxes – thus, every living being is a rarefaction. A rarefaction is more than an interception: an interception does not make a rarefaction, whereas a rarefaction is made solely from interceptions of fluxes.

We obtain schema 4, the schema of the living being or the body :

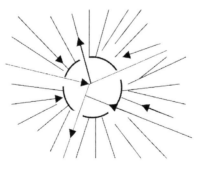

Schema 4: The Body

But we might then pose a new question, *viz*.: Is there a becoming of living beings? Or again: Is there an evental becoming of rarefactions? If we suppose it possible to think the living being, then there *must* be such a becoming. For if there was no becoming of rarefactions, one could only consider what a living being was made of, the matter that constituted its site. One could think what it is made of, but not what it is: one could think it as organism, but not as rarefaction. One could think the material substance of bodies, but not the bodies themselves as site of rarefaction, of the selection of images. But how to think the non-organic living being, since rarefaction itself is not made from nothing – since there does not exist any vital fluid, any matter other than that of physics, which would render singular the mode of being of a living being? One solution to this difficulty is the following: thinking the living being must come down to thinking the *becoming* of zones of rarefaction. There must exist a non-organic past of bodies – there must exist virtual rarefactions. We need a non-organic past of the living being, an inorganic becoming of bodies. Or further, we need a *body without organs*.[25] Then, if the foldings remain sufficiently coherent to constitute the foldings of rarefactions, we would be able to think life on the basis of its own evolution, and thus isolate a *typology* of vital becomings, becomings which cannot be identified with organic fluxes.

If we entrust to science the care of describing and thinking the states of things, that is to say the states of flux – we will reserve for philosophy the task of describing and thinking virtual becomings. Let us call *evaluation* every typology of becomings that are vital, but inorganic. What typology will be adopted by our evaluation? What are the major types of vital becomings admitted by the living being understood as discontinuous loop of interception? Two elementary

25. On the Body without Organs, see *Anti-Oedipus*.

cases present themselves: that of the narrowing and that of the broadening of discontinuities. The first *increases the power of disinterest* of the living being, the second signals itself through an *increased openness* to a part of the fluxes. We will call the second becoming *active*, the first *reactive*.

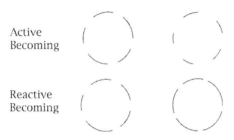

Schema 5: Active becoming, reactive becoming.

But before going further, it is time to show precisely in what way the interceptive model is distinct from that of pure perception according to Bergson – and why this distinction should interest us. The distinction is the following: Bergson begins with the postulate that there exist beings capable of acting freely – that is to say, centres of selection of images, the supposed selection being a selection of the *second type* (that which designates a *free choice* between various options). From this he then infers the nature of perception, which turns out to be a selection of the first type: an *unfree* selection from the terms of the choice. We have proceeded in the other direction: we gave ourselves *only* the first selections – unfree selections, that is – and then constituted the living being as a particular configuration of those first selections. Thereby, only part of the theory of pure perception is adopted:

because only one type of selection is introduced into the constructed model: unfree selection. These selections are then endowed with an unforeseeable becoming, alone capable of producing a novelty, thus making possible a distinction between two regimes of selection – active and reactive. We therefore understand that the advantage of the subtractive model is to allow *the grafting of Bergsonian selection onto Nietzschean selection.* For having removed from the Bergsonian model the notion of freewill recused by Nietzsche, we can bring together the two senses – the Nietzschean and the Bergsonian – of the term 'selection': that which designates the selection of images by perception, and that which designates the typology of vital becomings. A new effect of homology with Deleuze: the subtractive model allows us to think the meaning of his predilection for two philosophers who seem prima facie so very dissimilar. But in order to obtain this rapprochement rigorously, we must construct the concept of the active more precisely.

What is a reactive becoming, according to the present model? It is a becoming which manifests itself through a disinterested retreat inherent to the very constitution of the living being. This disinterest, precisely in so far as it is given as constitutive of the essence of the living being, we will give the name of *stupidity* [*bêtise*]. Stupidity, the stubborn stupidity of the proverbial mule, is for the living being always a way of conserving itself in its being, without opening out onto exteriority. On the contrary, an active becoming is always manifested through the fact that something *happens* – and more precisely, something *interesting.* So the categories of interesting and uninteresting are, for us, substituted for those of freedom and unfreedom. For the two becomings

– active and reactive (or stupid) – are both anterior to all free choice: they affect the space of choice, anterior to any choice being made. This is why becoming – and particularly active becoming – must be thought as essentially *passive*; must be thought, even, as an increase of the passivity of the living being, of its 'passability', a way for it to register an increased affectivity to a number of external fluxes. This increase is not itself material, since it is a folding: but it is a becoming which makes an increased flux of matter pass into the body. The concepts of encounter, of passivity, and even of affect – concepts resonant with the Deleuzian thinking of the event – thus take on a vital, not merely organic, significance here. To the active body, capable of an innovative, inventive becoming, something always happens: its increase of force does not come from an autonomous decision of a constitutive subject, but from an experience that is always undergone, an affective test in which a radical exteriority gives itself, an exteriority never before felt as such.[26]

By way of a conclusion, let us now come to that which seems to us to be the principal interest of the subtractive model.

The model allows us to give a precise response to a question that might suggest itself as regards the notion of life in Deleuze, and also in Nietzsche – a question which, we believe, already traverses the work of these two philosophers: how does the living being succumb to reactivity? A question that one might equally formulate as Deleuze does in *Anti-Oedipus*: are all forces doomed to become reactive?

---

26. On thought and its relation to stupidity, see particularly Chapter 3 of *Difference and Repetition*, and also François Zourabichvili's analysis in *Deleuze. Une philosophie de l'événement*, (Paris: PUF, 1994; republished in 2004 with a new introduction), 24-33.

That a vital becoming should be active is not difficult to understand: whether or not one agrees that a being tends to persevere in its being, it is easy to grasp that the living being tends to extend the surface of its relation to the world. But that a being should diminish its power, and thus diminish its receptivity – its inventive passibility – is obviously an enigma. It is an enigma that is reinforced when we consider that a reactive being can propagate its reactivity to other bodies, separate the active from what it can do, and that reactivity even seems ultimately to affect those experiences which in themselves are the most innovative, the most rev-olutionary. Indeed, the question is also that of dualism : because if we cannot manage to grasp in what way life is virtually reactive, we risk ending up with a separation between two modes of being whose communication will be averred unthinkable, even whilst it is, on the contrary, quite manifest. In short, how to understand that life should be complicit with reactivity ?

The subtractive model gives a precise response to this question. And this, for a simple reason: such a model leads us to maintain that there exist two types of death. *And it is because there are two types of deaths that there are two types of lives.*

Let us explain, and conclude.

Note firstly that we do indeed discover, in our model, an essential ambiguity of death. Because two deaths appear to be conceivable for inorganic bodies, two ways of 'erasing' the discontinuous loops: either by a *closing in*, and a progressive ossification of the loop of interception, or by *dissipation* and progressive disappearance of the loop itself. Or again: either a death by diminution of the surface of the loop (ossification of bodies), or a death by diminution of the loop (dissipation of bodies). This is what the following schema shows more clearly:

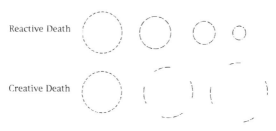

Schema 6: Reactive death, creative death.

We could say that death by diminution of the surface of the loop is equivalent to a monadological death, a death by vanishing: folded in upon itself, the body shrinks more and more, until completely annihilated. The *reactive* power of death might well be conceived in this way: for the reactive tends toward a death by narcosis, by exhaustion, by an ever-increasing indifference to the world. And we could name as the *priest* the conceptual persona heralding such a regime of death.

But how to think this other possibility of death, by diminution of the loop, by dissipation of the body, by an ever-wider opening of the latter onto the external flux, up to a complete dissolution? And what conceptual persona, this time, will incarnate such a deadly becoming?

It seems to us that it is the possibility of this second death that *affectively* dominated our very first reading of the beginning of *Matter and Memory*: reading this text, so gripping in many ways, we felt, however, at the same time, a vague terror. And this impression of terror was due to the following: as a good materialist, we had always considered death as a return of the body to inorganic matter – thus, for the subject, as a simple nothing. But if matter is what Bergson says it is, then death – the return to the material state – would not at all be identified with nothing, but rather with madness – and even an *infinite madness*. For becoming-material would be the effacement of the selection of images. And it would seem then that to make an image of death, we would have to conceive what our life would be if all the movements of the earth, all the noises of the earth, all the smells, the tastes, all the light – of the earth and of elsewhere, came to us in a moment, in an instant – like an atrocious screaming tumult of all things, traversing us continually and instantaneously. As if the nothing of death could not be understood as a simple void, but on the contrary only as a saturation, an abominable superfluity of existence. Death, thus understood, is the triumphant reign of communication. To die is to become a pure point of passage, a pure centre of communication of all things with all things. It will be seen, then, that the living being is not the emergence of pain in an atrophied world, but on the contrary the diminution of madness in a becoming-terror of chaos, bringing the latter to an infinite speed. Of this death-madness, this death-terror, one might say something like that which Deleuze says of chaos, in the conclusion to *What is Philosophy?*:

> We require just a little order to protect us from chaos. Nothing is more distressing than a thought that escapes itself, than ideas that fly off, that disappear hardly formed, already

eroded by forgetfulness or precipitated into others that we no longer master.[27]

The deadly becoming of communication thus brings with it an important difference from the reactive death of the priest: the fact that it *resembles active-becoming*, and is even, up to a certain point, indiscernible from the latter. As if the sciences of communication – advertising, marketing, etc. – which, Deleuze says (also in *What is Philosophy*?), have arrogated the concept to themselves – as if these disciplines were the terrifying continuation of authentic creation in the inconsistent and insignificant tumult of information.[28]

In the subtractive system, then, the *communicator* must be made an original conceptual persona, alongside the priest: he who founds becomings which are no longer reactive, but *creative* – becomings which decant death at the very heart of creation, by apparently marrying it with movement, and with words. Becomings which are not those of a stupidity closed in on itself, but which are rather those of a certain obstinate silliness, of a frenetic openness to whatever appearances of novelty come along. The terror of the philosopher before philosophies of communication, or at least certain of their avatars – the way the philosopher flees, as Deleuze says, as soon as they propose a 'discussion' – would be a terror before his own possible death – that which he courts dangerously: death-madness, death-inconsistency, and not death-narcosis. Degradation in the uninterrupted flood of communication, and not somnolence in the reinforced mutilation of affects.

---

27. *What is Philosophy?*, 201.

28. *Ibid.*, 10

We can see here, in passing, a second anti-Kantian characteristic of the subtractive model: not only does one attain the in-itself via a perception-ascesis, but what's more, that towards which the philosopher invites us to incline cannot be thought as Idea, even as regulative Idea. And this for a very simple reason: in this model, *there could be nothing worse than to achieve that towards which we tend*. One tends towards chaos when one invents, when one creates, but there is nothing one intends less than actually catching up with it. It is at once a tendential and an anti-regulative model: we must continually approach the chaos which governs the propensity to create, and continually guard against falling into it.

And so finally we clearly understand the source of the priest's power, that is to say the origin of the seductive force of the reactive over the living being: this seduction comes from the fact that the priest can at least promise us *a nice easy death*, a death that reinforces infinitely the process of birth, which was already originally a process of disinterest with regard to flux. The priest promises us a second birth, a birth that is an isolation, an indifference raised to the second power against the external world, a rarefaction greater than that of coming into the world – in short, a sort of immortality, after its own fashion. The model of the two deaths thus permits us, without founding any dualism, to understand the complicity of life with reactivity: *becoming-reactive is what defends life against its becoming-creative* – or more precisely: narcosis-becoming stops us from becoming-mad. For this is the great seduction of reactivity: which philosopher, faced with a communicator, wouldn't silently wish to become a priest?

In short, we have two deaths, one of which is worse than the other – and this is indeed why to think with Deleuze – really to think – is something as rare as it is difficult: because to think is to become a neighbour to the worst of the two, and to risk the becoming-chaos of life, its infinite becoming-creative. To think is twice victorious to cross the Acheron: it is to visit the dead, or rather death, and above all to succeed in returning; to remain a structured living being, having tested oneself against the nascent destructuration of new fluxes; to maintain oneself in the Outside, but to hold oneself close, thus to some degree closed, and thus to discipline into writing a chaotic experience. Or again, to say it even better, no longer with Nerval but with Deleuze: to think is *thrice victorious* to cross the Acheron.[29] For it is to have the courage to *set out once again* towards the worst of two deaths, after having escaped at least once before: it is to return to the worst, knowing all the while that it is the worst – because, after all, how could one do otherwise?

---

29. See *What is Philosophy?*, 202.

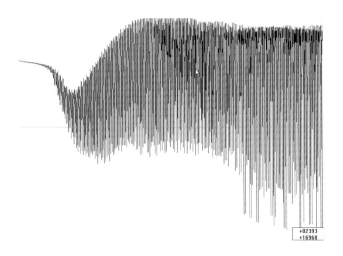

```
+02393
+16968
```

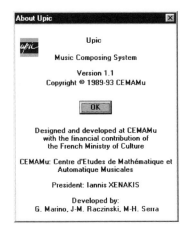

Blackest Ever Black

Haswell & Hecker

REDISCOVERING THE POLYAGOGY OF ABSTRACT MATTER[1]

As I see it, music is a domain where the most profound questions of philosophy, thought, behaviour, and the theory of the universe ought to pose themselves to the composer.[2]

The images in the following pages are screenshots taken during the drafting of the electronic 'score' of Haswell & Hecker's collaborative sound work, *Blackest Ever Black*,[3] composed using Iannis Xenakis's UPIC.[4] The conception and continued development of the UPIC – a digital system allowing the creation of music through the simple act of

1. Text by Robin Mackay in collaboration with Russell Haswell and Florian Hecker.

2. Xenakis, in H. Lohner, 'Interview with Iannis Xenakis', *Computer Music Journal* 10: 4, Winter 1986: 50-5, 54.

3. Warner Classics and Jazz (UK) WEA 64321CD / WEA 69972LP.

4. Unité polyagogique informatique du CEMAMu: See H. Lohner, 'The UPIC System', in *Computer Music Journal* 10:4, Winter 1986: 42-9; B. A. Varga, *Conversations with Iannis Xenakis* (London: Faber, 1996) 194-8; and Iannis Xenakis, *Formalized Music: Thought and Mathematics in Music*, trans. S. Kanach (NY: Pendragon, 1992), 329-34. CEMAMu, the Centre d'Etudes de Mathématique et Automatique Musicales, is a nonprofit co-operative founded by Xenakis in 1966 to conduct research and development in electronic and automated music (See *Conversations*, 118-33). On the aims of CEMAMu, see Lohner, 'The UPIC System', 43.

drawing – may seem, if not a departure, then something of a minor element of Xenakis's *oeuvre* (only a handful of Xenakis's works were composed exclusively using the UPIC). But an examination of the thinking behind this technology sheds much light on the philosophical importance and integrity of Xenakis's work, and its points of intersection with the philosophy of Deleuze (and Deleuze/Guattari).

Haswell and Hecker have spoken of the four movements of *Blackest Ever Black* as 'assist[ing] the experience of synaesthesia'.[5] And indeed, the UPIC emerged in the context of Xenakis's lifelong efforts to express in his work abstract forms which he saw as belonging essentially to no particular medium, any more than they were the exclusive province of the sciences or the arts. But what is the significance of synaesthesia, and of the UPIC's graphism-sound translation, in relation to Xenakis's interrogation of music?

For Xenakis, forms themselves were a sort of epiphenomenal 'froth' generated by the ordered relations between multiplicities of elements. To discover the mathematical structures underlying their emergence, and to understand what happened when the composer 'incarnated' them in time, was to require a series of mathematically-inspired conceptual 'generalisations', which saw Xenakis leave all musical tradition behind.

By the time of 1953-4's *Metastaseis*, Xenakis's key conceptual innovations – involving above all a thinking of the dialectical couplets unity/multiplicity, local/global and continuity/discontinuity – were already in place: The use

---

5. Curtis Roads, *Blackest Ever UPIC*, sleevenotes to *Blackest Ever Black*.

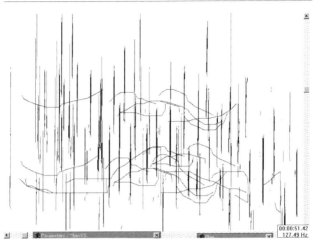

of 'sound masses', 'clouds' or 'complexes', defined through global textural and dynamic properties, and within which a multiplicity of individual lines are locally determined mathematically or statistically; giving rise immediately to the problem of continuity between one mass, state, or constellation, and another – precisely, metastaseis – whence Xenakis's characteristic use of glissandi.[6]

In a reprise of Leibniz's theory of *petites-perceptions*, according to which in perceiving the sound of the sea we operate an 'integration' of infinite unconscious perceptions of individual waves, a crucial inspiration for *Metastaseis* was the wartime experience of 'the transformation of the regular, rhythmic noise of a hundred thousand people into some fantastic disorder' – the mathematics of a

---

6. Equally so in his architectural work – the Philips Pavilion, constructed during his time working with Le Corbusier, and employing the same curve functions as the *Metastaseis* score, constituted 'a glissando in space' (Varga, *Conversations*, 24).

political singularity as native workers faced occupying Nazi troops.[7] The question of the nature of continuous transitions intersects with the question of the individuation of masses: why are certain clusters of frequencies registered as 'a' sound, and at what point does it change in nature, becoming many? Throughout *Blackest Ever Black,* simple units of sound gradually, insensibly shift and diverge into separate lines; as if, where there previously was a cloud or a swarm, we now see its constituent members, waves subtracted from the sea.

It was not only mathematics, but equally a close attention to the physical and perceptual parameters of sound as *material,* that would allow Xenakis to escape the impasse he diagnosed in serialism,[8] towards what could properly be called a structuralism, indeed a post-structuralism.[9] For the latter, serial music would be just another fetter to be shed,[10] a brake on the exploration of the objective Idea (in a quasi-Platonic sense, as we shall see) of music, informed by a sonic materialism.

According to Xenakis, serialism's baffling overcomplexity for the listener stems from its being based upon insufficiently interrogated categories of musical thought. The theoretical passing over of the greater part of the complex transformations that intervene between the tone-row and sound-matter itself, mean that what is quite systematic 'outside-time' becomes disarrayed 'in-time' as those dimensions

---

7. Xenakis, in Varga, *Conversations,* 52.

8. See I. Xenakis, 'Le crise de la musique sérielle', in *Gravesener Blätter*, Vol. 1, 1955: 2-4.

9. On Xenakis as structuralist, see T. Campener *Iannis Xenakis: strutturalismo e poetica della sonorità oggettiva*, at http://users.unimi.it/~gpiana/dm9/campaner/xen.htm.

10. Xenakis, in Varga, *Conversations,* 51.

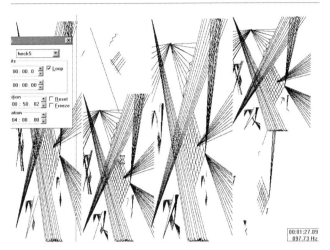

of sound suppressed under serialism's 'tautological unity'[11] emerge haphazardly in auditory experience, uncontrolled and unorganised. Serial music also leaves 'out of account the problem of continuity-discontinuity':[12] Although, naturally, continuous and discontinuous change took place within compositions, the problematic was not afforded the attention Xenakis believed it merited in music as in mathematics.[13] And so ultimately, the rigorous but arbitrarily-applied system of serialism failed the intelligence of the musical ear. To rectify this situation, Xenakis would seek an understanding of both the logic of musical perception and the mathematical structure of music, bringing them together into a new, generalised theory and practice.

11. Xenakis, *Formalized Music*, 204.

12. Xenakis, in Varga, *Conversations*, 76-7.

13. *Ibid.*, 72-3.

This would enable him to 'fertilize'[14] music with mathematics, rather than imposing formal systems upon music with little regard for the knot intricating together mathematics, music and the physical sciences since the dawn of Western Civilisation.[15] In order to theorise how 'to make the sound itself live', it had to be realised that 'the inner life of music is not only in the general line of the composition, of the thought, but also within the tiniest details'.[16] If on the macrocompositional level serialism represented a necessary escape from

---

14. Revault d'Allones's expression, in I. Xenakis, *Arts/Sciences:Alloys*, trans. S. Kanach (NY: Pendragon, 1985), 386.

15. As is well known, Messiaen's benificent influence on Xenakis began with his advice not to worry about conventional musical studies, but to use what Xenakis already had at his disposal: his knowledge of mathematics, and his Greek heritage. Xenakis's theoretical work is deeply rooted in his researches into presocratic thought (see Xenakis, *Formalized Music* 201-209).

16. Xenakis, in Varga, *Conversations,* 64.

the tonal,[17] its proponents' lack of attention to timbre[18] or to the analysis of sound masses bespoke a failure to listen to what the sound was telling them, beyond the overcoding they had imposed upon it. Ultimately the richness of sound overflowed their enterprise. The UPIC would need to apply a 'new simplicity', it would map the structure of music beginning with sound itself.

When Boulez later denounced Xenakis's music as 'too simple', Xenakis would argue that 'if music reaches a point where it has become too complex, you need a new kind of simplicity. Complexity is not synonymous with aesthetic interest.'[19] That the UPIC, in particular, was used as proof of lack of sophistication by Xenakis's detractors indicates a

00:02:39.85
5400.53 Hz

17. *Ibid*, 54.

18. *Ibid*.

19. *Ibid.*, 29.

failure to understand the principle at work: 'a maximum of calculated sobriety in relation to the disparate elements and parameters' is necessary in order to 'open onto something cosmic'; 'a sober gesture, an act of consistency, capture or extraction that works in a material that is not meager but prodigiously simplified, creatively limited, selected.'[20]

With the UPIC, Xenakis realised the plan (conceived during his time with *musique concrète* pioneer Pierre Schaeffer in the early 1960s)[21] of extending to the *molecular* level of sound the theories that he had already applied to *molar* statistical aggregates on a macrocompositional level in exploring the problems of continuity and individuation of sound masses. With the use of computers, 'the circle would become complete, not only in the field of macroform but also in the smallest domain, that of sound synthesis.'[22]

But within this domain also, Xenakis immediately identified – and set to work breaking from – conventional wisdom: electronic sound-synthesis at the time was based exclusively upon Fourier's demonstration that any complex wave can be analysed into a series of simple sine waves.[23] Rather than assembling sound from such notionally 'natural' ready-mades (virtual regularly oscillating bodies), CEMAMu's approach would be to 'take the pressure versus time curve as a starting point – that is, what we hear' – a continuous series of intensities (differences in pressure) of arbitrary complexity: 'Instead of going backwards, we start with the curve', says Xenakis;[24] 'I wanted to take possession

---

20. *A Thousand Plateaus*, 344-5.

21. Xenakis, in Varga, *Conversations*, 42-4.

22. *Ibid.*, 43.

23. *Ibid.*, 43-4.

24. *Ibid.*, 119.

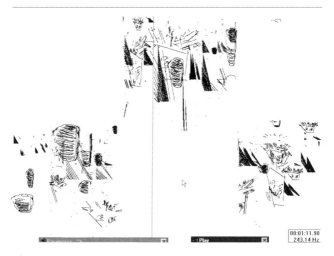

of the sound in a more conscious and thorough manner –
the material of the sound.[25]

But if the 'crisis of serialism' and the journey into
concrete sound helped break out of the stave, reinforcing
the fact that 'sound is much more general than pitch',[26] and
that '[i]t's important [...] to go beyond the limits of the pitch
versus time domain',[27] Xenakis had already been instinctively drawn to 'impure' sounds, the 'rougher [...] richer'
tones possible through unconventional usages of acoustic
instruments, precisely because they produced effects falling
outside 'the traditional pitch versus time relationship and
the musical idea that is linked to it'.[28] So that when he

---

25. *Ibid.*, 44. Italics ours.

26. *Ibid.*, 67.

27. *Ibid.*

28. *Ibid.*, 67.

came to work with Schaeffer, Xenakis found no difficulty in understanding why the latter 'despised sine waves' and worked instead 'with concrete sounds because they are really alive,'[29] and soon set about providing the enabling technology for the experimental electronic 'biology' of this sonic life.[30] In the wake of works such as *Metastaseis*, with their gigantic hand-drawn scores, and ever-enthusiastic for a 'generalisation' of methods and technical automation (Xenakis, for whom the orchestra is 'a machine [...] which makes sounds'),[31] in the late 60s he began work on what would become the UPIC, a system allowing the composer to experiment interactively, using graphical gestures, with 'the material of the sound'.

Just as serialism demanded specialist knowledge and codes, so early computer music systems demanded a detailed technical knowledge. Again, the UPIC aimed to break decisively from this, using a simple pen and tablet interface to focus attention on the act of composition. The composer would be given the simplest and least intrusive tool to realise their musical ideas, and would meanwhile participate implicitly in Xenakis's probing of the alliance between mathematical structure, the physics of sound, and the psychology of musical perception; between abstract structures, material synthesis, and artistic composition.

The UPIC puts the composer in control of every level of what is presented as a minimal hierarchy of composition – from the creation of waveforms that will determine the

29. Xenakis, in Varga, *Conversations*, 44.

30. To "study the evolution of timbres, dynamics, and register [...] to make chromosomes of attacks" – Xenakis, quoted in Harley, 'Electroacoustic Music', 35.

31. Xenakis, in Varga, *Conversations*, 67.

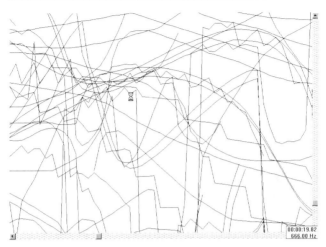

```
00:00:19.82
666.00 Hz
```

timbre, volume and intensity of the sounds to be employed, to the 'orchestration' of these voices into 'pages' of the score, and the mixing and layering of pages into a final recording. Importantly, no level of the hierarchy need ever be closed off in order for the composer to work on the next;[32] one might then describe the system as one of 'transparent stratification', rendering completely open to experimentation the levels of organisation necessarily in play in any musical composition. In addition, the UPIC user decides how, in Xenakis's terms, to bring the 'outside time' pages of the score 'into time': A page of music could be assigned, in the first version of the UPIC, a duration from 0.2 seconds to 30 minutes,[33] in later versions from 6 milliseconds to 2 hours.[34]

32. Lohner, 'The UPIC System', 46.

33. *Ibid.*, 48.

34. Roads, 'Blackest ever UPIC'.

This unprecedented elasticity of musical time encouraged by the UPIC is present as an ordering principle in *Blackest Ever Black*, where Haswell & Hecker use elements whose family resemblances are barely consciously recognisable, as they undergo extreme transformations, morphing from the instantaneous to the highly attenuated.

> The molecular has the capacity to make the *elementary* communicate with the *cosmic*: precisely because it effects a dissolution of form that connects the most diverse longitudes and latitudes, the most varied speeds and slownesses, which guarantees a continuum by stretching variation far beyond its formal limits.[35]

This simultaneous harnessing of the cosmic and the elementary makes of the most radical material experimentation at the same time a radical democratisation

---

35. *A Thousand Plateaus*, 308-9.

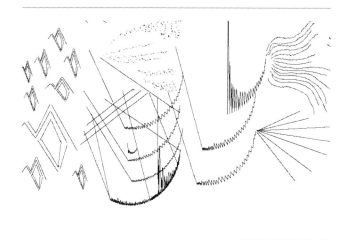

of means. *Contra* any theoretical elitism, the UPIC's lines of sound provide a 'more universal'[36] medium to 'produce, explore, and create new musical worlds' – 'everybody can understand a line'.[37] Theory-laden avant-garde practices ultimately operated a new overcoding of the music they had liberated from the classical tradition, at once constituting a new priestly caste versed in particular theories, and cutting off whole tracts of unexplored terrain, creating, in Xenakis's word, new musical 'islands'.[38] Whereas the stave is an unresolved mix of the symbolic and graphical, and whereas serialism tended only to exacerbate this condition whilst at the same time reterritorialising upon

---

36. Xenakis, in Lohner, 'Interview', 51.

37. *Ibid.*

38. Xenakis, in Varga, *Conversations,* 54, 59. Xenakis would later identify mathematically the transformations of serialism with the Klein Group.

a model drawn from badly-analysed structural composites (the twelve tones and their transformations) – as if one had dismantled the house of music only to rebuild it using an esoteric new system of construction, rendering it uninhabitable in the process – with the UPIC, Xenakis sought to attain maximum deterritorialisation by using a technology unmediated by theories because based exclusively on elementary acoustics,[39] but allowing the composer, through the graphical interface, sensitively to construct a new *habitus*, a minimum reterritorialisation ('just a little order [...] to protect us from chaos'):[40] a tool that operates not with overcoded conventional points, but with 'graphisms',[41] '*arcs sonores*'.[42]

It is this twofold goal of maximum deterritorialisation and universal accessibility that Xenakis calls *polyagogy*.[43] And it is important to observe that the UPIC was not conceived merely as a way to make experimental composition more efficient for the composer, but moreover as a way to make it literally 'child's play'. Xenakis's commitment to opening up these new spaces of musical freedom to all was indicated at the founding of CEMAMu, which sought to establish 'a new general level of awareness' through the recognition, and practice, that 'everyone is creative,'[44] and by enabling and encouraging children to 'evolve away from the tonal

---

39. Xenakis, in Lohner, 'Interview', 51.

40. *What is Philosophy?*, 201.

41. Xenakis, in Lohner, 'Interview', 52.

42. Lohner, 'The UPIC System,' 48.

43. '"*Polyagogique*" is my coinage – "*agogie*" means training or introduction into a field; "*poly*" means many.' Xenakis, in Varga, *Conversations*, 121.

44. Lohner, 'The UPIC System', 43.

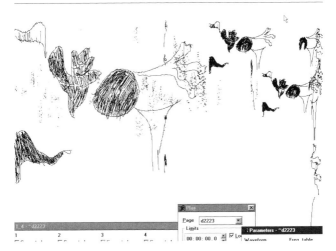

system still generally prevalent in Western civilization.'[45]
It is not that the child can 'play at' being a composer,
but that the composer finds himself raised to the status
of the child in relation to sound, having to jettison all he
'knows' about music: solfeggio, harmony, counterpoint,
and so on, all turn out to be obstacles in the way of a real
becoming-music (just as Messiaen had divined in the case
of Xenakis himself). The employment of manual gesture
creates a direct coupling between sound and mind ('direct
to the *mind*';[46] 'The hand is the organ of the body that is
closest to the brain'[47] – with the UPIC, 'we can solve the
problems of the composition directly, with our hands.')[48]

45. *Ibid.*

46. Xenakis, in Lohner, 'Interview,' 51.

47. *Ibid.*

48. Xenakis, in Varga, *Conversations*, 120.

It is not so much any particular piece composed with the UPIC that matters, but this *becoming* in which the user learns a 'hand-eye-ear' coordination as novel to the seasoned composer as to the child, an 'interdisciplinary pedagogy through playing'.[49]

Blackest Ever Black recovers the power of this vision, thirty years after the first working model of the UPIC was completed, and in an age where the digital manipulation of sound has become ubiquitous to the point of banality. Xenakis's vision for a mass-market production of the UPIC[50] failed, of course; but in certain sense his pioneering explorations of sound did presage modern pop producers for whom 'sonic construction' is the object of meticulous technical adjustments quite divorced from any traditional

49. This is carried even further in the latest versions of the UPIC which allow realtime manipulation.

50. See Lohner, 'The UPIC System', 44.

musical concerns. But equally, in an age of digital sampling, where a second of the most anodyne pop recording has been subjected to more electronic manipulation than Stockhausen's entire *oeuvre*, we might ask how the UPIC can stand as anything other than a relic of a highbrow dream, whose austere, uptight, still too-classical sensibility was overturned even as its aims were realised in popular musics.

The evolution of electronic instrumentation has taken us from a machine where the musician must physically link up circuits and oscillators, through keyboards with banks of pre-programmed sounds, to sampling technology, where any sound can become a ready-made instrument. Now hard-disk recording, like the UPIC, gives access directly to 'the curve', to a base-level sonic material which is transparently stratified and editable on all levels. Indeed, it is quite possible using HDR to 'draw' waveforms onto the screen just as in the UPIC. But the extreme facility and infinite potential of this technology seems to fail Xenakis's test of the power of simplicity, and in contemporary dance music the gap is all too often filled by barely-remixed tradition and modish cliché. Despite honorable exceptions, for the most part dance musics remain tonal and monorhythmic, composed of recognisable samples or fourier-synthesised tones.[51] It is tempting to venture an analogy between music and videogames (1978 being the year of *Mycenae Alpha* and *Space Invaders* alike): where the rudimentary technology of

---

51. It is also noteworthy, and reflects some of the paradox of Xenakis's legacy, that whilst UPIC aims at a maximal 'generalisation' in all dimensions, as Curtis Roads remarks, 'the sound palette of the UPIC is utterly singular' (Roads, 'Blackest Ever UPIC') – unlike HDR, it is, properly speaking, a musical instrument. Unless used in a spirit of deliberate obfuscation its sound-space is quite characteristic and has real integrity. Of course, this recognisable consistency owes something to the fact that Xenakis's aim with UPIC, as with his composition, is never to explode and destroy, but to isolate just what it is that holds things together: what is sonic consistency?

early games demanded a real and compelling synaesthetic becoming between human and machine, contemporary games, with their immaculate representational capabilities, can, and all-too often do, fail to create that symbiotic bond, becoming glossy representational entertainment instead.

The key to appreciating the UPIC's continued importance, therefore, is to understand it in the context of the polyagogical campaign to liberate children from Western musical heritage before they had been encultur-ated into it. Now, it may well be that in reterritorialising the abstract matter of sound back upon the landscape of excitational attractors and rhythmic tics, the outer edges of pop music initiate a slow drift of the human towards the plane of abstract sound, through a rhythmic contagion that we might place side-by-side with this polyagogy. Indeed, this subterranean kinship is dramatised in the lightshows and quaking electronic sub-bass eruptions of Haswell and Hecker's 'UPIC diffusion sessions', which continue a tradition of 'disorienting, hallucinatory light-shows'[52] engineered by Xenakis himself. But popular electronic music tends to thrive on producing excitation via jarring, violent sonic alienations; whereas, if simply listening to *Blackest Ever Black* heralds the shock of an encounter with sound as if for the first time, this should not obscure the fact that Xenakis envisioned a participatory and continuous process of sonic re-education (or de-education), with the hand-eye interface of the UPIC providing the graceful 'glissando' between the natural proclivities of the human ear and the vast virtuality of sound.

Creating a 'plane of consistency' between the hand-eye

---

52. J. Harley 'The Electroacoustic Music of Iannis Xenakis' *Computer Music Journal* 26:1, Spring 2002: 33-57, 33.

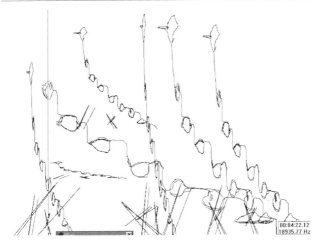

00:04:22.12
18935.77 Hz

apparatus and sonic materiality, the UPIC realises an abstract phylum that spans both and which is the seat of synaesthesia. In occluding forms and their production behind opaque codes, symbolic practices (such as serialism) militate against synaesthesia: the 'section' they take through musical possibility is not a clean enough cut. Of course, synaesthesia is not a goal in itself, either for Xenakis, for the UPIC, or for Haswell & Hecker; but it seems to play the role of a sign that one has accessed forms no longer belonging to the human organism and its perceptual system, but traversing it from the outside.

Beyond this vision of a 'becoming', polyagogy might also be said to correspond in certain respects with Deleuze's call for an experimental programme of 'transcendental empiricism'; it initiates an encounter that lays bare the *audiendum* – that which can only be heard, and therefore

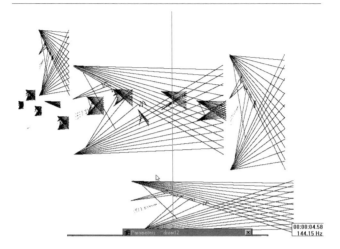

cannot be heard qua (re)cognisable;[53] that is to say, sound-material as series of intensities, or differences in molecular pressure – the 'phenomenon closest to the noumenon':

> [W]e are in a kind of continuum from [...] usual objects that we use in music down to the aspects of music that are inaudible, but which produce these events on a higher level.[54]

Further, it offers a theoretical possibility of accounting for how this material is integrated, individuated, amassed into recognisable forms, opening the way to a 'disjointed, superior or transcendent exercise'[55] of the musical faculty.[56] The UPIC reinstates a phylogenetic link to the noumenal continuum or the hidden in-itself of sonic difference,

53. See *Difference and Repetition*, 138-45.

54. Xenakis, in Lohner, 'Interview', 53.

55. *Difference and Repetition*, 143.

56. See *Difference and Repetition*, 138-45.

allowing us to render sonorous that which cannot/can only be heard. Whereafter, '[i]t is now a problem of consistency or consolidation: how to consolidate the material, make it consistent, so that it can harness unthinkable, invisible, nonsonorous forces';[57] 'to elaborate a material of [sound] in order to capture forces that are not sonic in themselves.'[58]

This raises the question of expression: In *Blackest Ever Black* Haswell & Hecker use the UPIC as a stenographer to translate into sound graphisms ranging from images of contemporary events, to their own designs, and finally surrealist automatic drawings. But of course there is no question of 'dumbly literal sonic analogy'[59] here. The UPIC may 'allow the child to find out what a fish, a house, or a tree sounds like,'[60] just as Haswell & Hecker give us the opportunity to 'listen to the shapes of leaves, terrorist atrocities and kebabs.'[61] But neither invite us to play a game of recognition, but instead draw us into a polyagogical *dérive*. Just as synaesthesia, far from being a sort of harmony between recognisable forms, is a sign that one is encountering something from outside, so what is 'expressed' in UPIC works are these structures that intersect us obliquely: it is the machine that will *instruct* us as to what the drawings are really 'of' so that we are momentarily transported outside ourselves; inciting us to further polyagogical investigation.[62]

---

57. *A Thousand Plateaus*, 343.

58. *Ibid.*, 342.

59. D. Fox, 'Seen and Heard', *Frieze* 98 (Apr. 2006).

60. Xenakis, in Varga, *Conversations*, 121.

61. Roads, 'Blackest Ever UPIC'.

62. In relation to the notion of expression, it should be noted that for the 1976 defence of his doctorate (published as *Arts/Sciences: Alloys* – see note 14 above), Xenakis chose

Throughout its four movements *Blackest Ever Black* is haunted by fugitive figures from outside, sonic personae in closely-marshalled crowds. The listener naturally tries, but ultimately fails, to apply to them the test of recognition: cicadas, screaming fireworks, foaming waves, crackling clouds of static, swarmachines of sound. Sometimes the glissandi and the sonic latitude recall those 'cosmic' instruments that lurk in the margins of the orchestra, indicating the spaces beyond – the onde martinot beloved of Messiaen (which 'make[s] audible the truth that all

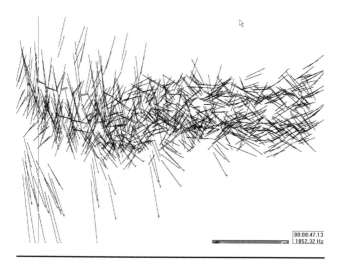

00:08:47.13
1852.32 Hz

Michel Serres as one of the panel; the Serres whose *Le Système de Leibniz* (Paris: PUF, 1969) advocated reading Leibniz as a proto-structuralist, for whom the relations uncovered by different modes of knowledge were more or less distinct expressions of a universal structural order. From this point of view, one might profitably investigate the relation between Leibniz's *mathesis universalis*, Xenakis's 'global morphology', and the work of A. Lautman (recently republished as *Les mathématiques, les idées et le réel physique*, Paris: Vrin, 2006).

becomings are molecular'),[63] the theremin, the reputedly madness-inducing hydrocrystalophone or glass harmonica, or the inharmonic spectra of the mark tree. But during periods of densely-differentiated sound, the listener feels rather as if she is eavesdropping on an encrypted transmission from another planet,[64] being absorbed into some unknown material in a state of extreme torsion, or witnessing the catastrophic collapse of microphysical filamentary structures, the breakdown of cells or gradual processes of liquefaction; and every so often, an echo of Xenakis's war, the ominous whine of warplanes on the horizon.

Thus *Blackest Ever Black* invokes a universe of unnameable phantom objects, colliding, brushing, scraping, resonating and devouring each other, suddenly expiring or becoming incandescent; sometimes metallic and buzzing with electricity, sometimes mobile and animate (usually insectoid – from Messiaen to Xenakis, 'the reign of birds seems to have been replaced by the age of insects, with its much more molecular vibrations, chirring, rustling, buzzing, clicking, scratching and scraping').[65]

According to Xenakis, time, pitch, interval, and intensity can all be characterised as real numbers; but, in the midst

---

63. *A Thousand Plateaus*, 308.

64. 'When astrophysicists receive signals from space with radio telescopes it's important that they should recognize the quality and quantity of periodicity so that they can draw conclusions with regard to the phenomena that occur in space [...] messages transmitted by intelligent beings have to be differentiated from natural signals [which] are more or less periodical [...] [T]he messages sent by intelligent beings also arrive in the form of periodic signals to a certain extent, otherwise the result would be just noise [...] [This] very profound problem [...] corresponds exactly to the question of pattern recognition in the field of sound synthesis and melodic patterns.' – Xenakis, in Varga, *Conversations*, 92.

65. *A Thousand Plateaus*, 308

of this mathematical regime according to which 'we are all pythagoreans',[66] *timbre* is not structural and cannot be ordered; it is a matter of vague zones of indiscernibility, connected in topologically unforeseeable and manifold fashions[67] – ORGAN PIPE TO MEET LITTLE FLUTE ON THE PLANE OF CONSISTENCY.[68] The system of heterogeneous series of quantitative multiplicities is coupled with a qualitative multiplicity of the Bergsonian-Riemannian (the conjugation is Deleuze's, of course) continuous manifold type, on the basis of a subterranean play of pure difference. And, in this sound-world of 'protoplasmic-like material'[69] ('material [as] molecularised matter')[70] which so scandalised Xenakis's peers, continuity is the rule. Terrestrial instruments become families of topological invariants (varying according to size and elasticity of materials); and outside their multidimensional, infinite yet circumscribed zone, lurk instruments with which we are by rights, as Leibniz would say, incompossible. The 'stretching [of] variation far beyond its formal limits'[71] precipitates a type of cosmic regression to the embryonic state of music – *before music was born, there was the great vibrating cosmic egg, the organ-without-organs*: 'Embryology

---

66. Xenakis, *Formalized Music*, 202.

67. 'We can't say that between two timbres only one path can be traced.' – Xenakis, in Varga, *Conversations*, 83.

68. '[...] take the low G tone on an organ, the waveform has a certain complexity. As you go towards higher pitches, the complexity diminishes until it becomes almost a sine wave [...] So [...] the more you gravitate toward the higher notes, it converges toward the sound of a little flute.' Xenakis, in Lohner, 'Interview', 52.

69. Xenakis, in Varga, *Conversations*, 35 (Serialist Antoine Goléa's description of *Metastaseis* upon its first performance in Donaueschingen in 1959).

70. *A Thousand Plateaus*, 342.

71. *Ibid.*, 309.

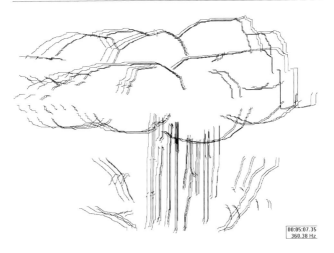

already displays the truth that there are systematic vital movements, torsions and drifts, that only the embryo can sustain: an adult would be torn apart by them.'[72] As Haswell & Hecker duly demonstrate, the UPIC's polyagogy gently returns composer and audience alike to a larval state, giving us a way of traversing and inhabiting this whole extended sonoverse, with 'just a little order'[73] to survive these wrenching transformations. Rather than throwing us in at the deep end, polyagogy, comprising a cartography of the objective Idea of music, teaches us to swim in sound; as described by Deleuze:

---

72. *Difference and Repetition*, 118; '"Regression" will be misunderstood as long as we fail to see in it the activation of a larval subject, the only patient able to endure the demands of a systematic dynamism' – Deleuze, 'The Method of Dramatisation' in *Desert Islands and Other Texts*, 98.

73. *What is Philosophy?*, 201.

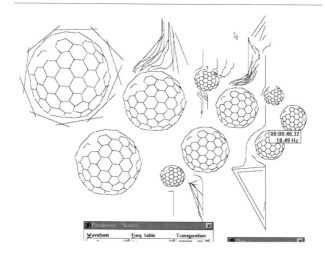

To learn is to enter into the universal of the relations which constitute the Idea, and into their corresponding singularities [...] To learn to swim is to conjugate the distinctive points of our bodies with the singular points of the objective Idea in order to form a problematic field.[74]

Polyagogy as discipline of becoming and problematisation of the body: What Xenakis says of performers of his music surely filters down to the audience also: 'I do take into account [their] physical limitations [...] but what is limitation today may not be so tomorrow.'[75] 'It is the composer's privilege to determine his works, down to the minutest detail'[76] but this also will 'give the artist [...] the joy

---

74. *Difference and Repetition*, 165.

75. Xenakis, in Varga, *Conversations*, 65.

76. *Ibid.*, 56.

of triumph – triumph that he can surpass his own capabilities'[77] in an encounter with a higher order of generality that reunites and reconnects actually-existing-musics ('islands')[78] into an pangaeic, cosmic Idea in continuous variation:

> We should be able to construct the most general musical edifice in which the utterances of Bach, Beethoven or Schönberg, for example, would be unique realisations of a gigantic virtuality.[79]

Regardless of whether Xenakis regrets the 'perpetual compromise'[80] that prevents him from being a 'pure ontologist' like Parmenides, he realises that such 'perpetual compromise' is also a 'perpetual exploration'[81] of this virtuality, a transcendental empiricism. For music is in fact nothing *but* this compromise between the mathematical and the biological, between structure and hand, between the Idea 'outside time' – a continuous plane populated by 'tones without sound'[82] – and their qualitative manifestation under certain conditions of selection, those of the duration which 'we' are. Here we remark Xenakis's proximity to his contemporary, and Deleuze's mathematical inspiration, Albert Lautman, whose Platonism speaks of a dialectic (comprising precisely those couplets discontinuous/continuous, local/global, unity/multiplicity, which underpin Xenakis's *oeuvre*) eternally inaccessible to us except through an ongoing

77. *Ibid.,* 66.

78. Xenakis, in Varga, *Conversations,* 51, 59.

79. Xenakis, *Formalized Music,* 207.

80. Xenakis, in Lohner, 'Interview', 55.

81. *Ibid.,* 54.

82. Lohner, 'The UPIC System', 46.

speculative contemplation of the mathematical theories that 'incarnate' it.[83] Ideas, or problems, are just those things that lie out of reach, that we struggle to grasp, making life both unbearable and bearable, and music recalls this struggle, as 'dream or nightmare'.[84]

This allows us to say that synaesthesia is the *anamnesis* proper to the polyagogical apprenticeship: A sensation of that which can neither be heard or seen, 'colours of sound',[85] a 'transcendent employment' of the faculties and the collapse of their borders – it is the remembrance of mathematics in its purest form, disincarnated from even the symbolic. Is music anything else?

As well as his endorsement of the Leibnizian theory of *petites-perceptions*, Xenakis himself also seems to personify a type of 'transcendental deduction' that recalls the hallucinatory theory of perception put forward by Deleuze:[86] the legacy of the war – chronic tinnitus, a lost eye – obliges Xenakis to reconquer the world through abstract principles, venturing 'generalisations' like a solitary musing Beckettian, or one of Kafka's animals, from inside 'a deep

83. See Lautman, *Les mathématiques, les idées et le réel physique, op.cit.*

84. Deleuze, 'The Method of Dramatisation', 99.

85. Xenakis, in Varga, *Conversations*, 72; 'Increasingly, it is the "colour" of the sound that matters' (*What is Philosophy?* 191). Messiaen himself insisted that he *saw* the colours of music – as 'musician's colours, not to be confused with painter's colours.' – appearing all at once, as in the stained-glass at the Sainte-Chapelle in Paris, which according to Messiaen was a 'luminous revelation' to him. And Xenakis himself (in Varga, *Conversations*, 173) will invoke the 'Inner Colour' that cannot be predicted, even by an experienced composer, from the clusters of individual notes involved. *Cf. A Thousand Plateaus* 347-8: 'the phenomena of synaesthesia [...] are not reducible to a simple colour-sound correspondence; sounds have a piloting role and induce colours that *are superposed* upon the colours we see, lending them a properly sonorous rhythm and movement'.

86. See *The Fold*, 93-4.

well [...] and I'm still there, so that I have to think harder than if I were able to grasp reality immediately.'[87] An undoubted advantage given that, as Bergson showed us, the 'immediate given is not immediately given';[88] and we saw how the UPIC aimed to reproduce this 'becoming-child' in forcing the composer to jettison all they knew about music. This emphasis on reconstructing the world from within sets Xenakis and Deleuze alike against a zen-like model of con-templation: As Deleuze and Guattari argue, in a passage that resonates with Xenakis's rather withering dismissal of Cage's attempts to 'let the universe speak' by suppressing the agency of the composer:[89]

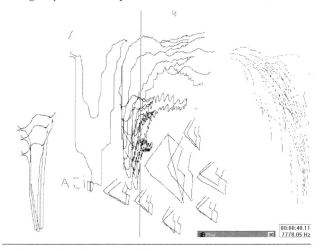

87. Xenakis, in Varga, *Conversations,* 48-9.

88. Deleuze, 'Bergson 1859-1941', in *Desert Islands and Other Texts,* 23.

89. 'We all have fortuitous sounds in our daily life. They are completely banal and boring … Silence is banal … I'm not interested in reproducing banalities' (Xenakis, *Alloys,* 94-5). Nevertheless Xenakis respected Cage greatly and was an early supporter of his work – see Varga, *Conversations,* 55-6.

The claim is that one is opening music to all events, all irruptions, but one ends up reproducing a scrambling that prevents any event from happening [...] instead of producing a cosmic machine capable of 'rendering sonorous'.[90]

Contemplation is already action, selection, composition,[91] in so far as this contemplation takes the actively exploratory form of a transcendental empiricism: not content to 'let music be', it attentively probes the being of music in order to discover its material basis and its life.

In writing electronic music you also have to direct the invention of new tools.[92]

If the greatest creative act is to create something with which to create – to imitate '*physis physeôs*'[93] – then the UPIC could be said to be, if not Xenakis's most important work, then certainly a most significant, if still latent, part of his creative legacy to future musicians, more of whom it is to be hoped will take up the gauntlet of *Blackest Ever Black*'s 'grand celebration of Xenakis's sound universe'[94] and put the polyagogy of abstract matter back into practice, creating a music that 'moves the soul, "perplexes" it'.[95] A music, then, to be accompanied by a philosophy that likewise 'tends to elaborate a material of thought in order to capture forces that are not thinkable in themselves.'[96]

---

90. *A Thousand Plateaus,* 343-4. Deleuze & Guattari do, in fact, go on to mention Cage.

91. See A. Villani, present volume, 62.

92. Xenakis, in Lohner, 'Interview', 50.

93. See Villani, present volume, 62.

94. Roads, 'Blackest Ever UPIC'.

95. *Difference and Repetition*, 140.

96. *A Thousand Plateaus*, 342.

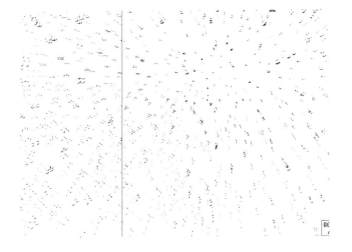

ÉTUDES

SUR

LA MATHÈSE

OU

ANARCHIE ET HIÉRARCHIE

DE LA

SCIENCE

avec une Application spéciale de la Médecine

DU DOCTEUR

Jean MALFATTI de MONTEREGGIO

TRADUCTION DE
CHRISTIEN OSTROWSKI

INTRODUCTION DE
GILLES DELEUZE

Scientia vita, in vita scientia

EDITIONS DU GRIFFON D'OR

PARIS

1946

Mathesis, Science and Philosophy[1]

Gilles Deleuze

It might be interesting to define mathesis in terms of its relations with science and philosophy. Inevitably, such a definition remains to some extent external to mathesis itself; it is simple, provisional, and tends only to show that, beyond any particular historical moment, mathesis describes one of the great ever-present attitudes of mind. That is to say that one will find in the following only a critique of the arguments that scientists and philosophers tend to invoke against mathesis, and above all a specification of how the word 'initiated' ought to be understood. Not that we should forget, certainly, the plane of Indian civilisation within which mathesis was deployed; this is most essential. For we will not say that mathesis can be abstracted, in any measure, from this civilisation; but only that at the heart of our Western mentality can be discerned certain fundamental needs which, already, can only be satisfied by mathesis – as a sort of introduction, a preface to itself. From this point of view, Dr. Malfatti's book presents a capital interest. No doubt, other works have since appeared which delve deeper into Indian consciousness, but few introduce the notion of mathesis in itself, in terms of its relations with science and philosophy, better than the present work.

1. Deleuze's text appears as an introduction to Jean Malfatti de Montereggio's *Études sur la Mathèse ou anarchie et hiérarchie de la science* (Paris: Éditions Du Griffon D'Or, 1946).

It is not easy to understand the exact sense of the discussions that periodically oppose philosophers and scientists – they do not speak the same language. Science installs itself within the object, reconstructing or discovering reality itself at the level of the object of thought, without ever posing to itself the problem of the conditions of possibility. The philosopher, on the contrary, situates the object, as representation, in its relation to the cognising subject. It is of little consequence to him, M. Alquié remarks, to know what matter might ultimately be – atoms, say – since the latter, like every other representation, have a philosophical status only in reference to the mind that represents them. And it is hard to see what difference even the latest discoveries in modern physics could make, for example, to the conceptions of Berkeley, dating from the eighteenth century. Thus a fundamental dualism poses itself within knowledge, between Science and Philosophy – the principle of an anarchy. It is basically the Cartesian opposition between extended substance and thinking substance.

The Cartesian case is all the more interesting in that Descartes never renounced the unity of knowledge, the *mathesis universalis*. And it is intriguing to see how the latter is situated on the theoretical plane: the knowing mind, as distinct as it might be in itself from the extension with which it appears to have strictly nothing in common, nonetheless deploys the order of things in thinking the order of its representations. At the very moment where unity is affirmed, this unity breaks apart and destroys itself.

But in being broken apart, Descartes now remarks, unity finds its true sense in re-forming upon another plane, where it finds its true meaning. In so far as the theoretical disunion of thought and extension is affirmed, so too is the fact of their practical union, as a definition of life. Unity does not come about at the level of an abstract God transcending humanity, but in the very name of concrete life; the Tree of Knowledge is no mere image. The unity, the hierarchy beyond all anarchic duality, is the unity of life itself, which delineates a third order, irreducible to the other two. Life is the unity of the soul as the idea of the body and of the body as the extension of the soul. Moreover, the two other orders, science and philosophy, physiology and psychology, tend to rediscover their lost unity at the level of living man. Beyond a psychology disincarnated in thought, and a physiology mineralised in matter, mathesis will be fulfilled only in a true medicine where life is defined as knowledge of life, and knowledge as life of knowledge. Hence the motto, 'Scientia vitae in vita scientiae'. A threefold consequence follows from this.

Firstly, to believe that mathesis is merely a mystical lore, inaccessible and superhuman, would be a complete mistake. This is the first misunderstanding of the word 'initiated' that is to be avoided. For mathesis deploys itself at the level of life, of living man: it is first and foremost a thinking of incarnation and of individuality. Essentially, mathesis would be the exact description of human nature.

Yet does not mathesis surpass this living human nature? For it defines itself as a collective and supreme knowledge, a universal synthesis, 'a living unity incorrectly deemed human'. Here we must agree: it must be realised that such a definition cannot be immediate but is posited last of all, receiving a precise sense. Prefiguring the relations between man and the infinite, the natural relation unites the living being with life. Life, in the first instance, seems to exist only through and within the living being, within the individual organism that puts it in action. Life exists only through these fragmentary and closed assumptions, each of which realises it on its own account and nothing more, in solitude. That is to say that universality, the community of life, denies itself, gives itself to each living being as a simple outside, an exteriority that remains foreign to it, an Other: there is a plurality of men yet, precisely, each one must in the same way assume his life for himself, without common measure with others, on his own account; the universal is immediately recuperated. And in this sense life will be defined as complicity, as opposed to a crew. For the crew is the realisation of a common world whose universality cannot be compromised or fragmented, and such that in the process of this realisation the substitution of crewmembers becomes both possible and indifferent. Such is science, on the side of the object of thought; or philosophy, on the side of the thinking subject; in both cases we have a dead crew, theoretical, non-practical and speculative. The only living Crew is that of God, and this because there is only one God, whose symbol is the circle, the perfect, indifferent figure all of whose points are an equal distance from the centre. In complicity, on the contrary, there is indeed a common world, but one whose community comes into effect, once more, through each member realising it for himself without a common measure with others, on his own account, and with no possibility of substitution. Clearly, the principal human realities of birth, love, language and death describe this same profile: Under the sign of death, everyone exists as non-substitutable and cannot have himself replaced.

And this, precisely, is the universality of death. In the same way, life is that reality wherein the universal and its proper negation are as one.

What characterises complicity is precisely that it can be ignored, denied, betrayed. The term 'everyone' denies the universal so effectively, at the very moment it affirms it, that it is easy to notice only this negative aspect. Thus, the u consists in passing from a state of latent, ignorant complicity to a complicity that knows and affirms itself as such. Not, certainly, the point where each loves as everyone, but where everyone loves in their singular manner. It is at the very moment when the living being persists stubbornly in its individuality that it affirms itself as universal. At the moment when the living being closed in upon itself, defining the universality of life as an outside, it did not see that it had, in fact, interiorised that universal: realised the universal on its own account, and defined itself as a microcosm. The first goal of mathesis is to assure this awareness of the living in relation to life and thus to ground the possibility of a knowledge of individual destiny.

Beginning with a purely natural and unconscious complicity where each individual only posits himself in opposition to others, and more generally to the universal, it is a question of passage to a complicity that knows itself, where each grasps himself as '*pars totalis*' within a universe that he already constitutes. In other words, federation. Ostrowski, the translator of this work, saw federation in a most curious fashion: 'At a moment [1849] where ancient Germany seeks to reconstruct its federative unity, lost for centuries, but probably to be rediscovered within our own, it will not be without interest to examine the efforts undertaken by this people of bold thinkers to return science to the unity it enjoyed at the outset – back to its common centre.' What is proposed is a federation as a definition of life, not a unity founded upon a cult of force.

Thus we see that unity comes about at the level of concrete man; very far from transcending the human condition, it is its exact description. It must simply be remarked that such a description must position man in relation to the infinite, the universal. Each individual exists only by virtue of denying the universal; but in so far as man's existence refers to plurality, the negation is carried out universally under the exhaustive form of each and every one – so that it is but the human way of affirming what it denies. We have called this mode of affirmation conscious complicity. And initiation is nothing other than this. Initiation does not have a mystical sense: it is the thought of life and the only possible way of thinking life. Initiation is mysterious only in the sense that the knowledge that it represents must be acquired by each person on their own account. The initiate is living man in his relationship with the infinite. And the key notion of mathesis – not at all mystical – is that individuality never separates itself from the universal, that between the living and life one finds the same relation as between life as species, and divinity. Thus, the multiplicity of living beings which knows itself as such refers itself back to unity, which it describes in inverse relief, the circle as the simplest case of the ellipse. This is why we need to take Malfatti's words literally when he reminds us that the circle, the wheel, represents God: 'Mathesis would be for man in his relations to the infinite, what locomotion is to space.'

Mathesis is therefore neither a science, nor a philosophy. It is something else: a knowledge of life. It is neither the study of being, nor the analysis of thought. Furthermore, the opposition of thought and being, of philosophy and science, have no meaning for it, seeming illusory, a false alternative. Mathesis situates itself on a plane where the life of knowledge is identical with the knowledge of life; it is simply awareness of life. Malfatti announces its *cogito* thus: *sum, ergo cogito*; *sum, ergo genero*. That is to say that its method will be neither scientific nor philosophical. To its object, which is quite particular, must respond a particular method.

*

* *

Scientific method is explanation. To explain is to account for a thing through something other than itself. Heat is movement, water is composed of H_2O, but movement as object of thought is only constituted by negating that which it explains – heat qua system of sensible qualities. Equally, when we arrive at H_2O, there is water no longer. We may call these sensible qualities appearances, but it would still be the case that the very definition of the appearance is that it is not given as such. At the other extreme, philosophical method is description in the widest sense of the word; it is that reflexive analysis whereby the sensible world is described as the representation of the cognising subject – that is to say that, here once again, it receives its status from something other than itself. In the two cases of scientific and philosophical method, we discover a new opposition – that of thought and the sensible.

We had defined the object of mathesis on the basis of the opposition between science and philosophy, between the object and the subject of thought. But that was merely a first aspect of the anarchy. For the object of thought is not merely 'thought' as thinking subject; it is also 'object', as sensible object. This gives a new depth to the opposition. Everyday life traces its path within the objectivity of the sensible; objects are outside of us, they owe us nothing, they are their own significations. Philosophically speaking, colour may be a secondary quality, a representation of the cognizant mind; scientifically it may be reduced to the object of the thought 'vibration', as the last word of reality. But it is no less certain that it is given in itself to the individual, without reference to anything other than itself. The individual knows very well that things haven't been hanging around waiting for him in order to exist. The point will be raised that the object is given to me according to a certain aspect, a certain profile, depending on the point of view it is observed from. But this is not a sign of the object's dependency. On the contrary, it is the manifestation of its total objectivity. It is well known that the contemplated object detaches itself from a ground constituted by the set of other objects. Yet, precisely, the object could not sustain any relationship whatsoever with others if this relation remained external to it. For such an object to detach itself as a form upon a ground of other objects, it must first already be its own ground. So that the 3 faces through which the profile of the cube is always given – 3 faces and no more – are already all 6 faces: the cube must already be its own ground. This phenomenon refers the object to itself and not to he who perceives. But to say that the 3 faces are already 6 faces, is to posit the identity of extension (3) and comprehension (6) in the sensible object. Why this identity? Why are the 6 faces given as 3? It is simply because everyday space is 3-dimensional. In taking a moment to reflect, it will be seen that the 6 faces as such only make sense in reference to a plane. The only way for 6 faces to exist *en bloc* in a space of 3 dimensions is to present 3 of them. The identity of extension and comprehension therefore simply defines space. Which is to say that within this space, the sensible object in general, in the name of such an identity, is none other than the concept: the word 'concept' here no longer signifying 'object of thought'.

Let us keep this in mind, it being only one of the moments of the theory of numbers in mathesis. Take the number 7, as analysed by Malfatti: Firstly, 7 is represented by means of straight lines but never by the curved line: it is the appearance of three dimensions. It indicates the truth that every (individual) body can be considered as an extension of surface (4), operating in 3 directions, length, breadth and depth. Secondly, on the other hand, 7 is concept: it does not yet represent the individual become real, but is 'the multiple development of the universal in innumerable individualities; it is the father of time and his image before the divisible time that tumbles in space upon the undulating images of appearance [...] it moves above the appearance.' A philosophical or scientific critique of this conception would surely lead to error: it does not belong to the same domain, nor to the same method.

We saw that this method of mathesis found itself before an opposition to be surpassed: that of the object of thought and the sensible object. For science explains the sensible object through something other than itself, through

149

the object of thought – a new duality, that must in turn be reduced, by reducing this object of thought back to the sensible, quantity to quality. Let us remark generally that this is the very reduction performed by the symbol. The most simple examples suffice to demonstrate this: When I say that the flag is a symbol of the homeland, I essentially present a sensible object as the incarnation of an object of thought, some piece of knowledge. Further, this sensible object is this very incarnation of knowledge. Earlier, in terms of explanation, the object of thought was the *explanans* which could only be constituted through the annulment of the sensible object it sought to explain. In contrast, in the case of the symbol, the symbolising agent is now the sensible object, and the knowledge which it symbolizes is identified totally with it. Fundamentally, the essential symbolic procedure is the poem. Take for example Mallarmé's Fan. Its subject is certainly movement in itself, as pure object of thought, beyond all sensible manifestation. It, also, moves above appearance, which keeps it at a safe distance:

Whose imprisoned stroke thrusts back
The horizon delicately

The poem's whole argument consists in incarnating in a sensible object the thought of movement, in transforming it in this object: and not merely in the open fan, which is not yet sufficiently profoundly mortified within a sensible matter, but in the fan as thing, the closed fan. Mallarmé indicates expressly this passage from the open to the closed: 'The sceptre of pink shores'; 'This closed white wing you place'.

This is but one example, indicating to us the general sense of the symbol, the incarnation of knowledge, the movement of mathesis. Unlike explanation, the symbol is the identity, the *encounter* of the sensible object and the object of thought. The sensible object is called symbol, and the object of thought, losing all scientific signification, is a hieroglyph or a cipher. In their identity, they form the concept. The symbol is its extension, the hieroglyph its comprehension. Whereupon the word 'initiated' takes on its full sense: According to Malfatti, the mysterious character of mathesis is not directed against the profane in an exclusive, mystical sense, but simply indicates the necessity of grasping the concept in the minimum of time, and that physical incarnations take place in the smallest possible space – unity within diversity, general life within particular life. At the limit, we could even say that the notion of the initiate is rationalised to the extreme. If *vocation* defines itself through the creation of a sensible object as the result of a knowledge, then mathesis qua living art of medicine is the vocation *par excellence*, the vocation of vocations, since it transforms knowledge itself into a sensible object. Thus we shall see mathesis insist upon the correspondences between material and spiritual creation.

Let us apply this symbolic approach to man. The thought of the human condition – that is, its comprehension, defines the former as existence separated from its essence. But to say that in man in general, essence and existence are dissociated, is to say that there are several men (extension). For 'if, for instance, there existed in nature twenty men, it would not be enough to investigate the cause of human nature in general' (Spinoza).[2] That is to say that each existence finds its proper essence outside of itself, within the Other. Which is to say that fundamentally, man is not only mortal: he is 'natal'. And if the parents bestow their existence upon their child, for him to do with it as he will, inversely, does not the child see in his parents the very principle of his intelligibility, his proper essence? In so far as the comprehension of the human is defined by the separation of existence and essence, the extension which is correlative to it – identical to it, even – comes down to sexuality: 'man and woman exist in two separate bodies, each one possessing the body of the other within it'. We now see that it is through man that the concept, as identity of extension and comprehension, comes into the world. In other words, *it is sexuality that grounds sensible qualities*; and Malfatti cites the words of Hippocritus: 'Man is dual, and if he were not dual, he would have no sensation.' But we have seen that sensation refers to three dimensions: So that it is not so much sexual duality as the triadic character of love, that should be remarked upon. 'What would individual life be without love of self, which alone can lead it to the life of the species, by reproducing it as eternal being, infinite, in the species? Dualism does not contain real life. Sexual love conciliates the other two, egoism and heroism.' Moreover, it is the life of the world that is established under the ternary sign: becoming qua addition, that is, birth; duration, as the multiplication through which the act of becoming is conserved; and destruction or subtraction.

What will be the human concept *par excellence*, then? God, unity of essence and existence, is conceptualised

2. [Letter 39, to Huyghens. – trans.]

by the circle: equivalence and rest, indifference of the interfocal zone, and pregenesthetic life. With the ellipse, however (or rather the ellipsoid, always in movement), we will rediscover separation, duality, the sexual antithesis of foci. Space is the passage from the unlimited circle to the limited ellipse, time the passage from the unity of the centre to the dualism of foci: the three dimensions are born. We might define this passage as the birth of the equivocal, with the ellipsis defined as an equivocal circle. Recall how the very object of mathesis was to be found in the problem of life, of complicity: 'It is at the very moment,' says Malfatti, 'when the individual momentarily puts himself in the place of nature, that he returns his own life to the life of nature'. In this sense, sexual love is at the same time love of self and love of the species, man-become-interior and man-becoming-exterior. Let us recall on the other hand the correspondence that presides over the relations living being/universal life and universal life as species/divinity. Thus we will see Malfatti insist on the fact that the genesthetic and the pregenesthetic are inseparable because one describes the other in negative relief: 'Before I was round. Now, I am extended in the form of an egg.' Through engenderment humanity pursues its own immortality, constitutes time as the mobile image of the eternal, seeks the completion of the ellipse in the circle. To be precise, ecstasy is nothing other than the act by which the individual is raised to the level of the species. For the species can only be thought at the limits of the circle – before the fall Adam existed as *humanitas*.

It comes as no surprise that the method of mathesis rejoins its very object. It is through the same movement that mathesis situates itself beyond the opposition thinking subject/object of thought, and also that other opposition object of thought/sensible object. We will see this even more clearly with the problem of numbers. On the one hand, number exists only within the decade, that is to say, within numeration: it seems to be constructed by a mental act, transparent to itself, in the process of which we merely add a unit to the preceding number. So that number seems to be on the side of the thinking subject; and yet it is revealed as object of thought qua opacity, endowed with unforeseeable properties to the point where the mental act, supposedly transparent to itself, engenders veritable natures. It is this privilege, on the other hand, that explains why mathesis has granted number a very particular importance: the symbol *is the thought of number become sensible object.* It is intriguing to see the reproach Malfatti addresses to the comparable studies of the Greeks: Their error was to have sought the signification of number in a purely geometrical connection, thus confining it to the object of thought. But, quite on the contrary, it is the symbol, in its full sense, that must be extricated from number. The decade begins with 0, hieroglyph of man and the world, and finishes with 10, unity realised within a complete spiritual and corporeal organism. Malfatti writes of 10 that it 'wearies neither with the action of entering nor with that of leaving. It is the sovereign of the little world (microcosm) within man.'

The definition of mathesis was twofold: In its object, in relation to the duality thinking subject/object of thought; and in its method, in relation to that other duality object of thought/sensible object. We reach a point where these two themes incessantly intersect one another, are identified with each other. The first theme led us to lay down a system of correspondences *between the individual (microcosm) and the universal*; the second, *between the corporeal and the spiritual.* Do not seek, then, a philosophical 'explanation' for the union of the soul and the body. Attempt no longer to critique scientifically the correspondences established between the individual and the universe, under the grand themes of fire, of fermentation ... etc.[3] Mathesis evolves in another domain, in the double depth of the symbol: here it finds its accomplishment, as the living art of medicine, ceaselessly establishing a system of ever-closer correspondences, embracing increasingly individual realities.

---

3. Similarly, it would be pointless to seek to refute those physiological conceptions put forward, for example, in the Third Study: they belong elsewhere, to 'romantic medicine' and to 'natural philosophy'. These scientific elements drawn upon by Dr Malfatti de Montereggio were far too fragmentary to be sufficient for a complete construction. The author therefore fills the voids with bold teleological hypotheses. It is his weakness, but it is also the inevitable fate of every *a priori* synthesis.

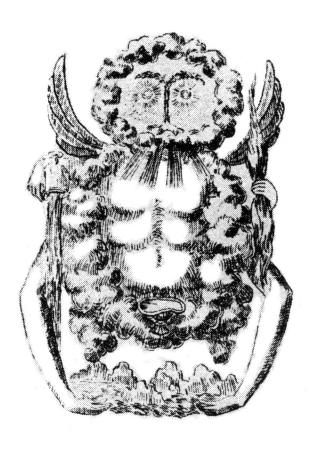

Malfatti's Decade

'Incognitum'

Malfatti's 1845 Studies in Mathesis *attempt to recover the ancient science of mathesis, the 'great unitary system of the contemplation of the world*[1] *from its fatal declination into, on the one hand, metaphysics, and on the other, mathematics* stricto sensu. *The* First Study*' claims to elucidate the metaphysical import of the decade through an examination of its importance in Hindu myth. The correspondences described by Malfatti in this study are elaborated on the basis of some strange and fascinating images from German scholar Nicolas Müller's 1822* Glauben, Wissen und Kunst der alten Hindus *(Faith, Knowledge and Art of the Ancient Hindus). Malfatti avows his indebtedness to Müller, one of those few 'who sought to penetrate the innermost meaning of the materials […] bequeathed us by this greatest of nations to whom we owe the highest of human discoveries'.*[2] *A number of these figures from Müller are reproduced in the 1946 Griffon d'Or edition of the* Studies.

---

1. J. Malfatti de Montereggio, *Études sur la Mathèse ou anarchie et hiérarchie de la science* (Paris: Éditions du Griffon d'Or, 1946), 57.

2. *Ibid*, 16.

In the 'First Study' Malfatti will set forth 'the Indian Organon of mathesis' in the form of a 'symbolic exposition enclosed in an elliptical hieroglyphic, deduced from the ten divine preformative powers and represented through the medium of the ten numerical signs'.[3]

According to Malfatti, the decade must be subdivided into three triads, Brahma ruling over the first triad, Vishnu the second, Shiva the third: Creation (3x1=3: the domain of unity, addition as becoming), Conservation (the domain of multiplication, through which becoming is conserved: 3x2=6), and Destruction (the domain of individuation in creation and destruction, as subtraction qua transformation; 3x3=9).[4] Thus the first three ciphers (1, 2, 3) will describe 'the passage from the sphere and the circle into the genesthetic in the form of the ellipse or ellipsoid, or revelation of the former in the latter', the emergence of the Trimurti (Brahma, Vishnu and Shiva), the 'metaphysical trinity of divine forces'.[5] The sequence of the second triad (4, 5, 6) will represent the passage from hermaphroditism to sexuation, the final triad (7, 8, 9) the passage from the general to the individual.[6]

Through the latter triads, the 'primary divine Trimurti […] passes into an external revelation […] of seven precreative powers […] the primary septuple metaphysical development personified by the allegories of Maya, Oum, Hiranyagarbha, Purusha, Prajapati, Prakriti and Prana […] [T]he cipher 4 belongs to Maya, 5 to Oum,

---

3. *Ibid.*, 57.

4. *Ibid.*, 59-60. On individuation *Cf.* Deleuze, *Mathesis*, present volume, 146.

5. *Ibid*, 17.

6. *Ibid.*, 17-8.

6 to Hiranyagarbha, 7 to Purusha, 8 to Prajapati, 9 to Prakriti, and 10 to Prana'.[7]

Malfatti reconstructs mathesis by setting forth the obscure but necessary relation of each of these ciphers to the metaphysical principle personified by the respective deity. The following pages, in which we reproduce selections from Müller's images, along with extracts from Malfatti's text, can only give a reductive and partial impression of the latter's highly involved exposition.

7. *Ibid.*

Brahma = 1, 2, 3: 'instead of eyes, we find two waterlilies in a form approximating most closely that of the cissoid; beginning together, these two lilies' stems form the radius (stem) in place of the nose, then are divided in two opposing curves, stop at the curve of the eyebrows – in the middle the curves cross, in the place of the eyes, two lotus flowers, bringing with them the representation of the symbolic spirit – cosmo-generic.'[8]

---

8. Malfatti, 22.

'Maya $= 4$ […] as [Maya] opens the second triad of the pregenesthetic decade, so the cipher 4 opens that of the second triad of our genesthetic decimal […] According to doctrine, Maya is the exercise of the threefold force of the Trimurti, as ex-engenderment of the latter […] the passage of the circle into the ellipse […] Female yet endowed with virile force, she is hermaphrodite […] She is half Brahma, half Maya: According to the Veda, the spontaneous act of the separation of double sexuality in the original form of feminine and virile demi-divisibility […] Through a careful examination of her image, we find, around the centre of her stomach, four groups of hanging pearls, the first signification of the number four. But the principal ornament of her clothing consists in a rich and prominent emblem composed of an ellipse enclosed within a parallelogram […] It is to be remarked, and it confirms our point of view, that the paralellogram which encloses the ellipse has the form neither of a square nor of a rectangle parallelogram, but rather that of a lozenge such as one might arrive at by repeating an iscosceles triangle upon its base – which precisely symbolises the deployment of the Trimurti in Maya. – The square, set in motion, becomes a lozenge, as the circle does an ellipse.'[9]

---

9. Malfatti, 26, 28-9.

'Oum = 5 [...] The image of Oum, where a circle symbolising infinite time (the serpent of eternity) circumscribes a square in the middle of which is found suspended a triangle.' Oum is 'a proclamation of all that becomes; a prototype of the first cosmogenetic development; a breath of original life; the container of a nature to come; the envelope of science; the mystical body of Brahma – the soul of all with and within Brahma.'[10]

---

10. Malfatti, 31-2.

Oum 'represented in human form, as masculine and feminine in the act of coupling'.[11]

---

11. *Ibid.*, 32.

'Hiranyagarbha $= 6$': 'in 6 [...] is substantialised not only the totality received from the ideal and real hermaphroditism as genre, as spirit of the world closed in on itself as the egg of the world [...] but also the idea of a development outside itself of finite sex in the third power of $2 = 8$, a sex which, in the third triad, is expressed in an infinite individuality.'

'The allegorical image of Hiranyagarbha consists in an altar decorated with a great altarpiece. An enormous tree-trunk plunging its roots into water, the earth and fire rising below a sky of clouds and lights. In the branches, this tree of the world holds a circle composed of fourteen heads, representing the spirit of the world which reigns in all things. – Inside, enclosed by the circle of heads, is the sea of light and of devouring flames, within which, like tongues of flame, swim the multitude of future individual souls, like golden carp in waters dappled silver by the sun.'[12]

---

12. Malfatti, 37-8.

'Purusha = 7 [...] opens the third triad as passage from the general to the particular, from the species to the individual, and as realisation of the conversion indicated in the second triad of hermaphrodism to sex; only by this token can it be a question, in the third triad, of a truly achieved individuality [...] 7 does not however yet represent the individual become real, but firstly the thought of the development of the divine Trimurti through Maya, Oum, Hiranyagarbha, as intermediate members in matter [...] The idea of matter can be understood sometimes as atomistic [...] and sometimes as dynamic [...] The figure of Purusha conforms perfectly to this analysis [...] It is a statue of large dimension, before which Brahma moves [...] beneath the veil of Maya [...] as a sun with powerful rays; thus the atomistic side is indubitably signified by the massive statue, as is the dynamic side by the radiating sun [...] But in the middle of the massive pedestal, we see emerge from the egg in the very direction of its axis of longitude, 4 + 3 powerful jets of fire; the same thing happens in the transversal axis, but in such a way that the 4 lower jets extend themselves in breadth and depth, as if in a determined triadic and tetradic manner [...] as 4 as two times 2 represents geometrically germination in space (but so far only in ideally – as surface), so also 7 can be understood as 6+1 or 4+3. – In the first case, it is the passage from the second into the third triad through the medium of a new development; in the second case, it is that geometric truth, that every (individual) body can be considered as an extension of surface (4), operating in three directions (length, breadth, depth).'[13]

---

13. Malfatti, 43-4; *Cf.* Deleuze, present volume, 149.

'Prajapati = 8 [...] In eight, individuality is finally obtained, as is seen in the figure of the cipher 8 closed in on itself with a perfect symmetry [...] Eight, the third power of the first number pair (more precisely, the feminine principle, reproductive of those that went before), gives the idea of space extended in three directions; not merely geometrically-empty space, but already corporealised space, whereas the interlaced double-ellipse indicates to us, since it signifies an operation of ever-living activity, the individuality which never separates from the world of the universal; – the dualism of mind and body (sex), already expressed in the act of becoming; – the two foci in man, reason and sensibility.'[14]

14. Malfatti, 47.

COLLAPSE III

'Prakriti = 9 [...] Just like Prakriti's position in the allegories, the relation of the number 9 to the ciphers is that of a conclusion of the third triad of the decimal: 3x3=9. The idea of the individual, which – according to its geometrical meaning, in regard to its participation in the passage from the circle to the ellipse, and properly the sphere into the ellipsoid – is so well symbolised in the number 8. This idea, however, suggested to the profound contemplative faculty of the Indians an aspect of the dependence of the individual, namely that of the triple life of the egg of the world, as sidereal life, telluric life and atmospheric life. – In man it is on one hand the head, the stomach and the chest; on the other hand reason, sensibility, and heart [the soul] [...] The image of Prakriti is a woman's figure with the shield of Maya at her feet, seated on a throne whose triangular base has nine surfaces; encompassed by the crown radiated by Brahma which passes across the chains of gold of the pleasure of the senses, she is charged from head to foot with interlaced chains and attaches to the head with points turned above. – In her lap are seated the divine image of the Trimurti, with most significant attributes. – Brahma holds the Veda and a lotus, Vishnu, the circle of the rotation of the world; Shiva, the flaming trident; – Prakriti throws with two hands the models of the forms of Maya into an apron attached in front, and mixes them together. – On the pedestal we see Maya, shifting the veil of the image of the world [...] Prakriti was considered to be the fundamental principle of phenomenal change into the intellectual, and, in the physical sense, as the fundamental principle of the immersion of the mind in the bonds of matter.'[15]

15. Malfatti, 50-1.

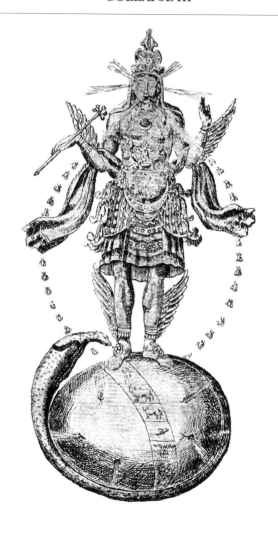

'Prana $= 10$ [...] Prana was considered to be the original form of the breath of the world, vivifying all, at the same time that Oum was its mystical body [...] The principle of movement in the original form of time and space, the pulsation of nature and the movement of the wind and spiritual pulse (the five winds of life) [...] His relation with the external world is expressed by the powerful rays which shine from his eyes, nostrils, ears and mouth, through which he makes the divine essence of life ebb and flow [...] Just as the sun radiates above his head, so we see shining, on his chest, the moon with the circle of clouds around his navel. He sits, as king of the breath of life, upon the egg of the world, from which, from five openings visibly give forth the currents of Prana (as image of the universe outside of man).'[16]

---

16. Malfatti, 53-5.

Aiôn and Chronos:
Deleuze and the Stoic Theory of Time

John Sellars

Gilles Deleuze outlines a supposedly Stoic dual theory of time: on the one hand there is aiôn, *comprising an infinite past and future; on the other there is* chronos, *the extended present. In the scholarly literature on Stoicism, however, either a single theory is reconstructed or the evidence is dismissed as too thin and incoherent. I offer an explanation for this distance between the Deleuzian and scholarly presentations of the Stoic theory of time. I conclude by answering the question to what extent, if any, the Deleuzian theory of* aiôn *and* chronos *deserves to be called Stoic.*

In his 1969 book *The Logic of Sense* Gilles Deleuze embarks on an unexpected engagement with the ancient Stoics.[1] His project in that book is to give an account of

---

1. See G. Deleuze, *Logique du sens* (Paris: Minuit, 1969); *The Logic of Sense*, trans. M. Lester (New York: Columbia University Press, 1990), hereafter abbreviated to *LS*, followed by French/English pagination. The present article forms part of a larger project concerned with Deleuze and Stoicism. A number of other articles have recently issued from this project, notably 'An Ethics of the Event: Deleuze's Stoicism', *Angelaki* 11/3 (2006), 157-71 and 'Deleuze and Cosmopolitanism', *Radical Philosophy* 142 (2007), 30-37. These follow on from a much older article, 'The Point of View of

linguistic meaning or sense as a non-existing entity, and in order to do this he draws upon Stoic philosophy of language, in which linguistic meaning is classified as one of four incorporeal entities outside the category of 'being' but within the broader category of 'something'.[2] According to Deleuze, Stoic ontology posits a surface populated on its two sides by corporeal causes and incorporeal effects,[3] although in fact this bears little relation to the ontology of the ancient Stoics.[4] This concern with the ontological status

the Cosmos: Deleuze, Romanticism, Stoicism', *Pli: The Warwick Journal of Philosophy* 8 (1999), 1-24. For literature on Deleuze and Stoicism by others see J. Simont, 'Se vaincre soi-même plutôt que la fortune (Le stoïcisme chez Sartre et Deleuze)', in G. Idt, ed., *Sartre en sa maturité*, 'Études sartriennes' VI (Paris: Université Paris X, 1995), 175-91; T. Bénatouïl, 'Deux usages du stoïcisme: Deleuze, Foucault', in F. Gros and C. Lévy, eds, *Foucault et la philosophie antique* (Paris: Kimé, 2003), 17-49; S. Bowden, 'Deleuze et les Stoïciens: une logique de l'événement', *Bulletin de la Société Américaine de Philosophie de Langue Française* 15 (2005), 72-97; A. Beaulieu, 'Gilles Deleuze et les Stoïciens', in A. Beaulieu, ed., *Gilles Deleuze, héritage philosophique* (Paris: Presses Universitaires de France, 2005), 45-72. There are also discussions of Deleuze and Stoic ontology in V. Bergen, *L'Ontologie de Gilles Deleuze* (Paris: L'Harmattan, 2001), esp. 117 ff. and 273 ff.

2. See *LS* 13-21/4-11. Here Deleuze draws upon Émile Bréhier's *La théorie des incorporels dans l'ancien stoïcisme* (Paris: Vrin, 1928; 9th edn 1997). For a brief overview of Stoic ontology see J. Sellars, *Stoicism* (Chesham: Acumen / Berkeley: University of California Press, 2006), 81-6.

3. These incorporeal effects are, for Deleuze, also identified with events.

4. There is indeed a contrast between existing bodies and subsisting incorporeals in Stoic ontology but it is quite different from the two-sided ontology that Deleuze develops in *LS* and credits to the Stoics. The Stoics in fact posit four types of incorporeal, of which linguistic meaning or sense (*lekton*, 'that which is said', often translated as 'sayable') is just one (the other three are time, place, and void). Deleuze's supposedly Stoic 'incorporeal effects' are merely examples of these incorporeal linguistic predicates. There is no Stoic concept of an 'incorporeal event' along the lines that Deleuze suggests. Nor is there any conception of parallel series of bodies-causes and incorporeal-effects inhabiting two sides of a single surface. Deleuze draws upon Sextus Empiricus, *Adversus Mathematicos* 9.211 (*Stoicorum Veterum Fragmenta* [hereafter *SVF*], ed. H. von Arnim, 4 vols (Leipzig: Teubner, 1903-24), 2.341; A. A. Long and D. N. Sedley, *The Hellenistic Philosophers*, 2 vols (Cambridge: Cambridge University Press, 1987), 55B) and takes Sextus's reference to incorporeal predicates as if it were a reference to incorporeals as such. Sextus's incorporeal predicates

of linguistic sense is the principal reason why Deleuze turns to the Stoics but his engagement with Stoicism in *The Logic of Sense* is by no means confined to their theory of incorporeals. He also discusses Stoic ethics and the Stoic 'image of the philosopher'.[5] One might say that Deleuze's principal theme of the logic (or ontology) of sense provides him with a way into a much broader exploration of ancient Stoicism.

Of the various aspects of Deleuze's engagement with the Stoics, it is his account of the Stoic theory of time as a dual theory of *aiôn* and *chronos* that is probably most widely known. In the wake of Deleuze's enormous influence in the English-speaking world these supposedly Stoic concepts of *aiôn* and *chronos* have taken on a life of their own and a quick internet search will turn up a wide range of references to 'the Stoic theory of *aiôn* and *chronos*' in publications from right across the spectrum of Humanities disciplines – from literary theory, film theory, architectural theory, feminist theory, and many others.

However, if one turns to the standard English-language scholarship on Stoicism one will find no reference to such a dual theory of time and no discussion of the terms *aiôn* and *chronos* with the sense that Deleuze attaches to them. The aim of what follows is to ask the question to what extent, if any, are Deleuze's concepts of *aiôn* and *chronos*

---

caused by bodies are merely *lekta* and as such are examples of but one of the four types of incorporeal proposed by the Stoics. On the basis of this misreading Deleuze goes on to construct his two-sided ontological surface. His account is, moreover, inconsistent, sometimes placing sense on the incorporeal side of this surface, other times locating sense on the boundary between the two sides. For discussion of Stoic *lekta* see Sellars, *Stoicism*, 61-4.

5. For Deleuze's remarks on Stoic ethics see the 20th and 21st series; for the 'image of the philosopher' see the 18th series.

Stoic concepts and, if not, to ask where they came from. This is a fairly modest scholarly task and I do not claim that any serious philosophical consequences follow from my response to these questions. I shall begin by outlining Deleuze's account of these terms and locate his principal source. I shall then turn to the early Stoics and see what has been said about their theory of time. Then I shall move on to the later Stoic Marcus Aurelius who, as we shall see, is particularly significant for this question. We shall also briefly touch upon the discussions of time in Henri Bergson and William James, in so far as they inform the interpretations of Stoicism under discussion. I shall conclude by offering an answer to my question, namely whether the concepts of *aiôn* and *chronos* are really Stoic concepts at all.

1. DELEUZE ON AIÔN AND CHRONOS

According to Deleuze the Stoics proposed two distinct readings of time.[6] Rather than conceive time as a continuum divided into the three parts of past, present, and future, Deleuze suggests that the Stoics separated the present from the past and future. On the one hand the Stoics conceived time as *chronos*, the extended, but limited, living present. On the other hand they conceived time as *aiôn*, the unlimited past and future:

> Thus time must be grasped twice, in two complementary though mutually exclusive fashions. First, it must be grasped entirely as the living present in bodies which act and are acted upon. Second, it must be grasped entirely as an entity infinitely

---

6. The conceptual distinction is introduced at *LS* 14/5 and elaborated in the 10th and 23rd series, with passing references throughout. For a general discussion see P. Mengue, 'Aiôn / Chronos', in R. Sasso and A. Villani, eds, *Le Vocabulaire de Gilles Deleuze*, Les Cahiers de Noesis 3 (Nice, 2003), 41-7.

divisible into past and future [...]. Only the present exists in time and gathers together or absorbs the past and future. But only the past and future inhere in time and divide each present infinitely. These are not three successive dimensions, but two simultaneous readings of time.[7]

Under *chronos*, the present moment has a certain extension or duration (*étendue ou durée*),[8] an extension that can expand or contract – the present discussion, the present day, the present year, for instance. It can even expand to encompass all of time, becoming what Deleuze calls the cosmic present.[9] From the perspective of *chronos* the past and future are merely parts of some larger present that subsumes the current present: 'the past and future indicate only the relative difference between two presents'.[10] The past and future of the present day – yesterday and tomorrow – are merely parts of the larger present that is the present week. Thus there exists a series of presents of differing extensions enveloping one another, all ultimately enveloped by the cosmic present.

Under *aiôn*, the relationship between the present on the one hand and the past and future on the other is reversed. Instead of a present that can expand and absorb the past and future, under *aiôn* the extended present evaporates in a process of subdivision into part of the past and part of the future.[11] The extended present is replaced by the instant,

7. *LS* 14/5. See also *LS* 77/61 and 190/162, where Deleuze labels these two readings *chronos* and *aiôn* respectively.

8. See *LS* 190/162.

9. See *LS* 77-8/61; see also 190/162: 'God experiences as present that which for me is future or past, since I live inside more limited presents'.

10. *LS* 78/62; see also 190/162.

11. See *LS* 78/62.

a mathematical limit without thickness or extension that stands between past and future.[12] If ever we think we have isolated a present moment with any extension in between past and future, it will always be possible to divide it once again into part of the past and part of the future. On this reading no event is ever truly present, having either just happened or being just about to happen: 'no one ever dies, but has always just died or is always going to die'.[13] With *aiôn*, then, we find an echo of Aristotle's discussion of time in *Physics* 4.10, where Aristotle wonders whether time really exists if some of it is in the past and so no longer exists and some of it is in the future and so does not yet exist. The 'now' (*nun*) for Aristotle is an instant without extension separating past and future, and so neither does this exist, for it does not refer to a period of time that is ever actually present.[14]

It should be clear that these two conceptions of time attributed to the Stoics are radically opposed to one another.[15] The idea of an extended present with a certain temporal extension or duration is incompatible with the idea of a present defined as an abstract mathematical limit. Thus we have two diametrically opposed conceptions of

---

12. See *LS* 78/62, where he calls this a *pur instant mathématique*, and 193/164, where it is 'the instant without thickness and without extension' (*l'instant sans épaisseur et sans extension*).

13. *LS* 80/63.

14. See Aristotle, *Physics* 4.10, 217b29-218a8. For the 'now' being an instant without extension see *Physics* 4.13, 222a10-20. For the infinite divisibility of a continuum such as time see *Physics* 6.1, 231a21-b18. For discussion see R. Sorabji, *Time, Creation, and the Continuum* (London: Duckworth, 1983), esp. 7-16.

15. We can also note that, for Deleuze, the extended present of *chronos* is intimately connected to the interactions of existing bodies, while the infinite and infinitely divisible past-future of *aiôn* is associated with the subsisting incorporeal effects of the event. These are the two sides of his pseudo-Stoic ontological surface.

time involving two different conceptions of the present moment (and in order to avoid confusion Deleuze labels the present without extension 'the instant').[16] For Deleuze, the Stoics do not conceive time as something composed of the three elements of past, present, and future. Rather, they read time in two distinct ways: as an expanding and contracting extended present on the one hand (*chronos*), and as an infinitely divisible line of past-future divided by an instant without thickness on the other (*aiôn*)

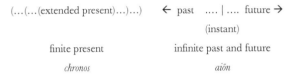

Figure 1. Two Conceptions of Time

Deleuze straightforwardly presents this as an ancient Stoic theory and he cites as his source for this theory a book by the French scholar Victor Goldschmidt on the 'Stoic System and the Idea of Time'.[17] If one has any doubts about whether this really is an ancient Stoic theory then one must turn to Goldschmidt and assess his account and examine the ancient sources that he cites in its support. We shall do this shortly, but first let us turn directly to the ancient Stoics and some of their other modern interpreters.

---

16. See *e.g. LS* 78/62 and 193/164, noted above.

17. See *LS* 78/340 ('Victor Goldschmidt in particular has analyzed the coexistence of these two conceptions of time'), with V. Goldschmidt, *Le système stoïcien et l'idée de temps* (Paris: Vrin, 1953, 4th edn 1979). Deleuze also cites É. Bréhier, *La théorie des incorporels dans l'ancien Stoïcisme* (Paris: Picard, 1908; 9th edn Vrin, 1997) as a source for his reading of Stoicism, although he relies on this mainly for his account of the Stoic theory of incorporeals rather than the theory of time.

2. THE EARLY STOICS ON TIME

None of the works of the early Stoics survive and so in order to consider their theory of time it is necessary to rely upon quotations and doxographical reports of their views. These are inevitably partial, partisan, and sometimes contradictory. The task of determining what the early Stoics thought is by no means easy, then, and this is especially true when it comes of their thoughts about time. The matter is complicated further by the fact that the label 'early Stoics' covers a number of thinkers, each of whom may well have revised their position at some point. It is sometimes assumed by both modern readers and ancient doxographers that there exists just one early Stoic position on any given philosophical topic, but this is not necessarily the case. Moreover, ancient doxographers and modern scholars sometimes assume a philosophical identity between the early Stoa as such and the work of its most prominent figure, Chrysippus. In short, determining what the early Stoic theory of time actually was is a scholarly minefield. With that warning in place, let us turn to consider the evidence.

There are in fact just three texts that report what the early Stoics thought about time, and these are in Diogenes Laertius, Plutarch, and Stobaeus. The last two are longer and include reports relating to different early Stoics so I shall divide both of these in two, giving us five ancient texts to consider:

(a) Diogenes Laertius 7.141: Time (*chronos*) too is incorporeal (*asômatos*), being the measure (*diastêma*) of the world's motion (*kinêsis*). And time past and time future are infinite (*apeiron*), but time present is finite.[18]

---

18. This text is *SVF* 2.520. It is not included in Long and Sedley.

(b) Stobaeus 1,106,5-23: Chrysippus said time (*chronos*) is the dimension (*diastêma*) of motion (*kinêsis*) according to which the measure of speed and slowness is spoken of; or the dimension accompanying the world's motion. And (he says) every single thing moves and exists in accordance with time [...] Just as the void in its totality is infinite (*apeiron*) in every respect, so time (*chronos*) in its totality (*panta*) is infinite (*apeiron*) on either side (*eph' hekatera*). For both the past and the future are infinite (*apeiron*). He says most clearly that no time (*chronos*) is wholly present (*holôs enistatai*). For since continuous things are infinitely divisible (*tomê*), on the basis of this division every time (*chronos*) too is infinitely (*eis apeiron*) divisible (*tomê*). Consequently no time (*chronos*) is present exactly (*kat' apartismon enestanai*), but it is broadly (*kata platos*) said to be so. He also says that only the present belongs (*huparchein*); the past and future subsist (*huphestanai*), but belong (*huparchein*) in no way, just as only predicates which are [actual] attributes are said to belong (*huparchein*), for instance, walking around belongs to me when I am walking around, but it does not belong when I am lying down or sitting.[19]

(c) Plutarch, *On Common Conceptions* 1081c-1082a: The Stoics [...] do not admit a minimal time (*elachiston chronon*) or wish the now (*nun*) to be partless (*ameres*) but claim that whatever one thinks one has grasped and is considering as present (*enestos*) is in part future and in part past. [...] Chrysippus [...] says in his book *On the Void* and elsewhere that the part of time (*chronos*) which is past and the part which is future subsist (*huphestêkenai*) but do not belong (*huparchein*) and only the present belongs. But in *On Parts* Books, 3, 4, and 5 he maintains that one part

---

19. Cited according to volume, page, and line of C. Wachsmuth, *Ioannis Stobaei Anthologii Libri Duo Priores Qui Inscribi Solent Eclogae Physicae et Ethicae*, 2 vols (Berlin: Weidmann, 1884; repr. 1958). This text is Arius Didymus fr. 26 (in H. Diels, *Doxographi Graeci* (Berlin: De Gruyter, 1879; Editio Quarta 1965), 461,23-462,3), *SVF* 2.509, and Long and Sedley 51B.

of the present time (*enestêkotos chronou*) is future and the other past. So it turns out that he divides the belonging constituent of time into non-belonging parts of what belongs, or rather that he leaves nothing at all of time belonging, if the present has no part which is not future or past.[20]

(d) Plutarch, *On Common Conceptions* 1081e: Archedemus says that now (*nun*) is a kind of joining and meeting of the past and future [...] now (*nun*) is not a time (*chronos*) but a limit (*peras*) of time (*chronos*).[21]

(e) Stobaeus 1,105,17-106,4: On Posidonius: Some things are infinite (*apeira*) in every respect like the whole of time. Others in a particular respect like the past and the future. For each of them is limited only by reference to the present (*paronta*). His definition of time (*chronos*) is as follows: dimension of motion or measure of speed and slowness. And he holds that that time which is thought of in terms of 'when' is partly past, partly future, and partly present. The last consists of a part (*meros*) of the past and a part of the future, encompassing the actual division (*diorismon*). But the division (*diorismon*) is point-like (*sêmeiôdê*). Now (*nun*) and the like are thought of broadly (*en platei*) and not exactly. But now (*nun*) is also spoken of with reference to the least perceptible time encompassing the division (*diorismon*) of the future and the past.[22]

---

20. This text is *SVF* 2.517-9 and Long and Sedley 51C. I have made use of the helpful text with translation in H. Cherniss, *Plutarch, Moralia: Volume XIII, Part II* (Cambridge, MA: Harvard University Press, 1976).

21. This text is Archedemus fr. 14 (in *SVF* 3) and Long and Sedley 51C.

22. This text is Arius Didymus fr. 26 (in Diels, *Doxographi Graeci*, 461,13-22), Posidonius fr. 98 (in L. Edelstein, and I. G. Kidd, *Posidonius, The Fragments* (Cambridge: Cambridge University Press, 1972; 2nd edn 1989)), and Long and Sedley 51E.

These texts are complex and in certain respects seemingly contradictory. The challenge of reconstructing the Stoic theory of time from these meagre remains has not surprisingly led to a number of conflicting interpretations. On the basis of text (a) some have suggested that the Stoics posited a finite present with a certain extension or duration sitting between the past and future each of which are limited by the present on one side but unlimited on the other.[23]

← infinite past … (extended finite present) … infinite future →

Figure 2. Tripartite Theory of Time

This is clearly the polar opposite of Deleuze's reading. Others have suggested that while there is a mathematical limit between past and future, there is also an extended present that overlaps with part of the past and part of the future,[24] in effect combining Deleuze's two opposed readings into one.

instant

← infinite past … | … infinite future →

(extended present)

Figure 3. Revised Tripartite Theory of Time

---

23. I. G. Kidd, *Posidonius II: The Commentary*, 2 vols (Cambridge: Cambridge University Press, 1988) suggests this was Zeno's position. Sorabji, *Time, Creation, and the Continuum*, 25, attributes this interpretation to G. E. L. Owen (although not citing this text).

24. See *e.g.* Sorabji, *Time, Creation, and the Continuum*, 25, who considers (but does not endorse) this reading along with the previous reading as 'two rival interpretations of Chrysippus'.

The reading that has tended to dominate modern scholarly discussions rejects both of these possibilities. It argues that for the Stoics the present does not have any extension of its own and when we talk as if it does we are merely talking about a fictitious or specious present. This is the position adopted by Sorabji after considering and then rejecting the other two readings and it is also the position adopted by Long and Sedley in their influential sourcebook.[25] The latter note that according to the sources 'time is infinite in extension and infinitely divisible'.[26] While time as a whole is infinite, past and future are infinite on only one side, limited on the other side by the present. Long and Sedley take 'the present' and 'the now' to be synonymous, being an indivisible durationless point (*i.e.* Deleuze's 'instant'). 'But', they say, 'we are allowed to speak of the present as if it had a duration or existence of its own. That is acceptable at the level of perception, but under strict analysis the present is specious since it "consists of a part of the past and a part of the future"'.[27] In other words, the extended present is merely a popular but ultimately mistaken way of talking (and not a second theory of time). On this reading, there is no extended present of *chronos*, only the infinite past-future of *aiôn*.

There is one piece of ancient evidence that this reading does not take into account. It is the claim reported by Plutarch and Stobaeus that while the past and future 'subsist' (*huphestanai*), the present moment 'belongs' (*huparchein*).[28]

---

25. See Sorabji, *Time, Creation, and the Continuum*, 21-6; Long and Sedley, vol. 1, 307.

26. Long and Sedley, *ibid.*

27. Long and Sedley, *ibid.*

28. On this distinction see A. A. Long, 'Language and Thought in Stoicism', in A. A. Long, ed., *Problems in Stoicism* (London: Athlone, 1971), 75-113, at 89-93; V.

This word translated as 'belong' (*huparchein*) has sometimes been translated as 'exist'.[29] The present moment belongs or exists in the same sense that the predicate 'I am walking' belongs to me when I am actually walking but not when I am sitting. The important point is that the present is said to have a greater ontological status than the past and future, and this seems at odds with the claim that the present is merely specious.

It has been suggested by Kidd that the Stoic Posidonius tried to overcome this problem by drawing a distinction between two senses of the now (*nun*).[30] According to Kidd, the first Stoic, Zeno, held a tripartite theory of time divided into past, present and future, positing a finite present with a certain extension sitting in between the past and future. Chrysippus rejected the idea of a finitely extended present due to the problem of its infinite divisibility (raised by Aristotle in *Physics* 6.3, 234a11-24), and so was left with only the past and future separated by a limit. However, this left Chrysippus with the paradox of claiming that the present 'belongs' even though it isn't really there. Posidonius overcame this paradox in Chrysippus' position (in which the present is reduced to nothing but still 'belongs') by distinguishing between two senses of now (*nun*), one conceptual and one temporal – the dividing limit and the specious present (these are Deleuze's 'instant' and 'extended present'). While the conceptual present is a mathematical

Goldschmidt, '*Huparchein* et *huphistanai* dans la philosophie stoïcienne', *Revue des Études Grecques* 85 (1972), 331-44; F. H. Sandbach, *Aristotle and the Stoics*, Cambridge Philological Society Suppl. Vol. 10 (Cambridge: Cambridge: Philological Society, 1985), 79-80; Long and Sedley, vol. 1, 164.

29. See *e.g.* Long, 'Language and Thought in Stoicism', 89; Sorabji, *Time, Creation, and the Continuum*, 22.

30. See Kidd, *Posidonius II: The Commentary*, vol. 1, 395-403.

concept, the temporal present is an extension or interval between two limits where the extent of the interval is not fixed, and so the present can expand or contract, although it remains specious.

Zeno:

← infinite past ... (extended finite present) ... infinite future →

Chrysippus:

instant

← infinite past ... | ... infinite future →

Posidonius:

conceptual instant

← infinite past ... | ... infinite future →

(temporal extended present)

Figure 4. Kidd on Zeno, Chrysippus, and Posidonius

Kidd goes on to draw a parallel with William James,[31] suggesting that the philosophically correct use of the notion of the present is to refer to a durationless limit or instant. This is the conceptual present. However, the foundation for our conception of time is a pre-philosophical specious present of lived time, which is necessarily vague and imprecise. Again, like Sorabji and Long and Sedley, the extended present of *chronos* is rejected as specious and we are left with the infinite past-future and durationless instant of *aiôn*. More recent scholarship has continued with this

---

31. Kidd cites W. James, *The Principles of Psychology*, 2 vols (London: Macmillan, 1890), 1,631.

line of interpretation. In the nine hundred pages of *The Cambridge History of Hellenistic Philosophy* we get just one paragraph on the Stoic theory of time: 'To the Stoics time is an incorporeal continuum which can be infinitely divided. For this reason no time is wholly present inasmuch as the present consists of a part of the past and a part of the future. Past and future are parts of time and stretch out infinitely on one side but are limited by the present, which acts as a kind of joining'.[32] This is again the Deleuzian time of *aiôn*. No attempt is made here to reconcile this with the ancient claim that, while the past and future subsist, the present 'exists' or 'belongs' (*huparchein*).

By way of summary thus far, we can see that according to the recent scholarly consensus the Stoics held a theory of time close to Deleuze's conception of *aiôn*. However, there remains a tension within the ancient sources that is uncomfortable. Indeed, most modern accounts fully acknowledge this and their readings are offered as the most plausible reconstruction of some messy and possibly contradictory doxography. The tension that remains is this: while on the one hand time infinitely extends into the past and future and the past and future are separated by a durationless instant, on the other hand the present moment is said to be extended and to 'belong', which accords it a greater ontological status than the past or future.

Plutarch, who is explicitly looking for contradictions within Stoic philosophy, sums this up best in text (c) above. There he says that while Chrysippus says in his book *On the Void* that 'part of time which is past and the part which is

---

32. D. M. Schenkeveld, 'Language', in K. Algra *et al.*, eds, *The Cambridge History of Hellenistic Philosophy* (Cambridge: Cambridge University Press, 1999), 177-225, at 191.

future subsist (*huphestêkenai*) but do not belong (*huparchein*) and only the present belongs (*huparchein*)', in his other book *On Parts* 'he maintains that one part of the present time is future and the other past'. Consequently Plutarch charges Chrysippus with dividing 'the belonging constituent of time into non-belonging parts of what belongs, or rather that he leaves nothing at all of time belonging'. This is the tension that modern scholars try to explain away. The fact that Plutarch cites from two different works by Chrysippus (*On the Void* and *On Parts*) should not be overlooked, and Kidd may well be right to try to sketch a development in Stoic thinking about time.[33] What we may have here are fragments of two different positions held by Chrysippus at two different stages in his philosophical development. But of course such a claim can be no more than speculation.

There is also an issue of translation here. In the two passages from Stobaeus it is said that the present is *kata platos* and *en platei*.[34] Long and Sedley render these as saying that the present is 'broadly said to be' and is 'thought of broadly', implying imprecisely.[35] We say that the present moment exists but this is imprecise because strictly speaking the present is merely part of the past and part of the future. However, others translate these passages as saying that the present *is* broad or has a certain extension. (Goldschmidt has 'étendue'; Rist has 'extension'; Hadot has 'thickness' in Chase's translation; Brunschwig has 'extended'; Sorabji has 'broadly', to imply thickness, even though he rejects

---

33. The only other reference we have to *On the Void* is from Diogenes Laertius 7.140 (*SVF* 2.543) who helpfully tells us that in *On the Void* Chrysippus discusses the void. There are no other references to *On Parts*. See Appendix II in *SVF* 3, 200.

34. See Wachsmuth, 1,106,18 and 1,105,26, in texts (b) and (e) above.

35. See Long and Sedley, vol. 1, 304 and 305.

this reading.)[36] On this reading the present is real and is not specious. How we translate this phrase will affect how easily the tension within the doxography can be reconciled. However, one tension will not go away. For even if we dismiss the supposedly extended present as specious, we are still faced with the claim that only the present belongs. Yet it seems odd to say that the 'now' conceived as a durationless mathematical limit can 'belong' in a way analogous to the way in which walking 'belongs' to me when I am walking. On the contrary, walking sounds precisely like a present activity that takes place in an extended, albeit unspecified, duration of time.

3. MARCUS AURELIUS ON TIME

As we have seen, usually the Stoic theory of time is read as a single theory of time, although one with a few loose ends not fully explained. However we can also see, especially in the testimony of Plutarch, that it might not be unreasonable to see two distinct conceptions of time in the ancient evidence, one with an extended present that belongs and another with a durationless instant separating past and future. But there is nothing to suggest that the Stoics held on to two distinct readings of time as part of one theory, nor is there any evidence to suggest that two such readings were referred to by the terms *aiôn* and *chronos*. Indeed, *chronos* is simply 'time', so what we have been examining thus far is simply the Stoic theory of *chronos*, although the philosophical position that we have uncovered is usually read as one

---

36. See *e.g.* Goldschmidt, *Le système stoïcien et l'idée de temps*, 37; J. M. Rist, *Stoic Philosophy* (Cambridge: Cambridge University Press, 1969), 278; P. Hadot, *The Inner Citadel: The Meditations of Marcus Aurelius*, trans. M. Chase (Cambridge, MA: Harvard University Press, 1998), 136; J. Brunschwig, 'Stoic Metaphysics', in B. Inwood, ed., *The Cambridge Companion to The Stoics* (Cambridge: Cambridge University Press, 2003), 206-32, at 215; Sorabji, *Time, Creation, and the Continuum*, 22.

that is close to what Deleuze calls *aiôn*.

If *chronos* is simply 'time' then what about *aiôn*? This might be straightforwardly translated as 'eternity', although depending upon the context it is also sometimes rendered as 'time'. In the standard collection of the fragments of the early Stoics *aiôn* appears just once, in an obscure etymological observation reported by Varro, who says that Chrysippus defined *aiôn* ('eternity') as *aei on* ('always existing') – if something is eternal it exists always.[37] In short, there is no explicit early Stoic discussion of *aiôn* in the surviving evidence. If we want to find this term in Stoic texts we must move forward some four hundred years from Chrysippus to Marcus Aurelius.[38] In Marcus's *Meditations* there are 21 instances of *aiôn* and it is from Marcus that Victor Goldschmidt takes the term in his discussion of Stoic time, a discussion upon which Deleuze's account of the Stoic theory of time is based.

Goldschmidt argues that there are indeed two conceptions of time in Chrysippus, the extended present that belongs and the infinite past-future separated by the durationless instant, but Goldschmidt suggests that Chrysippus was negligent when it came to terminology. However, that failure was rectified much later by Marcus, who used the term *aiôn* to refer to the infinite time of past-future. In support of this claim Goldschmidt cites *Meditations* 4.3, in

37. See Varro, *De Lingua Latina* 6.2 (*SVF* 2.163): 'Aevum ab aetate omnium annorum (hinc aeviternum, quod factum est aeternum): quod Graeci *aiona*, id ait Chrysippus esse *aei on*.'

38. For Marcus Aurelius I have used the editions by C. R. Haines, *The Communings with Himself of Marcus Aurelius Antoninus* (London: Heinemann, 1916), A. S. L. Farquharson, *The Meditations of the Emperor Marcus Antoninus*, 2 vols (Oxford: Clarendon Press, 1944), and J. Dalfen, *Marci Aurelii Antonini Ad Se Ipsum Libri XII* (Leipzig: Teubner, 1987), the last of which contains a complete Index Verborum.

which *aiôn* is conjoined with *apeiros*:[39]

> Shall mere glory distract you? Look at the swiftness of the oblivion of all men; the gulf of infinite eternity (*apeirou aiônos*), behind and before; the hollowness of applause, the fickleness and folly of those who seem to speak well of you, and the narrow room in which it is confined. This should make you pause. For the entire earth is a point (*stigmê*) in space, and how small a corner thereof is this your dwelling place, and how few and paltry those who will sing your praises here.[40]

However, Goldschmidt fails to note *Meditations* 2.14 and 10.31, in which *apeiros* is conjoined with *chronos*:

> Always remember, then, these two things: one, that all things from everlasting are of the same kind, and are in rotation; and it matters nothing whether it be for a hundred years or for two hundred or for an infinite time (*en tôi apeirôi chronôi*) that a man shall behold the same spectacle; the other, that the longest-lived and the soonest to die have an equal loss; for it is the present alone of which either will be deprived, since (as we saw) this is all he has and a man does not lose what he has not got.[41]

> For in this way you will continually see that man's life is smoke and nothingness, especially if you remind yourself that what has once changed will be no more in infinite time (*en tôi apeirôi chronôi*).[42]

---

39. Goldschmidt, *Le système stoïcien et l'idée de temps*, 39. See also É. Alliez, 'Aiôn', in B. Cassin, ed., *Vocabulaire européen des Philosophies* (Paris: Le Robert / Seuil, 2004), 44-52, at 45, who cites the same text for the same thesis.

40. *Meditations* 4.3; translation by Farquharson, modified. Farquharson translates *apeirou aiônos* as 'endless time'; Haines has 'infinite time'. Clearly neither thinks that a contrast between *aiôn* and *chronos* is implied here.

41. *Meditations* 2.14; translation by Farquharson.

42. *Meditations* 10.31; translation by Farquharson.

These other passages indicate that Marcus was not using *aiôn* as a technical term to refer to time conceived as infinitely extending into the past and future. Indeed, a careful reading of the 21 instances of *aiôn* and the 31 instances of *chronos* in the *Meditations* makes clear that Marcus uses neither term in any technical sense to refer to a specific conception of time.[43] As we can see from the passages above, Marcus is keen to stress how small a portion of time each of us is allotted compared with the infinite expanse of time, in order to highlight the paltry insignificance of human life, but there is no evidence to suggest a philosophical theory about the nature of time. In these passages Marcus uses the terms *aiôn* and *chronos* synonymously and interchangeably;[44] elsewhere he does use them to draw a contrast between the *chronos* of a human life and the *aiôn* of the cosmos, but again this is merely to draw a contrast between the limited amount of time allotted to each human life and the infinite time of which it is an insignificant part.[45] As we have seen, *chronos* is also used to refer to that same infinite time.[46]

At this point I want to turn to Pierre Hadot's reading of Marcus Aurelius, which involves one of the few explicit discussions of Goldschmidt's thesis.[47] In the *Meditations*,

43. For *aiôn* see *Meditations* 2.12, 4.3, 4.21, 4.43, 4.50, 5.24, 5.32, 6.15, 6.36, 6.59, 7.10, 7.19, 7.70, 9.28, 9.32, 9.35, 10.5, 10.17, 11.1, 12.7, 12.32; for *chronos* see 1.17, 2.4, 2.14, 2.17, 3.7, 3.11, 4.6, 4.32, 4.48, 5.10, 6.15, 6.18, 6.23, 6.25, 6.36, 6.49, 7.29, 7.35, 7.46, 8.5, 8.7, 8.11, 8.44, 9.14, 9.25, 10.1, 10.17, 10.31, 12.3, 12.18, 12.35.

44. Compare *Meditations* 2.14, 4.3, and 10.31, cited above. See also 10.17 where they are used synonymously and where Farquharson translates both as 'Time'.

45. For *chronos* as a finite human lifespan see *e.g. Meditations* 2.4, 2.17, 3.7, 4.48, 6.49, 7.46.

46. For *chronos* as infinite time see *e.g. Meditations* 2.14, 10.17, 10.31.

47. See Hadot, *The Inner Citadel*, esp. 131-7.

Hadot argues, there is a specific attitude towards the present, a concern with focusing one's attention on the present moment. Hadot relates this to the early Stoic theory of time, and quotes Stobaeus (text (b) above). What we find in this report are 'two diametrically opposed conceptions of the present',[48] Hadot suggests: on the one hand the present is merely a limit between past and future, without any extension; on the other hand the present does have a certain duration, reflecting the intention and attention of the individual subject. Rather than try to reconcile these two opposed conceptions of the present, Hadot draws a parallel with the philosophy of Henri Bergson who, in a lecture originally delivered in Oxford in 1911, drew a distinction between the present as a mathematical instant and the present as a certain duration or extension determined by one's attention.[49] For Bergson, the present conceived as a mathematical instant is a pure abstraction without any real existence, unable to constitute part of time for all the reasons outlined by Aristotle. The present that we experience, by contrast, has 'a certain interval of duration':

> Our consciousness tells us that when we speak of our present we are thinking of a certain interval of duration. What duration? It is impossible to fix it exactly, as it is something rather elusive. My present, at this moment, is the sentence I am pronouncing. But this is so because I want to limit the field of my attention to my sentence. This attention is something that

48. Hadot, *The Inner Citadel*, 135. Note also the summary in his *What is Ancient Philosophy?*, trans. M. Chase (Cambridge, MA: Harvard University Press, 2002), 192.

49. See Hadot, *The Inner Citadel*, 136. Bergson's Oxford lecture was first published in *La Perception du Changement: Conférences faites a l'Université d'Oxford, les 26 et 27 mai 1911* (Oxford: Clarendon Press, 1911), reprinted in H. Bergson, *La Pensée et le mouvant* (Paris: Félix Alcan, 1934), 143-76, and translated in *The Creative Mind*, trans. M. L. Andison (New York: Philosophical Library, 1946), 153-86.

can be made longer or shorter, like the interval between the two points of a compass.[50]

For Bergson this interval can be expanded or contracted by one's attention, and even expanded so far as to include a substantial portion of one's past. But as soon as we stop paying attention to a particular moment it falls into the past and no longer forms part of our present. Thus the distinction between past and present for Bergson is fluid and dependent upon one's level of attention. In the light of both Marcus's focus on the present moment and Bergson's pri-oritization of lived duration over mathematical abstraction, Hadot understands Chrysippus's extended present not as a specious pre-philosophical present that evaporates before our very eyes when submitted to philosophical analysis, but rather as a lived present that truly 'belongs' (*huparchein*) to us. When Marcus exhorts us to focus our attention on the present moment he is referring to this extended present, Hadot suggests, and by adjusting our attention we can also expand or contract this extended present along the lines outlined by Bergson.

According to Hadot, Goldschmidt claimed that, for Marcus, this extended present could contract right down to an instant without duration.[51] Hadot rejects this reading of Marcus. He also rejects the claim that, when discussing eternity (*aiôn*), Marcus is conceiving the present as a dura-tionless limit. On the contrary, he is highlighting the limited extension of the present compared with the infinities of past and future. Although Marcus in places describes the present

---

50. Bergson, *La Pensée et le mouvant*, 168-9; *The Creative Mind*, 178-9.

51. See Hadot, *The Inner Citadel*, 137, and Goldschmidt, *Le système stoïcien et l'idée de temps*, 195.

as a point,[52] the context makes clear that this is to emphasize its relative smallness rather than its non-existence. Marcus's term *stigma*, sometimes translated as 'point', is a pin-prick or a mark rather than a mathematical limit.[53] It has a size, albeit a small one. For Marcus, according to Hadot, the present is always the extended lived present. Goldschmidt's attribution of a durationless instant to Marcus reflects his attempt to find a theory of infinite past-future in the *Meditations* and connect it with the evidence for the early Stoa which, as we have seen, does not stand up to close scrutiny.

According to Hadot's Bergsonian reading, then, there are indeed two distinct Stoic conceptions of the present moment: the first is the durationless mathematical limit or instant conceived by Chrysippus and the second is the extended (expandable and contractible) present meditated upon by Marcus.

Chrysippus:

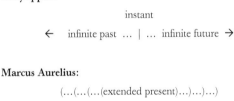

instant

←   infinite past … | … infinite future →

Marcus Aurelius:

(…(…(…(extended present)…)…)…)

Figure 5. Hadot on Chrysippus and Marcus Aurelius

---

52. See *e.g. Meditations* 4.3, cited above, and 6.36: *pan to enestôs tou chronou stigmê tou aiônos*, which Farquharson translates as 'every instant of time, a pin-prick of eternity'.

53. However, Aristotle does use this term to refer to a mathematical limit; see *e.g. Physics* 4.13, 222a14-17.

Turning Goldschmidt's claim on its head, according to Hadot it is Chrysippus who is the theorist of unlimited *aiôn*, while Marcus is the theorist of the extended present of *chronos*.

4. TWO APPROACHES TO THE PRESENT MOMENT: BERGSON AND JAMES

So far we have seen Anglo-American scholars dismiss the extended present as specious and French scholars affirm the extended present as primary. While some of the former turn to William James for philosophical inspiration, some of the latter turn to Henri Bergson. As both Bergson and James have been brought into the discussion by these scholars of Stoicism, it may be instructive to consider briefly the relationship between their two positions.[54] This should help us to clarify the difference between Hadot's reading of the Stoic theory of time and the reading dominant in the English-language scholarship.

It is well known that Bergson and James corresponded, met, and had great respect for each other's work.[55] They developed their dual theories of time independently of one another but they do share a striking structural similarity.[56] James in particular often stressed his

54. One should also note Sambursky's appeal to Whitehead in his account of the Stoic theory of time. In particular, he cites Whitehead's distinction between a moment and a duration. See S. Sambursky, *Physics of the Stoics* (London: Routledge & Kegan Paul, 1959), 105.

55. See R. B. Perry, *The Thought and Character of William James*, 2 vols (London: Oxford University Press, 1935), 599-636, which also reproduces their correspondence.

56. Bergson's position was first outlined in H. Bergson, *Essai sur les données immédiates de la conscience* (Paris: Félix Alcan, 1889), James's in his 1890 work *The Principles of Psychology*. For a rejection of the claim that there was any influence one way or the other see Perry *The Thought and Character of William James*, 599-600.

philosophical proximity to Bergson.[57] Proximity, however, is not identity. In fact, it would be more accurate to say that their two theories are diametrically opposed to one another, one being the reversal of the other. Bergson and James share a position involving two conceptions of the present moment: an extended present of duration on the one hand and a conceptual mathematical limit between past and future on the other. For Bergson, it is the extended present of duration that truly exists, while the conceptual instant between past and future is a mere confusion that cannot grasp the reality of time. For James, by contrast, the extended present is a specious present, a pre-philosophical everyday confusion that should be replaced with the scientific concept of the extensionless instant.[58] (These at least are their opening positions, as I understand them; James may well have amended his position later after discovering Bergson's philosophy.)[59] Both agree that the extended present is our primary experience, but – initially at least – they differ as to its value. James, for instance draws upon psychological studies that try to measure the extended present, and he suggests a maximum duration of 12 seconds. One suspects that Bergson would not have been impressed by such attempts. Indeed, Bergson would

---

57. See in particular James's 'Bergson and his Critique of Intellectualism' in W. James, *A Pluralistic Universe* (London: Longmans, Green, and Co., 1909), 225-73. Bergson also wrote on James; see Bergson, *La Pensée et le mouvant*, 239-51 (translated in *The Creative Mind*, 248-60), first published as the preface to the French translation of James's *Pragmatism*.

58. See James, *The Principles of Psychology*, esp. 608-10. James borrows the phrase 'specious present' from E. R. Clay.

59. See *e.g.* James, *A Pluralistic Universe*, 235: 'all these abstract concepts are but as flowers gathered, they are only moments dipped out from the stream of time, snap-shots taken, as by a kinetoscopic camera, at a life that in its original coming is continuous'.

have rejected the very phrase 'extended present' to describe his concept of 'duration', for it involves an implicit spatialization of time which is precisely what his theory is trying to overcome. The thought of trying to measure duration simply misses his point.[60]

As one can see, an appeal to Bergson or to James when trying to reconstruct the Stoic theory of time will imply quite different attitudes towards the extended present, the conceptual instant, and the relationship between the two. It is precisely this relationship that is central to understanding Deleuze's account of *aiôn* and *chronos*. However, an appeal to either James or Bergson when trying to comprehend the Stoic position runs the risk of anachronism.

5. A STOIC THEORY?

We should now be in a position to answer the question whether Deleuze's theory of *aiôn* and *chronos* is really an ancient Stoic theory of time. In the light of our discussion a number of points should be clear. Firstly, there is no explicit ancient Stoic theory of *aiôn* and *chronos* and the word *aiôn* is nowhere used in Stoic texts as a technical term within a philosophical theory of time, whether one looks at the doxography for the early Stoics or at a late Stoic text such as the *Meditations* of Marcus Aurelius. Secondly, although scholars have attempted to construct a single theory of time out of the evidence for the early Stoics, tensions remain, and it *is* possible to read within the evidence two distinct conceptions of time. However, the evidence is far too thin to attribute to the early Stoa a twofold theory of time,

---

60. Later, James may well have agreed with this: the phrase 'specious present' appears in James's 1890 *Principles of Psychology* but it is absent from his 1909 essay on Bergson which contains nothing to suggest that James disagreed with Bergson on this point.

and the tensions may equally be explained in terms of a development of the Stoic position over a period of time. Thirdly, Marcus Aurelius is concerned with the notion of an extended present and this does contrast with the durationless instant attributed to Chrysippus by modern scholarship. However these two conceptions of the present moment, corresponding to Deleuze's *chronos* and *aiôn* respectively, come from philosophers separated by four hundred years and there is no evidence to suggest that they should be taken together as parts of an explicitly dual theory of time.

As we have also seen, Deleuze is dependent upon the work of Victor Goldschmidt. Notwithstanding Hadot's criticisms of Goldschmidt, which I think are well founded,[61] Goldschmidt and Hadot share a broadly Bergsonian reading of the ancient Stoics on time in which there are two distinct conceptions of the present moment. In contrast to the Jamesian readings of the English-language scholarship in which the extended present is dismissed as specious, both Goldschmidt and Hadot affirm the reality of the extended present. One can see why the Bergsonian Deleuze would be attracted to the Stoic theory of time when presented in such Bergsonian terms.[62] However, *contra* Goldschmidt, it is

61. I agree with Hadot's criticism of Goldschmidt over the interpretation of Marcus Aurelius. However, do not accept all of Hadot's account of the Stoic theory of time, which, with regard to Chrysippus, does not do justice to the tensions in the surviving evidence. On the basis of the meagre evidence available to us, I would suggest that Plutarch's charge of inconsistency is well founded. But before we praise Plutarch too much we must also remember that our evidence has in part been shaped by Plutarch's own selective quotations from Chrysippus, no doubt informed by his own polemical agenda. On this final point see G. Boys-Stones, 'Plutarch on *koinos logos*: Towards an Architecture of the *de Stoicorum repugnantiis*', *Oxford Studies in Ancient Philosophy* 16 (1998), 299-329.

62. It is worth noting that Deleuze uses very Bergsonain descriptions in his account of the Stoic theory of time, calling *chronos* the 'living present' and *aiôn* a 'being of reason' (see *e.g. LS* 80/63).

to Chrysippus (and not Marcus) that we must turn to find what Deleuze calls the Stoic theory of *aiôn* and it is with Marcus that we shall find the extended present of *chronos*. Whether any ancient Stoic actually held both of these conceptions at once, as a dual theory of time, is a matter about which we must ultimately suspend judgement. There is certainly no evidence to confirm that the theory of *aiôn* and *chronos* made famous by Deleuze was in fact a Stoic theory.

It should be borne in mind that Deleuze made no pretensions to be an expert in ancient philosophy, and this is equally clear from his account of Stoic incorporeals.[63] Nevertheless, it is necessary to be clear about the differences between the Deleuzian and Stoic theories of time if we are to grasp the significance of either of them.[64] The theory of *aiôn* and *chronos* is an interesting element in Deleuze's philosophy that takes its inspiration from a speculative reading of the ancient Stoics, but it is not an ancient Stoic theory.

As I acknowledged at the outset, this relatively minor scholarly point does not claim to raise any philosophical objections to the use that Deleuze makes of this dual theory of time. The same may be said about his confusions regarding the Stoic theory of incorporeals. But it is ironic that it is these aspects of Deleuze's engagement with the Stoics that have become best known. Deleuze's supposedly Stoic ontology in *The Logic of Sense* is not really Stoic at all. By contrast, his comments on Stoic ethics in the same book,

---

63. On Deleuze's misreading of Stoic incorporeals see n.4 above. For a discussion of his methodological approach to the history of philosophy see J. Sellars, 'Gilles Deleuze and the History of Philosophy', *British Journal for the History of Philosophy* 15/3 (2007), 551-60.

64. For a similar point see Mengue, 'Aiôn / Chronos', 45.

although based upon an equally brief acquaintance, are much closer to the spirit of ancient Stoicism.[65] Both Marcus Aurelius and Epictetus would have welcomed Deleuze's statement that 'Stoic ethics [...] consist of willing the event as such' and that the ultimate task of ethics is 'not to be unworthy of what happens to us'.[66] It is in the realm of ethics, and not ontology, that Deleuze comes closest to Stoicism.

---

65. This claim has been elaborated at greater length in Sellars 'An Ethics of the Event: Deleuze's Stoicism' (cited in n.1 above).

66. *LS* 168/143 and 174/149.

Matisse-Thought and the Strict Quantitative Ordering of Fauvism[1]

Éric Alliez and Jean-Claude Bonne

The revolution inaugurated in painting by Matisse during his 'Fauvist' period of 1905-6 consisted in substituting for the traditional qualitative conception of painting, subordinated to the representation of (the forms of) things and/or the exposition of the medium, a rigorous, intensive conception for which the reciprocal differential quantities of colours are *their qualities, no longer being covered or mediated by phenomenal qualities in whose service their creative power had hitherto been placed. The intensity of colours, which Matisse pushed to its full extent, will fuel the expansiveness of the canvas, energising it from within, ultimately taking it beyond its limits, in other words beyond the Canvas-Form of painting. But this could only be achieved through a 'strict quantitative ordering' at odds with any post-romantic understanding of Fauvism, and implying a rigorous new constructivist conception of expression. An appreciation of Matisse's experimental practice during this period allows a new understanding of the significance of Fauvism for his later work; whilst also reaffirming the philosophical pertinence of a Nietzschean-Deleuzian thinking of intensity and extensity, the qualitative and the quantitative.*

---

1. Translated extract from E. Alliez & J-C. Bonne, *La Pensée-Matisse: portrait de l'artiste en hyperfauve* (Paris: Le Passage, 2005), 75-84.

THE QUANTITATIVE FOUNDATION OF THE QUALITATIVE

For Matisse, decorativity implies that *colour only exists qua constructive expression of the relation of forces* between colours. Furthermore, the *relation of quantity* between coloured surfaces would then constitute the *quality* of colour. In the case of a painting which, like his, employs pure (unmixed) pigments, Matisse's formula – '[…] even colour can only be a creation' – only makes sense in envisaging the quantitative determination of the quality of colours[2] – A quantitative creation which seizes hold of the totality of the construction of the painting through the '*all-over*' *organisation of colour* ('this *whole* [*ensemble*] the painting constitutes').[3] 'Organisation of forces – colours are forces'; 'to organise sensations'; 'organisation of his brain' … Matisse comes back continually to this: 'painting requires organisation'.[4] *Organisation is the Matissean name for composition*, for the *global composition* which 'is modified along with the surface to be covered'[5] and consequently is no longer, qua creation in the making, that *classical design* (*disegno*) that would project an *idea* onto an inert matter. Idealist (Italian, Latin) ideation

---

2. 'Rôle et modalités de la couleur' in H. Matisse, *Écrits et propos sur l'art*, ed. D. Fourcade (Paris: Hermann, 1972 [Henceforth EPA]), 201; the complete formula is: 'Everything, even colour, can only be a creation'.

3. Yve-Alain Bois was the first to insist, quite rightly, on the importance of the quantitative in the all-over conception of colour in Matisse (see 'Matisse and "Arche-Drawing"' in *Painting as Model*, Cambridge, MA: The MIT Press, 1998).

4. See H. Matisse, 'Entretien avec Léon Degand', in 'Matisse à Paris' EPA 301-3; 'Notes d'un peintre' EPA 51 ('to organise sensations'). Matisse declares of Cézanne: 'There were such possibilities in him that he needed, more than any other person, to put some order into his brain', Jacques Guenne, 'Entretien avec Henri Matisse', *L'Art Vivant*, no. 18, September 1925; EPA 84.

5. H. Matisse, 'Notes d'un peintre', EPA 43.

is replaced by the announcement of the materialist idea of the medium, an idea excluding 'preconceived forms' (Derain); an idea whose proper logic is that of the quantitative working of the surface by its freed forces, freely organised in the *all-over conception*. But it is the same Matisse who writes, in his 'Notes of a Painter': 'For me, all is in the conception. It is thus necessary to have, from the very start, a clear vision of the whole [*l'ensemble*].'[6] For, as opposed to the pre-visionary idea of the *study*, this envisaging of the whole is none other than the 'consciousness of the forces that one employs', as one proceeds, 'driven by an idea that one does not truly know except in so far as it develops with the growth [*la marche*] of the painting.'[7] Far from being any sort of 'reportage' of a mental image, its necessity is a *function* of the impossibility of a difference/différance of the conception from its *realisation* (a Cézannian term if ever there was one, to which the painter of Aix opposed the *esprit littérateur*). Or once again: in the absence 'of rupture between thought and the creative act',[8] conception is of importance only inasmuch as it *surfaces* in a continuous becoming. This processual materialism is antipodeal to the post-romantic

---

6. *Ibid.*

7. H. Matisse, 'Notes d'un peintre sur son dessin', EPA 163. One thinks here of the passage in Bergson's *Creative Evolution* where he speaks of the portrait which one cannot predict in advance, 'for to predict it would have been to produce it before it was produced' (H. Bergson, *Creative Evolution,* trans. A. Mitchell, NY: Dover, 1998, 6).

8. H. Matisse, remark reported by André Verdet, *Prestiges de Matisse*; EPA 47 n11. It is necessary to have a vision of the global state at each moment: 'everything must be envisaged correlatively in the course of the work.' ('Notes de Sarah Stein', 1908, EPA 71). 'I never know in advance what I'm doing' (correspondence with Jean and Henri Dauberville, EPA 47 n11). On the absence of rupture between conception and realisation, see Yve-Alain Bois, 'Matisse and "Arche-Drawing"', *op. cit.* 28*sq.*

exasperation to which the Fauvist 'movement' has been reduced. Matisse does not even balk at evoking a *strict quantitative ordering* in a formula which constitutes, in our view, his most technical definition of Fauvism: 'At the time of the "Fauves", what constituted the *strict ordering of our paintings was that the quantity of colour was its quality.*'[9] In what Matisse calls 'expression', a Nietzschean intuition of the greatest purity will always animate Fauvism: The intuition that *quality is nothing other than the difference of quantity which corresponds to it in each force in relation to all other forces;*[10] the intuition that unity can only make sense in the relational domain of the multiplicity of forces in terms of *the organisation of their mutual play*; the intuition of the liberatory function of art qua *destruction* of every type of ulterior world (the artist as 'spokesman for the "essence" of things', the 'telephone to the beyond');[11] and the *construction of a physiology of aesthetics,*[12] grounding itself *quantitatively* upon the forces of the universe, so as to extract from chaos the *varieties of a composition.* It is this *principle of immanence* which continually refers the 'Fauves' back to Nietzsche, offering his philosophy an alternative to the antagonism between romanticism and classicism which the thinker of the Great Midday sought to redefine by recusing 'most resolutely the classical method'.[13] To borrow

9. H. Matisse 'Visite à Henri Matisse', interview with Tériade, EPA 98 (italics ours).

10. See *Nietzsche and Philosophy*, 42-4 ('Quantity and Quality'), along with the fragments from *Will to Power* upon which Deleuze's argument rests.

11. See F. Nietzsche, *On the Genealogy of Morals* (trans. K. Ansell-Pearson, Cambridge:Cambridge University Press, 1994), 78 (Third Essay, §5).

12. The 'hitherto untouched and unexplored *physiology of aesthetics*' appears in *On the Genealogy of Morals*, 85 (Third Essay, §8).

13. See M. Kessler, *L'Esthétique de Nietzsche* Paris:PUF, 1998, 156 (along with the

from Deleuze and Guattari: Fauvism 'is not chaos but a *composition of chaos* that yields the vision or sensation, so that it constitutes, as Joyce says, a chaosmos, a composed chaos – *neither foreseen nor preconceived*'. If it 'takes up arms against chaos, it is in order to *borrow weapons from it that it turns against opinion*, the better to defeat it with tried and tested arms'.[14] (This 'composition of chaos' echoing the *organisation of chaos* put forward by Nietzsche at the end of the second *Untimely Meditation* – '*das Chaos* [...] *zu organizieren*'.) In the 1907 interview which Appollinaire, persuaded by Goldberg, succeeded in obtaining with Matisse despite the reticence of the latter, who held the poet for a poor art-critic, we find the formula: 'To order a chaos, that is creation'.[15] Directed against that 'opinion' which had begun by sealing the marriage between romanticism and impressionism, and then that of symbolism with a purportedly 'natural' classicism,[16] the strictness of the ordering indicated by Matisse also implies a rupture with every type of

---

whole of the second part, 'The genesis of classical formalism'). In the introduction, the author quite rightly posits that 'Far [...] from representing a brutal and massive force, the greatest will to power is a power of organisation and thus of the simplification of the original chaos of the universe. Beyond this minimal definition aimed at serving his own philosophical and aesthetic categories, classicism thus means nothing to Nietzsche'.

14. *What is Philosophy?*, 204 (emphasis ours).

15. *La Phalange* no. 2, December 1907, reprinted in EPA, 56; unlike other formulas, this is not given in inverted commas, as a citation of a remark of Matisse's but it does seem to correspond to his thought. On the circumstances of this interview, see H. Spurling, *The Unknown Matisse: Volume 1 - A Life of Henri Matisse 1869-1908* (London:Hamish Hamilton, 1998), 415-7.

16. Nietzsche already noted, in this fragment republished in *The Will to Power* (Trans. W. Kaufman and R.J. Hollingdale, ed. W. Kaufman, New York:Vintage, 1968), 447-8 (§849): 'One believed that classicism was a kind of naturalness! [...] The romantics in Germany do *not* protest against classicism, but against reason, enlightenment, taste, the eighteenth century'.

transcendental or spiritualist psychology wedded to the 'language of forms and colours'.

It will be objected that Matisse, in his interview with Tériade, says 'at the time of the "Fauves"' – to which we will answer: Yes, because the quantitative equation crystallises the *trans-historical* dimension of this continued revolution which, in Matisse's words, sees Fauvism at the 'base of everything'. With the principle '*1cm² of blue is not as blue as a square metre of the same blue*',[17] Fauvism is inscribed at the base, as the fundament of a *scienza nova* of colour, composing through its differences of quantity a rigorous processual machine of 'requalification' of the world that *exceeds the art-world*. For it does not announce the same thing as Gauguin did when he said to Cézanne: '*A kilo of green is more green than half a kilo.*'[18] For Matisse, the substitution of surface for weight implies a radical rejection of all metaphorisation of quantity, as a result of the severance of all ties with the symbolism of colour: the intensity of colour depends upon a regime *at once superficial and relative* from which every 'in-itself' has been banished – even one *weightily* carried to saturation-point. From this point of view, despite the debt owing to Gauguin, the painter of flat colour planes, for escaping 'the tyranny of Divisionism',[19] Matisse will affirm that 'the basis of Gauguin's work and that of

17. Remark by Matisse, reported by Aragon in *Henri Matisse, roman* (Paris: Gallimard, 1998), 830; EPA 129 n95 (emphasis ours).

18. 'In a golden book I have seen at the house of Marie Gloannec, at Pont-Aven,' specifies Matisse (EPA 129 n95). On this problematic attribution, see Yve-Alain Bois' scrupulous analysis, in 'Matisse and "Arche-Drawing"', *op cit.* 36-9.

19. Matisse will confide: '[…] fundamentally Gauguin was more answerable than the neo-impressionists for making me take a step in my own direction' (EPA 95 n43).

my own, are not the same', discerning the essential point: 'Gauguin cannot be counted among the Fauves, for he lacks a construction of space by means of colour, which latter he employs as an expression of feeling.'[20] Matisse is rather hard on Gauguin – for the latter had indeed also *constructed* space by means of colour. But it must be admitted that this construction plays more upon a qualitative sentiment of colour than upon the quantitative – in other words upon the sentiment of the vital force immanent to colour. This judgment clearly confirms, then, that for Matisse there is a clear difference between vital expressivity and psychological expressionism, since he explicitly opposes himself to the idea of colour as 'expressive of feeling', even though he sometimes formulates his own conception of colour in precisely these terms![21] Thus Matisse sets himself up against a sentimentalism of colour to which is attributed a shared but internally-conflictual symbolism running 'from Eugène Delacroix to neo-impressionism', up to Kandinsky's 'spiritual turn' – a sentimentalism which takes on the cast of a regression or counter-revolution. As Nietzsche wrote: 'We are enemies of *sentimental emotions*.'[22]

The summer of 1905 spent in Collioure (in the Eastern

---

20. H. Matisse, remark collected respectively by G. Duthuit, *Les Fauves* (Paris:Michelon 2006), and Russell Warren Howe, 'Half an hour with H.M.', *Apollo*, February 1949 (EPA 95 and 94 n43). We cite once more Matisse's phrase concerning Gauguin, reported by Escholier, where it is difficult not to hear the echo of symbolism: "I instinctively fled his *already fixed* theory' (EPA 95).

21. For example, in 'Notes of a Painter', 1908, he writes: 'My choice of colours does not rest upon any scientific theory: it is based on observation, on feeling, on the experience of my sensibility', EPA, 48 *sq.* (but this passage is significantly followed by a first formulation of the quantitative principle, *cf. infra.*)

22. Nietzsche, *Will to Power*, 448 (§850 'The nihilism of artists').

Pyrenees) in the company of Derain, is a period of disquiet and feverish research, leading in diverse and sometimes contradictory directions, very much in Matisse's manner.[23] But Collioure is also the moment when Matisse will begin to experiment with the new, and no longer with the contemporary. The exploratory character of this period translates into products of very heterogeneous appearance, as can be seen by a superficial comparison of *Paysage à Collioure* and *La Moulade, Collioure*, both dating from that summer. The first painting is highly vibratory and effervescent, with explosive coloured patches, hatched brushstrokes, large coloured spots [*pastilles*]: it has a more animated and disruptive character than the other. The second has an entirely different texture, produced through the assemblage of taut surfaces, better circumscribed and more homogeneous, even if we also find here discontinuous brushstrokes, in short strips. These two aspects might be considered as symptomatic of two components – one destructive, the other constructive – traditionally associated with Fauvism. But we will see that these components come as a pair and in fact are both to be found in each of the two paintings, as indeed in all his Fauve paintings.

It is true that during the period in question, the liberation in colour of its (vital) energy sometimes takes on

---

23. Indeed, as Phillipe Dagen says: 'Between 1895 and 1905, from twenty-five to thirty-five years old, he dedicated ten years to recapitulating in an exhaustive and methodical manner the modern pictorial styles that had appeared between 1874 and the moment when he set to work.' And, having enumerated them (impressionism, Gauguinism, neo-impressionism, Cézannism, japonism ...), the author concludes: 'With subjects chosen with regard to the effects they allow him to experiment with, Matisse reviews references and models, sometimes taking literal inspiration from them, sometimes combining them into strange, mixed forms of painting.' P. Dagen, *Le Peintre, le poète, le sauvage. Les voies du primitivisme dans l'art français*, (Paris:Flammarion 1998), 8.

an appearance that was deemed disorderly and violent. To face this violence of colour that he had already tested and exploited before the Fauve summer (for example during his 1898 sojourn in Corsica) and to try to control it without renouncing its intensity, Matisse had sought in 1904 (but this was not the first time) a solution by way of neo-impressionism, and certain paintings from Collioure still bear the mark of this solution. But he was soon to discover that Divisionism, by parcelling out colour, destroyed its force. To shake off the yoke of the past and the present alike was indeed to imply a 'destructive' effect, one that would even be qualified as 'chaotic'.[24] It is true that, in certain works, Matisse goes further than all who came before him in challenging the representational conception of colour and of line. The various impressionisms did not go so far as to question radically an optical or symbolic *finality* of the image internal to their paintings, even if they displayed a strong pictoriality quite free from illusionism. But alongside, and intertwined with, this 'destructive' aspect, what also came to light at Collioure was a 'constructive' aspect founding the *maximum* expressive power of colours upon the global quantitative organisation of their relations of forces in such a way that they did not mutually diminish each other. ('An avalanche of colours remains without force. Colour only attains its full expression when it is organised.')[25] Certainly, the constructive stakes of the quantitative are not yet formulated as such at Collioure, but certain canvases are

---

24. One finds this adjective used by Matisse historians precisely with regard to *Paysage à Collioure*.

25. H. Matisse, 'Rôle et modalités de la couleur', remark collected by Gaston Diehl in *Problèmes de la peinture*, EPA 200.

already distinguished by its being (experimentally) taken seriously into account. This must, in any case, have been clear enough to Matisse for him to maintain, retrospectively, that 'at the time of the "Fauves", what constituted the strict ordering of our works, was that the quantity of colour was its quality', a formula already cited, but which must be linked to what follows it, because here Matisse adds a further important specification: 'It had to be right [*juste*] from all points of view. That was what was opportune at the time.'[26] To speak of paintings from the period of historical Fauvism (1905-1906) in terms of a *strict quantitative ordering* will seem surprising to many. Yve-Alain Bois, who so rightly brought into strong relief the importance of the quantitative in Matisse, does not recognise its true employment in painting (after its discovery in the line of the woodcuts of 1906) until after this period, from *Bonheur de vivre* in winter 1905-1906.[27] But he agrees that, despite the *eclecticism* of the Fauve summer and even of the beginning of 1906, 'the most important canvases [of that period] are [...] those in which the equation quantity = quality was being sought, before being isolated in the woodcuts', even if this equation as yet only concerned limited parts of the paintings and not their overall construction.[28] Rather than suggest that Matisse is researching something but that he does not know what, we prefer to say that Matisse utilises

26. 'Visite à Henri Matisse', interview with Tériade, EPA 98-9, emphasis ours (Matisse then explains that this leads to a simplification of forms).

27. This is the thesis first formulated by Yve-Alain Bois in 'Matisse and "Arche-Drawing"', *op.cit.*, 53: 'According to my hypothesis, *Le Bonheur de vivre* marks at once the end of Fauvism and the birth of the 'Matisse system'; a thesis reprised in 'L'aveuglement', in *Henri Matisse 1904-1917*, exhibition catalogue, 42.

28. Bois, 'Matisse and "Arche-Drawing"', *op.cit.*, 52.

practically and deliberately (but without yet formulating it) the equation quantity = quality as a *research programme*, and that the object of his experimentation is the possible ways in which this equation might be applied. It is not the object of an exclusive choice, because it is still competing with other solutions. It is therefore not stabilised: all of which results in an eclecticism which, for our part, we would qualify as quite methodical. But it is in this equation that Matisse was to recognise, in the aftermath of a lengthy period of practice, the positive contribution of Fauvism, once its fecundity had been verified and recognised through effects that would have been impossible to anticipate. Such is our hypothesis, but there can be no *a priori* decision on this debate. It is through a 'strict' analysis of the complete 'ordering' of certain paintings that we can put to the test the exactitude of Matisse's assertion *as regards Fauvism itself*. Unless this can be demonstrated, we would have to maintain that Matisse misunderstood himself completely with regard to the nature of his own paintings from the time of the Fauves, and that he is the victim of a very curious retrospective illusion with regard to a crucial aspect of his work. It remains to discover the precise meaning of this equation.

THE INTENSIVE AND THE EXTENSIVE

We will start from the first explicit presentation. A first concern with the *general quantitative adjustment* of at least certain of the qualities of colours appears in 'Notes of a Painter', written in 1907-8. The passage is interesting in that Matisse opposes himself on this point to neo-impressionism, with which he had had to break after having experimented with it. 'Inspired by certain pages of Delacroix's, an artist like Signac becomes preoccupied with complementary colours, and a theoretical knowledge of them leads him to employ, here or there, this or that tone.'[29] That is, Signac makes simple local applications of a general principle that is purely qualitative because thought, and applied, from an exclusively theoretical point of view (as established by Chevreul). For example, the contrast in itself between red and green – naturally, of one particular green and one particular red, but as if their coupling had a purely qualitative identity independently of their quantity.[30] Signac does indeed think (complementary) colours in terms of relations, but simply qualitative relations, quantity – for example the division (the 'mechanical' division, Matisse says) of brushstrokes into regular units – intervening only as one of the several optical qualities of colour. To which Matisse opposes *his practice* of colour: 'For myself, I seek simply to use colours that render my sensation.' Matisse therefore does not start from principle ('we have nothing to do with laws');[31] he observes and follows the singular expressive-vital 'growth' [*«la marche»*] of colours within his painting. The setting of colours is internally governed, without being (tightly) subordinated to a form (which would give it a qualitative identity as colour *of* that form or that figure) or to a symbolism (which would act upon it in the same way). Because – and this is stated directly – 'there is *a necessary proportion of tones* [whose pursuit] can lead me to modify the form of a figure [which latter tends to impose 'its' form on the colour] or to transform my composition. As long as I have not obtained [this proportion] *for all the parts, I seek it, and I continue my*

29. H. Matisse, 'Notes', EPA 49.

30. Matisse will say of the neo-impressionist conception, in an interview with Rayssiguier on 5 February 1949: 'it is too narrow: blue, red, green, yellow, *according to the quality between them*'. In H. Matisse, M.-A. Couturier, L.-B. Rayssiuguier, *La Chappelle de Vence. Journal d'une création* (ed. M. Billot, Paris: Cerf, 1993), 141: italics ours.

31. In response to a question from Russell Warren Howe on complementaries ('Half an hour with Matisse', EPA 49 n14).

work. Then, there comes a moment when *all parts have found their definitive relations*, and from then on, it would be impossible for me to retouch anything in the painting without entirely remaking it' (italics ours). What exactly is to be understood by the 'proportion of tones'? Signac, in his manifesto, means 'by *hue* the quality of a colour [in other words its chromaticity] and by *tone* the degree of saturation and luminosity of a hue', whilst recognising that the two words are often employed the other way around.[32] So perhaps the word 'tone' here captures for Matisse these two *intensive* qualities of colours – unless it is simply a synonym for colour, as might be suggested by the way the word is used in the preceding phrase and by the context more generally.[33] Nonetheless, the notion of proportion implies, in any case, the idea of *quantitative relations* (which takes us beyond the pure quality of Signac's 'hue').

But what precisely is the 'quantity' of colour? One could, indeed one must, understand it in two senses, as both extensive – quantity of surface (of 'hue', if you like) – and as intensive – the force of saturation and luminosity (of 'tone'). Thus a double process is put into play here, or rather a double dimension of the process which Matisse does not make explicit, doubtless because the two aspects are indissociable, thus lending a certain ambiguity to his formulae. It is fitting to remove this ambiguity. For Matisse sometimes says that quantity *is* quality, and sometimes that it is what *gives* quality – which is not the same thing. Could it be that these two different ways of formulating the quantitative principle correspond to these two different ways of understanding quantity?

---

32. P. Signac, *D'Eugène Delacroix au néo-impressionisme* [1899] (republished Paris: Hermann, 1978), 35n.; note that Signac's 'tone' conflates saturation and what we call luminosity.

33. In favour of this identity, this formula: 'A mere tone is just a colour; two tones together is an accord, it is life. A colour counts for nothing apart from its accord with its neighbour' (cited by Gaston Diehl in *Henri Matisse* (Paris: NEF, 1970) EPA 67 n41.

In first place, the intensive quantity – the force – of colours varies for Matisse with their reciprocal extensive quantity. The most famous statement of this principle – the statement that '1cm^2 of blue is not as blue as a square metre of the same blue' – is wholly theoretical in so far as it abstracts from the relations between a colour and its 'neighbours'; now, since the latter can change, a colour is able to change in intensity and thus in quality (as the result of a change of contrast, for example) without its 'surface quantity' being modified. (To re-establish an equivalent intensive relation one or other, or both, of the quantities would have, in turn, to be modified). It is intensive quantity alone, but qua differential, that must be said to *be the quality* of the colour, according to the most radical formula of the equation quantity = quality which Matisse formulates *precisely* with regard to Fauvism. The intensive, or difference of force of colour, constitutes its entire quality for Matisse (following the Deleuzian argument: 'each intensity […] reveal[s] the properly qualitative content of quality' in expressing the difference in quantity).[34] The intensive is *ontologically* and *operationally* primary in that the extensive results from the relations of forces with each another (Deleuze again: 'Everywhere intensity is primary in relation to organic extensions').[35] This is what Matisse's *oeuvre* demonstrates, in so far as extension (figures) and space (where they take place) appear in it not as given in and through forms, but as *resultants* (to use a word of Derain's) of a moment of *the equilibrium of the forces of colours*. What Matisse

---

34. *Difference and Repetition*, 222.

35. *Ibid*, 251.

seeks are 'energetic and harmonious relations'[36] – *harmony* (that commonplace in art discourse, whose sense he also displaces) must be understood in Matisse as that decorative or *all-over* character which, precisely, gives a work its *equilibrium,* which must be made through, and with, the 'mutual impact' of colours.[37] Thus, extensive differences must be regulated as a function of the intensive differential: the painter who 'wants to give an *expressive* character *to the uniting of many colour surfaces*' must take into account 'pure colour, *with its intensity, its reactions on neighbouring quantities*' – this is the 'difficult task' of the painter. Even if the intensive has naturally always been in play in painting to some degree or other, it is Matisse's Fauvism which operated a systematic and thus wholly affirmative laying-bare of *chromatic energy* (in so far as it is no longer mediated) – an expressivity which is the sensible reason of vitalism, and without which Fauvism would lose its principle of immanence. Or, once more: colours *are not* identitarian qualities, as in a 'representative' system which necessarily cuts off forms from the *differential of forces* constituting the material basis of their production, in order to make appear the identity which stabilises them and allows them to be recognised in their *formal, and thus structural, differences* (resemblance is the law of

36. This expression is found in a letter from Matisse to Pierre Gaut, director of Établissements Linel, 25 March 1946, reproduced by Antoinette Rezé-Huré, 'Une lettre de Matisse à Pierre Gaut' (*Cahiers du Musée national d'art moderne* 84, 13 July 1984), 28 (Établissements Linel were responsible for finding the typographical inks for the reproduction of the plates of *Jazz*).

37. 'For me, colour is a force. My paintings are composed of four or five colours which collide with each other, giving sensations of energy.' – A statement, around 1942, by the ever-'Fauvist' Matisse to Pierre Courthion (reported in P. Courthion, 'Avec Matisse et Bonnard', in *D'une palette à l'autre. Mémoires d'un critique d'art* [Geneva: La Baconnière Arts, 2004] 173).

quality as *form of representation*). When intensive difference is submitted to representation and thus to identity, 'quality then comes to cover over intensity', as Deleuze concludes in the pages where he takes colour as his example.[38] When, on the other hand, representation is submitted to the differential of forces, the field of their confrontation overwhelms formal differences, *bearing and sweeping them away* into its chaosmosis. See *Paysage à Collioure*: Non-identitarian, the colours are nonetheless energetic individuating differentiations whose singularities always enter into relations of forces amongst themselves; relations of forces which assure their resonance and/or their internal/external expansivity in this intense field of individuation which the canvas *is*, which it *becomes*. Every individuating force thus affirms itself in communicating immediately with others in an 'aesthetic of intensities' whose processual, *chaosmic* immanence might be called the 'implicated art of intensive quantities' in so far as it ex-plicates the 'fluent world of Dionysus' in restoring the difference of intensity as vital being of the sensible.[39]

We will not say of *extensive quantity* that it *is*, properly speaking, the quality of colour, but only that it actualises it and, in this sense, produces its *intensive quantity* (in other words its differential quality). This is what can be surmised from formulas such as: 'The quantities being different, their quality changes: when colours are employed quite overtly,

---

38. *See Difference and Repetition*, 245: '[A] multiplicity such as that of colour is constituted by the virtual coexistence of relations between genetic or differential elements of a particular order. These relations are actualised in qualitatively distinct colours, while their distinctive points are incarnated in distinct extensities which correspond to these qualities'.

39. *Ibid*. See also in *Difference and Repetition* the Nietzschean conclusion of the chapter 'Asymmetrical Synthesis of the Sensible'.

it is their relations of quantity which *make* their quality'; or again: 'it is the proportion of colour which *gives* [the stained-glass windows of Chartres Cathedral] their quality'[40] – remember that the 'Notes of a Painter' spoke of 'a necessary proportion of tones'. Given that *to make* and *to give* do not mean *to be*, these formulas are probably better understood as alluding to extension, or 'quantity of surface', but one might also suppose them to refer to quantity in general, in so far as it always implies the intensive and the extensive.[41] As far as the extension of colours is concerned, above all the point must be made that, apart from the quantity of surface properly speaking (its area), this extension also refers to *spatial qualities* capable of affecting the intensity of colours, and so these must be taken into account in regulating their reciprocal extension. It is probably this aspect of the quantitative that Matisse is addressing when, after having declared that 'at the time of the "Fauves", what constituted the strict ordering of our works, was that the quantity of colour was its quality', he adds, as will be remembered, this crucial specification: 'It must be *right from all points of view*', and insists: 'That was what was opportune at the time' (emphasis ours). Matisse does not enumerate 'all the points of view' according to which the intensive quantity of colour (and necessarily the extensive also) must 'be right' – that is to say strictly

---

40. Respectively, H. Matisse, letter to Alexandre Romm, January 1934 (correspondence published in the catalogue of the exhibition *Henri Matisse*, Moscow, Musée des Beaux-Arts Pouchkine, and Leningrad, Musée de l'Ermitage, 1969), EPA 146, and 'Notes on colour', EPA 206.

41. The formula concerning the stained-glass of Chartres is immediately preceded in 'Notes on Colour' by a formula that we have cited above on 'pure colour with its intensity, its reactions on neighbouring quantities'.

ordered/arranged – because, since they are innumerable, an exhaustive inventory cannot be made of them. We must be content with suggesting the principal ones. Intensive quantities are to be adjusted not only as a function of the proportions of their sizes (brushstrokes, colour-patches, masses of colour, larger surfaces …) but also of their forms (precise or indeterminate, figurative or not, with clear or degraded borders, compacted or explosive …); of their placement in the field (peripheral, central, high, low …); of their density (thick or transparent …); of their texture (smooth flatness, worked matter, homogeneous, fluid or taut …); of their orientation (uni- or multidirectional, centrifugal, centripetal …); of the frequency and modes of distribution of these different surfaces (unicity, multiplicity, aleatory or ordered rhythmicity …), not forgetting the chromatic interactions (complementarity, simultaneous contrasts …). Thus, to take this last case, the theoretical quality of contrasting complementary colours varies practically, for Matisse, with the reciprocal quantities of these colours.[42] The (intensive) quality of colours is thus not only a function of their 'surface quantity',[43] as certain formulae suggest,[44] it must also be *quantitatively adjusted* as a function of other spatial properties of the surfaces. It is in these conditions that the *quantitative ordering* of *all* of the painting imposes itself as the discovery of Fauvism. The question of

42. In 'Notes of a Painter' Matisse writes, after the declaration on the proportion of tones: 'In reality, I hold that the very theory of complementaries is not absolute' because 'one could […] push back the frontiers of the theory of colours as currently accepted', EPA 49.

43. EPA 149.

44. This is also, if we understand correctly, what is suggested in Yve-Alain Bois' 'Matisse and "Arche-Drawing"', *op.cit.*

the quantitative is thus complex and cannot be the object of a finite calculation but only of an open evaluation on the part of a spectator who must, as far as possible, estimate it according to the 'points of view' implicated in the construction of the painting (as so many *factors forcibly entering, entering into force*). All the forms of the quantitative being, practically, mutually intricated and indissociable, we can speak globally of the quantitative (as does Matisse), leaving implicit what it comprises of the extensive and the intensive.

No longer being directly mediated by an external finality (which, on the contrary, is now but a medium in the service of energetic vitalism), the qualities of colours no longer depend on anything but their relations of quantity (intensive and extensive). It is true that the relatively large and homogeneous flat colour plane renders particularly sensible the importance of the quantity of surface in the force of colour. This is what Matisse will practice in the compositions of large coloured surfaces *after* the epoch of historical Fauvism. He will indeed declare with regard to the works of 1909-10 that put into play only a few colours, in large surfaces: 'When I undertook *La Danse* and the Moscow *Musique* – I was determined to put the colours into surfaces, without nuances [...] What seemed to me *essential was the surface quantity of colours.*'[45] That this was what *then* appeared essential to him does not at all mean that he was indifferent to the other 'points of view' (to realise this one need only look at a reproduction of his paintings in inverse: 'the surface quantity' being unchanged, all the relations of colours are completely upset). This point, naturally, is decisive for the treatment of the question of the

45. H. Matisse, letter to Alexandre Romm, October 1934, EPA 149 (emphasis ours).

quantitative in the Fauve period, during which Matisse does not yet resort, or very little (in any case not systematically) to significantly large flat colour planes, because he has not yet come fully to realise the importance of the extensive. Still, the accumulation of enlarged brushstrokes coming together as a mass through an identity of colour, the coloured patches and, *a fortiori*, the more considerable applications of colour, already function as (quantities of) *surfaces*, in the twofold sense of marks which are given as literally applied to (the surface of) the canvas, and which maintain a certain surface area there (*qua* isolated elements or multiplicities of variable density).[46] The spacing of brushstrokes is certainly not the best way to *intensify* colour *to the maximum*, but it is already a way to *quantify it differentially*. If one refuses to recognise the (intensive) quantification of colours in a 'strict ordering' (necessarily including the extensive) as the contribution of Fauvism, on the pretext that the colours do not yet occupy a sufficient 'surface quantity' (a 'large' flat colour plane), it is because one wrongly identifies intensive quantity and *maximal* intensification. Furthermore, a response must be given to this rather absurd question: 'at what level of "surface quantity" does/will a surface begin to function quantitatively (= qualitatively)?' It appears to us decidedly problematic to say that the Matisse-system does not begin until *Le Bonheur de vivre*. The quantitative equation functions already in Fauvism, and from Fauvism

---

46. Even though in 1912, the following remark of Matisse's already makes sense for the epoch of historical Fauvism: 'Do not apply different little brushstrokes, but masses, because it is through quantity, through mass, that your tone acts in your painting.' Reported by Marcel Sembat in his 'Cahiers noirs', date of 29 April 1912. Taken up again in *Matisse-Sembat, Correspondence. Une Amitié artistique et politique, 1904-1922*, ed. C. Phéline and M. Baréty (Lausanne:La Bibliothèque des Arts, 2004), 170.

onward, because colour has no other finality in principle apart from its immanent vital expressivity; it is this alone that *imposes* this equation, not the extensive as such. Will not Matisse-Thought have demonstrated anew a tremendous historical *and* theoretical pertinence, in its formulation of the quantitative principle 'at the time of the "Fauves"'? For this formulation implies that it can only be a question of intensive quantity – as that which *is* the quality of colour – and not particularly of its (large) extensive quantity, whose importance had not yet been either truly recognised or isolated, and which was thus *implicitly* numbered amongst 'all the points of view' according to which 'quantity' must be adjusted. To *intensify* intensity, thereby to assure a greater grasp of the quantitative on the qualitative, Matisse was to be led, *at the end of the Fauve experimentation and as one of its direct developments*, to simplify and to augment the dimensions of the colour surfaces, and thus to *make explicit* the importance of extensive quantity. This will certainly be an important evolution in the conception of the quantitative equation, but not at all a rupture marking its appearance.

With regard to the epistemological importance of the quantitative factor in the interpretation of human phenomena at the end of the nineteenth century and the beginning of the twentieth, one cannot but bring together the name of Nietzsche with that of Freud who, very early on, will aim to 'discover what form the theory of mental functioning assumes when one introduces the notion of quantity into it, a sort of economy of nervous forces'. In developing this economy, the psychic processes will be linked to displacements, investments and discharges of a 'quantum of affect', which 'corresponds to the drive in so far as the latter is detached from representation and finds an expression adequate to its quantity in processes which become sensible to us as affects';[47] with the result that the affect will be defined as 'the qualitative expression of the quantity of drive energy and of its variations'.[48] The quantitative principle which thus brings together Matisse and Freud is all the more striking in that the latter has no affiliation with the intellectual references of the former.

Let us return to the question(ing) of form, to which our reflection here belongs. It can easily be seen that the quantitative principle which founds the Matissean aesthetic as an energetics of colour implies that form should be thought in terms of active, not static, surface, and still less in a purely linear fashion. If a painting really obeys a system of *all-over* construction in which the forms do not isolate themselves one from another by detaching themselves from the ground, their qualities do not belong to intrinsic properties of contours, but are rather relative to the relations of (intensive and extensive) quantities of coloured surfaces, relations within which the line that recip- rocally delimits these surfaces is itself also held. Naturally, the colours present qualities that are not directly quantita- tive, in other words not intrinsically vital – representational, expressionist, pictorial qualities … Matisse always strives to treat them also in terms of relations of force, so that they might participate in a constructive fashion in his vitalism. Which necessarily implies treating them quantitatively,

---

47. Respectively, a letter from Sigmund Freud to Wilhelm Fliess, 25 May 1895 (see *The Complete Letters of Sigmund Freud to Wilhelm Fliess, 1887-1904*, ed., trans. J.M.Mason. Cambridge, MA: Harvard University Press, 1985) and 'Repression' (in *On Metapsychology – The Theory of Psychoanalysis*, London: Penguin, 1991; cited after J. Laplanche and J.-B. Pontalis, *The Language of Psychoanalysis*, trans. D. N. Smith, London: Karnak, 1996, 390).

48. Definition of the term 'Affect' in *The Language of Psychoanalysis, op cit,* 13.

since the quality of a force lies in its quantity relative to another. 'The essence of force is its quantitative difference from other forces, and [...] this difference is expressed as the force's quality'.[49] By bringing together this Nietzschean formula of Deleuze's with Nietzsche's own question – 'To what extent is art immersed in the essence of force?' – one might measure the proximity of Matisse-Thought to Nietzsche, and risk a (possible) response.

---

49. *Nietzsche and Philosophy*, 50.

infinitely tiny things differential relations that will make possible an integration of the sum — in other words, a clear and distinguished perception. It is a filter, a selection. Now, on the one hand, I am not always capable of doing so at all times, but only in a particular zone that varies with each monad, and such that, for each monad, the greatest part remains in a state of detached dizziness, un-differentiated, unintegrated, in an absence of accord. All that can be said, to the contrary, is that no part of the world can be taken in the zone of *a* determinable monad, and that does not carry accords produced by this monad. But on the other hand especially, the linkages produced by a monad can be very different. Leibniz's writings clearly guarantee a classification of accords.

It would be wrong to seek a direct transposition of musical chords in the way they are developed in the Baroque; and yet it would also be erroneous to con-clude with Leibniz's indifference in respect to the musical model: the question, rather, involves analogy. And we know that Leibniz was always trying to bring it to a new rigor. At its highest degree, a monad produces *major and perfect accords*: these occur where the small solicitations of anxiety, far from disap-pearing, are integrated in a pleasure that can be continued, prolonged, renewed, multiplied; that can proliferate, be reflexive and attractive for other accords, that give us the force to go further and further. This pleasure is a "felicity" specific to the soul; it is harmonic par excellence, and can even be felt in the midst of the worst sufferings, such as in the joy of martyrs. In this sense the perfect accords are not pauses, but, on the contrary, dynamisms, which can pass into other accords, which can attract them, which can reappear, and which can be infinitely combined.[23] In the second place, we speak of minor accords when the differential relations among the infinitely small parts only allow integrations or instable combinations, simple pleasures that are inverted into their contrary, un-less they are attracted by a perfect accord. For, in the third place, integration can be made in pain. That is the specific character of *dissonant accords*, the accord here consisting in preparing and resolving dissonance, as in the double operation of Baroque music. The preparation of dissonance means integrating the half-pains that have been accompanying pleasure, in such ways that the next pain will not occur "contrary to all expectations." Thus the dog was musical when it knew how to integrate the almost imperceptible approach of the enemy, the faint hostile odor and the silent raising of the stick just prior to its receiving the blow.[24] The resolution of dissonance is tantamount to displacing pain, to searching for the major accord with which it is consonant, just as the martyr knows how to do it at the highest point and, in that way, not suppress pain itself, but suppress resonance or resentment, by avoiding passivity, by pursuing the effort to sup-press causes, even if the martyr's force of opposition is not attained.[25] All of Leibniz's theory of evil is a method to prepare for and to resolve dissonances in a "universal harmony." A counterexample would be furnished by the damned, whose souls produce a dissonance on a unique note, a breath of vengeance or

Unknown Deleuze

Mehrdad Iravanian

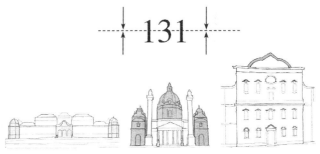

Two 'unknown Deleuze'*s and one* 'un'*: an approach to deciphering the collective symmetrical manner of the central page (page* 131*) of* The Fold (518 *words*) *– carrying out a logical carto-graphical composition of abstract topological elements (monads, words, etc.). The baroque nature of* 131 *can be distinguished through two references: firstly, the central piece (*3*) has an identical architectural form to baroque facades (Santa Maria della Pace, Saint Ivo della Sapienza, Sant'Andrea al Quirinale); secondly, the same central piece (*3*), as surrounded by symmetrical pieces (*1-1*), manifests the voluptuousness of a curvilinear, growing, unfolding form, immanently symmetrical. As a form,* 131 *presents the elements of symmetrical order of the early baroque.*

'An expression of states and relations which are inflected, which evolves a process shaped by different types of information before, during and after a building is materialized.' This is how a boogazine – a hybrid type of publication, often employed by architects and combining the heterogeneity and topicality of a magazine with the referential and comprehensive approach of a book – describes the comic-book-like format through which it re-edits an event (*viz.,* any product: building, piece of writing, art object), usually after the event has found the solid ground necessary in order for it to be instituted as an object.

The proper place to seek the unfolded Deleuze is within the collective information that he has processed, not outside the content: the unknown is within.

More precisely, in relation to the subject at issue: With regard to its sources, *The Fold* diagrams the unpleating function.

Chapter title: *The New Harmony* – a most appropriate title for this new arrangement of unread characters.

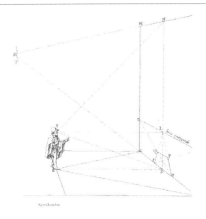

The following graphitext critically examines this type of processing whilst (1) avoiding the vulgar comic-book tendency toward collage (instead invoking the baroque sense of perpetual development of a term); (2) receding to a lower profile of difference: The dominant modes and techniques of visual literacy are based on creating a relation between (graphical) elements in a grammatical manner – puzzle-solving on a monodimensional surface. It ought to be understood, however, that their effects (the perceived visual production) ultimately take place in the distance between the observer and the work (as related to the monodimension). Control of this space (the inderdimensionality between the observer and the work) can be achieved by influencing the networks of a series of focal points, the difference between the members of which is only a matter of distance (either as color or shape: hue, gradient, saturation, etc.). So that this management of distances between focal points from the observer is another way of creating 'work' – a lesser-known type of visual literacy amongst graphic artists.

233

EXAMINATION OF TEXT: SEARCH FOR HIDDEN SUBJECTS

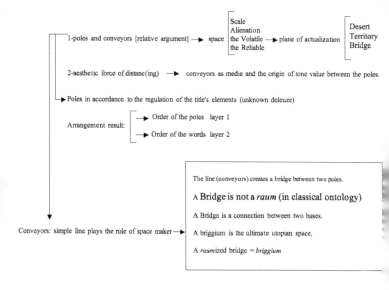

1-poles and conveyors [relative argument] → space | Scale / Alienation / the Volatile / the Reliable → plane of actualization | Desert / Territory / Bridge

2-aesthetic force of distanc(ing) → conveyors as media and the origin of tone value between the poles.

Poles in accordance to the regulation of the title's elements (unknown deleuze)

Arrangement result:
→ Order of the poles layer 1
→ Order of the words layer 2

Conveyors: simple line plays the role of space maker →

The line (conveyors) creates a bridge between two poles.

A **Bridge** is not a *raum* (in classical ontology)

A Bridge is a connection between two bases.

A briggium is the ultimate utopian space.

A *raum*ized bridge = *briggium*

LETTERS FIND DIRECTION

'Unknown Deleuze', as semantic unit, is non-directional, whereas:

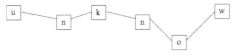

– is directional.

unknown deleuze = solid

= raum

Solid vs. raum

Separation and re-connection create a spatial, multidirectional statement. This process evolves the original statement into an unpleated state.

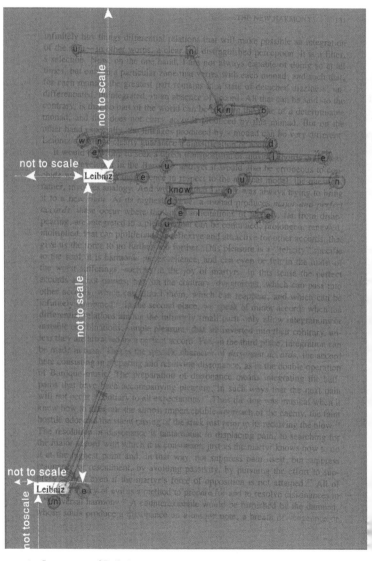

infinitely tiny things differential relations that will make possible an integration of the ... — in other words, a clear and distinguished perception. It is a filter, a selection. Now, on the one hand I am not always capable of doing so in all cases, but only in a particular zone that varies with each monad, and such that, for each monad, the greatest part remains in a state of detached dizziness, un-differentiated, unintegrated, in an absence of accord. All that can be said is: on the contrary, no two parts of the world can be ... ... of a determinate monad, and it does not cease... ... ... by this monad. But on the other hand, the little accords or little folds produced by ... monad can be very different.

Leibniz ... does not guarantee ...

It would ... to seek a ... composition ... ... in the Baroque ... it would be too ... to ... ... in respect to the ... ... rather, in ... an analogy. And ... ... was always trying to bring it to a ... ... As at the ... ... a monad produces *major and perfect accords*: these occur where the little ... ... can be prolonged, enlarged, are integrated in a pleasure ... ... far from disappearing ... multiplied, that can proliferate, be reflective and attractive for other pleasures, that give us the force to go farther and farther. This pleasure is a "felicity" peculiar to the soul; it is harmonic *par excellence*, and can even be felt in the midst of the worst sufferings, such as in the joy of martyrs. In this sense the perfect accords ... not pauses, but on the contrary dynamisms, which can pass into other accords, which can attract them, which can reappear, and which can be infinitely combined. In the second place, we speak of minor accords when the differential relations among the infinitely small parts only allow integrations or suitable combinations ... simple pleasure, that, inverted into their contrary, inverted they ... a pain when a certain accord. Yet, in the third place, integration can be made in pain: this is the specific character of *dissonant accords*, the accord here consisting in preparing and resolving dissonances, as in the double operation of Baroque music. The preparation of dissonance means integrating the half pains that have been accompanying pleasure, in such ways that the next pain will not occur contrary to all expectation... That the dog was musical when it knew how to integrate the almost imperceptible approach of the enemy, the faint, hostile odor and the silent raising of the stick just prior to its receiving the blow. The resolution of dissonance is tantamount to displacing pain, to searching for the major accord with which it is consonant, just as the martyr knows how to do it at the highest point and, in that way, not suppress pain itself, but suppress ... resentment, by avoiding passivity, by pursuing the effort to suppress ... even if the martyr's force of opposition is not attained... All of ... a way of evolving a method to prepare for and to resolve dissonances in a ... total harmony. A counterexample would be furnished by the damned, whose souls produce a dissonance on a unique note, a breath of ...

2. Briggium

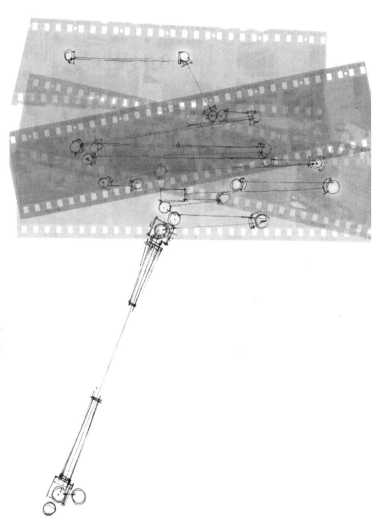

3. Concentration of Memory

4. Poles Cast Shadows

239

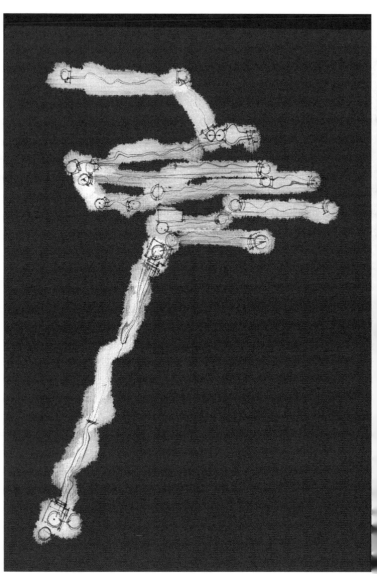

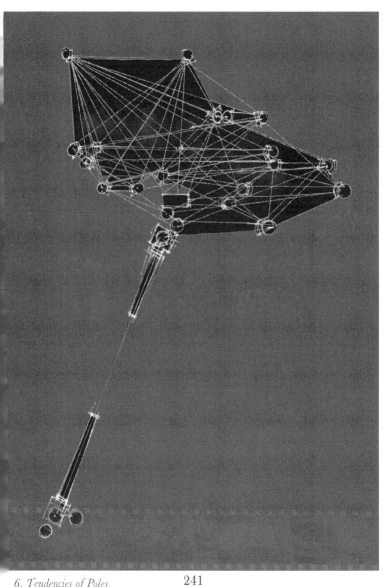

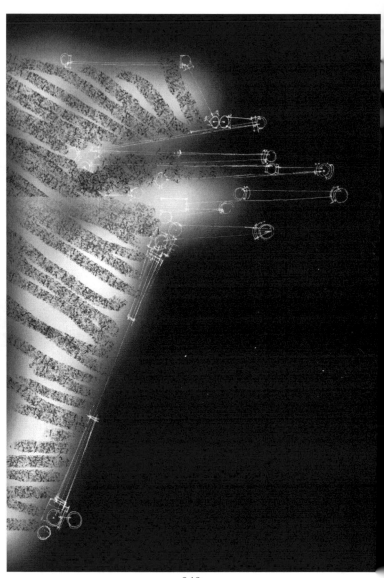

In Memoriam: Gilles Deleuze (1925-1995)

Thomas Duzer

> Between the intensive and thought, it is always by means of an intensity that thought comes to us.
> (Deleuze, *Difference and Repetition*)
>
> *
>
> Young man, do not incriminate the gods!
> (Sartre, *The Flies*)

On 4th November 1995, Gilles Deleuze committed suicide by throwing himself from the window of his Paris apartment. He was 70 years old. In 1969, after having completed his major thesis (later published as *Difference and Repetition*), he was rushed to hospital, and diagnosed with tuberculosis; emergency pulmonary surgery immediately followed. With the passing years his health slowly deteriorated, and by the end of his life, he was dependent upon a machine: an artificial respirator.

Obviously, the question of Gilles Deleuze's suicide remains a problem which can quite properly be considered as a part of his philosophy. Indeed, by overstepping

Spinoza's prohibition, he would choose to withdraw from the scene at his own chosen moment. Ultimately it was stoicism that the vitalist philosopher chose, faced with the compounded forces which had appropriated the extensive parts subsumed under his modal essence. But perhaps these are not the best terms in which to pose the question of the ultimate meaning of his philosophy. Didn't Deleuze's thesis director, Maurice de Gandillac, emphasise his student's visceral Nietzscheanism and keen interest in Diogenes Laertius's doxographies? From the moment he began his studies at the Sorbonne, behind each philosophical system Deleuze sought the philosopher as individual: Which body? Which thought? Every philosophy is a vital and affective evaluation, an animal perspective, and a theoretical bringing-into-engagement. Every philosophy is the theory of a practice, or the systematization of an immanent way of living, of *a singularity*: For Deleuze, *every ethics is the correlative of an ontology*. In this, he is absolutely Spinozist.

This is the secret centre of the long and patient years he dedicated to the history of philosophy. In his early monographs, Deleuze does not interrogate a philosophy so much as a philosopher – which explains the strange character of these works. For in reading them, one becomes aware that, although there is no doubt that the Deleuzian commentary concerns the same author treated in classical erudite tradition, a sort of rupture is always in evidence, a sort of *Unheimlichkeit* and a problematisation that is difficult to situate. But this is so only in so far as one attempts to locate the Deleuzian reading within the perspective of a classical history of philosophy, whose logic of exposition is that of a chronological procession of concepts and systems.

For his part, Deleuze preferred to refer to a time that he called 'stratigraphic.'[1] It is certainly important that philosophies succeed one another in time. Nevertheless, these philosophies are *virtually* coexistent. Every philosophy is *virtually* contemporary with every other, even if certain logics creep into those that preceded them, and certain concepts are reclaimed in their original form. Thus, *in the present*, every system of ethics rivals every other, since, *in reality*, all logics are in non-dialectical conflict with each other. More precisely, according to Deleuze, any philosopher worthy of the name – that is to say, any philosopher-creator – traces out a plane within chaos. For concepts are born of thought's confrontation with chaos. Or, in other words: concepts must be *created*. They are dated and signed, even if later philosophers must divert them from their original function, hijacking their components and their flows. This means that every new plane, if it is to inaugurate a truly new philosophy, even if it should have originated from an anterior plane, must distinguish itself from and find its own autonomy from the latter. But how? Most fundamentally, it is through assuming his own problematics – even if these problematics are not explicitly thematized – that the philosopher has a chance of tracing such a plane. And, on this plane, a new consistency may be given to chaos, by means of the singular creation of the arsenal of connected concepts that populate it. For Deleuze, the style *is* the philosopher.

And it is from somewhere close to this *active centre* of Deleuze's philosophy that Badiou's attack seeks to draw

---

1. See *What is Philosophy?* and also the distinction between *Aiôn* and *Chronos* in *Logic of Sense*.

its force. With an incisive gesture, Badiou takes Deleuze's *continuous variation*, a major element in his philosophy and his style alike, and annexes it to one of his enemy constellations: *phenomenology*.[2] This judgement may seem reasonable at first, but on further consideration becomes absurd. For Deleuze declares, as a Spinozist, his hostility towards all philosophies of the *Cogito*. Clearly, for him, there is no subject.[3] Every philosophy that concedes any legitimacy to the Ego is anathematised. Even the non-thetic[4] *Cogito* of

---

2. A. Badiou, *Deleuze: The Clamor of Being*, trans. L. Burchill. Minneapolis: Minnesota University Press, 1999.

3. The critique of the Subject has been a *topos* in post-Cartesian philosophy ever since the *Objections to the Metaphysical Meditations*. However, after the Humean episode, it was generalized following Mach and Nietzsche, who, as a matter of fact, later spawned two divergent philosophical tendencies. Similarly, psychoanalysis profoundly modified the notion of the subject through the notion of the unconscious; Heidegger, having broken away from Husserlian phenomenology founded on Kant's inherited and enhanced *Cogito*, replaced the classical and transcendental subject with *Dasein*. The list of subjectivity's detractors in the twentieth century is certainly a long one. Nevertheless, the notion, although drastically modified at times, was never abandoned. But Deleuze affirms in a 1988 interview entitled *Signs and Events* that there is 'no subject [...] there are only processes, sometimes unifying, subjectifying, rationalising, but just processes all the same.' (*Negotiations*, 145). Undeniably, from *Empiricism and Subjectivity* onward, Deleuze asked, through the works of Hume, whether or not subjectivity is constituted within the given, within the 'flux of the sensible'. It seems, in fact, that the critique of subjectivity comprises a guiding thread in Deleuze's *oeuvre*. As a question it certainly intersects with his major problems and concepts, and turns out to be one their conditions of possibility: desire, multiplicity, BwO, 'to be done with judgement,' plane of immanence, and domain of transcendence ... But this critique cannot be reduced to a simple questioning of the subject. Deleuze promotes another type of individuation, a 'non-personal individuation,' *haecceities* and singularities. The construction of these concepts intersects and enriches the problematics of other philosophers such as Foucault, Klossowski, Blanchot, or Artaud amongst others. With the help of Guattari, moreover, this construction opposes psychoanalysis in order to substitute a machinic unconscious for a theatrical unconscious. In short: 'there is no longer a subject, but only individuating affective states of an anonymous force.' ('Spinoza and Us,' in *Spinoza: Practical Philosophy*, 128).

4. For Sartre, consciousness, being spontaneous, is effected within a 'prereflexive *cogito*', unlike a cognition that implicates the object-subject couple; *conscientia* is not

Sartre, Deleuze's admired *maître*,[5] is rejected. What does this mean? All philosophy that claims to found itself on the central positing of an *Ego* plainly privileges substance over process. Why reject this? Because it is the triumph of reactivity. It is apparent that what makes a rhizome of the postwar Nietzscheans is ultimately a reading of Kant's Copernican revolution as *reactionary* – making the object turn around the subject changes the order, but *not the places*.[6] If the Ego, the World, and God are transcendental illusions of theoretical reason, they remain regulative ideals and, as noumena (objects of thought and not of knowledge), lose none of their force and pertinence in Kant's philosophy, at the heart of practical reason. Whereas, on the contrary, the Nietzschean revolution leads thought into an *a*subjective becoming: a comet-thought, the wandering star whose variations in speed and whose creativity constitute its coherence.

Thus, Badiou describes Deleuze's conceptual creations as virtuoso *phenomenological* apparati. His philosophy, especially when 'machined' with that of Guattari, will be ultimately monotone and repetitive. But this reading of Deleuze *fails*, in the sense that one might say of an encounter that it failed. For as we well know, one must refrain from suggesting some sort of general falsification of Deleuze

cum scientia. Such a prereflexive *Cogito* therefore insists on a presence-to-self that is immanent and anterior to the 'return to self' engendered by reflection. Consciousness is 'to be for oneself' and refuses to settle as object: it is non-thetic.

5. 'He Was my Teacher', in *Desert Islands and Other Texts*, 77-81.

6. This is a strictly structuralist discovery: the symbolic – implying that in a structure, the position, the place, is primary with regard to that which occupies it. See 'How Do We Recognise Structuralism?' in *Desert Islands*, 170-92.

on Badiou's part.[7] Indeed – and the sly Badiou certainly knows how to remind orthodox Deleuzians of this – for a Nietzschean, the distinction between the true and the false never makes for a strong argument. In fact, Deleuze always favored the problematic of stupidity over that of error – that is to say, that of sense over that of truth. This is a corollary of the destitution of substance in favour of process. One of its consequences is the absolute rejection of a foundational subject or, as we have already seen, of any *Cogito*, whether it be Cartesian or Kantian, or indeed any analytic of *Dasein*. Deleuze's principal weapon against stupidity naturally turns out not to be a Heideggerian anti-humanism – which continues to concede rather too much to its opposite, even if only in order to situate itself, in Hegelian manner – but rather a strict *inhumanism*. At this point, Artaud is convoked as schizophrenic, *i.e.,* practitioner of the theory. For this is exactly what interests Deleuze so deeply about schizophrenia: that intensities are consumed *directly*. Thought articulates itself upon the body as its obverse and reverse. Within this intensive machinism, the 'Theatre of Cruelty' reveals the factories of the unconscious. Presentation is presented in its purity, without the mediation of representation: *incarnation* replaces identification and recognition.[8]

Truth and error, both structures of recognition, are merely the result of the correspondence or non-correspondence of a given case with a rule. On this point it is essential

---

7. See, for example, the diverse receptions of Badiou's *Deleuze* in the review *Multitudes* (formerly *Futur Antérieur*).

8. Schizoanalysis does not make 'points,' but 'lines' ('On *A Thousand Plateaus*', in *Negotiations*, 33); it is closer to Bacon's pictorial experiments and therefore closer to 'meat' than to the 'flesh' invoked by phenomenology.

to note that to consider, as Deleuze did, that truth[9] is not an 'interesting' category doesn't indicate that it is refused wholesale, but rather that it is ratified but *not made sacred*.[10] To deny or to affirm a proposition implies that this is done according to truth, and thus according to eternity. Nevertheless, in the 'power of the false', as endorsed by Nietzsche, for example, there is something more than a simple negation of truth. *Anti-dialectically* speaking, affirmation cannot result from the negation of a negation. And this is why the problem of stupidity and consequently, that of the remarkable, the interesting, the singular, and the novel, are *transcendental*. For, following Bergson, it is a question of applying the test of truth and falsity to the problems themselves. Here, not only are the rule itself and its legitimacy interrogated, they are *experimented* with – it becomes necessary to ask not just 'what the principles are, but what they do'.[11] Thus, morality, together with the substantialisms of the Same, is abandoned in order to constitute an ethics, as experimental and processual science. In the wake of William James and American pragmatism, Deleuze proposes a *transcendental empiricism*, which can be expanded into a cartography of intensities conceived as *patchwork*, *computation*, and non-diplomatic immunity.[12] Consequently, if, as Littré says, truth is 'the quality by which things appear as they are,' then we

9. For Deleuze, the distinction Badiou makes between truth (*vérité*) and the veridical (*véridicité*) does not exist. For truths are confined to the domain of knowledge (*savoir*) and do not harbour an evental dimension as they do in Badiou's philosophy.

10. 'There are imbecile thoughts, imbecile discourses, that are made up entirely of truths [...]' *Nietzsche and Philosophy*, 105.

11. *Dialogues II*.

12. See T. Duzer, 'On the Mathematics of Intensity: A Logic of Self-Belonging', in *Collapse* Volume 1, 245-60.

can affirm that a transcendental empiricism is the activity through which beings *become* what they are.[13] It has been possible to paint Deleuze, as does Mattéi,[14] as contemptuous toward the *archê*, the Father, or the Master, but it is the One he adamantly challenges, in favour of a pluralist philosophy (the power of the indefinite article – *an* archê, *a* Father, *a* Master ...) Following Nietzsche's example, then, it is Platonism, but Platonism *qua* inherited philosophy, that he seeks to invert: To reject, not Plato as creator, but Plato as leader of a school, father of the *Diadochi*; to challenge the principle of succession which Plato made possible by positing the created concept as increate Idea. Thus it is not at all a question of indifferentiation, or a nihilist principle of abolition, as Mattéi maintains. Indeed, as Badiou himself recalls, 'contrary to all egalitarian or "communitarian" norms, Deleuze's conception of thought is profoundly aristocratic.'[15] Thus, Deleuze chooses the 'Platonism of encounters'[16] over that of the 'Good beyond Being'.

The statement is clear: *the given is constructed.* No 'innate opinion', no phenomenological *Urdoxa*. *The Deleuzian philosophy is neither a sophistics,[17] nor a phenomenology; it is a*

---

13. Knowing that, as Badiou said, interpreting Pindar, 'we are only that which we become' (A. Badiou, *Briefings on Existence: A Short Treatise on Transitory Ontology*, trans. N. Madarasz, NY: SUNY Press, 2006, 68).

14. J.-F. Mattéi, *L'étranger et le simulacre: essai sur la fondation de l'ontologie platonicienne.* Paris: PUF, 1983.

15. A. Badiou, *Deleuze, op.cit.,* 11.

16. I owe this expression to Guillaume Destivère. Further, he adds: 'from this point of view, [Deleuze] has preempted Badiou, "the intermediary of encounters with truths", on all fronts. And Badiou knows it.' (personal correspondence).

17. Indeed, we should note that if the sophists insist on the question of nature, convention, and the concrete, it is Parmenides himself that reminds the young

philosophy. The Badiousian stratagem backfires, for Deleuze is truly Spinozist. Philosopher *sans Cogito*, he is also a philosopher of the concept, which is to say a para-*doxa*-cal philosopher. In this, he is a philosopher of complete freedom, meaning absolute necessity and power. On this point, the Stoic and the Spinozist, quite coherently and logically, are as one – *as ethicists*. So that Deleuze, this considerable contemporary, himself finds a place in the subterranean and volcanic line of rare philosophers who are irreducible to the official history of philosophy. *A life* – 'It is at this mobile and precise point, where all events gather together in one that transmutation happens: this is the point at which death turns against death; where dying is the negation of death, and the impersonality of dying no longer indicates only the moment when I disappear outside of myself, but rather the moment when death loses itself in itself, and also the figure which the most singular life takes on in order to substitute itself for me.'[18]

This is why there is nothing but the nomad.[19] That which 'deterritorializes,' crosses boundaries, goes beyond limits in order to go to the end of its powers, which distributes and is distributed in a smooth space. It is that which, because it is a pure multiple, *consists* and thus cannot be

---

Socrates of the rights of hair, dirt, and mud to benefit from an appropriate Idea.

18. *Logic of Sense*, 173-4.

19. The nomad, who, although quite capable of austerity, is *desiring*, and thus certainly does not pursue the ascetic ideal stigmatised by Nietzsche.

subdivided.[20] We could call 'nomad's checkmate'[21] the move that Bergson's Riemannian disciple intuitively pulled off against Badiou,[22] the ex-Maoist turned Platonist. From *Theory of the Subject* to *Being and Event* to *Logics of Worlds,* Badiou refuses to abandon a non-phenomenological concept of the subject, inspired by Lacan, but brought together with post-Cantorian mathematical set theory as well as category theory. We must distinguish between conceptual personae here: the preeminence of the nomothete[23] over the judge is the preeminence of the one who constitutes over the one who is constituted. In passing from the former to the latter, something is lost. The distinction is neither dialectical nor logical; it is *ethical.* For joy differs, absolutely, from sadness, power from helplessness. He who gives the rule is free, while he who judges *according* to the rule is free only through the mediation of the rule which constitutes him, and through servitude to the rule he institutes. Such is the meaning of this

---

20. Here, the psychoanalytic *Ichspaltung* and Lacan's divided subject are to be contrasted with Artaud's BwO, the Deleuzian planomenon, or the intensive multiplicity posited by Bergson, which differs from extensive multiplicity (divisible *partes extra partes*); being 'defined by the number of dimensions it has [...] it cannot lose or gain a dimension *without changing its nature.* Since its variations and dimensions are immanent to it, *it amounts to the same thing to say that each multiplicity is already composed of heterogeneous terms in symbiosis, and that a multiplicity is continually transforming itself into a string of other multiplicities* [...]" (*A Thousand Plateaus,* 249).

21. 'Nomad's mate' (*mat du nomade*) alludes to – and contrasts with – the 'Shepherd's mate' (*mat du berger*), a chess move known in English as the 'Scholar's mate'.

22. Indeed, for Bergson, it is within intuition that the absolute is given. If it is not a question of *intellectual* intuition, which Kant refused Plato, neither is it a question of sensible intuition. It is more a matter of *metaphysical* intuition, which is not an intuition of immutable essences or simple phenomena. Instead, it is the intuition of pure duration conceived as indivisible time and considered as *in-itself,* given that 'reality is mobility itself.'

23. 'The philosopher [...] is legislator.' 'Nietzsche', in Deleuze, *Pure Immanence,* 66.

heterological representative operation: For the hot cruelty of the theatre lauded by Artaud, and for crowned anarchy, is substituted the internal coldness of the world of Masoch, who, *aparallel* and heterogeneous to sadism, establishes a suspension of the law of the institution, by means of the contract. Which can be summed up thus: pleasure is the benchmark of *a desire that lacks nothing* since, according to the classic axiom and the Parmenidean (which is to say pre-anti-Platonic) legacy, *nothingness has no properties.*

In conclusion, if effects of transcendence do indeed occur, it is only qua denaturing of pure immanence, a denaturing whose frequency gives the exact measure of the rarity Badiou attributes to the event. For it is a commonplace that the conflict between Deleuze and Badiou's philosophies lies essentially in their respective articulation of the concepts of the whole [*tout*] and of the set; at least, this is the ambiguous *postmortem* angle of attack taken up by Badiou, holed up in the citadel of set theory.[24] If Kant makes of totality a category of understanding (under the rubric of quantity) and presents it as a synthesis of unity and plurality, for him it will consequently be a question of a principle of closure. For such a synthesis forecloses plurality, that is to say it makes it a whole through the mediation of unity. Deleuze, on the contrary, defines the 'whole […] through relation' specifying further that relation is 'not a property of objects.' The relation is 'exterior to its terms',[25] and belongs to the 'whole' on condition that the whole is thought in an exceptional way, *i.e.* not as quantity, but as *continuum*, as

---

24. However, the brief note dedicated to *Being and Event* in *What is Philosophy?* (151-2) seems almost to justify such an attack.

25. *Cinema 1: The Movement-Image*, 10.

an indivisible continuity[26] like a 'thread' that connects sets and keeps them open. Thus it is a question of a *nomadological autonomisation of the relation*,[27] a process which consitutes the originality of Deleuzian ontology,[28] and not a mere devaluation of the 'closed,' as Badiou would have it. The latter asks: Which infinity? Which multiplicity?[29] Deleuze, however, has already responded: not with the One-All, as the master mathematician of the rue d'Ulm affirms, but with *a* multiplicity, the whole as 'paradoxical link',[30] the event as 'lightning'.[31]

---

26. 'The real whole might well be, we conceive, an indivisible continuity' (H. Bergson, *Creative Evolution*, trans. A. Mitchell, NY: Dover, 1998).

27. A relation that, as we have seen, is external to the terms that effectuate it (and which thus *become* through the relation's intervention). Therefore, the relation is not a correlation, but rather constitutes the properly Deleuzian absolute; the relation not as being or necessary essence, but as event, or in Nietzschean terms, as '*Himmel Zufall*.' In particular, it is of course not easily assimilated to the 'count-as-one' of set-theoretical belonging.

28. More so, in fact, than the primacy Deleuze grants to Life, or even to Difference (which he declares, during the period of *Difference and Repetition*, is 'in the air of the times'), particularly through the notion of the structuralist-inspired 'differential relation'.

29. A. Badiou, 'One, Multiple, Multiplicities' in R. Brassier and A. Toscano (eds., trans.) *Theoretical Writings* (London: Continuum, 2006), 67-80.

30. *Cinema 1: The Movement-Image*, 11.

31. See for example: *L'Abécédaire de Gilles Deleuze* (Éditions Montparnasse DVD, 1996), 'Z comme Zigzag' [see C. Stivale's summary at http://www.langlab.wayne.edu/CStivale/D-G/ABC3.html], or the theory of the 'dispars' in *Difference and Repetition*.

Another World

J.-H. Rosny the Elder

ROSNY AND THE SCIENTIFIC FANTASTIC[1]

The pseudonymous J.-H. Rosny (1856-1940) was 'already multiple', even before Belgian brothers Justin and Joseph-Henri Böex subjected him to a belated fissure, thus giving birth to Rosny 'the Younger' and Rosny 'the Elder'. It was Joseph-Henri, 'Rosny the Elder', who would achieve notoriety in the late nineteenth century as one of the group of writers whose 1887 *manifeste du cinq* broke acrimoniously with Zola's naturalism, declaring it a pandering and sterile form.[2] J.-H. Rosny the elder became a prominent literary figure, later presiding over the *Academie Goncourt*

---

1. Introduction by Robin Mackay,

2. See http://www.berlol.net/chrono/des5.htm.

and publishing over 150 books in almost every genre, from historical romance to what he dubbed *le merveilleux scientifique*, in virtue of which he is now recognised as a pioneer of Science Fiction. A minor 'rediscovery' in the 1970s saw his SF stories republished in the original French,[3] with a few being translated for US paperback editions, and a 1981 film of his prehistoric tale *Quest for Fire*, but to this day Rosny's legacy remains undeservedly overshadowed by those of Verne and Wells.

Only Deleuze's patronage saves Rosny from equal obscurity as a philosopher, even though a contemporary placed him in the most exalted company, dedicating a volume saluting a 'philosophical revolution' to 'Bergson, Einstein, le Dantec and Rosny the Elder'.[4] Deleuze was familiar with Rosny's fantastic fiction (a 'naturalism in intensity'),[5] but it is the reference to two key theses of the philosophical work *Les sciences et le pluralisme*[6] that confirm

---

3. The most complete collection is *Rosny: récits de science-fiction*, ed. J.-B. Baronian (Verviers: Marabout, 1975).

4. J. Sageret, *La Révolution Philosophique et la Science*: *Bergson, Einstein, Le Dantec, J.H.Rosny aîné* (Paris: Alcan, 1924).

5. See *Difference and Repetition* 326-7n. 2.

6. *Les sciences et le pluralisme* was published in 1922 by Félix Alcan, a publisher who, in the first decades of the twentieth century, assembled a remarkable stable of philosophers of science (Lachelier, Renouvier, Brunschvicg, Bergson, not to mention Gabriel Tarde, Jean Wahl and Michel Souriau, to name only those cited in *Difference and Repetition*) who would exert a profound, if subterranean, influence upon French philosophy for the rest of the century. Alcan's name is attached to a group of authors who, rather than embodying a common ethos, saturated, through a sort of philosophical chromaticism, every philosophical possibility the epoch offered to the field.

The philosophical programme of philosophy of science inaugurated by Lachelier and Boutroux, and later renewed by Cavaillès and Bachelard, was, of course, finally interrupted by the Occupation, subsequently to be obscured by the 'return to the

that Rosny's contribution to *Difference and Repetition* was far from marginal:

(1) Resemblance presupposes difference; it is differences that resemble one another;

(2) Difference alone allows us to conceive of being.[7]

Rosny's book attacks the 'monist' presupposition that science proceeds by annulling differences through a reduction of the heterogeneous and complex to the homogeneous and elementary;[8] and that any dissenting, pluralist position must lead to nothing more than a 'confusionism'.[9] In so far as scientific thought implies simplifications and abstractions, like Bergson, Rosny regards it as continuous with cognition *per se*, and with life as such: Noting that 'each of our senses is constructed so as to

concrete' – but continued to operate beneath the surface, as is evident equally from the work of Badiou and Deleuze. See present volume, 35-6n. 90. A particularly clear account of the origins and mutations of this tradition is given by C. Imbert 'La fin d'une période : de Lachelier à Cavaillès et de Boutroux à Bachelard', at http://tlrdoc. free.fr/pages/philosciences.htm.

Alcan was one of the first French publishers to cede editorial control of scholarly journals to the scholars themselves, privileging innovation over tradition. This made Alcan the focal point of a new social network which would later lead to the formation of the *Quadrige* alliance of academic publishers, later PUF. For a detailed analysis of the role of *alcanisme* in the formation of the allied *Presses Universitaire de France* (PUF), and Alcan's impact in French publishing culture and the nascent figure of the intellectual, see V. Tesnière, *Le Quadrige: un siècle d'Édition universitaire, 1860-1968.* (Paris: PUF, 2001).

7. *Difference and Repetition* 327n. 2.

8. The most prominent advocate of such a thesis was Emile Meyerson, according to whose anti-positivist nihilistic ontology the underlying principle of science is an elimination leading to a uniform 'void' of absolute identity lacking all qualities. See E. Meyerson, *Identity and Reality* trans. K. Loewenberg (NY: Dover, 1962 – first published in French by Alcan in 1908).

9. J.-H. Rosny Aîné, *Les sciences et le pluralisme* (Paris: Alcan, 1922), 1.

"neglect" what does not interest it',[10] he takes up Bergson's example of the 'contraction' of light, suggesting that '[i]n the same way' that we 'contract' trillions of vibrations into a single qualitative sensation, 'science continually neglects, totalizes, symbolizes.'[11] But for Rosny this abstraction always exists and acts alongside *experimentation*,[12] which continually puts thought back in touch with the infinite complexity of the real, there to discover new differences, the disequilibria that drive scientific revolutions and refoundations.

Like the process of evolution, the progress of scientific thought constantly wards off a passage to the limit in either direction, to monism or 'confusionism'. But although we cannot therefore do without either the concept of difference or that of resemblance, Rosny claims that the former encompasses the latter: 'the concept of difference, since it is irreducible, radically suppresses the concept of resemblance, whilst the latter does not at all suppress that of plurality.'[13] The pluralist conception subtends the monist one, which tacitly presupposes it, and this, for Rosny, in so far as pluralism, 'the only possible method, the only one that has been implicitly practiced, the only one conforming to intellectual activity issued from instinctive activity'[14] necessarily implies a theory of difference: 'There can be no unity if difference is essential to the constitution of things; but there can be any number of resemblances, resemblances of every order,

10. *Ibid.*, 2.

11. *Ibid.*, 3

12. *Ibid.*

13. *Ibid.*, 5.

14. *Ibid.*, 7

"different" resemblances, so to speak, in an indefinitely varied and variable universe';[15] 'we perceive more and more clearly summations of differences, where before we thought we saw resemblances.'[16] Like his contemporary Gabriel Tarde, whose 'differential epistemology' proposed that the infinitesimal and its integration were 'the key to the entire universe',[17] Rosny discovers the magical equivalence 'PLURALISM=MONISM'[18] through the promotion of difference as primary and fathomless; whence the formula repeated in *Difference and Repetition* to illustrate that there is nothing behind difference but difference:

> All (calculable) energy implies factors of the form $E - E'$, in which E and E' themselves conceal factors of the form $e - e'$, and so on indefinitely.[19]

This differential pluralism extends from Rosny's philosophy of science into his science fictions, for if 'experimentation indefinitely dominates speculation' this implies the tantalising fact that 'we only ever know a tiny portion of things in relation to the immensity and diversity of the universe. It makes us see that there exist innumerable series whose existence will never be revealed to our feeble powers of discrimination'.[20] In the final chapter, where Rosny makes this connection explicit, *Les sciences* begins to answer to Deleuze's ideal definition: philosophy becomes

---

15. *Ibid.*, 5.

16. *Ibid.*, 6.

17. See J. Milet, *Gabriel Tarde et la philosophie de l'histoire* (Paris:Vrin, 1970).

18. *A Thousand Plateaus*, 20.

19. Rosny, *Les sciences*, 6; *Cf. Difference and Repetition*, 117, 222.

20. Rosny, *Les sciences*, 8.

truly 'a kind of science fiction', written 'at the frontiers of knowledge',[21] and invoking the central theme of Rosny's fantastic tales: strange alien beings just beyond the reach of our limited knowledge:

> [T]here is no reason why the terrestrial surface, since it is traversed by immense energies, should not have produced organic systems equal in complexity to our own. No more than there is any reason that it might not produce another organic realm once ours has disappeared. My *Xipehuz*, *Moedigen* and *Ferro-Magnetics* are perhaps pale symbols of anterior and future realities.[22]

Indeed, these were already the stakes of Rosny's first SF tale, 1887's *Les Xipehuz*, whose nonorganic aliens announced, as surely as do the 'Moedigen' of 'Another World', the arrival of a non-anthropomorphic SF.

Along with this obsession with radically different orders of living beings, Rosny's rejection of the hubristic aspiration to a unification of knowledge unites him with another writer favoured by Deleuze: The following is Rosny, but it could easily have been written by the American weaver of weird tales H.P. Lovecraft (1890-1937):

> Revolting against our infirmity, if we cannot traverse and dominate the universe, at least we might conceive it. Vain dream of ephemeral beings, whose race will last but an instant in the innumerable succession of phenomena […] [23]

Both Rosny and Lovecraft drew on contemporary scientific advances, and did not hesitate to extrapolate wildly

---

21. *Difference and Repetition* xx-xxi.

22. Rosny, *Les sciences*, 215.

23. Rosny, *Les sciences*, 8.

from them. Both created weird tales in which 'the world of normality hardly ever appears',[24] even as a dramatic foil for preternatural occurrences. Both had a taste for materialism, scientific rationality, and precision that showed through in the meticulous construction of their alien worlds and creatures; both showed a will to estrange the reader with scientifically-plausible abstract-cosmic theses, with creatures that went beyond any biological comprehension but exemplified the most outlandish findings of physics (in Rosny we find creatures that are geometrical constructs of pure energy, helicoidal ferromagnetic forms, fluid, spiral, cones of magnetically-charged matter – all in perfect keeping with Lovecraft's bizarre hexagonal barrels, four-dimensional protoplasms and ineffable yet material presences). Both authors seal this alienation with their weird creatures' unpronounceable names – Rosny's 'Wanawnanabm' and 'Kzamms' for Lovecraft's 'Nyarlathotep' and 'Cthulhu' – and by overegging their tales with weighty adjectival invocations of the noumenal.[25]

---

24. J.P. Vernier 'The SF of J.H. Rosny the Elder', *Science Fiction Studies*, #6, 2:2, 1975.

25. 'First of all there are certain words – always the same, always identical, almost piercing, like incantatory fomulae: fearful, formidable, terrible, prodigious, savage, gigantic! […] As if the author had deliberately wanted to define his literary universe, as if he had sought, by resorting to a singular vocabulary, the most accurate adumbration of his real and precise ambitions […]' – Jean-Baptiste Baronian, 'Les Fins et les Manieres', preface to Rosny, *Récits*, 5.

'In this register Lovecraft has never been equalled. One may copy his manner [...] but one can never imagine oneself emulating those passages where he loses all stylistic reserve, where adjectives and adverbs accumulate to the point of exasperation, where he lets loose exclamations of pure delirium [...] [T]his is the true goal of his work. One could even say that the often subtle and elaborate structures of the "major works" have no other purpose apart from preparing the way for passages of stylistic explosion [...] The adjectives and the exclamation marks multiply, the fragments of incantation spring to his mind, his heart is lifted with enthusiasm; he plunges into a true ecstatic delirium [...]' – M. Houellebecq, *H.P.Lovecraft: Against the World, Against Life*, trans. D. Khazeni (NY: Believer Books, 2005). Translation modified.

But as well as the difference in their scientific expertise (Lovecraft, though invariably well-researched, was ever the gentleman-amateur, whereas Rosny was something of a polymath and was in direct contact with the scientific luminaries of his day, including – as Deleuze notes – Marie Curie) the two authors display a marked difference in moral outlook. Although both perceived with utmost clarity the extent to which modern science had dislodged man from the centre of the universe, whilst Lovecraft revelled in repeatedly hammering home man's powerlessness in the face of impersonal cosmic forces (see Houellebecq's suberb account),[26] Rosny maintained a faith in man which survived the ravages of darwinism, atomic physics and relativity.

Both invoke weird and frightening creatures beyond our ken; but whereas in Lovecraft's quasi-Faustian tales an unhealthy taste for science is often to blame for bringing unhappy protagonists into contact with beings they ought to have left well alone, for Rosny these beings can, through the power of scientific thought, be brought within the purview of a positive scientific knowledge, in the process altering our own perception of the universe – a cognitive evolutionism, then, inspired no doubt by the enthusiasm for the mechanisms of adaptation and mutation in Bergson and his contemporaries.

Although Lovecraft and Rosny share a fascination for the seething world of particles and energy and for the apparent impossibility of defining what constitutes a living being, by constantly emphasising man's biological kinship with 'lower' and 'higher' forms of life alike and

26. Houellebecq, *op.cit.*

his consequent interconnectedness with the universe, Rosny finds a paradoxical sort of comfort wholly lacking in Lovecraft's visions of cosmic desolation. This theme of a sort of abstract community is keenly argued throughout Rosny's work: he believes in a sort of primacy of a *structure of life*; and inversely the 'meaning of life', in the higher form of advanced scientific thought, is the search for structure. Rosny's hymns to experimental research – including 'Another World' – are in some sense the inverse of Lovecraft's grim counsel against meddling with the hostile indifference of the physical universe. Perhaps this can be attributed to Rosny's personal involvement with the science that rendered Lovecraft awestruck from afar; Rosny's faith in the human involvement in the fundamental questing impulse of science fending off the Azathothic terror brought on for Lovecraft in contemplating its actual findings:

> Modern research, you who have made of the abstract a tool rather than a limit, oh incommensurable spiral – reaching into the depths of the spaces where the human spirit ascends [...] [27]

As we know, for Lovecraft, there is no mistaking that this spiral is a *descent* ... Furthermore, for Rosny, universal community becomes a link between the everyday world of emotion and sociality, and the arid calculus of exact science; thus suggesting a very definite view of science's positive historical and social import: it is, after all, this intuition of structure common to all life that, in Rosny's *Les Navigateurs de l'infini,* allows a human to fall in love with a six-eyed

---

27. Vernier, *op.cit.*

martian 'of ternary symmetry'![28] The instinct for beauty, an *a priori* for all possible consciousness and recalling the role of purposiveness in Kant's aesthetics, reflects the cosmic dominance of structure, and therefore implies the possibility of bringing the human into harmony with a universe full of uncharted inhuman forms of life. Rosny's touching suggestion – utterly unthinkable for Lovecraft – is that we can even come to empathic terms with 'luminous networks of phosphorescent matter' – as ridiculous as it might seem, perhaps not such a very different sentiment from the spirit that inspired the plaque on the Voyager space probe.

What intervened in between 'Another World' and 'The Mountains of Madness', between the cosmic optimism of diaphanous, playful lifeforms and the absymal horror of tentacular crawling chaos, was the Great War – technological arsenals unleashed in a senseless, implacable and indifferent manner that Lovecraft perhaps saw as a revelation of the very eternal truth of the universe.[29] Nevertheless, Rosny is no mere anti-Lovecraft, any more than he is merely anti-Meyersonian. In fact it is the black romantic Lovecraftian vision of dissolution into confusionist schizophrenic chaos[30] that is the reverse image of the Meyersonian glacial ascent to monolithic identity. Rosny's differential ontology means that his pluralism can affirm both simplification and complexification, in a non-dialectical relation; differentiation

---

28. Rosny, *Récits de science-fiction*, 40-91.

29. See China Miéville's introduction to H.P. Lovecraft, *At the Mountains of Madness* (NY: Random House, 2005); Note also that 1910 saw the publication of Rosny's *Mort de la Terre*, where the parallel life-forms – this time 'ferromagnetic beings' – finally turn on man, killing off the human race.

30. See *A Thousand Plateaus*, 73-4, 240, 245, 248.

and selection together with a univocity that preserves an empathic opening to the cosmic. Seeing no contradiction between an immediate aesthetic apprehension of the universe (beauty) and scientific knowledge (structure), arguing for the equal importance of conceptual reduction and an experimental/experiential immersion, Rosny's work is a unique, lyrical vitalist-structuralist apology for pluralism.

'Another World' typifies the Rosny narrative arc: an alienated being is reconciled with our world through systematic scientific experimentation, conducted by the sympathetic figure of the curious but prudent and objective Doctor van den Heuvel.[31] A mediation is achieved between 'durations' which would otherwise exist in parallel, unknown to each other; ending in a union which promises more experiments, more differentiations, to come.

---

31. Note that the protagonist of 'Another World' finds both social acceptance and the scientific expertise necessary to bring him into engagement with the wider world, in the cordial cosmopolitan setting of *the city*, which, for Lovecraft, promised only the horror of pullulating 'shoggothic' masses (see Houllebecq, *op. cit.*).

COLLAPSE III

ANOTHER WORLD

I

I am a native of Gelderland. Our inheritance had dwindled to a few acres of heather and yellow water. Pine trees lined its borders, quivering and rustling with a metallic sound. The farmhouse had hardly any habitable rooms, and was crumbling, stone by stone, in its solitude. We were a clerical family of old, once numerous, now reduced to my parents, my sister and myself.

My destiny, so dark to begin with, has become as wonderful as I could ever have dreamt of: I have met with those who understand me; they have learnt that which I alone amongst men know. But I suffered for such a long time, I despaired, prey to doubt, to the solitude of the soul, which ended up corroding even absolute certainties.

I came into the world with a unique constitution. From the start, I was an object of astonishment. Not that I seemed maladapted: I was, so they told me, more graceful of body and countenance than is normal in a newborn. But I had a most extraordinary complexion, a sort of pale violet hue – very pale, but most definite. In lamplight, especially that of oil-lamps, this tint became even more pale, turning into a peculiar whiteness, like a lily submerged in water. That was, at least, what other people saw: myself, I saw it differently, as I saw differently all objects in the world. For this first peculiarity was to be supplemented with others which would reveal themselves later on.

Although born with all the appearance of good health, I grew very slowly. I was thin, I cried endlessly; at eight months old, no-one had ever seen me smile. They soon began to despair of the prospect of raising me. The doctor from Zwartendam declared that I was stricken with a physiological infirmity: he could recommend no other remedy than a strict regime of hygiene. But this did not prevent my wasting away; it seemed that, day by day, I was just fading away. My father, I believe, was resigned to it, his *amour-propre* – the *amour-propre* of a Dutchman of order and regularity – somewhat injured by the bizarre nature of his child. My mother, quite against the grain, loved me all the more in proportion to my bizarreness, having eventually found the tone of my skin lovable.

Things stayed just so, until a rather simple event came to my rescue: but, just as everything was abnormal for me, this event too was to be an occasion for scandal and fear.

Upon the departure of a servant, to replace her we took on a vigorous young girl from Friesia, full of honesty and enthusiasm for work, but with a weakness for drink. I was entrusted to the new arrival. Seeing me so weak, she came up with the idea of giving me, in secret, a little beer and water mixed with jenever: a remedy, according to her, for all ills.

The most curious thing is that I wasted no time in regaining my full vigour, and that from that time onwards I demonstrated an extraordinary predeliction for alcoholic drink. This fine girl secretly rejoiced, not without a certain relish at the puzzlement of my parents and the doctor. Put on the spot, she finally solved the mystery. My father flew into a violent rage; the doctor railed against superstition and ignorance. Strict orders were given to the servants; and my nurse was sent back to Friesia.

COLLAPSE III

I began to get thinner again, to waste away, to the point where, hearkening only to her love for me, my mother put me back on the regime of beer and jenever. At once, I regained my vigour and vivacity. The experiment was conclusive: alcohol was revealed to be indispensible to my health. My father took it as a humiliation; the doctor took charge of things by arranging for medicinal wines to be brought, and after this my health was excellent: although one would be forgiven for presaging for me a career of drunkenness and debauchery.

A little after this incident, a new anomaly struck those around me. My eyes, which first of all had appeared quite normal, started to become strangely opaque, taking on a calloused appearance, like the hard wingcases of certain beetles. The doctor predicted that I would lose my sight; all the time avowing that the condition seemed absolutely inexplicable to him and that he had never had occasion to study anything remotely similar. Soon the pupil was so amalgamated with the iris that it was impossible to tell the one from the other. It should be remarked, meanwhile, that I was able to look at the sun with no apparent unease. In truth, I was not in the least bit blind – in fact it would have to be admitted in the end that I saw extremely well.

Thus I attained the age of three years. I was, according to the opinion of those of the neighborhood, a little monster. The violet colour of my skin had hardly changed; my eyes were now completely opaque. I spoke poorly and with incredible speed. I was nimble with my hands and well adapted for any movements that demanded more speed than strength. It could not be denied that, if I had had a normal complexion and normal eyes, I would have been graceful and pretty. I showed signs of intelligence, but with certain gaps which those around me could not fathom, especially as – apart from my mother and the Friesian girl – they did not like me at all. For strangers I was an object of curiosity, for my father a continual source of mortification.

If, however, the latter may have nursed hopes of seeing me one day become equal with other men, time served only to dash them. I was to become more and more strange, in my tastes, in my conduct, in my qualities. At six years old, I nourished myself almost uniquely on alcohol. Only very rarely did I take a few mouthfuls of vegetables or fruits. I grew prodigiously fast, I was incredibly thin and light. I mean light in a quite specific sense – something different to merely thin people: I swam with the slightest of effort, I floated like a plank of poplar-wood. My head didn't sink any more than the rest of my body.

I was nimble in proportion to this lightness. I ran as fast as a deer; I leapt over ditches and obstacles which no man would even try to clear. In the blink of an eye, I could climb to the top of a beech-tree; or, what is even more surprising, I could jump right onto the roof of our farmhouse. On the other hand, even the slightest burden exhausted me.

*

All of these, in sum, were only phenomena indicative of a peculiar nature, which would not, on their own, serve to distinguish me or make life hard for me: none of them categorised me outside the bounds of humanity. No doubt I was a monster, but certainly no more than those born with the eyes or ears of an animal, with the head of a calf or of a horse, fins, no eyes or an extra eye, four arms, four legs, or no arms or legs at all. My skin, despite its surprising tint, was near enough to being just a tanned skin; my eyes were not particularly repugnant, despite their opacity. My extreme agility was an asset; my need for alcohol could have passed for a simple vice, the result of a family legacy of drunkenness: in any case, rustic folk like our Friesian servant would see in it only a confirmation of their ideas about the 'potency' of jenever, a particularly acute proof of their tastes. As to the speed of my speech, its volubility, which made it impossible to follow, this might have been mistaken for faults of pronunciation – stuttering, stammering, lisping – common to so many small children. I therefore did not have, properly speaking, any striking traits of monstrosity, even if the whole was extraordinary in its combination: for the most curious aspect of my nature escaped those around me, because none of them could know that my vision differed strangely from normal vision.

If I saw some things less well than others, I also saw a great number of things that others did not see at all. This difference was especially manifest with regard to colours. Everything that is called red, orange, yellow, green, blue, indigo, appeared to me as a more or less dark grey, whereas I perceived violet, and the series of colours beyond it, colours which are nothing at all for normal men. I recognised later on that I could thus distinguish about fifteen colours as dissimilar as, for example, yellow and green – with, of course, an infinity of gradations.

Secondly, transparency does not manifest itself to my eye in the usual way. I saw quite poorly through glass and through water: glass is very densely coloured for me; so is water, noticeably, even when quite shallow. Many so-called diaphanous crystals are more or less opaque to me, and inversely many supposedly opaque bodies are no barrier to my vision at all. In general, I can see through things more often than you; and translucidity, semi-transparence, is so commonplace that I might say that it is, for my eyes, the rule for nature, whereas complete opacity is the exception. Thus it is that I see objects through trees, leaves, the petals of flowers, magnetised iron, coal, *etc.* However, as their thickness varies, these bodies become an obstacle: such as a large tree, water a metre deep, a thick block of coal or of quartz.

Gold, platinum, mercury are black and opaque, ice is blackish. Air and water vapour are transparent, but somewhat coloured, like certain types of steel, certain very pure clays. Clouds do not prevent me from seeing the sun nor the stars. However, I can perceive the clouds suspended in the atmosphere.

This difference between my vision and that of other men was, as I have said, very little remarked upon by those close to me: it was known that I distinguished poorly between colours, that was all; and that is too common a problem to draw much attention. It was without great consequence for the day-to-day proceedings of my life, since I saw the forms of objects the same – and perhaps even more subtly – than most people. The designation of an object by its colour, when meant to differentiate it from another object of the same form, was only a problem if they were new to me. If someone called the colour of one waistcoat blue and that of another red, the real colours in which the waistcoats appeared to me mattered little: blue and red became purely mnemonic terms.

Along these lines, you can well understand that there

emerged a certain sort of accord between my colours and the colours of others, and that ultimately it became just as if I saw their colours. But, as I have already written, I perceived red, green, yellow, blue, etc. when they were pure – as are the colours of a prism – as darker or lighter shades of grey; they simply were not colours for me. In nature, where no colour is pure, things are not the same: some substances called green, for example, are for me a certain composite colour;[32] but another substance called green, and which to you looks exactly the same shade as the first, is not at all the same colour for me. You can therefore see that my palette of colours does not correspond to yours: when I agree to call both brass and gold 'yellow', it is a little as if you were to agree to call both a cornflower and a poppy 'red'.

II

If the difference between my vision and normal vision had stopped there, this would, certainly, have been extraordinary enough. It is nothing, however, in comparison to what remains for me to tell you. The world coloured differently, differently transparent and opaque – the faculty to see through the clouds, to see the stars even on the most overcast of nights, of seeing through a wooden partition what is happening in an neighbouring room or outside a house – what is all that, compared to the perception of a LIVING WORLD, of a world of animated beings who move alongside and all around man, without man ever being conscious of it unless he is alerted to them by some sort of immediate

---

32. And this composite colour, of course, does not contain green, since green is but a shadow for me.

contact? What is all that, compared to the revelation that there exists on this earth a fauna other than our fauna, one which does not resemble ours whatsoever, either in form, organisation, or behaviour, nor in the way it is born, grows, and dies? A fauna which lives side-by-side with ours and beyond ours, influences the elements which surround us and is influenced by them, is nourished by these elements, without our ever suspecting their presence. A fauna which – as I will demonstrate – knows nothing of us just as we know nothing of it, and which has developed in complete isolation from us just as we have in complete isolation from it. A living world, with just as much variety as ours, just as significant as ours – and perhaps more so – in terms of its effects on the face of the planet! A kingdom, finally, moving across the oceans, in the atmosphere, in the soil, modifying these oceans, this atmosphere and this soil, in a completely different way than we do, but with an assuredly formidable energy, and in that way acting indirectly upon us and on our destinies! ... This, nonetheless, is what I saw, what I see, alone among man and beasts; this is what I have studied fervently for five years, after having spent my childhood merely observing it.

III

Observing it! For as long as I can remember, I instinctively supressed the attraction of this creation so alien to our own. At first I confused it with other living things. Perceiving that no-one else took any notice of its presence, that everyone, on the contrary, seemed utterly indifferent to it, I made no effort to point out its peculiarities. At six years old I knew perfectly how to distinguish it from the plants of the fields, the animals of the farmyard and stable, but I sometimes still confused it with inert phenomena such as fire and light, or the motion of water and clouds. These beings were intangible: when they touched me I felt no sensory effect from their contact. Meanwhile their forms, however highly varied, had the peculiarity of being so thin in one of their three dimensions, that one might compare them to drawn figures, to surfaces, mobile geometrical lines. They traversed all organic bodies; on the other hand, they seemed sometimes to be blocked, entangled in invisible obstacles … But I will describe them later. For now, I want only to indicate, to affirm, the variety of their contours and lines, their almost complete absence of thickness, their impalpability, along with the autonomy of their movements.

*

Around the time of my eighth year, I finally realised definitely that they were just as distinct from atmospheric phenomenon as from the animals of our natural kingdom. Enraptured by this discovery, I tried to express it. I could never succeed in doing so. As well as my speech being nearly completely incomprehensible, as I have said, the extraordinary nature of my vision rendered what I said suspect. No-one would bother to spend the time to decipher my gestures and my phrases, any more than they would be minded to admit that I could see through wooden partitions, however many times I might furnish proofs of so doing. There was, between myself and others, an almost insurmountable barrier.

I fell into discouragement and reverie; I became a sort of solitary child; my presence caused unease – and I could sense it – when in the company of children my own age. I was not exactly a victim, since my speed put me well out of the reach of childhood malice and gave me the means to wreak revenge easily. At the least sign of trouble, I would be far away, leaving the pursuer floundering. No matter what numbers they came in, children could never hope to surround me, much less get a hold of me. It was not even any use to try to grab me by stealth. As weak as I was when it came to bearing a load, my speed was irresistible, and I would escape instantly. I could return unexpectedly and overcome the adversary, or even adversaries, with prompt and sure blows. So they left me alone. They took me at once for an innocent and something of a sorceror, but one whose brand of sorcery was apparently so limited that he deserved scorn. By degrees, I began to live a life apart, insular, meditative, and not completely devoid of peaceful moments. Only the kindness of my mother humanised me, even if, busy most of the day, she found little time for caresses.

IV

I will try to describe summarily several scenes of my tenth year, before making more concrete the preceding explanations.

It is morning. A large lamp lights up the kitchen, a lamp which is a pale yellow for my parents and the servants, very different for me. Breakfast is being served, tea and bread. But I do not take any tea. They just give me a glass of jenever with a raw egg. My mother busies herself tenderly with me; my father questions me. I try to answer him, I slow down my speech; he only understands one syllable here, one there, and shrugs his shoulders.

"He'll never speak! …"

My mother looks at me compassionately, convinced that I am a little simple. The domestic staff and the servants are not even curious any longer about the little violet monster; the Friesian returned to her homeland a long time ago. As for my sister – she is two – she plays around me, and I feel a great fondness for her.

The meal finished, my father goes on his way, along with the servants, and my mother begins to attend to the daily chores. I am in there in the courtyard. The animals gather around. I regard them with interest, I love them. But all around, the other Kingdom shifts and changes and captures me even more: the mysterious domain that I alone know.

On the brown earth, there are various scattered forms; they move, stop, palpitate across the expanse of the ground. They are of many types, differentiated by their shape, their movement, and above all by their behaviours, the contours and the hues of the curves which traverse them. These curves constitute, in sum, the principle of their being and, even as a child, I could see this quite well. Whilst the greater part of their form is dull and greyish, the lines are almost always sparkling. They form very complicated webs, they emanate from centres, they radiate, until they die out, becoming indiscernible. Their hues are innumerable, their curves infinite. These hues vary for one single line, as they do also, but less so, for the whole form.

Taken as a whole, each being is described by a contour,

rather irregular but very distinct, by centers of radiation, by multi-coloured, multiply intersecting lines. When it moves, the lines vibrate, oscillate, the centres contract and dilate, whilst the contour hardly varies.

All of this, I saw quite well, already, even if I was incapable of defining it; I was penetrated by an exquisite charm in contemplating the Moedigen.[33] One of them, a colossus ten metres long and almost as wide, passes slowly across the courtyard, with great centres like eagles' wings, interests me greatly and almost frightens me. I spend a moment following it, but then others claim my attention. They are of all sizes: some are no bigger than our most common insects, whereas I have seen some attain more than thirty metres in length. They proceed on the ground only, as if they are attached to solid surfaces. When a material obstacle – a wall, a house – presents itself, they clear it by moulding themselves to its surface, always without any significant modification of their contours. But when the obstacle is of matter that is living or has lived, they pass directly through it: I have seen them thus, a million times, emerging from a tree and under the feet of an animal or a human. They also pass through water, but prefer to remain on the surface.

These terrestrial Moedigen are not the only intangible beings. There is an aerial population, marvellous and splendid, of an incomparable subtlety, variety, and lustre, besides which the most beautiful birds are dreary, slow and heavy. Here again, a contour and some lines. But the

---

33. This is the name which I spontaneously gave them during my infancy, and which I have kept for them, even if it does not correspond to any quality or form of these beings.

bottom is not greyish; it is strangely luminous; it sparkles like the sun, and the lines detach themselves from it in vibrating veins, the centres palpitating violently. The Vuren, as I named them, are more irregular of form than the terrestrial Moedigen, and generally speaking they direct themselves with the aid of rhythmic behaviours, crossings and uncrossings whose nature, in my ignorance, I could not determine and which confounded my imagination.

Meanwhile I had taken my route across a recently-mown lawn: the combat of one Moedig with another drew my attention. These combats are frequent; they intensely excited me. Sometimes, it is a combat between equals; most often the attack of a strong one against a weak (the weak is not necessarily the smallest). In the present case, the weak one, after a summary defense, takes flight, pursued briskly by its aggressor. Despite the speed of their progress, I follow them, and I succeed in not losing sight of them, up to the moment when the battle recommences. They fall on one another, firmly, rigidly even, each one solid against the other. At the shock, their lines phosphoresce, are directed towards the point of contact, their centres blanching and contracting. At first, the struggle remains fairly equal, the weaker expending energy the most intensely, and even succeeding in obtaining a respite from its adversary. It profits from this by fleeing anew, but is rapidly caught up, attacked with force and finally seized upon, that is to say consumed through an opening in the contour of the other. This is precisely what it had sought to avoid, by responding to stronger shocks with less energetic, but more sudden shocks. Now, I see all of its lines vibrating, its centres pulsing despairingly; and, in proportion to this, its lines fading, growing finer, the centres becoming more indistinct. After a few minutes, it is granted its liberty: it moves away slowly, dimly, debilitated. The antagonist, on the contrary, sparkles yet brighter, its lines are more highly coloured, its centres more distinct and more rapid.

This struggle has profoundly moved me; I re-imagine it, I compare it to battles which I have seen sometimes between our animals; I grasp confusedly the fact that the Moedigen, essentially, do not die, or only rarely so; that the victor contents itself with taking energy at the expense of the vanquished.

The morning wears on, it is nearly eight'o'clock; the Zwartendam school will open soon: I make a leap back to the farmhouse, I gather my books, and there I am, amongst my classmates, where no-one divines the profound mysteries which pulsate all around us, where no-one has even the most confused idea of the living things which all humanity traverses and which traverse humanity, with no indication of this mutual penetration.

I am a truly awful scholar. My writing is but a halting trace, unformed, unreadable; my speech remains uncomprehended; my distraction is obvious. The schoolmaster continually cries:

"Karel Ondereet, are you finished watching the flies buzzing around? …"

Alas! Dear master, it is true that I watch the flies buzzing, but how much more my soul follows the mysterious Vuren which move through the room! And what strange sentiments haunt my young soul, in observing everyone else's blindness, and above all yours, grave pastor of minds!

V

The most painful period of my life was from twelve to eighteen years old.

Firstly, my parents tried to send me to college; there I knew only miseries and vexations. At the cost of exhausting difficulties, I was able to express in an almost comprehensible manner the most common things: slowing my syllables with great effort, I spat them out maladroitly and with the accent of a deaf person. But, as soon as it was a question of something more complicated, my speech reverted to its inevitable speed; and once again no-one could hope to follow me. I could not hope therefore to make my progress known orally. On the other hand, my writing was atrocious, my letters squashed up one on top of the other, and, in my impatience, I missed out syllables, words: it was a monstrous gibberish. In any case, writing was for me a torment perhaps even worse than speaking: – of an asphyxiating heaviness and slowness! – If, on occasion, by sheer painful force of will, and sweating great drops, I managed to begin some work, soon I was at the end of my energy and patience, and felt I was about to faint away. So that I preferred the remonstrances of the masters, the punishments, the scorn, to this horrible labour.

Thus, I was almost totally deprived of any means of expression: an object of ridicule, already, because of my skinniness and my bizarre colouring, because of my strange eyes, I now also passed for some sort of idiot. I would have to remove myself from the school, resign myself to being a peasant. The day when my father decided to renounce all hope, he said to me with unaccustomed kindness:

"My poor boy, you see, I have done all I can … all I can! Do not reproach me for your fate!"

I was intensely moved; I cried hot tears: I had never felt with such bitterness my isolation from the world of men. I ventured to embrace my father tenderly; I murmured:

"But still, it isn't true that I'm an imbecile!"

And, in fact, I felt myself superior to those who had been my colleagues. For a while now, my intelligence had taken a remarkable turn. I read, I understood, I did some guesswork, and I had sufficient occasion for meditation, far more than others, in this universe visible to me alone.

My father did not decipher what I said, but he softened to my embrace.

"Poor boy!" he said.

I looked at him; I was in dreadful distress, knowing more than ever that the void between us would never be filled. My mother, by some intuition born of love, saw in that moment that I was not inferior to other boys of my age: she beheld me with great tenderness, mouthing naïve pleasantries from the depths of her being. But I was nonetheless condemned to cease my studies.

Because of my feeble muscular power, they entrusted me with the care of the livestock. I acquitted myself marvellously; I never needed a dog to keep the herds or a foal under control, no stallion was more agile than I.

I lived, then, between the ages of fourteen and seventeen, the solitary life of the shepherd. It suited me more than any other. Given over to observation and contemplation, and also to much reading, my brain never ceased to develop. I compared ceaselessly the double creation I had before my eyes, drawing from this some ideas on the constitution of the universe; I vaguely fabricated hypotheses and systems. If it is true that my thoughts could not have at this time a perfect correlation, did not form a lucid synthesis – for they were the thoughts of an adolescent, uncoordinated, impatient, enthusiastic – they were nevertheless original and fecund. That they were only of value to my unique constitution, I would not deny at all. But not all their force came from this. Without the least pride, I believe I can say that they surpassed appreciably, in subtlety and in logic alike, those of ordinary young people.

They were the sole source of consolation in my sad life of a semi-pariah, without companions, without real communication with those around me, even my beloved mother.

*

At seventeen, life became decidedly unbearable for me. I was sick of dreaming, sick of vegetating in a desert island of thought. I fell into languor and boredom. I spent long hours immobile, disinterested in the whole world, inattentive to everything that happened within my family. What did it matter to me to know things more marvellous than other men, since in any case this knowledge was to die with me? What use to me was the mystery of the living beings, and even of the duality of the two vital systems traversing one another without any knowledge of each other? These things could have intoxicated me, filled me with enthusiasm and ardour, had I been in any way able to teach them or to share them. But what hope of that! Vain and sterile, absurd and miserable, they rather contributed to my perpetual psychic quarantine.

Many times, I dreamt of writing, of setting down, all the same, at the price of continual efforts, some few of my observations. But, since I had left school, I had completely abandoned the pen, and, such a poor writer before, now, even when I applied myself fully, I could barely write the twenty-six letters of the alphabet. If I could have still conceived of some hope, perhaps I might have persisted! But who would take my miserable lucubrations seriously anyhow? Where was the reader who would not think me insane? Or the sage who would not dismiss me with disdain or irony? What purpose, then, could I adduce for such a vain task, such a tiresome devotion – something like the obligation, for an ordinary man, to carve his thoughts on tables of marble, with a hammer and chisel! Any writing of mine would have to be stenographic – and what's more, a stenography more rapid than the usual!

Thus I had not the courage to write, but nevertheless I hoped fervently for some unknown, some happy and singular stroke of destiny. It seemed to me that there must exist, in some corner of the earth, impartial, lucid, rigorous minds, able to study me, to understand me, to be able to speak with me and to communicate my great secret to others. But where might these people be? And what hope did I have of ever meeting them?

And I fell again into a vast melancholy, into desires for immobility and annihilation. For a whole autumn, I despaired of the universe. I languished in a vegetative state, from which I only emerged to give voice to great laments followed by dolorous revolts.

I became thin again, to the point of becoming fantastically so. The people of my village called me, ironically, Den Heyligen Gheest, the Holy Ghost. My silhouette trembled like that of the old poplars, light as a reflection, and, at the same time, I attained the stature of a giant.

Slowly, a project was born. Since my life was sacrificed, since none of my days held any appeal to me, since all was darkness and bitterness to me, why stagnate in inactivity? Even supposing that no soul existed which could respond to mine, surely it was worthwhile to make the effort to convince myself of it. At least it was worth quitting this morose land, going to find the great cities of scientists and philosophers. Wasn't I, after all, an object of curiosity? Before even calling attention to my superhuman cognitions, could I not excite the desire to study my person? Weren't the physical aspects of my being alone worthy of analysis: my sight, the extreme quickness of my movements and the peculiarity of my nutrition?

The more I reviewed these thoughts, the more it seemed reasonable to hope, and the more my resolution grew. The day arrived when it became absolutely firm, and I revealed it to my parents. Neither of them really understood, but both ended by ceding after repeated insistences: I obtained the means to take myself to Amsterdam, and to return should the outcome be unfavourable to me.

I left one morning.

VI

From Zwartendam to Amsterdam it is around a hundred kilometres. I made this distance easily in two hours, with no particular incident apart from the extreme surprise of those coming and going at seeing me run with such speed, and some gatherings at the outskirts of small towns and large market-towns which I passed. To be sure of my route, I addressed myself to two or three solitary old people. My sense of direction, which is excellent, did the rest.

It was around nine'o'clock when I got to Amsterdam. I entered resolutely into the great city, I walked the length of its beautiful dreamy canals where the commercial flotillas live. I did not attract as much attention as I had expected to. I walked fast, amongst people who were busy, suffering here and there the gibes of a few young urchins. I decided not to stop, however. I walked around the city a little in every direction, until finally I resolved to enter a cabaret, on one of the quays of the Herengracht. The location was peaceful; the magnificent canal stretched out, full of life, between fresh rows of trees; and amidst the Moedigen which I saw circulating on the banks, I seemed to see a new species. After a moment of indecision, I crossed the threshold of the cabaret and, addressing myself to the patron, as slowly as I could manage, I asked him to be so good as to tell me the way to a hospital.

The host looked at me with a mixture of stupor, defiance and curiosity, took his big pipe from his mouth and put it back, many times, then finished by saying:

"You are from the colonies, no doubt?"

As it was perfectly useless to contradict him, I responded:

"That's right! …"

He seemed enchanted by his own perspicacity; he set

285

me a new question:

"Perhaps you come from that part of Borneo where no-one has yet set foot?"

"The very same! …"

I had spoken too fast: he opened his eyes wide.

"The very same!" I repeated more slowly.

The host smiled with satisfaction:

"You can't speak Dutch too well, eh? … Well, it's a hospital you want … You're ill, are you?"

"Yes …"

Some customers had approached. The rumour was already going round that I was a cannibal from Borneo; nevertheless, they looked at me more with curiosity than antipathy. Some men ran up from the road. I became nervous, disquieted. Nevertheless I kept a straight face, and said, coughing:

"I'm very ill!"

"Just like the monkeys from that country," offered a very fat dutchman cordially, "the Netherlands kill them!"

"What funny skin!" said another.

"And how does he see?" asked a third, indicating my eyes.

The circle drew nearer, enveloping me with a hundred curious looks, with new arrivals constantly entering the room.

"How tall he is!"

It is true that I was taller than the tallest of them by a head.

"And thin!"

"He doesn't seem to be getting much nourishment, this cannibal!"

None of the voices seemed particularly malevolent. A few sympathetic individuals protected me:

"Don't push him like that, he's ill!"

"Come on, friend, courage!" said the big fat man, seeing my nervousness. "I'll take you to a hospital myself."

He took me by the arm; he set about pushing through the crowd, shouting:

"Make room for an invalid!"

The dutch crowd were not particularly fierce: they let us pass, but tagged along after us. We strode along the canal, followed by a compact multitude; with people crying:

"It's a cannibal from Borneo!"

*

Finally, we got to the hospital. It was visiting time. They led me to an intern, a young man with blue glasses, who received me sullenly. My companion said to him:

"It's a savage from the colonies."

"What, a savage!" cried the other.

He removed his glasses to look at me. For a moment his surprise held him immobile. He asked me brusquely:

"Can you see?"

"I see very well …"

I had spoken too fast.

"It's his accent!" said the fat man proudly. "Say it again, friend!"

I repeated it, and made myself understood.

"They are not human eyes …" murmured the student. "And the colour! … Is that the colour of your race?"

I said, making a terrible effort to slow myself down:

"I've come to be seen by a scientist!"

"You're not ill then?"

"No!"

"And you're from Borneo?"

"No!"

"Where are you from then?"

"From Zwartendam, near Duisbourg!"

"So why did your companion claim that you were from Borneo?"

"I didn't want to contradict him … "

"And you want to see a scientist?"

"Yes."

"Why?"

"To be studied."

"To make some money?"

"No, nothing like that."

"You're not a poor person? A beggar?"

"No!"

"Why are you so keen to be studied?"

"My constitution … "

But I had again, despite my efforts, spoken too fast. I had to repeat myself.

"Are you sure that you can see me?" he demanded, looking fixedly at me. "Your eyes are like callouses … "

"I see very well."

And, moving right and left, I swiftly picked up objects, put them down, through them into the air and caught them.

"Extraordinary!" continued the young man.

His voice now softer, almost amicable, filled me with hope:

"Listen," he said finally, "I think doctor Van den Heuvel might well be interested in your case … I'll go and tell him about it. You wait in the next room … And, about …. I forgot … you're not ill, then?"

"Not at all."

"Good. Come on … in here … the doctor won't be long … "

I found myself seated amongst monsters conserved in alcohol: foetuses, children of bestial form, colossal frogs, vaguely anthropomorphic reptiles.

This is definitely, I thought to myself, my waiting-room … Aren't I a candidate for one of these formaldehyde sepulchres?

VII

When doctor Van den Heuvel appeared, emotion overwhelmed me: I had the frisson of the promised land, the joy of touching it, the fear of being banished from it. The doctor, a large bald man, with a powerful analytical gaze, a soft but stubborn mouth, examined me in silence, and, as with everybody, my excessive thinness, my great height, my encircled eyes, my violet complexion, were causes for astonishment.

"You say that you would like to be studied?" he asked finally.

I responded with great force, almost violence:

"Yes!"

He smiled in an approving manner, and then posed the customary question:

"Do you see well with those eyes?"

"Very well … I can even see through trees and clouds …"

But I had spoken too quickly. He shot me a disquieted glance. I reiterated, sweating great drops:

"I can even see through trees and clouds …"

"Really! That would be extraordinary … Well then! What do you see beyond that door … there?"

He indicated to me a long-disused door.

"A large glass-fronted bookcase … a large carved table …"

"Really!" he repeated, stupefied.

My chest expanded, a profound peace descended upon my soul.

The scientist remained in silence for a few seconds, then:

"You speak with great difficulty."

"Otherwise I speak too fast! … I can't speak slowly."

"Alright, then tell me something in your usual voice."

I recounted then the episode of my entry into Amsterdam. He listened with great attention, with an air of intelligence and observation that I had never before encountered from my own people. He did not understand anything I said, but he displayed great sagacity in his analysis:

"If I'm not mistaken … you pronounce between fifteen and twenty syllables per second, that is to say three or four times more than the human ear can perceive. Your voice, also, is far more acute than anything I have heard from a human voice. Your gestures, excessively rapid, correspond to your speech … Your constitution is probably as a whole more rapid than ours."

"I run," I said, "quicker than a greyhound … I write …"

"Ah!" he interrupted. "Let's see your writing …"

I scribbled a few words down on a blotter he handed to me, the first quite legible, the others more and more mixed-up, abbreviated:

"Perfect!" he said, and a certain pleasure was mixed with his astonishment. "I really think that I can count myself lucky in making your acquaintance. It will assuredly be most interesting to study you."

"It's my most dear, my only desire!"

"And mine, obviously … Science … "

He appeared preoccupied, in a reverie; he finally said:

"If only we could find some more easy way to communicate … "

He paced the room from end to end, his brow furrowed.

All of a sudden:

"Am I stupid! You must learn stenography, by jove!...
Eh! ... eh! ... "

A jovial expression appeared on his face:

"And I forgot about the phonograph ... the perfect
confidante! It will allow us to turn it slower for listening
than for recording ... That's it then: you will stay with me
during your stay in Amsterdam!"

The joy of a satisfactory vocation, of never having to
spend vain and sterile days! Before the intelligent person
of the doctor, in this scientific milieu, I felt a delicious
well-being; the melancholy of my soul's solitude, the regret
for my lost faculties, the long misery of a pariah that had
crushed me for so many years, all disappeared, evaporated
in the sentiment of a new life, a real life, a destiny saved!

VIII

The next morning the doctor made all the necessary
arrangements. He wrote to my parents; he arranged
a stenography teacher for me and procured some
phonographs. Since he was extremely rich, and science
was everything to him, there was no experiment he wasn't
ready to try, and my vision, my hearing, my musculature,
the colour of my skin were subjected to scrupulous investigations, the results of which made him more and more
enthusiastic, crying:

"What wonders!"

I realised with marvel, after the first few days, how
important it was that things were carried out methodically,
from the simple to the complex, from the simple abnormality

to the marvellous abnormality. I myself also had recourse to a little skill of mine, of which I made no secret with the doctor: that is, only to reveal my faculties bit by bit.

It was the rapidity of my perception and my movements that occupied him first of all. He hypothesised that the subtlety of my hearing corresponded with the speed of my speech. Graduated experiments on more and more fugitive sounds, which I was able to repeat back with ease, the sound of ten or fifteen people speaking at the same time, each of which I was able to understand perfectly well, proved the point clearly enough. The speed of my vision was no less proved by experiment; in comparative studies of my ability to decompose into separate images the gallop of a horse or the flight of an insect, and the same task carried out with instantaneous photographic apparati, demonstrated the superiority of my eye. As to my perception of ordinary things, the simultaneous movement of a group of people, of children playing, pebbles thrown in the air or little balls thrown in an alley to be counted as they flew – it amazed the family and friends of the doctor.

My walks in the large garden, my bounds of twenty metres at a time, the instantaneity with which I seized objects or replaced them were even more admired, not by the doctor, but by those around him. And it was a totally new pleasure, for the children and the wife of my host, on a walk in the country, to see me run ahead of a rider at a gallop or to follow the flight of swallows: there was no thoroughbred that I could not outrun by two-thirds, whatever the running, no bird that I could not easily outdo.

As for the doctor, more and more satisfied with the results of his experiments, he defined me thus: "A human being endowed, in all his movements, with a speed incomparably superior, not only to other humans, but to that of all known animals. This speed, found in every particular of his organism just as in the whole, makes him a being so distinct from the rest of creation that he merits a new category for himself alone in the animal hierarchy. As to the most curious disposition of his eye, as for the violet tint of his skin, we must consider them as simple indices of this special state."

Verification made of my muscular system, he found nothing remarkable, except for an excessive thinness. Neither did my ears seem to show any peculiar characteristics; nor, for that matter did my epidermis, except of course for its unusual colour. As for hair, of a rich dark colour, a violet-black, it was fine like a spider's web, and the doctor made a meticulous examination of it:

"We shall have to dissect you!" he sometimes said laughingly to me.

Time passed most pleasantly. I had picked up stenography very quickly, thanks to the intensity of my desire to do so, and the natural aptitude which I displayed for this method of rapid transcription, to which I actually introduced further new abbreviations. I began by taking notes, which the stenographer transcribed; and for the rest, we had phonographs, made to a design specially formulated by the doctor, and which we found perfectly suited to rendering my speech, at a slower speed.

The confidence of my host, over time, became unreserved. In the first weeks, he had not been able to avoid the suspicion – quite natural, of course – that the peculiarity of my faculties was not unaccompanied by some form of insanity, some cerebral derangement. Once disabused of this fear, our relationship became wholly cordial, and, I believe, equally captivating for both parties. We made an analytical examination of my perception of objects through a great number of different substances said to be opaque, and of the darkish coloration which water, glass and quartz had for me when a certain thickness. You will remember that I saw very well through wood, the leaves of trees, clouds and many other substances, but that I could distinguished but poorly the bottom of a pool of water half a metre deep, and that glass, although it might be transparent to me, was less so than for the common man, and was of a dark colour. A large piece of glass appeared almost black to me. The doctor was able to convince himself at leisure of all of these peculiarities – and was struck above all by observing how I was able to make out the stars on cloudy nights.

It was only at this time that I began to tell him how colour also seemed different to me. Experiments showed beyond doubt that red, orange, yellow, green, blue and indigo were as completely invisible to me as infra-red and ultra-violet to the normal eye. On the other hand, I was able to demonstrate that I could perceive violet, and, beyond violet, a range of graduated shades, a colour spectrum at least twice the range of that which extends from red to violet.[34]

This astonished the doctor more than all the rest. His

---

34. Quartz gave me a spectrum of around eight colours: extreme violet and seven colours beyond it within ultra-violet. But there remained about another eight colours which quartz did not separate further but which other substances separated more or less.

study of it was lengthy, minute, and, meanwhile, conducted with infinite art. It became, in the hands of this able experimenter, the source of some very subtle discoveries in the order of the sciences, providing the key to phenomena as far removed as magnetism, affinity, inductive power, and guiding them towards new notions of physiology. To know that a certain metal contained a series of unknown gradations, which varied under pressure, temperature, electrical charge, that the finest gases had distinct colours, even when very thin; to learn of the infinite richness of tones of objects that appear more or less black, but which display a gamut of tones more magnificent in ultra-violet than all the known colours; to know lastly how an electrical circuit, the bark of a tree, the skin of a man, vary in unknown nuances during a day, an hour, a minute, – it is easy to imagine all the many lines of research an ingenious scientist might initiate on the basis of such notions.

With his study, whatever it might be, the doctor was plunged into the delight of scientific novelty, set against which the products of the imagination are cold like ashes from the fire. He never ceased exclaiming to me:

"It's clear! Your extra-perception of light is, essentially, just an effect of the great speed which your organism has developed!"

We worked patiently for a whole year without my making any mention of the Moedigen – I absolutely wanted to convince my host, to give him innumerable proofs of my visual faculties before venturing to bestowing on him the supreme confidence of this disclosure. Finally, the moment came when I felt I could reveal all.

IX

It was one morning, during a lovely autumn full of clouds, which had rolled along for a week in the dome of the sky, without any rain having fallen. Van den Heuvel and myself were walking in the garden. The doctor was silent and thoughtful, completely absorbed by speculations of which I was the principal object. Finally, he began to speak:

"It's a lovely dream to be able to see through the clouds … to penetrate right to the ether, whereas we … blind as we are … "

"If only I saw just the sky!" I replied.

"Ah! Yes, the whole world is so different for you … "

"Even more different than I've told you so far!"

"How?" he cried, with avid curiosity, "have you hidden something from me?"

"The most important thing of all!"

He stood before me, staring at me fixedly, with a look of veritable anguish mixed with who knows what mystical intuition.

"Yes, the most important thing!"

We had arrived outside the house; I called for a phonograph. The instrument they brought me was of a scale perfected for my friend, able to record a long discourse; the domestic placed it on the stone table where the doctor and his family took their coffee on sunny summer days. The apparatus, a miracle of clockwork, lent itself admirably to discussions. Thus we pursued our conversation almost like a normal conversation:

"Yes, I hid the main thing from you, wanting to make sure first that I had your full trust. And even now, after all the discoveries my organism has allowed you to make, I still think it will be hard for you to believe me, at least at first."

I stopped to repeat the phrase using the machine: I saw the doctor become pale, the pallor of great scientists observing a new disposition of matter. His hands trembled.

"I will believe you!" he said with a certain solemnity.

"Even if I tell you that our creation, I mean our animal and vegetable world, is not the only life on earth ... that there is another, just as vast, just as multiform ... invisible to your eyes?"

He suspected some sort of occultism and couldn't stop himself from saying:

"The world of the afterlife ... souls, the ghosts of departed spirits?"

"No, no, nothing like that. A world of living beings condemned like us to a brief life, to organic needs, to birth, to growth, to struggle ... a world as precarious and ephemeral as our own, a world subject to laws just as fixed as ours, if not identical, a world that is also a prisoner of the earth, just as helpless before its contingencies ... but nevertheless totally different to ours, without any influence on us, as we are without influence on it, – except for changes which it can effect upon our common ground, the earth, or by parallel modifications that we can make to this same earth."

I no longer knew whether Van den Heuvel believed me, but had no doubt he was in the throes of intense emotion:

"Are they fluid, then?" he asked.

"This is something I can't answer, because their properties are too contradictory to the idea which we have of matter. The earth is resistant to them as to us, the same for most minerals, although they can enter a little into a humus. They are totally impermeable, solid, in relation to each other. But they pass through, if with some difficulty, plants, animals, organic tissues; and ourselves, they pass through us in the same way. If one of them could perceive us, we would appear to them perhaps as fluid in relation to them, as they appear so in relation to us; but it would probably be unable to conclude anything, it would be so struck by parallel contradictions … Their form has the strange quality that it has no thickness at all. Their size varies to infinity. I have known one reach one hundred metres in length, other common ones as small as our smallest insects. Their nutrition is taken, for some of them, from the earth and from meteors; with others, from meteors and from other individuals of their kingdom, without this ever being cause for murder as it is with us, since it suffices that the strongest takes some energy and that this energy can be tapped without exhausting the sources of life."

The doctor said brusquely:

"Have you seen them since childhood?"

I suppose that he suspected some more or less recent disorder in my organism:

"Since I was a child!" I answered energetically … "I can give you all the details you want."

"Do you see them now?"

"I see them … the garden contains a great many… "

"Where?"

"On the path, on the lawns, on the walls, in the air … because, you see, there are terrestrial and aerial varieties … and also aquatic ones, but those ones rarely leave the surface of the water."

"Are there many of them everywhere?"

"Yes, but less in towns than in the fields, less in houses than in the streets. Those which like to be indoors tend to be smaller, doubtless because of the difficulty of moving about, although wooden doors are no obstacle to them."

"And iron … glass … brick…"

"They are impermeable to them."

"Can you describe one to me … one of the larger ones?"

"I can see one near to that tree. Its form is extremely elongated, quite irregular. It is convex on the right, concave to the left, with bulges and notches: one might imagine it as the projection of a gigantic, squat larva. But its structure is not typical of the Kingdom, because structure varies a great deal from one species (if you can use the word) to another. Its infinite thinness is, on the other hand, something common to all of them: they are never more than a tenth of a millimetre, whereas they are five feet long and forty centimetres at the widest point. What defines them most of all, and their entire Kingdom, are the lines which traverse them, in every direction, finishing in webs which get finer between two systems of lines. Each system of lines has a centre, a sort of slightly raised patch beneath the mass of the body, or sometimes on the contrary, sunken. These centres have no fixed form, sometimes almost circular, or elliptical, sometimes circumscribed or spiraloid, occasionally divided by many loops. They are astonishingly mobile, and their size varies from hour to hour. Their outline palpitates strongly, with a sort of transversal undulation. Generally, the lines which lead out from it are thick, although they can also be quite fine; they diverge, ending up in an infinity of delicate traces which gradually disappear. Some lines, meanwhile, far paler than others, don't belong to any centre; they remain isolated in the system and grow without changing in colour: these lines are able to move around the body, and to vary their curves, whilst the centres and the lines radiating from them remain stable in their respective places … As to the colours of my Moedig, I can't hope to describe them: there is nothing perceptible to the register of your eye, none of them have a name for you. They are extremely bright in the webs, less so in the centres, very faint in the independent lines which, however, do have a sheen, a metallic ultra-violet sheen, if I could describe it like that … I have collected various observations on the way of life, the nutrition, and the autonomy of the Moedigen, but I don't want to give them to you now."

I became silent; the doctor replayed several times the words inscribed on our impeccable intermediary, and then remained a long time in silence himself. I had never seen him in such a state before: his face was rigid, frozen, his eyes glassy, cataleptic; sweat ran down his temples and dampened his hair. He tried to speak but could not. Trembling, he made a round of the garden, and, when he reappeared, his look and his mouth expressed a violent, fervent, religious passion: one might have taken him for a disciple of some new faith rather than a serene researcher of phenomena.

Finally he murmured:

"You've got me beat! Everything you say seems hopelessly lucid, and have I really the right to doubt you, after all the marvels you have revealed to me?"

"Doubt," I said to him warmly, "Doubt as strongly as you can … Your experiments will only be more fertile for it!"

"Ah!," he replied in a dreamy voice, "it is a veritable miracle, and so magnificently superior to the vain miracles of legend and fable! … My poor human intelligence is so tiny compared to such knowledge! ... but my enthusiasm is infinite. However, something in me still doubts …"

"Then let us begin work on dissipating your uncertainties: our efforts will be repaid a hundredfold!"

X

We worked. It took several weeks for the doctor to fully dispose of his doubts. Ingenious experiments, irrefutable correspondences between each of my affirmations, two or three lucky discoveries about the influence of the Moedigen on atmospheric phenomena, left no remaining place for equivocation. The addition of the eldest son of Van den Heuvel, a young man full of the greatest scientific aptitude, increased yet more the fecundity of our work and the certitude of our findings.

Thanks to the methodical spirit of my companions, thanks to their power of investigation and classification – faculties which I was assimilating more and more – that which, in my understanding of the Moedigen, was unco-ordinated and confused was transformed in no time. Discoveries multiplied, rigorous experiments gave firm results, from evidence which, in ancient times and even in recent centuries, might have suggested at most some fanciful speculations.

It is now five years that we have been pursuing our research: they are far, very far, from finished. The first report of our work will not appear for some time yet. We are, however, determined as a strict rule not to submit to haste: our discoveries are of too important an order to be reported but in the greatest of detail, with the greatest of patience, and with the most minute precision. We have no other researcher to compete with, no brief to follow nor any ambition to satisfy. We exist at such heights that vanity and pride are no longer an issue. How can we reconcile the delicious joys of our work with the miserable enticement of human fame? In any case, isn't the random chance of my constitution the source of the whole affair? In which case, how base it would be of us to glorify ourselves because of it!

We live passionately, always on the verge of marvellous things; but also we live in an immutable serenity.

*

Something has happened to me which may add to the interest of my life, and which, in my rest, has brought me infinite joy. You well know how ugly I am, how strange, fit to scare away any young lady. However I have found a companion who has been able to accept my affections to the point of our being happy together.

She is a young girl, a hysteric, with a nervous illness, who we encountered one day in a hospice in Amsterdam. You would say she had a miserable look about her, as pale as plaster, hollow-cheeked, wild-eyed. But to me, her aspect seemed agreeable and her company most charming. My presence, far from astonishing her, as it did all the others, seemed from the first to please and to comfort her. I was touched by her, I wanted to see her again.

It did not take long to notice that I had a beneficial effect upon her health and her well-being. On closer examination, it appeared that I affected her magnetically: my approach, and above all the touch of my hands, communicated a gaiety to her, a serenity, a truly restorative spiritual equilibrium. In return, I found great joy being with her. Her face appeared so pretty to me; her paleness and her thin body were the fondest delicacy for me; her eyes, capable of seeing the glow of lovers, like those of many hyperesthetics, hadn't for me in the slightest that character of wildness of which she was accused.

In a word, I felt a great affection towards her, which she reciprocated with passion. So that I took the decision to marry her, and arrived easily at this goal, thanks to the goodwill of my friends.

The union was a happy one. My wife's health returned to her, although she remains extremely sensitive and frail; I tasted the joy of being, in principle at least, equal to other men. But my destiny has been even more enviable since six months ago: a child was born to us, and in this child are united all the characteristics of my constitution. Colour, vision, hearing, extreme rapidity of movement, nutrition – he promises to be an exact replication of my organism.

The doctor watches him grow up with delight: a delicious hope has come to us – that the study of the life of the Moedigen, of that Kingdom parallel to our own, that study which demands such time and such patience, shall not end when I am no more. My son will continue it, no doubt, in his turn. And why should he not find collaborators of genius, capable of taking it to new heights? Why should he also, in turn, not father new witnesses of the invisible world?

And may I not myself expect more children, may I not hope that my dear wife will give birth to new offspring of my flesh, just like their father? … In thinking of it, my heart trembles, an infinite beatitude overcomes me, and I feel blessed amongst men.

Goldsmiths
UNIVERSITY
OF LONDON
Centre for the Study of
Invention and Social Process

COLLAPSE
Independent Journal of
Philosophical Research and Development
www.urbanomic.com

Speculative Realism

A One-Day Workshop
1–7pm, Friday 27 April 2007
Lecture Hall, Ben Pimlott Building
Goldsmiths, University of London
New Cross, London SE14 6NW

Participants: Ray Brassier (Middlesex), Iain Hamilton Grant (UWE), Graham Harman (American University in Cairo), Quentin Meillassoux (Ecole Normale Supérieure)

Contemporary 'continental' philosophy often prides itself on having overcome the age-old metaphysical battles between realism and idealism. Subject-object dualism, whose repudiation has turned into a conditioned reflex of contemporary theory, has supposedly been destroyed by the critique of representation and supplanted by various ways of thinking the fundamental correlation between thought and world.

But perhaps this anti-representational (or 'correlationist') consensus – which exceeds philosophy proper and thrives in many domains of the humanities and the social sciences – hides a deeper and more insidious idealism. Is realism really so 'naïve'? And is the widespread dismissal of representation and objectivity the radical, critical stance it so often claims to be?

This workshop will bring together four philosophers whose work, although shaped by different concerns, questions some of the basic tenets of a 'continental' orthodoxy while eschewing the reactionary prejudices of common-sense. Speculative realism is not a doctrine but the umbrella term for a variety of research programmes committed to upholding the autonomy of reality, whether in the name of transcendental physicalism, object-oriented philosophy, or abstract materialism, against the depredations of anthropocentrism.

Schedule
Chair: Alberto Toscano (Sociology, Goldsmiths)
1–1.15 Welcome
1.15–2.30 Ray Brassier
2.30–3.45 Iain Hamilton Grant
3.45–4.15 Break
4.15–5.30 Graham Harman
5.30–7.00 Quentin Meillassoux
7.00–8.00 Drinks

for further information, and advance excerpts of speakers' work see http://www.goldsmiths.ac.uk/csisp/
THIS EVENT IS FREE, BUT PLEASE REGISTER BEFOREHAND BY EMAILING a.toscano@gold.ac.uk

Speculative Realism

Ray Brassier, Iain Hamilton Grant,
Graham Harman, Quentin Meillassoux

'Speculative Realism: A One-Day Workshop' took place on 27 April 2007 at Goldsmiths, University of London, under the auspices of the Centre for the Study of Invention and Social Process, co-sponsored by **COLLAPSE**. Rather than announcing the advent of a new theoretical 'doctrine' or 'school', the event conjoined four ambitious philosophical projects – all of which boldly problematise the subjectivistic and anthropocentric foundations of much of 'continental philosophy' while differing significantly in their respective strategies for superseding them. It is precisely this uniqueness of each participant that allowed a fruitful discussion to emerge. Alongside the articulation of various challenges to certain idealistic premises, a determination of the obstacles that any contemporary realism must surmount was equally in effect. Accordingly, some of the key issues under scrutiny included the status of science and epistemology in contemporary philosophy, the ontological constitution of thought, and the nature of subject-independent objects.

However, as workshop moderator and co-organiser Alberto Toscano indicated, a common feature of the work presented was the implication that from a genuine interrogation of the continental tradition necessarily ensues a repudiation of the orthodoxies symptomatic of that tradition's conceptual exhaustion (the most visible of which being the seemingly endless deluge of insipid secondary literature and the 'X-ian' identity of its authors), thus rendering the task of doing philosophy 'in one's own name' essential once again. 'Speculative Realism', then, forces contemporary philosophy to make a decision, but it is not so much one concerning idealism or realism. Rather, at stake here is the possibility of a future for audacious and original philosophical thought as a discourse on the nature of reality – or, as one might otherwise call it: philosophy itself.

Presentation by Ray Brassier

Rather than reading a paper, I'm just going to make some general remarks about what I take to be the really significant points of convergence and divergence between Iain, Graham, Quentin, and myself. The fundamental thing we seem to share is obviously a willingness to re-interrogate or to open up a whole set of philosophical problems that were taken to have been definitively settled by Kant, certainly, at least, by those working within the continental tradition. This is why, as I'm sure everyone knows, the term 'realist' in continental philosophy is usually taken to be some kind of insult – only someone who really hasn't understood Kant could ever want to rehabilitate something like metaphysical realism, or any form of realism which does not depend upon some kind of transcendental guarantor, whether that guarantor is subjectively instantiated by pure apperception, or construed in terms of linguistic practices, or a communicational consensus, etc. Much of the mainstream of nineteenth and twentieth century post-Kantian philosophy is about simply redefining, generalising, specifying, these transcendental structures or conditions of cognitive legitimation. And in a way, it doesn't really matter whether you claim to have replaced the subject and the object with some form of communicational consensus or being-in-the-world or any variant of the latter on these issues: The transcendental function has been variously encoded in different versions of post-Kantian continental philosophy. But the thing that seems to be assumed within this tradition, the thing that actually Graham's work first brought out to me, is the notion that whatever structure there is in the world has to be transcendentally imposed or generated or guaranteed, which is to say that objectivity can only be a function of synthesis. And it's striking that in post-Kantian philosophy the difference between Kant and Hegel seems to be that where Kant will localise the synthesising function in something like pure apperception or wholly on the side of the subject, Hegel and the various forms of objective idealism will say that reality itself is self-synthesising, that there is a kind of principle of synthesis encoded in objective reality itself. So that, famously, in Hegel's objective idealism, the relational synthesis which Kant takes to be constitutive of objectivity is simply transplanted from its localisation in the subject and construed rather as the relation between subject and object, which Hegel recodes as the 'self-relating negativity' that yields the structure of reality. So the question is: If you refuse to say that synthesis – the synthesis which produces objective structure – is anchored in a subject, does this mean that you have to idealise the real by attributing to it this capacity for self-relation? A capacity for self-synthesis whereby a continuum of relation itself yields the type of discontinuity that gives rise to discrete objects? In other words, is there a principle of intelligibility encoded in physical reality?

This is absolutely the key issue, I think, in Iain's book on Schelling.[1] And according to Iain's reconstruction, Schelling proposes an alternative variant of objective idealism, one wherein structure and objectivity are intrinsic to nature, but the ideal structures that are intrinsic to or inherent in physical reality are no longer construed in terms of a dialectic of opposition and contradiction. In Iain's brilliant reconstruction of Schellingianism, what you get is something like a 'transcendental physics', a physics of the All, where ideas are differential dynamisms, attractors immanent to and inherent in material reality. So, nature is self-organising. And the ideal structure of nature produces the structure of thinking. But if cognition is a result, a product – if it's every bit as conditioned as any other natural phenomenon – the question then becomes whether there's any reason to suppose that thought can limn or grasp the ultimate structure of reality at any given moment, any specific historical juncture. Because the key thing, if you're committed to a transcendental realism, of which Iain provides a powerful reconstruction in his book, is that it is the structure of material reality that generates the structure of thinking. But this means that one must discount any appeal to intellectual intuition, which is to say, the idea that thinking can simply transcend its own material,

---

1. Iain Hamilton Grant, *Philosophies of Nature After Schelling* (London: Continuum, 2006).

neurobiological conditions of organisation and effectuation and grasp the noumenal structure of reality as it is in itself. The problem is this: If the structure of reality produces the structure of thinking, then the challenge is to avoid both transcendentalism and a kind of pragmatism which would say that evolutionary history simply guarantees the congruence between representation and reality as a function of adaptational necessity, so that only creatures that have a cognitive apparatus that is appropriate to their kind of biophysical environment will be able to survive. And this is a claim that fuels much of naturalised epistemology, but one that I think is metaphysically problematic, because there is no reason to suppose that evolutionary adaptation would favour exhaustively accurate beliefs about the world. There's no reason to suppose that evolution would infallibly provide human organisms with a cognitive apparatus that can accurately track the salient features or the deep structure of reality. So in other words, there seems to be a kind of incompatibility between any pragmatic, adaptationist rationale for cognitive functioning, and scientific realism, which says that the physical structures of reality, as articulated by the natural sciences, can't simply be explained in terms of their usefulness as viable survival strategies. And the force of Iain's book is to try to propose what he calls a 'transcendental naturalism' – which claims that you can explain the emergence of the structure of ideation from the ideal structure of physical reality, so that ideation would be capable of tracking the ideal dynamisms, the transcendental dynamisms, that underlie merely empirical or merely somatic reality.

An important distinction in Iain's book is between the Aristotelian-Kantian reduction of materiality to somatic or corporeal reality – the idea that to be material means to be some sort of body with a set of perceptible properties – and the transcendental materialism that Iain ascribes to Schelling, where the real material structures are the abstract differential dynamisms that generate and produce bodies, organisms, and spatio-temporal objects, but can never be reduced to them. But here's one consequence of this: if the structure of ideation is a function of the ideal structure of material self-organisation, then the process is ongoing – and Iain emphasises this – so it's simply not the case that biological history has reached some sort of apex in human consciousness. And if the process is still ongoing and will keep going, then not only is there more to know about the structure of *reality* than we currently know just now; there's also more to know about the structure of *ideation* than we currently know. And I think this presents a quandary for someone who's committed to a version of speculative realism: transcendental physicalism insists that there are real conditions of ideation but that these conditions have an ideal structure. The question then is: can the specific conceptual details of these ideal physical structures be satisfactorily identified using the currently available resources of conceptual ideation? What does this mean? It means using either the available registers of mathematical formalisation available to contemporary science; *or* – if we are thinking in terms of transcendental philosophy – a set of suitably generic conceptual categories. But then, can we be sure that any of the abstract conceptual categories in terms of which we propose to reconstruct these ideal structures

Ray Brassier

are applicable? Can we be sure that these self-organising features of material reality can be linguistically encoded and encapsulated? In other words, are the resources of natural language sufficient to successfully articulate the transcendental dynamisms that fuel material processes? Or do we need to discover more about the machinery and structure of ideation before we can confidently specify the physical structure of nature? So, as regards the characterisation of ideas as 'phase space attractors', the question is whether that could ever satisfactorily characterise the underlying dynamisms of physical nature. More importantly, with regard to the category of 'dynamism', which, as Iain shows, goes back to Plato and Aristotle: Is it enough simply to supplant a somatic or Aristotelian metaphysics, which equates material reality with constituted bodies, products, organisms, and objects with a metaphysics of dynamisms as the real, underlying motors of self-organisation, or ultimate generators of material structure?

So, I guess what I'm asking is: what is the status of dynamism in speculative physics? Is it truly adequate to physical infrastructures? Or might it not be contaminated by certain folk-physical prejudices? I agree with Iain about re-inscribing the machinery of ideation within the physical realm, and about the need for a transcendental naturalisation of epistemology, but wonder whether that re-inscription provides a warrant for what he calls 'speculative physics'. What is the relationship between the dynamic structure of the idea and the mathematical register deployed for its formalisation? So my question to Iain then is really about the status of epistemology within transcendental materialism: Although the advantages of the latter vis-à-vis the pragmatic variants of naturalised epistemology are fairly evident, I think there's an issue here about what articulates ideation and the mathematical resources of ideation that have been crucial in ridding us of this parochial Aristotelian model of physical reality. It was the mathematisation of nature that definitively ruined and shredded the medieval Book of the World. And the question is, can we rehabilitate a form of transcendental or speculative materialism or realism that would also explain the success of mathematical formalisation in supplanting the old, pre-Galilean models of physics and metaphysics?

One final point, concerning the nature of dynamism, and this is a general point related to process philosophy:

If you privilege productivity, if these ideal generative dynamisms that structure and constitute material reality can be characterised in terms of the primacy of production over product, then the question is, how do we account for the interruptions of the process? How do we account for discontinuity in the continuum of production? And while I have no doubt that it's possible to do so, I think it's a significant problem for any process philosophy that wants to defend or prosecute a form of ontological monism based on something like 'pure productivity', 'pure becoming', 'duration', or whatever one chooses to call it. Because then it seems that you always have to introduce or posit some sort of conceptual contrary, some principle of deceleration, interruption, disintensification or whatever, in order to account for the upsurges of stability and continuity and consistency within this otherwise untrammelled flux of becoming and pure process. So even if one then goes on to reintegrate it into the former as a mere moment, one still has to explain why there is anything but pure process or why the processual flux is ever momentarily stabilized. It's striking that you see this in Bergson: the idea that you need something to explain what interrupts the process, what produces or introduces discontinuity into the flux of becoming.

And I think Graham's contribution lies precisely in this key area. The idea is that if you begin with some form of preliminary methodological dualism of production and product or, in its classic Bergsonian articulation, something like duration and space, then you need to explain what interrupts the continuum – how duration ever externalises itself or coagulates into something like a spatial fixity or stasis. And Graham gets around this problem by simply having a metaphysics of objects, which in a way removes the question of synthesis altogether. What's striking about Graham's account is that you don't need to explain how objects are synthesised, because you simply take objects as nested within one another. You have this kind of infinite nesting of objects within objects within objects … Every relation between objects itself unfolds within another object. So Graham turns the question around by showing how the problem consists in showing how discontinuous, autonomous objects can ever enter into relation with one another – his answer is that they do so on the inside of another object. In other words, every relation is itself another object. So what you have then is a kind of egalitarian objective univocity, a kind of ontology of pure objectivity: there are nothing but objects, objects nested within one another, and the really significant metaphysical challenge is explaining their interaction.

But I have two questions vis-à-vis Graham's project: First, Graham explains the interaction between objects in terms of their sensual properties, *i.e.*, no object ever exhausts the ultimate reality of another object. It engages or interacts with it on the basis of a set of sensual or perceptible properties, and it is these that provide the basis for the reciprocal interaction between objects. And my question is: what is the criterion for distinguishing sensible from non-sensible properties for any given object? Is it possible to provide such a criterion without giving it some sort of epistemological slant or formulation? In other words, in order to interact with one another, it seems that objects need to 'know' something about one another. The fire must 'know' that the cotton is not rock; the rock must 'know' that the ice is not water. Whatever kind of interaction objects have, the fact that their interface is possible on the basis of this recognition of something like sensual properties, which are capable of locking together and causing the interaction – well, I think the question is whether it is possible to explain how objects discriminate between the sensual or perceptible and the imperceptible properties of any other object. And this ties into a second question, which is about the status of the distinction between real and imaginary objects for Graham, because, for Graham, it makes no sense to ask whether something is real: everything is real, everything is objective, so nothing is more real than anything else. He provides us with an absolutely egalitarian, flat ontology of objects. But the danger then is – and Graham and I have spoken about this before – that this would simply license too much or result in too liberal a construal of objectivity. For instance, what would be the distinction between a hobbit and a quark here? This is a very serious metaphysical question! And Graham maintains that the properties of the hobbit or any other kind of fictitious, contrived, artificially generated example would be purely imaginary, and of course one can contrive and generate imaginary qualities for imaginary objects. But how do we make the distinction, given that we know that imaginary objects or fictitious entities such as the Virgin Mary or Yahweh or phlogiston seem perfectly capable of producing real effects – it's perfectly possible for these things to generate real effects in so far as people believe in them and do things in the world on the basis of their belief in them. If we say that this is a misdescription, and that there's actually a real object underlying the imaginary object, and it is this real object that causes things to happen, then the question is: on what basis do we make this distinction if not by invoking some form of epistemological criterion that distinguishes between real and imaginary properties or objects?

In other words, my question to Graham is: Is it possible to prosecute an ontology of objects without explaining *how it is that we are able to do so*; *i.e.* how we seem to have to *know* something about objects? This is not to reintroduce the Kantian primacy of the subject, but just to say that even objects seem to have to know certain things about one another in order to interact, just as we seem to have to know something simply in order to be able to describe and identify objects. And Graham is clear that the episte-mological relation, which Kantianism took to be absolutely primary and fundamental – *i.e.*, the subject-object relation-ship – is merely a relation between objects just like any other. It has no kind of epistemological or transcendental primacy, so that explaining how we're able to know the laws of mechanics is an interesting question, but it's not really fundamentally different in kind from explaining how fire is able to burn cotton, or how a marble is able to interact with a table. But I think I want to problematise this issue further – my conviction is that it's not so clear, and that philosophy should do more than simply generate a formal metaphysics of objects; my conviction is that describing or reconstructing the structure of interaction between objects does not exhaust the task of philosophy.

And finally, I'm just going to say a few things about Quentin and how I situate myself vis-à-vis his work. My key reservation concerns the status of intellectual intuition.

Quentin defends the claim that mathematical ideation, mathematical intellection, has a grasp of things-in-themselves. It grasps the intelligible structure of reality. He has an extremely interesting hypothesis about why it's precisely the meaninglessness or the insignificance of mathematical inscription that allows you to grasp what he calls the 'absolute contingency' of reality. But he explicitly wants to rehabilitate the Cartesian project, where mathematical ideation accurately describes the objective structure of reality as it is in itself, against the Kantian one, which would limit the scope of scientific cognition to the phenomenal realm. My question is very simple: Is it possible to abstract ideation from the physical reality which it grasps or apprehends, given what we know since Darwin, *i.e.*, that the capacity for mathematical ideation which underwrites the objectivity of scientific cognition is the result of a long process of evolutionary development? And the question here again is: Can one concede that ideation, even the most sophisticated form of abstract conceptual ideation as it's deployed in mathematical science, simply supervenes on a set of fundamental neurobiological processes? Can one grant this without reducing cognition and ideation to pragmatic expediency – *i.e.*, the claim that we represent the world in the way we do because evolution has guaranteed this congruence between mind and world (a claim which I think provides an extremely feeble warrant for scientific realism)? In other words, can one reject pragmatism, and naturalist pragmatism in particular, without ascribing some kind of mysterious transcendence to thinking; without saying that thinking, and specifically scientific cognition, is this mysterious kind of capacity that human beings have either stumbled upon or had bestowed upon them by some mysterious sort of process, and which it's impossible to try to understand in more rudimentary terms? And I think that arguably *the* most significant philosophical development of the twentieth century is the emergence of a science of cognition; that is, the idea that the process of cognition can be re-integrated into the realm of objective phenomena studied by the empirical sciences. In other words, there's a circle here, and a circle which, I think, is too quickly disqualified as vicious by transcendental philosophy. Husserl tried to disqualify psychologism on the grounds that if you reduce ideation to a set of psychological processes, then you remove the dimension of necessity, of logico-mathematical validity, which is the guarantor for the cognitive authority of the natural sciences. In other words, you reduce scientific discourse to a discourse like any other discourse, simply a way of speaking, and you basically turn into Richard Rorty.

So, as I see it, the key challenge for speculative realism is: Can one be a realist about the sorts of entities and processes postulated by the sciences without having to shore up that commitment to realism with some sort of pragmatism on the one hand, or transcendentalism on the other? Can one be a naturalist without turning into Richard Rorty, and can one maintain that what science says is true without becoming a Husserlian or something of that ilk? And I think this is a really interesting question; I think this is where some kind of communication is needed between the speculative audacity which is a characteristic of so-called 'continental philosophy' and the really admirable level of engagement with the empirical sciences which is a feature of the most interesting work being done specifically in the kind of Anglo-American philosophy of mind that engages directly with, or that sees its project as continuous with, cognitive science. So, can one be a transcendental realist without idealising ideation, but without reducing it to a set of pragmatic functions either?

*

IAIN HAMILTON GRANT: This is fascinating, Ray, not least because I've never heard anyone talk about my work before! But several things you mentioned brought to mind certain features which I think are perhaps necessary to any speculative project. One of them is a certain commitment to a variety of realism, and the question is, which realism? And my question is: Is it possible that there is a realism which is in some sense eliminativist? Because if so, then there are all sorts of ontological problems with that. If not, then, if nothing can be eliminated, then we have a situation where it no longer makes sense to ask, 'What is the difference between a hobbit and a quark?', or for that matter, between Rorty and Husserl! Actually, is there one? Or rather what are the differences? There are several differences between these entities, but to use a difference as a disqualification for their being 'real' or not is simply to beg the question about realism, fundamentally. And for that reason, it seems to me that a non-eliminative realism is committed to becoming a form of idealism, in which case we merely extend realism to the Ideas: In which case we no longer have the problem of the separativity, the subtraction, of ideation from nature, which you were suggesting might be a problem; nor do we have the reducibility to a simple state of affairs whose mere existence guarantees an equilibrium reached between the forces of nature and this highly evolved product or what have you – what you've described as 'pragmatism'. So really my question to you is – and this is also in the light of what reading I've done of your book,[2] really – what are the grounds on which it would become possible for any realist to say, '*x* or class *x* or category *x* cannot and does not enjoy being'?

RB: Well, the traditional way, although it may be completely implausible, is to say that to be real is to make a difference. Anything that makes a difference is real. And of course, then you have to say, 'Well, it has to be a *real* difference, so what do you mean by *real* difference?' And one traditional response to this is that anything that has effects, anything that produces effects, must be real, no matter how else it might be qualified. And this is the key question for Graham, who refuses any distinction between the real and the imaginary, so that it doesn't make sense to ask if anything is more real than anything else. I can see why, because it seems that the difficulties attendant upon trying to articulate a difference between what is real and what isn't just seem insuperable. But it seems to me that if you're willing to grant that we know more about the world than we used to – which I know some people are not willing to grant, but which I'm kind of desperately wedded to – then it seems that you want to say that what happens when we discover something real about the world is that we discover the real causal mechanism, we discover what is *actually* making the difference – so it's

2. Ray Brassier, *Nihil Unbound: Enlightenment and Extinction* (Basingstoke: Palgrave Macmillan, 2007).

not the Virgin Mary who's making the difference, it's a complicated set of processes for which the Virgin Mary is some sort of figurative shorthand. In other words, I'm not simply saying there is no such thing as the Virgin Mary, because clearly there is, in the same sense simply in which there are such things as hobbits or unicorns: the sense in which all these things have made a difference to *our* world, at least. But the claim would be that this is a kind of a folk-language, a kind of linguistic shorthand to describe something else, something that is inapparent, and whose proper description would invoke complex configurations of psychological, as well as socio-historical, processes. In other words, this stuff happens, everyone knows it: why is it that people's apparently false beliefs can have real consequences in the world? The answer would be because we can account for how things can happen even when we ourselves as agents of that happening are deluded about the causally salient factors. There is a way of describing what the salient mechanisms are that produce what's happening. And I think the question of scientific realism is: What are the salient mechanisms that make a difference in the world, that produce difference? In the history of science, phlogiston, calorific fluid, etc. – these things were thought to be viable explanatory categories, and when we dispensed with them, when we said, 'No, that's not an adequate explanation for heat, etc.', we realized we were misconstruing or misdescribing the relevant factors or mechanisms. My conviction – and I think it's a necessary conviction if you want to be a transcendental realist – my conviction would be that we can always misdescribe the structure of reality, but that doesn't mean that there isn't a kind of underlying, deep structure, even if there's always going to be something unsatisfactory or superficial about the mechanisms that we describe. For instance, when Newtonian physics was supplanted by Einsteinian physics – did Einstein 'falsify' Newton? Well, not really, he just showed that his physics had only a limited domain of applicability. And it seems to me that that's the dynamic, the cognitive dynamic that underlies science. It's not that we discover that what we knew was false, but rather that it was limited. This is what it means to find out more about the world, that there's much more going on, and that it turns out to be more complicated, and that we need to forge new resources in order to be able to adequately describe or identify these complex processes. So, in a way, the distinction then wouldn't be between what's real and what isn't real, but between degrees, I suppose – possibly between degrees of adequation. And I think it's possible to describe what adequation would be, what it means for thought to be adequate to its object, without resorting to a Kantian framework. But I'm still groping at this. I really haven't got anything worked out, so these are just kind of intuitions.

GRAHAM HARMAN: Ray also mentioned a few things about my work that I can respond to. First I want to say, though, in your response to Iain you mentioned defining the real as that which has effects, and I would encourage you to stay away from that definition, because then it seems like you're defining the real by something outside the real. So it's not the real in its own right, but something outside of it – potential or something. We can argue about this, but this is why I shy away from that definition, just as I shy away from the definition 'reality means resistance', which you see in Heidegger and Max Scheler and others. That might be a way we measure reality, but that can't be reality in itself, because *something* is resisting. The resistance itself is at best a way of *knowing* the reality.

The last thing you asked about my work was whether I think that this theory of relations between objects exhausts philosophy, and at this point I'm not in a position to say yes or no – but that's definitely my project, that's what I'm trying to say. And just in the last week in London I've decided what I'm going to do for the second half of this next book, which is go through every one of the metaphysical problems that Kant throws out and try to rehabilitate every one of them – such as, 'is there a smallest possible unit of substance, or does the division go on forever?', 'is there freedom or no freedom?' It would be fun to try to rehabilitate all these problems in terms of objects and the relations between them. I was struggling with how to organise that metaphysical part of the manuscript, but I think this is the way to do it, since Kant is the one who destroyed all these problems, according to everyone. Why not just go right in his face and try to bring them all back? Who knows if it will work or not, but it should be fun.

The hobbit and the quark, I think, was the second point, and that's actually easier to deal with than the first. I'm a Latourian on this point. For Latour, every kind of object is real, and you simply judge an actor by how many allies it has, and what sorts of … – I almost said 'effects', I'm contradicting myself – how well it resists tests of strength that are made against it. Clearly a hobbit has to be a real object in some sense, because I can ask 'What is a hobbit?', 'What does a hobbit do?', 'How does it behave?', and this will never be completely reducible to all the things that Tolkien says in all of his novels, because you can imagine new scenarios. You can ask, 'Could a hobbit fit in a Lovecraft story?', 'Could a hobbit fit in a Proust novel?' I would say no. Now why is that? It's never been tried, so why is it that when I mention these possibilities we immediately reject them? It's because you have a sense of what the hobbit is beyond all of the things that have been said about hobbits in films and novels that we already know. So I'd say a hobbit is real. Okay, of course you don't want to say a hobbit is as real as a quark – why not? Or to take an even sharper example, you don't want to say that five hundred imaginary crowns are the same as five hundred real crowns. And the way I would deal with that problem is as follows: The traditional pre-Kantian solution was to say there isn't really anything different in the two. God creates the five hundred real crowns, being becomes a real predicate in the real ones that wasn't there in the imaginary ones. And then Kant says it's not a real predicate, it has to do with our position, namely their relation to us. But why not say that the five hundred real crowns and the five hundred imaginary crowns do not have the same qualities in the first place? They differ in essence, not just existence. That's my solution, and it's not fully worked out yet. The shiny gold lustre of the real coins is not the same as that of the imaginary coins, because somehow qualities are borrowed from the parts of a thing, I would say, and the five hundred real crowns have real parts, the five hundred imaginary crowns do not. So that's the direction I would go in, to answer that: to say that everything is real, and that the qualities of things are not universals. The qualities of things come from individual parts. And then you have to explain what universals are, which is another problem I haven't even touched yet – how do you explain what 'red' means?

The first question you asked was the hardest. Objects interact on the basis of essential properties. In order to interact, objects need to know something of one another. I'm not sure if this answer will satisfy you, but what I say is that objects do not interact with each other directly, but simply somehow allude to each other, and what they're coming in contact with are qualities of each other, that somehow allude to the things. And I think you see this in metaphor, and this is the example I used in *Guerrilla Metaphysics*[3]: The example Max Black uses was 'man is a wolf', which is a different metaphor from 'wolf is a man', it has a completely different effect. When you've got 'man is a wolf' in Black's example you have some sort of elusive human thing there that's being orbited by wolf qualities that are transformed in a human direction. But somehow those qualities allow you access to the human underneath that wolf-man thing, whatever it is. So, things do interact but they interact only on the interior of another object where one of them is merely sensible, or an intentional, object, and you're trying to point at a real object in that way.

I don't want to hog the time here, but I was going to answer Iain's rhetorical question about whether there's a difference between Husserl and Rorty. I think there is a difference, and the difference is that the key to Husserl is the intentional objects. Husserl *is* speaking of the phenomenal

---

3. Graham Harman, *Guerrilla Metaphysics: Phenomenology and the Carpentry of Things* (Chicago: Open Court, 2005).

realm, but he's also speaking of a phenomenal realm broken up into objects that are never fully exemplified by our specific perceptions of them – I think that's his great discovery. These are different from real objects that withdraw and hide as in Heidegger and in various realists. In Husserl what you have are objects that are already there yet somehow covered over with too much detail, so you have to eidetically vary them and circle the thing from many different directions and finally, asymptotically perhaps, get at what the thing is by looking at it from all the different possible angles. And you certainly don't see that in any of the empiricists. Objects are merely arbitrary bundles imposed by us on sense data, for empiricists. Whereas I think the object is really there, organising the qualities, and Merleau-Ponty actually does a nice job on this. I'm not the greatest fan of Merleau-Ponty, but he does a nice job arguing that the black of a pen is not the same as the black of a coat – there's a connotation to the blackness that is different in each case, because the quality is somehow impregnated with the object to which it belongs. So … I will let our visitor from Paris take the reins now.

QUENTIN MEILLASSOUX: Thank you, Graham. I would say the following about formalisation, mathematics, in relation to the world: I don't want to demonstrate that there is a necessary relation between mathematics and reality. My problem is a problem of *possibility*. In *After Finitude*,[4] the problem that I encounter is that of explaining the possibility

4. Quentin Meillassoux, *Après la finitude: Essai sur la nécessité de la contingence* (Paris: Seuil, 2006), translated into English by Ray Brassier as *After Finitude: An Essay on the Necessity of Contingency* (Continuum: London, forthcoming 2008).

of science, physics, being able to describe a world without humans. For a transcendental philosopher, for what I call 'correlationism', this makes no sense – it is an absurd question to ask, 'What would the world be if there were no humans?' 'What would the world be like if we didn't exist?' – This is an absurd question, *the* absurd question, I think, for every Kantian or post-Kantian philosophy. But the problem is that sciences are supposed precisely to explain what the world is like even if there are no humans. What is the world before humanity? What could the world be after humanity? So, my problem is just a problem of possibility. What distinguishes scientific description is its mathematicity. So, the problem that I encounter is to explain how mathematics might possibly be able to describe this world. Of course this description may be deficient, it may be that there is far more in the world than mathematics is able to describe. But at least we must explain the possibility that the theory – a theory which may be refuted in the future – a physical theory, might be able to describe the world. That is the fact I want to explain. I don't feel that contemporary theories are necessarily true – maybe they are false, but maybe they are true; this 'maybe' must be explained. So, it is really a modest position. I just want to explain the possibility of mathematical explanation. For I think this possibility is a condition of an explanation of science itself. By which I mean: how it is possible that mathematics could be able to describe the world, even a world without humans. This is the problem of science.

About Rorty and Husserl, I would say this. I think that every time a Rortian speaks and argues, he always has the following position. He always says that, 'Your discourse is a contingent discourse, a discourse among other possible discourses'. And he will say that about mathematics. So, I will say he has this sort of primitive theme in his mind: Maybe there could be some non-human organism, some extra-terrestrial, that would be able to have a radically different relation to the world – a different perception, different conceptual apparatus, etc. So all discourses are historically or maybe biologically contingent. So I would say that contingency is the ground of every relativist theory. What we have in common with every human or non-human discourse is that we think we are able to be Rortian – even an extra-terrestrial can be Rortian. And imagine an extra-terrestrial which was Rortian – what would he say? He would say the same as the terrestrial Rortian, he would say, 'Maybe all discourses are contingent, maybe there could be other possible discourses, *etc.*'. So contingency is a common property of all relativisms of all times, on all planets. That's why I made contingency the real ground, the universal and eternal ground, of every relativism in the universe – I'm sure of that. So, if there is a certain sure ground of every discourse, which would be accepted by every Rortian – human or non-human – I would say it would be contingency. So, my problem is very simple: are we able to derive, to deduce, from this eternal ground – which, according to me, is contingency – the capacity of mathematics to possibly be able to describe a world without humanity? I have the ground, I have the problem. Between them what I try to show is, if contingency is eternally true, maybe there are determinations of contingency itself. Maybe to be contingent, you must be *a* or *b* or *x*. Because you can't be just anything if you want to

330

be contingent. My hypothesis is that to be contingent you must not be contradictory, because if you are contradictory you are everything and you can't change. So if I can derive, deduce – but I don't yet do this in *After Finitude* – if I could derive from contingency a condition which explains the possibility of mathematics describing a world without humanity, okay, bingo. I didn't do that in *After Finitude*. But I think it's possible. And in that case, you know, we would be sure to be immune from Rortian refutation, because Rortian refutation is always grounded on contingency; and on the other hand, we would have explained what must be explained to understand the capacity of sciences to possibly describe a world without us.

RB: Okay. It's a question of scientificity here: whether mathematical formalisation or mathematical science can and should be the privileged paradigm of scientificity. Because there's another issue here, which is that lots of what we know about the world before and after humans is not mathematical knowledge. Lots of biology and geology is not mathematically formalised. And yet surely we want to say that we know that dinosaurs existed, and that we know quite a lot about the morphology of brontosauruses. I mean, I know the question of dating is crucial here, but it's not just that we know that the accretion of the earth happened 4.5 billion years ago because we have a mathematical way of determining the date, but that we know much more. We know about the processes involved, which are geological, physical, chemical processes, just as we know an incredible amount about the pre-human world, about pre-human flora and fauna. And surely it's important

to be able to defend the reality of the claim that brontosauruses had such and such a property. There's very little
that is mathematical about what we know about brontosauruses. And my worry is that if you turn mathematisation into the criterion of scientificity, you accidentally or
unwittingly compromise the authority of all sorts of non-
mathematical knowledge, which surely we want to say is
objective: geology, biology, etc. And this can be turned
around, because lots of people will say – an idealist will
say – certainly mathematics is the only reliable guarantor
of objectivity, the irrefutable canon of objective validity,
and they will use that to discount biology and all sorts of
other things. And this position has been used to disqualify
lots of other areas of knowledge which are deemed not to
be scientific just because they haven't been formalised. So
I wonder, is it possible to loosen or weaken the criterion
of scientificity in order to guarantee the same degree of
insuperable objective validity to biological, geological, and
even zoological discourse, without saying that science is
purely about a set of stipulative conventions and criteria
of legitimation? And I think this is a really profound epistemological problem, and that's why I want to refuse the
idea that Kant definitively resolved the epistemological
problematic. Kant gave a bad answer, it's not a satisfactory
answer, because of what we know about the contingency of
thought and consciousness. We know that thought and consciousness are not ineliminable features of reality, and that
reality would have many of the same characteristics even
if thought were not there. As Steven Jay Gould said, if the
dinosaurs hadn't been wiped out by whatever wiped them
out, they would have carried on, evolution would have

followed some other trajectory, in which consciousness and all those characteristics and peculiar cognitive prowesses exhibited by sentient creatures would simply never have come into existence, and yet reality would have been the way it is. So I want to generalise, I want to be able to say that we can describe a non-human world, or the inhuman world, without mathematics. Because if you cast doubts upon the objectivity of these non-mathematical discourses, then it seems a very … well, it's a concession that I'm not willing to make, because it simply seems to open the door to all sorts of obscurantism, which I think really need to be exterminated.

The basic thing I want to talk about is the philosophical problem of nature, and I think this is a springboard for speculation – not opportunistically, but necessarily. I think that if philosophy of nature is followed consistently it entails that speculation becomes necessary, as the only means not of assessing the *access* that we have, but of the *production* of thought.

I'll start from two things that I think everyone would accept and see if we can work outwards from there. I think that, unless you're some kind of convinced dualist, it's absolutely necessary that we accept that there's something prior to thinking, and that there are several layers of dependency amongst what is prior to thinking. It's not just one thing, it's an entire complex series of events. Now we could articulate that by means of some form of causation. We could try to establish, as it were, a direct line between the event we're trying to analyse, the event we're trying to account for in naturalistic terms, and all the causes that might have contributed toward its production, and so on. Such a task is inexhaustible in principle, not merely in fact. It's inexhaustible in principle because the conditions that support the event that's produced also support the production of other events. So if we accept that there are naturalistic grounds for the production of thought, then we have to accept that the naturalistic grounds for the production of thought are not themselves evident in thought except in so far as thought is regarded as part of nature.

So that's the starting point, and I take this to be Schelling's central contribution to philosophy. Schelling, of course, is known as a transition engine. He was a sort of facilitator, a go-between, for philosophical history. He sits between Fichte – who we all equally understand because, after all, Fichte talks about ethics – and Hegel – who no one understood but who everyone would like to. Schelling had neither of these benefits nor deficits, and in consequence, no one could understand him nor wished to! However, Schelling also produced this monumental series of works on the philosophy of nature, this extraordinary series of overtly speculative works – and when I say that, there's partially a descriptive element here. It's like a genre of writing, at one level. That is to say, the commitment to getting it down as it's coming out, is not merely that of a poet under inspiration – it's also an ideational requirement, really. If the thought as it's happening is to have any impact whatsoever on the world in which it's happening, then it's absolutely necessary that it be got down. So if you look at Schelling's output, it's hideous, it's absolutely frightening. No wonder people hated his guts: he was writing six books a year – and that's not counting essays and journals edited and so on. It was frightening – he turned out more than a novelist. So there's this extraordinary record of production of works on the philosophy of nature. And to distinguish the philosophy of nature as Schelling propounds it or explicates it successively, again and again – and not always in the same way or according to central shared principles – it's convenient to call it 'speculative physics', as indeed he did in the journal he edited under that name, the *Journal of Speculative Physics*. I don't know about you, but the very idea of combining those two things seems an absolute recipe for heaven on Earth. This is building particle accelerators that cost billions, that bankrupt countries, sinking great tunnels into the centre of mountains in order to capture sunlight from aeons ago, starlight from aeons ago – this is speculative physics. So the combination isn't at all strange to us at one level, but at another level it's strange to see it coming out of a philosopher's works.

So those really are the two things. Speculative physics: what is entailed, on the one hand, vis-à-vis the nature of philosophy; and on the other, what it entails for the nature of thought. Those are the two areas I'm particularly interested in. And the reason I think these are significant – beyond the fact that they happen to interest me, which isn't significant – the reason I think these are interesting at all is that they present us with an idealism which is wholly and utterly different. And to illustrate this I'm going to cite, paradoxically, Bernard Bosanquet. I'm very concerned to show that idealism, as it were, doesn't look like we think it does. I'm very concerned that we see and acknowledge this to be the case, because the speculative tools that it has built into it are immense. This is from a book that Bosanquet wrote called *Logic, or the Morphology of Knowledge*. It's a book on logic. One question is, why are the idealists so fascinated by logic? Why are they all experimenters in logic? Why do we get vast tomes, repeatedly, from idealists on logic? There are many possible answers to this, and I'll come to one of them later. But this is what Bosanquet has to say at the very conclusion of his book. Upon starting it out he has two epigrams, one from Hegel, from the *Science of Logic*, the other from Darwin, from *The Origin of Species*, and his avowed aim is to bring these two things together. I won't use the phrase 'evolutionary epistemology', although obviously there's a certain kinship between these strategies

– but there is certainly something about knowledge that entails that it is evolutionary, if it is knowledge of nature. This is what he has to say:

> In knowledge, the universe reveals itself in a special shape which reposes on its own nature as a whole and is *pro tanto* proof against contradiction. The detail that the universe presents in the form of cognition is true *of* the universe, although falling within it, because the universe *qua* object of cognition, in it's self-maintenance against self-contradiction, in that form, shows that it must take the detailed shape it does and no other. And to know it is to endow it with that form, making the given more and more of itself.[5]

Now this has got a lot in it, but the two things to pull out of it are: 1) the fact that there is, again, this nature that precedes the production of logic – and incidentally, in the quote from the *Science of Logic*, is Hegel talking about, you know, how evolution is significant if and only if we can account for the production of the syllogism in evolutionary terms, which is fair enough, really: a true philosopher, there. But this is not Bosanquet's project. He thinks that the universe is actually manifesting logical laws and their expression is largely indifferent. What we will find is that nature does behave in this way. So there's this *prius*, this 'firstness', preceding, as it were, the production of the laws of logic in so far as they are *overt* laws of logic and are articulated by ourselves or some variant thereof. 'To know it is to endow it with that form', Bosanquet says; and that form is the form it necessarily has in so far as it is the universe, manifesting itself and maintaining itself against

5. B. Bosanquet, *Logic, or the Morphology of Knowledge* (Oxford: OUP, 1911), Vol. II, 322.

self-contradiction. There is a reality to the law of non-con-tradiction. It's not merely a formal thing, it derives from natural history. There is a production of non-contradiction which takes place constantly throughout the production of nature. The productivity of these logical constants can be measured in terms of existence. Beings are everywhere the fruit of the stated mechanism. It would be one and the same thing if we discovered any other law of nature. All that's happening here, all that Bosanquet is suggesting, is that the grounds for our being able to have a law of non-contradic-tion are supplied, as they are for all thought or all systems of thought, *not* from the ether, *not* from some non-physical cause, but from nature.

Now if we accept that, it seems to me that idealism is committed to a realism about all things, a realism that applies equally to nature and to the Idea. And in general terms I think this is true, I think this is what all idealism in fact does: it approximates, more or less. If you look at Plato, who is often regarded as the very archetype of the 'two-worlds' metaphysician, what does he say? He says fun-damentally that becoming is caused by the Idea which it can never be but can only approximate. This is a physics, this is fundamentally a physics. The Idea is a content-free point that denies accessibility, that determines, as it were, the chaos around it to be chaos around it. Why? Because the chaos around it cannot be what it is, because it is the only self-identical thing there is. There are several Ideas of course, so it's not just one, despite certain splits toward the end of the *Republic*.

Okay, so I think basically there are grounds to assume that idealism is realism about nature coupled with realism

Iain Hamilton Grant

about an Idea. In terms of the situation in which we find ourselves today, my question really is: does this or does this not, as it seemed to at the turn of the nineteenth century, provide an exit from the strictures of Kantianism? Clearly, I think it does, and it does so by denying that interiority plays any role whatsoever. The Idea is external to the thought that has it, the thought is external to the thinker that has it, the thinker is external to the nature that produces both the thinker and the thought and the Idea. There are a series of exteriorities between thinker, thought, Idea, the various strata of the nature necessary to produce that event – necessary but not sufficient, it should be stressed. So you can't say that this and only this nature could produce that event, but we can say that it's necessary. I've said a little about why, and that's a huge problem actually. It's simply that the problem of ground, naturalistically understood, presents us with a tremendous series of problems. If it is the case that the Idea is exterior to the thinking, the thinking is exterior to the thinker, and the thinker is exterior to the nature that produced it, then, inevitably, we no longer have a series of interiorities within which it's possible for anyone to recognise themselves in the production of their thoughts. It's simply a banal accident that we know what it feels like to have thoughts. That is not particularly significant. What's significant is the thought. The thought is the product, and of course there are events taking place that surround that thought. It's very difficult to imagine, as I said, that what's necessary for the production of a particular event in nature is sufficient for the production of *that* and only that event. In other words, we have no reason whatsoever to assume that our perception of our own interiority guarantees that that interiority is somehow reproduced in reality. It just isn't: that the Ideas are separate from the thinker that thinks them, the thinker that thinks them is separate from the thinking that he or she thinks, and the separateness of the thinker from the nature that *necessarily* produced it isn't sufficient *on its own* to produce it, seems to me to guarantee that.

So that's idealism. What does idealism therefore offer speculation? Why does it make it necessary? There are two reasons why, and I'm really going to concentrate on one – and this is part of an answer to one of the questions that Ray asked earlier concerning, 'how do you arrest the process of production, as it were?', 'how does the product intervene, as it were, in a process of production such that in some sense the process of production has an outcome?', because without that surely it isn't a process of production. So is this a dualism of principles or is there something else going on there? I'll begin this with a re-articulation of what Schelling did to Kant. This is brutal. If thought had an anatomy, and if a thinker were to have done this to an anatomy, then the owner of that anatomy would be completely dismembered. In other words, this is Schelling being the Furies chasing after Orestes in the forest. He rends Kant to shreds. He takes the *a priori* and the *a posteriori* and totally inverts their purpose. The *a priori* is intended to guarantee that prior to the production of any thought, there are certain laws in place of that thought that entail that that thought and only that thought can be legitimate within the sphere it's being thought. Schelling turns it around and says, 'No this is not *a priori*, this is a *prius*. It's firstness'. *A posteriori*, Kant wants to claim, is a matter of almost total indifference. Any science that studies, for example, as chemistry does, 'mere' sensible *a posteriori* evidences, is basically mistaking the product for the law that produced it, and is therefore pointless, not really a science but a cataloguing exercise – something, incidentally, that both Hegel and Darwin complain about in the epigrams in Bosanquet's book, this 'cataloguing exercise'. The *posterius* and the *prius* for Schelling – far from representing this divide between what is *a priori* true for all knowledge, for all knowing, and what is *a posteriori* going to be given, that *a priori* once granted – is to say that this is simply a firstness and secondness that belongs to a generative program. The firstness is firstness not merely by the nature of thought but by the nature of what it is that thought is. In other words, it's not an internal problem of thought that there is firstness – apriority, if you like – it's rather a problem of nature that there is a problem, that there is a question or an apriority. The *a priori* is nature. Unless there were a nature there would be no thinking, I think we can agree. If there were no nature there would be no thinking. The *prius* of thinking is necessarily nature. But the *prius* never goes, is never a *prius*, unless there's a *posterius* for it to be *prius* to. In consequence, the product and the productivity, the *posterius* and the *prius*, are two co-present and constant elements in the articulation of process. It's simple. It's a formal nugget at one level, but at another level, it's actually the way in which firstness and secondness – time, in other words, or its production – becomes particular, becomes particular entities, becomes particular thoughts, whatever kind of entities are produced down the line. All we have is sequencing, and the sequence is *prius* and *posterius*. But a *posterius* can never, no matter what it is, capture the sum total of the causes of its production. This applies to physical entities, it applies to mountains: Imagine a mountain trying to contain within itself and catalogue, lay out, merely to lay out and catalogue, all the elements that went into its production. '4.5 billion years. By God, that's a long life', says the mountain. 'How much further have we got to go? Only another 10 billion years, till we get back to the point where I catalogue all the events that are necessary to my production', and so on. It's as important to the production of physical entities, such as is commonly understood, as it is to thought. What is it that happens when thought pretends to chase its own tail? – the Ourobouros diagram from the front of the Macmillan edition of Kemp

Smith's translation of Kant's first *Critique*. What is it that happens when thought tries to catch its own tail, tries to trap its own conditions of production in its product? First of all, it can't happen, because, as for the mountain, the conditions of the production of the thought are simply far too extensive for it to be in principle possible for a thought to recover them. So there's a necessary asymmetry, if you like, between thought and what precedes it, and it's this asymmetry which means that thought is always different from what precedes it and always at the same time requires what precedes it as its necessary ground – necessary but not sufficient. So there we have a process of generation that's understood as one then the next, that is demonstrated, if you like, by the incapacity of thought or mountains, by the lithic or the noetic, to go back and to recover its conditions of production. It's simply not doable.

So that is the beginning of a problem, the beginning of a naturalistic interpretation, a speculative physical interpretation, of the question of ground, of the problem of ground, which, it seems to me, is a problem that we're all addressing. Several consequences flow from it which it seems to me are worth explicating, not in so far as they relate necessarily to this project but in so far as they relate, I think, to speculation in general. I would like to make certain claims, in other words: I would like to make the claim that speculation is entailed by natural productivity. We don't have, in other words, the comfort zone of an interiority which really masks an impossible reflex. We don't have that comfort zone to slip back into, and to say to ourselves, 'Ah, look, we have recovered the totality of the conditions under which thought is possible, and *only* possible'. We don't have that comfort zone, that interiority, and that's one reason why speculation's entailed … It also means something very bizarre epistemically at a quite mundane level, at the level of reference. What is it that happens when we have thoughts about things? Two things happen: there are things and there are thoughts. What's the basis of their relation? Well, the thought that specifically occurs at that point is the means by which they are related, and that if there is no other body of reference, are we talking about a world? No, the world's talking. Now, the question therefore becomes: If the world talks, if the world is articulate, and if, that is, nature thinks – and however many strata we want to place in between the agent and its product is fine by me, well, there ought to be loads … however many strata we want to place between the agent and its product, between the thinker and the thought is fine – but it seems to me that if nature thinks, then it follows that nature thinks just as nature 'mountains' or nature 'rivers' or nature 'planetises', or what have you. These things are the same to all intents and purposes. In other words, there are new products every time there are thoughts, which creates the problem of ground. And as I see it, the problem as it presents itself through these lenses, seems to me to focus on a single question: Are there one or many grounds? If there is one ground for example, the law of non-contradiction, such as Bosanquet espouses, being a fruit of nature – if there is one ground, then all of the fruits of nature can be related to that ground. Necessarily? Certainly. But sufficiently, no. If there is more than one ground, if there is ground every time there is event, then that becomes a question of what job it is that the ground is doing. Is the ground a *prius* or a *posterius*? And as a product, an entity, it must be *posterius*. So the reformulation of the question of ground, it seems to me, is the means by which we can guarantee a consistent speculation concerning the origins of thought as much of as the origins of stones. And that's where I'll stop and open it up …

*

ALBERTO TOSCANO: What's not entirely clear to me when we talk about realism is the particular relationship being proposed between thought, consciousness, cognition, and various other terms. Because on one level, this Schellengian idea that nature thinks in the same sense that nature planetises or blossoms or does whatever – that seems to give thought a kind of substantiality and materiality of sorts, although it's not entirely clear how one would define it. On the other hand, for instance, when Ray was speaking about a science of cognition, one of the things that's very striking in a lot of work being done on these issues is precisely a tendency towards something like a substrate-independent or matter-independent notion of thought, whereby indeed thought would be something that is perfectly compatible with a kind of inhuman horizon, inasmuch as it's not by any means necessarily individuated over human beings or intellects and so on. So in a sense it would be sort of radical anti-Kantianism that would also involve avoiding anchoring thought in any form of subjectivity. And so, I suppose, one of the issues is not just the question about a realist epistemology or epistemology's relationship to realism, but it's also a question about whether speculative realism is also a realism about thought. And if it's a realism about thought, does it necessarily depend on thinking of thought as something that has a substantiality and materiality? Another possible option would be to be a formalist about thought. I'm thinking, for instance, of the Churchlands. There's a point in one of the debates where they say, 'Well, if thought is to some extent or another understandable as a type of formalism' – you know, they talk about pattern activation vectors, etc. – 'then why can't thought be instantiated over a social collectivity or a network of computers or indeed whatever other assemblage or entity you might find?' And this seems to me very important vis-à-vis science, because if we start talking about science and realism and then act as if scientific discoveries take place in the sense of individu-ated human thought, it seems that the entire process of the generation of scientific statements is completely misrepre-sented. Because it seems to say that whatever statements are being produced about quarks or about galaxies and so on, involve the capacity of a single human scientist to think about the cosmos – which seems a totally farcical scenario about how science operates. It seems like a false epistemo-logical scenario. So I was wondering – I mean, obviously these are a broad set of questions – but vis-à-vis this kind of Schellingian line, what is the status of the reality of thought? Is it some form of substance?

IHG: I'd like to start from one of the points you make, because in the terms in which you put it I think the interesting point is this: If this is true, if there is an unrelated *prius* and *posterius* in the production of thought, and if this has the effect of making the thought particular to its conditions of production but incapable of reflexively recovering those conditions, then we are condemned to a complete particularity that would seem, on the face of it, to deny the prospect of collective work. So it certainly would make, for example, subatomic physics impossible. There would be no prospect whatsoever of collective work. So I'd like to start from an almost sociological point of view. I mean, it seems to me that clearly there is sufficient consistency across a range of individuals in laboratories and so on and so forth, to generate the sort of work that was done in early sociology. It seems there is, obviously, consistency. Theory itself, the very idea that there are theories, is dependent on some kind of consistency being reached that makes it irrelevant what the conditions of the production of thought are.

AT: In the individual?

IHG: In the individual, yeah. So the question is how this happens. And it seems to me that this is why the idealists are fascinated by logic. If it is true that we have nothing to go on other than the thoughts being produced, then the demand that the relations between thought, things, and so on be formalised becomes an imperative. It's the only way this could possibly happen. This is something I was thinking about while reading what you had to say, Quentin, on formalism, on mathematics, and about the *signe dépourvu du sens*. This seems to me to be necessary if there is going to be any kind of communication between sciences such that a programme becomes possible. However, what does that mean? It means, in effect, that there must be produced a series of reproducible patterns. The whole question ceases to be, therefore, a question of the conditions of production and starts being a question of the kinds of products required. The fact that they are available could of course then be used to trigger a rekindling of the transcendental. To some extent, the criterion of utility attaching to maintaining a scientifically realist epistemology, as it were, gives the game away here. We can't recover the conditions of its production such that it's possible for us to say, 'Well we know this because …', and so on. We might be able to do this in one particular case, but there will always be others, other cases that produce other thoughts, and that's why it becomes necessarily a question of ground once again. Is there one ground for all patterns, or are there several grounds for several patterns? In other words, how malleable are logics? How many possible formalisations are there? That seems to me the question that nature poses to thought.

ALI ALIZADEH: One word which is not being mentioned so often here is 'cognition'. You talk about consciousness and you want to talk about the difference between the ideal and nature, but how far would it take us away from Kantianism and transcendental philosophy altogether if we tried to abolish completely the synthetic unity of apperception? That's kind of what Ray mentioned as well. There is the difference between thought and thinker, as you said, and the difference between thought and Idea, but the problem is the implicit evolutionary theory here. And if you go for an evolutionary theory the move from nature to thought and from cognition to thought has to be gradual, it has to be linear, but we cannot really trace these trajectories all the way back from humans, who think self-consciously, to all the forms of inorganic life from which we emerged. But we do know that the difference between cognition and thought is disjunctive. It's a difference in quality. So that's the problem: Kant was not interested in finding the totality of the conditions of the production of thought, he was interested in finding the conditions of the possibility of cognition, whereas you're just interested in the former.

IHG: So Kant was also interested in necessary but not sufficient conditions also, as it were, in that regard: not the conditions of the production of this thought here and now but rather the necessary conditions if there is thought, the form it must take, and so on. Yeah, I agree, and I don't think, as it were, that there is no attraction to the transcendental. I don't think that the idea that Kant was just gloriously wrong and how we laughed when we look back and we think, 'Oh God, the eighteenth century, they were so dumb!' It's not really that. There is such a powerful attraction to the domain of the transcendental, the domain that is anchored by – not that anchors, and this is crucial – but is anchored *by* the transcendental unity of apperception. There is an attraction there, because it presupposes a domain, the one domain in all being, where everything can be ruled by what Freud called 'the omnipotence of thought', where it's sufficient for me to think to be able to determine what goes on. So I think, yeah, that aspect of Kantianism, that reason why Kantianism, or the transcendental apparatus in Kantianism, has become so embedded in our philosophical practice, is because of its powerful attractiveness – a domain wherein it's possible for thought to legislate for itself, not for others, not for anything outside itself, and not to be legislated to by anything outside itself. The problem is, it's impossible. There must be something that produces this, this must come from somewhere, unless of course it's parachuted in from Venus. It could be a Venusian Richard Rorty, I suppose, who legislates what we think. Thought comes from somewhere, and the somewhere it comes from is nature. To that extent, it's no longer going to be possible to consider that the transcendental unity of apperception is responsible for the transcendental. Rather, the transcendental is responsible for the unity of apperception. So, regard that as a product rather than the producer of the field. It's not the autonomous judge, it's rather the heteronomous satellite of the transcendental, if you like, turned around on the basis of a naturalism about how thought got here at all. And we simply have to give up the illusion that the domain of thinking that we call reflection is coextensive with the domain of thinking *tout court*, as it were. So, I think – although abrupt and hideous – that's what's necessary.

AT: Can I just follow up on that briefly? On what grounds, in the step beyond the critique of Kantianism, does one want to make the argument that the conditions, let's say, of the *genesis* of thought, however defined, are relevant to the *conditions of possibility* of thought? For instance, if you have a kind of substrate-independent notion of what are the formal or formalisable conditions for thinking, however defined, then whether it's arrived at by a particular genetic lineage, or whether it's artificially produced, etc., the argument would be that ... well, isn't it the case that if the Kantian project at its core remains persuasive, then in a sense whether it's evolutionary or machinic or whatever other genetic process is to some extent irrelevant? ... I mean, wouldn't that be the reply, to say that it seems to beg the question to say that somehow genesis is necessary to understand the immanent conditions of the possibility of thought? Unless obviously you totally pluralise thought in a way in which the thinking of the Venusian and our thinking are only the same thinking by convention rather than by a set of formal conditions.

IHG: Yes, one thing the transcendental entails, epistemically and metaphysically, is that it gives us license to be able to think a finitude of possible types of knowledge. If we don't have that, if we don't have the transcendental to rely on, then either we find some other mechanism that does the job without entailing that this finitude is active fundamentally in a subject or we just haven't got it.

AT: So there's no closure to whatever we might understand by thought?

IHG: No, no, no ... But I think that must be the case if we hold that time is to some extent involved in the production of nature. I put it that way around. I don't say that if we hold that, you know, neo-Darwinism is the correct account of genetic transfer, then, etc. ... I don't put it that way around. If there is time involved in the production of nature, then that time is the reason why the particular aspect of nature that happens to think, as it were, is what it is. It's necessary that it is, but its sufficiency is always in question. And what are the mechanisms by which it can be assessed? Well, inevitably, third-party ones. It can't be done by reflection.

There is the possibility of a morphology of thought, as it were, where we look at the patterns. This is the suggestion that Whitehead made years ago, and there are interesting suggestions in contemporary logical formalisms – for example, Graham Priest. There's a thing he's working on, a thing called 'dialetheism', which is basically a logic that makes self-contradictory propositions coherent elements of a formal system.[6] He says that two properties are contradictory – one is closure, the other is transcendence – and neither of them can be reduced, one to the other, and both are operative. This is a system which is entirely inconsistent but generates consistent systems. So the question of patterns might become more important. But then we don't have to ask the questions, or we're not tempted in the same ways, to ask the questions about 'what is the horizon of the possibility of these patterns', because the horizon of nature is possibilizing them – you know, nature is the reason.

GRAHAM HARMAN: I'll save some bits for my comments later, but Ray already alluded to a principle of 'retardation' in your book: so you have a primal flux or becoming that's pre-individual in some way, and retardation is what makes it crystallise into individual things such as rivers and mountains. Now, of course, we've seen this in other philosophers, where it's the human that's the retarding principle. So, for example, in Bergson, if not for humans time would go like that [*snaps fingers*]. And for the early Levinas: if it weren't for the human subject, being would be an *apeiron*. It would be a rumbling *il y a*, and it's only the human that

6. G. Priest, *Beyond the Limits of Thought* (2nd edition, Oxford: Clarendon, 2002).

breaks it into parts. But obviously you don't want to do that because you're a realist. So it can't be the human who does all the work. So how exactly is this retardation – I know it's a tough question – but what are some of the ideas you have about how the flux can be retarded to give rise to individual shapes?

IHG: It generally happens that when asked questions of this nature, the answer will strike me in about three days' time! But this in a sense illustrates the answer that I'm going to give now, which is, it seems to me, that if there is production there is product and vice versa, and there is no production if there is no product. And instead, therefore, of thinking of the question of how there is this substrate where the mobile is static, where it acquires form, we think about, you know, this is the conjunction of product-production, as the kernel of all possible production. Then, to some extent, the question disappears. Now I know that doesn't answer the question, so it's a solution that evidently I haven't thought through.

PETER HALLWARD: This is a way of going back to Alberto's question, but you said at one point that nature talks, or nature thinks, and I just wanted to know what that means, exactly. What does that add to our understanding of linguistics or the symbolic or the semiotic or, you know, conventional accounts of how language works, by saying that it's nature that's doing the speaking? How does that sharpen or inflect a research agenda in a way that people who work on linguistics, for example, might understand?

IHG: Two things, I suppose. One is, if we're talking about purely symbolic language, then clearly the answer to that question belongs to the answer I made to Alberto concerning patterns, concerning shared languages, a shared symbolism. But that is possible only on condition that the symbolism has no reference. The alternative would be that there is a way of accounting for the production of linguistic units in terms of referential signs. So you need to place the cart before the horse to some extent in so far as you're asking: Given that signs have this property of reference, how is it they get there; was it the natural production of reference, and so on? And this suggests that reference is an essential property of signs. But the principle I take Schelling to be espousing – and of course the possibilities for error are immense, not least because Schelling and consistency were only sometimes bedfellows – is quite simply that if, when it comes down to it, there is a process, a necessary process of nature, culminating in a particular product, and there's no alternative to that view, unless we accept some form of dualism, then what we can accept as being produced in this way exists by virtue of it. The ground is provided by nature. The production of anything else has to be simply accounted for in terms of abstract languages. So the abstract elements of it have their ground, as Bosanquet suggests, in nature. The question is, how many possible formalisms are there? How many possible abstract languages are there? – not really how this particular abstract language can be used to make, as it were, referential sense of a body of natural language, and how speakers use it. So I think the question may be the wrong way around, and that's how I would respond. Although one of the things which interests me, which I think is not just interesting but imperative, is to find ways of conjoining philosophical work with all the sciences. If idealism becomes an operating principle of any sort whatsoever, if it is true, there's nothing which can be ruled out *a priori*. And all the sciences become imperative, in the form of this idealism, and no-one can do all of the sciences. Therefore it becomes a cooperative labour. Therefore the question that Alberto's raising, and which I think you're raising just now, becomes imperative. But we can't, I think, do that so long as we do it through lenses that presuppose exactly what's being explained, as it were. That's a disappointing answer, I'm sorry …

DUSTIN MCWHERTER: I have a question that also kind of follows up on Alberto's question about the ontological status of thought, but also a question about how this plays out in your book. In the *System of Transcendental Idealism*, Schelling has an explicitly epistemological agenda, and it seems to me that that's elided a bit in your book, despite the brilliance with which that work is otherwise interpreted and explicated. So, how would you handle Schelling's epistemological agenda in the *System of Transcendental Idealism*? And furthermore, it seems as though, in that reading of the *System of Transcendental Idealism*, you construe ideation as simply a regional phenomenon in nature: Nature becomes an object to itself through organisms that can think. So it's merely regional; thought's not everywhere. But at other times it seems as though you're speaking of Ideas in the Platonic sense, as things that exist independently of thinkers – and I think this is a reflection of an inconsistency in Schelling's philosophical trajectory. So, those are my two questions: what about the epistemological agenda of the *System of Transcendental Idealism*? And, is there a kind of oscillation in your book between the regionality of ideation and a kind of universality?

IHG: To take the second question first, it's fascinating, I suspect my answer to this would have been different a few months ago. But I think that what's going on is effectively that thought isn't everywhere all at once, but there are thoughts, wherever, at various times, and there's no region for which we can rule out thought occurring prospectively at any particular point. However, it remains true that thought does happen at such and such locations. That's the bridge, as it were, between the nature of thought and the thinking doing it – which is the inversion that Schelling explicitly undertakes in the epistemological work that he does in *System of Transcendental Idealism* – but it's an inversion premised precisely on the unrecoverability of the conditions of genesis of thought. So, he says, for example, 'the lamp of knowledge points only forwards'. This lovely line provoked a great deal of consideration on my part, and I thought – well, actually this is definitely true. And there is no prospect, really, of it being otherwise. Even the reflexive recovery of the conditions of production of the thought that is pointing only forwards would entail a lapse of time. Whatever comes after it would be a second, with the lamp shining in one direction rather than another as its *prius, but* that gives determinacy at the same time as it denies the possibility of recovery. And so it's the question of determinacy which I think is core to the epistemological project that Schelling pursues. This is the vexed question of the presumed identity between nature-philosophy on the one hand and the transcendental philosophy on the other. This is why, I think, Schelling says at the outset of the *System of Transcendental Idealism* that it's necessary to consider this as an adjunct, to consider it to be simply true that there's always a double series involved in thinking about thought, because it tends to be that they're closely related, I take it, in time, although I'm not sure. I'm not satisfied with that answer. I mean, it seems phenomenologically apt, but whether it's got any basis in the principles he offers for a consistent priority and posteriority, I don't know, or the *prius* … there are ways it can be worked out, perhaps. But the final thing, therefore, is the question of identity, which comes back to the question of the Ideas, and why the Ideas might be one and at the same time many, and yet the thinking of them may be potentially everywhere, and so on. This is really the core of the problem. Is Schelling a Platonist, a neo-Platonist, or some form of hyper-Platonist? So long as the 'Good beyond being', as it were, is not taken as being the entire anchor to the system of Ideas, which structure is then reproduced here on Earth. Schelling's conception of identity seems to me to go a long way towards explaining the possible relations between Idea and thought. He actually makes this explicit in *Presentation of My System* and *Further Presentation of My System*. On the one hand there are Ideas which are identical. *They* are identical; but not to the things they are ideas *of*. They're not ideas *of* anything – they're Ideas, and their identity is their being as Idea, fullstop. And that means that everything which is not them is in chaos, in flux, and so on. So the means by which to relate the Idea to the thinking is the concept. The concept is a partial grasp of the Idea, or a finite and differentiating grasp of an infinite identity. That's his description of it, which seems to me to do quite a better job than the 'double series' claim. In other words, if the proto-phenomenology of the double series is an explanation of an epistemology, it seems to me not as good as the neo-Platonic exposition by way of the difference between concepts and Idea in the later work. But what we have not got to deal with is an absolute identity of thought here and being there, in this hideous symmetrical way in which Hegel will pretend, and which bad readers of Parmenides always maintain.

NOORTJE MARRES: This is a partly related but somewhat more general question, regarding realism as an epistemic question, a question of knowledge and of thought. Because listening to your talk, and also Ray's, made me think of other kinds of undoings of Kant in the twentieth century, because that's obviously taken many forms and has been launched on many different occasions. And one of them, I thought, had to do precisely with undoing the primacy of the epistemic. There you get arguments concerning realism as a question that must be taken out of the realm of epistemology if it is to be addressed pertinently, and this shift can take various forms. It can be a shift to historic ontology or a shift to ethics or embodied experience, with various consequences for the type of realism, obviously, that results. But I'm curious how, on the basis of the types of arguments you have presented now, what your position is on this question. Should it be preserved as an epistemic question, or is your mode of arguing actually moving along with this ontologising and making ethical of the question of realism?

IHG: I'm certainly ontologising, certainly *not* ethicising. I think one of the badges by means of which Kantianism is maintained, the reason why it remains a problem despite the various attempts to undo it, is because, all too often, the Good assumes authority over being, and it becomes possible to say things like, 'The universe ought to be…', and this statement is assumed to have philosophical significance. In fact, Fichte says just that. He started with an identity, a realism about, 'Here I am, what do I know about myself? Well, all this accidental stuff, plus I'm free, dammit! … and I'm gonna show it!' And that's the basis of Fichte's realism. He goes to great lengths to demonstrate this, but fundamentally, what he reserves the right thereby to do is to call realism the view that – and here I'm going to cite a passage from Kant – desire consists in being the cause, 'through one's presentations, of the actuality of the objects of those presentations'. It occurs in two places: in the *Critique of Practical Reason* and the *Critique of Judgement*.[7] What that means is that it's simply enough to will or desire it in order that it be, because being is secondary to acting. And that, it seems to me, is simply not true. It's transcendentally adequate only on certain conditions, and those conditions are that the remit of realism is maintained solely within the transcendental field, *i.e.*, solely within the field of possible reflection, so that I can always say, 'Oh well, I know I got run over by a bus, and I know that looks like the revenge of the not-I, but in fact I willed it thus!', which is what Nietzsche said, in effect. So I think there can be no liberality at that level, and realism can't be regionalised, as it were, nor said to be realism if it is dependent

---

7. *Ak*.V 9n. and *Ak*.V 177n., respectively.

on the willed suppression of some external condition. An ethical realism is precisely not a realism, in the same way that a political realism is not a realism. In the same way, in fact – and I know this is contentious, but it seems to me a point that needs to be made – a *critical* materialism is *not* a materialism. Fundamentally, it's a materialism oriented, driven, steered, designed, by critique. In other words, it's a theory of matter held by people with some use for certain bits of it and none for others. How is it possible for critical materialism to think that there can be a difference between what *matters* and crude *matter*, you know, things like plants? So I think that there can't be any liberality at that level, that would be my answer. And the very fact that such positions are perpetuated is the reason why this needs to be done again.

GH: I can guess what you think of Marxist materialism.

IHG: Love it! No, it's simply wrong. The idea that it's possible to invoke a diminished realm, as it were, for matter and to condemn whatever does not fulfil the economic, tele-ological purposes of certain types of agents to a sphere of 'merely crude matter', where it has absolutely no effects whatsoever, where it's left to one side of the philosophical and the political problem, seems to me a recipe for disaster. If you're trying to do politics, if you're trying to work out, 'we need to do *x*, how are we going to do *x*, we need a strategy', and so on. What's the first thing you do? You take account of the environment, and so on. What's the first thing critical materialism does? 'I want a theory of matter, what am I going to do? I know, I'll ignore half of it'. That's just not good metaphysics, fundamentally. It's not a good way of approaching reality, it seems to me.

PH: But what about cases where you *do* will something to be true, though, or to be the case? I mean, just banally, holding a promise, making a commitment. There are cases in which something comes to be because you will it so, and politics would be completely disarmed if you lost that.

IHG: There's the Spinozist response to that: what I think of as my freedom is my incapacity to explain the cause of the event that I'm trying to describe. I move my arm because I will it so, or do I just not know the causes of my arm moving? That's the Spinozist answer …

PH: And like I said, that disarms, well, that *is* the disarming of politics.

IHG: Yeah, yeah it is. I think … fundamentally it seems to be a question about consistency of effects, at one level. It's possible that a series of actions can be maintained despite having, let's say, punctual conditions of production. So there seems to be a consistency of events, and they're all tending in one direction. I want to raise my arm because I want the bus to stop. So I stick my arm out and the bus stops – a triumph for transcendentalism! I have achieved the stopping of the bus by means of my will alone. Let's say that happens. It really does seem to be about a question of consistency, and the problem from the perspective I come from is how to explain the consistency, and I do acknowledge that's a problem. But do we explain it any more by saying that it's an act of will? I don't think so. I think the reason we move our arms is because we have arms to move, first and foremost, and because there are certain contours of the world that make that a possible gesture and a significant gesture: naturalistically possible and socially practical. It has outcomes. But the question of whether we should hold ontology ransom to political expediency seems to precisely re-present the problem of transcendentalism, in so far as the latter concerns 'what are the spheres of my legitimate autonomy, over what can I legislate?'

AA: Action and will do not only belong to the practical realm of philosophy. They go back to Descartes, in a sense, because will and action are the very necessary elements of thinking itself. Without willing to think there is no thought – so before it becomes the practical element, it's epistemic.

IHG: Again, this is a solution, I think, that's often tried. Let's say we've accepted the point that in order to think I have to will it, yes? And let's say I'm not thinking yet, but I will to think. I will to think, and then comes the thought. How can I will to think prior to the thought that I will to think being there? I can't. So the idea that there is a will that thinks thought for me makes sense if and only if that will is outside of me, is nothing to do with me. So it's not *my* will that causes the thought to occur. If we call it 'will' that presumably serves some additional ontology, some additional metaphysics – Let's say the Fichtean one, which does subsume epistemology, the theoretical under the practical. Let's say that's the aim. Then it begins to make sense to do that, but only given those caveats. Fundamentally, however, I don't think it's true that my thinking is caused by my will. Would that it were! For God's sake, then practical problems like writing papers late at night would disappear!

AA: But you don't have any criteria for the intensity of the receptivity of sense data here – that is, whether or not I'm aware of the intensity of what I'm receiving, reinforcing that data, and that I'm not just receiving it in a kind of semi-unconscious state …

IHG: Yeah, put it in the form of a question: What is the impetus to thought? Where does thought come from? If you can answer that question, then we can say what the source of the thought is. And the necessary answer, I would contend, is that it comes from nature.

CECILE MALASPINA: And where does nature come from?

IHG: What's the ground of the ground? – absolutely. Why is there this nature rather than another, and so on? That's the principle of sufficient reason, that's the problem of ground. That's why I think it's an important question.

RAY BRASSIER: Obviously you claim that so-called transcendental metaphysics says that you can't be compromised by any concessions to folk-psychological superstitions. I wonder, then, what's the status of categories like 'production'? What happens to the conceptual register that you use – that Schelling used – to articulate this kind of transcendental philosophy? Given that transcendental philosophy, or even a nascent speculative materialism, is carried out using the semantic resources of natural language, doesn't there need to be a kind of dialogue between the critical and eliminative dimension of a properly scientific psychology which systematically undermines the viability of these folk-psychological categories, and the project of a transcendental metaphysics? In other words, this is why I think the relationship between ontology and epistemology can't be straightforwardly adjudicated from either side. For instance, imagine a Schellingianism informed by the Churchlands: recasting the categories of speculative metaphysics using the resources of dynamic vector activation patterns. So, doesn't this requirement for a dialogue with eliminativism mean that you have to kind of stipulate a revisability in terms of even the most fundamental conceptual categories you use, such as productivity or production?

IHG: Okay, let's start with the question about the Churchlands. It's not hard, actually, to make the Churchlands into Schellingians. In fact, at the end of Patricia Churchland's *Neurophilosophy* – the biggest manifesto ever written – she says, 'So it is that the brain investigates the brain […] and is changed forever by the knowledge',[8] which seems to me

8. P. S. Churchland, *Neurophilosophy. Toward a Unified Science of the Mind-Brain* (Cambridge, MA: MIT, 1990), 482.

perfectly Schellingian. There's an absolute symmetry there between what she's arguing and what Schelling discusses in his own epistemology. How do you anchor the knowing of things, as an extra product, in the being of those things that you want to know? So there's a new entity in being. That's the way of addressing the problem. So I don't think, philosophically, metaphysically, that there's a problem there. I do think, however, that there's a point when the epistemic demand makes demands on ontology that ontology can't meet, when we have to ask, 'is this a correct epistemological approach?' But that's the way around to do it, I suspect. So, for example, this is the method of eliminativism: I'm investigating an object, call it a car, and this car, it is alleged, drives by itself. Now my job is to explain how it is that the car drives, and at the end of the explanation it should be clear. The false explanations have been gotten rid of and a good explanation put in their place. So, let's say all those criteria have been satisfied, let's say that is achieved. What has the theory achieved at the epistemic level? It's managed to produce exactly that explanation. What's achieved ontologically? It's managed to commit itself to an ontology which requires that things that do not exist exist in order that they be eliminated. So it's ontologically inconsistent but epistemologically necessary. I can see its virtue, or I can see its requirement epistemologically. But the question must be put, I think, the other way around: If we work out what the ontology demands, then that provides a means of working out answers to the differences between good and bad explanations, whatever they might be. My suspicion is that otherwise we find ourselves backed into an unsustainable metaphysics of not-being. You called it a 'dialogue between the critical and the ontological' – but that's exactly what Kant maintains metaphysics should be replaced with, a critical dialogue where fundamentally Reason will have the ultimate say. So I think it really is a one or the other question, at that level. The question becomes, how do we think about the problem of epistemological rectitude without invoking, as it were, the transcendental categories?

Speculative Realism

Presentation by Graham Harman

Firstly, I'd like to thank Ray Brassier for conceiving of this event and organising it. This all started for me about a year ago, when Ray came back from Paris and he strongly recommended that I read Meillassoux's book, *Après la finitude*, which you should all definitely read. And from there I got into Iain's work, and from reading these works, there are definite points in common, which I've had plenty of opportunity to enjoy over the past year.

'Speculative Realism', first of all, is a very apt title, because realism, of course, is very out of fashion in philosophy. And I think one of the reasons it's out of fashion is that it's considered boring. Realism is the philosophy of the boring people who smack down the imaginative ones and force them to take account of the facts. G.E. Moore supposedly held up his hand and said: here it is, external objects exist. Yes, but that hardly exhausts the field of reality! And as yesterday's Lovecraft conference[9] title indicated, realism is always in some sense *weird*. Realism is about the strangeness in reality that is not projected onto reality by us. It is already there by dint of being real. And so it's a kind of realism without common sense. If you look at the work of all four of us, there's not much common sense in any of it. The conclusions are very strange in all four cases. In Ray's case you have a reductive eliminativism, and you end his book with the husks of burnt-out stars and the meaninglessness of everything. That's not something you usually get in G.E. Moore and those sorts of realists!

9. A one-day conference, 'Weird Realism: Lovecraft and Theory', held under the auspices of Goldsmiths Centre for Cultural Studies on 26 April 2007.

In Iain's book you have a pre-individual dynamic flux that somehow meets with retardations and becomes encrusted into rivers and mountains. In my work you get objects infinitely withdrawing from each other into vacuums and only barely managing to communicate across some sort of qualitative bridge. And of course in Quentin's philosophy you get no causal necessity whatsoever. Everything's pure contingency. These are not the sorts of notions one usually associates with realism. Metaphysics is usually thought to be concerned with wild, speculative sorts of ideas, and speculation is usually not considered a form of realism. You hear 'speculative idealism', not ' speculative realism'. Another obvious common link is a kind of anti-Copernicanism. Kant is still the dominant philosopher of our time. Kant's shadow is over everyone, and many of the attempts to get beyond Kant don't get beyond Kant at all. I think Heidegger is a good example of this. Heidegger's a great example of the 'correlationist', in Meillassoux's sense.[10] Obviously, we all think of Kant as a great philosopher. But that doesn't mean he's not a problem. It doesn't mean that Kant is the right inspiration for us, and in fact, I hold that the Kantian alternatives are now more or less exhausted.

One of the things I did to prepare for this conference is to put each of our names on an index card, and I was shuffling them around on my table in Cairo, trying to group us together in different ways. And you can come up with different combinations in this way, various differences between us despite the shared similarities. I came up with some interesting ones; but if you were going to say what distinguished each of us, I think it's fair to say – and they

10. For 'correlationism' see **COLLAPSE** Vol. II (March 2007).

can contradict me if I'm wrong – that Ray is really the only reductionist or eliminativist, Iain is the only dynamist, I'm the only phenomenologist, and Quentin is the only one opposed to causality *tout court* – there's no chance of any necessary relations between anything in his vision of the world. And you can also see different influences in each case. In Ray's case, I think: Badiou and Laruelle. Those are the two chapters that seem most central to me in his manuscript. And cognitive science, of course. In Iain's case: German Idealism, Deleuze, Bergson, and his own reading of Plato. In my case: Husserl and Heidegger, with a bit of Leibniz and a bit of Latour. And in the case of Meillassoux: Badiou, of course, but also, I see a lot of similarities between him and David Hume in many ways; not only the clarity of his writing style, but even some of the arguments, seem Humean in inspiration.

Before I comment on the work of the other three on the panel, maybe I should give a quick summary of my own work. It all started for me with Heidegger. I don't think I was ever quite an orthodox Heideggerian, but I certainly loved Heidegger very much. And early on in my graduate studies, I was focusing on the tool-analysis, the way things hide behind their facades as we use them. And it occurred to me at a certain point fairly early that all of Heidegger boils down to this. There's really just one fundamental opposition that keeps recurring, whether he's talking about being or tools or Dasein or anything else: a constant, monotonous reversal between the hiddenness of things and their visible presence-at-hand. And it started as just a reading of Heidegger, and there wasn't really any metaphysical inclination whatsoever at that point.

What first started doing it for me was when I was writing an article on Levinas a couple years after that, and trying to piece together Levinas's theory of how the human subject breaks up the unity of being and hypostatises it into individual things. And this struck me as so inherently preposterous. I'd never really thought of it that clearly before, but the more you think about it, why should it be that the human subject breaks the world up into parts? This actually has a precursor in the pre-Socratics; it was Anaxagoras, for whom *nous* makes the *apeiron* rotate very quickly, and it starts breaking up into fragments, and so it's mind's fault that the world has parts, and each of the parts contains all the others and mirrors all the others. But you see that in Levinas, too. And I realised I was opposed to that, but I didn't quite have the language to start defining why that was so. Then, for my dissertation – which is now *Tool-Being*,[11] the book – if you look closely at Heidegger's tool-analysis, what he's explicitly saying there is that the floor you're using now, the air you are breathing now, the bodily organs you are using now, tend to remain invisible because you're simply using them. You're not staring at them, you're not creating theories about them. Fine, it's a great concept, arguably one of the great insights of twentieth century philosophy. The equipment tends to remain invisible as long as it's functioning solely as equipment – fine. But that can sound like the old reversal between theory and practice. One of the great things about playing with an idea in your mind for a long time is that you become bored with it after a few years. That's why I think we often make progress, because

---

11. Graham Harman, *Tool-Being: Heidegger and the Metaphysics of Objects* (Chicago: Open Court, 2002).

we have a great idea, then we become bored with it and see its shortcomings – and that's what happened to me. I started realising: this is not going to be anything more than 'practice comes before theory', and 'praxis breaks down when the hammer fails'. It also occurred to me that praxis does not get at the reality of the object any more than theory does – that was the next step. Yes, by staring at this chair I don't exhaust its being, but by sitting in it I also don't exhaust it. There are so many deep layers to the reality of that chair that the human act of sitting is never going to exhaust. Even if humans created the chair, even if only humans see it as a chair, there will still be, I'd say, an infinite number of qualities in the chair itself that cannot be exhausted by any seeing or by any counting. So now I had both theory and practice over here, both on this side. On the other side, the causal relations seem to be happening in the depths. But the problem with causal relations is, you really can't say that inanimate objects exhaust each other either, and this doesn't even really get into the whole pan-psychism debate. Fire does not have to be conscious to turn cotton into a caricature. (I always use fire and cotton because that's the great example from Islamic philosophy, which I've read a lot of since moving to Cairo.) The cotton has a scent, a colour, numerous other attributes we can speak of, and they're irrelevant to the fire in those senses. And so, it became to clear to me that as soon as you move away from the idea that the world is a homogeneous unit, as Levinas or Anaxagoras think, then you have a world with many parts. And as soon as you have a world with many parts, they're going to interact. And if they interact they're going to have the same relationship of caricature to each other

Graham Harman

that we have. And reading Whitehead at about the same time really cemented that idea, that you cannot privilege the human relationship to the world of over any other kind of relation. Whitehead's still the best source for that, I think, even better than Leibniz, because for Whitehead it can happen at all different levels and sizes. With Leibniz there's always a privileged caste of substances that are natural, and you can't talk about an international corporation having relations with real things. But for Whitehead you can, and for Latour you also can. So Whitehead was one key, and another key was Zubiri, Xavier Zubiri, a Basque ontologist who studied with Heidegger and Ortega y Gasset, who's not as well known as Whitehead, of course, but who I think is a pivotal twentieth-century thinker. Because his idea is that the essence of the thing is never adequately expressible in terms of any relations or any interactions with it, and so that's where the kind of vacuum-sealed objects withdrawing from all relations came into my work, from Zubiri.

And then what I did in *Tool-Being* was that I more or less showed how a lot of things – Heideggerian concepts such as time and space and referential contexture, and all these things – boiled down to the tool-analysis; that was Chapter 1. In Chapter 2, I took that and used it as a weapon against all the things commentators usually say about Heidegger. In Chapter 3, I simply tried to turn in a more speculative direction. And I can make this short, because the real speculative problem that arises from this immediately is that if you have objects that are incapable of contact, why does anything ever happen? Given that it is in the nature of things to withdraw from all relations, you have a real problem with causation. One thing can't touch another, in any sense at all. And this immediately got me thinking about occasionalism in the history of philosophy, of course, where, before the French you had the Arabs – in Iraq you had the Ash'arite school of theology. And of course this fits a lot more easily in Islam than it does in Christianity, which never had any real occasionalists in the pre-modern period, because for the Muslims, in that period at least, if God sends an innocent man to hell, so be it. God is all-powerful. It doesn't create a paradox of free will, as it did for many Christians. So you see that first in the Arabs. It's not only a threat to God if other entities are creators, in the sense of creating the whole universe – obviously there has to be only one entity that can do that – but things like creating furniture and brewing coffee would also somehow denigrate God's power, if individual agents were able to do this themselves. And so God is there to explain all actions, recreating everything constantly. And although the theology seems a bit outrageous to us now, it's a very profound metaphysical idea, the idea that things cannot relate, inherently, that things-in-themselves are totally sealed off from each other. We see this come back in the seventeenth century in Europe of course, and historians of seventeenth-century philosophy are often extremely finicky about who they allow to be called an occasionalist: just Malebranche, Cordemoy, and maybe a couple of other French names. I see no reason not to expand it to include Descartes, and I would also say Spinoza, and Leibniz, and definitely Berkeley. I take the name occasionalism in a very, very broad sense: any time that individual entities do not have causal power you're giving in to a kind of occasionalism. And then Hume is the important final step. Skepticism in many ways is simply an upside-down occasionalism, and it's no accident that Hume was a great fan of Malebranche. Hume owned Malebranche's books, marked them copiously, and here you have a hardcore theist and there an unrepentant atheist. The connection between them is the fact that in both cases you have the problem of things being unable to relate directly, and the difference of course is that for the occasionalists, in the classical sense, you have independent things in the world that are apart from each other from the start and the question is how they relate. In a sense, with Hume you already have their relations. We're already born into a world where there are habits. Things are linked in my mind already, and the question is only whether they have any existence outside it. So Hume starts with relations, whereas Malebranche starts with substances. I think in both cases the solution is incorrect, because in both cases they're privileging one magical super-entity that is able to create relations where others cannot. So for the occasionalists: 'No one else can do it? Oh, God can do it'. For Hume, my mind does it, my mind creates objects ('bundles') through customary conjunction, creates links.

So, the question is how we can have a form of indirect causation that does not use God as the solution – which would lead us back into the discredited old forms of theological philosophy – and which equally does not use my mind as the solution, which would lead us ultimately to idealism, as Hume eventually did lead us. How do we have a realist version of occasional causation, without laying everything on God? And I coined the term 'vicarious causation'[12] just because whenever I mentioned occasional causation people always laughed – that was the first reaction, and I realised it was hopeless to keep this term for myself! It's too associated with doctrines that have been refuted by undergraduates for the past three hundred years, so I had to invent this new term. So I speak of a vicarious theory of causation; but where does this causation happen? That was a mystery to me for a long time, and the mechanics of it are still a mystery to me. The *Collapse* article is about as far as I've gotten; I've gotten only a little bit further than that. But I got the answer from Husserl, of all people, because what we have in Husserl is a second kind of object. Neither Heidegger nor Husserl are really realists, I would say. They both focused too much on human access to the world over

---

12. See **COLLAPSE** Vol. II, 171-205.

the world itself. But in Heidegger we have these tool-beings, these objects; they're real objects, they withdraw from us, they do things in the world outside of our access to them. What you have in Husserl – which is often confused with Heidegger's own discovery – are the intentional objects. If you read the whole first half of the *Logical Investigations*, after he's done refuting psychologism, his real enemy is British empiricism, and what he is up against is the notion that what we encounter are qualities, and that somehow the qualities are bundled together by us. Somehow the objects are not given for British empiricism. What's given are qualities, and those qualities are fused together by the human subject. That's what the entire phenomenological tradition most opposes, I would say, because in Husserl you have intentional objects. You have this table, which I'm only seeing the top surface of, I'm not seeing the front of, as these people [*indicates audience*] are. I'm not seeing the bottom of it. I could circle around it, crawl beneath it and look up at it. All of these changing perceptions, though, do not lead me to think I'm seeing a different object. I think I'm only seeing different aspects of the same object. This table is not hidden from me like the tool-being of the table, like the real table would be. It's here. I look at it, I see the table. I'm not seeing all aspects of it at once, but I am seeing the table, not just scattered qualities. Furthermore, this table is not the same as the real table in the world, doing its own independent work, because the one I think I see might not exist – hallucinations do occur. And so intentional objects are not the same as real objects, despite what Husserlians always tell me. There was a big fight in Iceland last year with the 'Husserlian mafia' – they tried to tell me that intentional objects are the same as the tools, because they want to say that Husserl discovered everything that Heidegger did eight years earlier. It's not true!

One other point about Husserl: Husserl made another bizarre discovery that no one ever talks about, which is that one object contains others: namely, consciousness. My intentional relationship with the table for Husserl can be viewed as a unit, the relation itself as a whole. Why? Because I can talk about this relation, I can retroactively think about it, I can have other people analyse it for me – because, that is, other phenomenologists can analyse my relationship to the table – and none of those analyses ever exhaust the relation, which is enough to make it an object. That's the definition of the object: not a solid, hard thing, but a thing that has a unified reality that is not exhausted by any relation to it, so that the intention as a whole is one thing. But then within that intention, notice there are two things contained. There's the table and there's I myself, both contained within the intention. And there's an asymmetry here because this table is simply phenomenal; I myself, however, am real. And you can reverse it: if the table's actually encountering me, which might not happen then in that case, when you look at the relation asymmetrically in the other direction, the table is the real object in that case and I am the phenomenal object being reduced by the table to a caricature of myself. I know it sounds strange. But I generalise from there to say causal relations always occur on the inside of a third entity. It's not just something that's true of human consciousness and phenomenology. Containment is what a relationship *is*. 'Relationship' means: a real object meeting a sensual or intentional object on the inside of a third real object. And there are incredible problems trying to work out exactly how this happens. There are paradoxes that arise, and I started putting together the puzzle pieces in *Collapse II* in that article 'On Vicarious Causation'. And that's where the project is today. So I hope that gives some idea of what I'm doing so I can better situate it with respect to the other three, who I think are a very good match for what I'm doing. I think Ray chose exquisitely in this case.

I'll start with Ray since he went first. What is always refreshing for me in dealing with Ray and conversing with Ray is his knowledge of and sympathy for the empirical sciences, which is extremely rare in our discipline. Especially in the case of cognitive science, because, probably like most of you, I grew up in an environment where the name of the Churchlands was always spoken with a wince and a sneer. I don't know the work of the Churchlands nearly as well as Ray does. I just picked up Metzinger and am looking forward to reading that, but I don't know these things that well. So that's extremely refreshing. Ray, like the rest of us, does not want to see the human subject privileged in its relation to the world. The idea that our relation to the world is special could be eliminated, that it is a kind of folk-psychology, perhaps, I agree with him on all that, definitely. The two ways in which we may differ … Ray is something of a reductionist, because you heard his objections to me earlier about the hobbits, and he's mentioned the tooth fairy to me before. These are good objections. Are they really as real as solid physical objects? I'll address that one first. The point is well-taken, and this is a flaw in the Latourian position, I think – the position from which I come. Since I diverged from Heidegger, Latour was one of the first life preservers I grabbed on to, since he treats all objects on an equal footing, and I like that part of him. But I think there is a problem. You have to be able to explain reduction, and the way he does it is from the principle of "irreduction", which is to say, yes, anything can be reduced to anything else, as long as you do the work to show how it's related. Now this puts too much of the power in the hands of the human scientist, I think. Isn't it necessarily the case that some things just *are* inherently reducible to other things? I think that's probably true, and so I wouldn't want to go the 'irreduction' route. I think there's got to be a better way to solve this problem.

Ray is also opposed to the ontological difference, which is something I've retained as a Heideggerian. I don't use that term, but for me the ontological difference is the difference between the thing itself and its relation to anything else. Now, I think Ray's rejection of the ontological difference goes hand in hand with his reductivism, because, for Ray, you wouldn't need anything hiding behind anything else, right? You see certain things as symptoms or epiphenomena of other things, which are in fact real. Then you get to that real level, and then you try to reach something that's different from where you started. Now, what I would ask Ray is, how do you avoid what I would call, not naïve realism or speculative realism, but '*disappointing realism*' – my term for Kripke, whom I like very much. Kripke is my favourite analytic philosopher by far. He explodes so much of analytic philosophy, and turns it into metaphysics, by simply saying that Russell and Frege are wrong. A name does not refer to all the qualities we know about a thing, because I can learn that some of the qualities

I thought I knew about you were false and yet I'm still pointing at the same person. So there is something there that I *stipulate* to be you that is deeper than the qualities somehow. And he even criticises Strawson and Searle, who give us the watered down 'cluster theory': 'well, you only have to be right about *most* of the qualities you knew about the person'. But does that mean 51 percent of them, or a group of the most important? And so I follow Kripke in his critical portions, that you have to be pointing at something deeper that is essential and the same, that is not reducible to surface qualities. But the reason I call it 'disappointing realism' is because it ends up being the physical structure of things, for Kripke, that is real about them. So what's real about gold is that it has seventy-nine protons. I find that very disappointing. What's real about each of you is that you had to have the two parents that you had – which, first of all, is genetically false, right? You could get the same DNA, by some outlandish chance, through two different parents. And it just doesn't quite seem like it's my essence, somehow, to have come from those two parents. So, yes, I would like to know if you are committed to such a reductionism. For me, it's easy to escape that problem because I have all these different levels, Latour has all these different levels, and even if we have a problem in showing how things reduce, the reductionist position has the more profound problem of explaining what that final level is that endows something with reality. Is it just the physical structure or is it something more? If it's not a physical structure then you could be in some kind of weird idealism, where you have, I don't know, brain-states floating around … Pan-psychism seems to be coming back in fashion among some of these people. Even rocks and tomatoes have some primitive form of intentionality. So I'd like to know what Ray ends up with as his final stage once eliminativism has succeeded. That would be my question to him.

I'll go on next to Iain – I'm going in the order of the programme. I was cheering him on the whole way as I was reading his book. I am completely sympathetic to the idea that metaphysics and physics are the same, because one of the problems with physics now is that it's not metaphysical *enough*, I would say. It doesn't ever really raise the question, for me, of what causation is, for example. It argues about whether causation is statistical or whether it's retroactively caused by the observer, but it never really gets into the nuts and bolts of what happens when one thing touches another. I think it needs to become more metaphysical, and in 'On Vicarious Causation' I suggest that this is how philosophy can get out of the ghetto. We've been so terrified by the sciences for the past two hundred and twenty years. We find ourselves in this ghetto of human discourse and language and power – probably because we're afraid of stepping onto the level of nature. We're afraid that we don't have the resources, but I think we do. I think in Iain's book you can see there are tools for this that we already have. I'm also very sympathetic to his idea that inversions of Platonism are completely useless, because they keep you trapped in the same two-world theory. So, Nietzsche – great, he flips it over – but then you still have the same opposition between appearance and Platonic Ideas. Another thing I love about Iain's book is that it finally made sense of the *Timaeus* for me. There was a great fad for the *Timaeus* in the 1990s due to Derrida's *chora* essay and, even worse, through John Sallis, which really turned me off! So I never really understood it. Three years ago I had to teach the *Timaeus* because I had to take over the class for someone at the last minute, and I wished he had ordered any other dialogue than the *Timaeus*. But finally, after reading Iain's book, it's starting to become real to me: *Timaeus* is the site of a one-world physics, a physics of the Idea in Plato – it's wonderful. Your critique of Kant, I like that, and you cite Badiou as saying we need to overturn Kant, not Plato. I agree with that. I also completely agree with the idea that life-philosophy is always an alibi. Life-philosophy is an alibi for refusing to deal with the inorganic. Why do people like David Farrell Krell always go straight to life and never talk about rocks? What's so sexy about life? You see, it's an alibi, and it's a way to stay close to the human while claiming that you're going deeper than that somehow. Iain also leans toward anti-eliminativism, as I do in my own temperament, which makes us different from Ray, to some extent. And finally, I think, another thing that unites us, maybe more than the other two panelists, is that we are more ambivalent towards Badiou, I've noticed, although we both respect him. You criticise Badiou for giving us only this alternative of 'number and animal', and say that this is not a real alternative. You point out that it fails to capture the geological and other things, and I would tend to agree with that. And I also miss a philosophy of nature in Badiou. For me, the problem is – as I said in my review of Meillassoux's book in *Philosophy Today*,[13] – is the inconsistent multiple in Badiou really multiple? It doesn't really seem

---

13. Graham Harman, 'Quentin Meillassoux: A New French Philosopher', *Philosophy Today*, Volume 51, no. 1, Spring 2007: 104-117.

to do anything other than haunt our current count, our current situation. But the proper multiple would actually need to interact apart from the subject. It doesn't seem to me that it does so in Badiou, and that's why I would not call myself a Badiouian, though *Being and Event* is a fantastic work of speculative philosophy, the best one I can think of since *Being and Time*. I really appreciate the ambition of it and many of his strategies for attacking certain things.

So those are some of the things we agree on. There's really just one central disagreement between me and Iain, and it's a huge one, and it leads into a disagreement about the history of philosophy. The big difference is that Iain is against what he calls "somatism" and I'm totally in favour of it. For him, philosophy is not about the bodies, it's about a deeper force prior to the bodies from which the bodies emerge. For me it's nothing but objects, there is no pre-individual dynamic flux that surges up into various specific individuals. And I suspect there's some influence of Deleuze here, in this position. The objects themselves don't seem to have the power to interact, it all happens at a deeper level. Now, that leads to a big disagreement about the history of philosophy, because he sees Aristotle as being on the same side as Kant. He sees Aristotelian substance as being on the same side as the Kantian phenomenon, which I wouldn't agree with. There are times when Aristotle refers to substance as equivalent to the *logos*, but I think there are more places where he says the real can never be adequately expressed in a *logos*. So I would never go so far as to say that an Aristotelian chair is the same as my perception of a chair for Kant. I would say Aristotle's one of the good guys if you're a realist. He traditionally has been seen that way, so Iain's making a radical move by saying Aristotle's actually on Kant's side, and Plato's one of us – counterintuitive, but interesting. I would say we need to retain Aristotle on our team. I would say the Aristotelian forms are not mathematical formalisations. They are substantial forms, and substantial forms can hide from the *logos*. In fact they do hide, because the *logos*, I would say, never adequately exhausts them. And I would also oppose Iain and defend product over productivity, which I know is very unfashionable. In recent decades the avant garde has always been about process and not product. I would defend product over process, because I think much of process is lost when the product is created, and you don't need to know the process. Much information is lost. Yes, it's true that causation is productive. This is DeLanda, actually, not Iain, but Iain might have said something like this. Causation is productive because there's always more in the effect than there was in the cause. It's also true that there is less in the effect than there was in the cause, because I think many things about the cause are eliminated from the product. Different processes can yield the same object. But my question to Iain would be: Why not just have objects all the way down? Why do we need to have a unified dynamic nature? And notice he talks about geology, but he never, unlike Latour, talks about technological objects – oil rigs and things like that – because the different kinds of objects are less important for Iain than the deeper natural forces that all objects stem from.

Now, on to Meillassoux. There are so many things to admire about Meillassoux's book. Stylistically, it's very clear and economical. You never feel that he's wasting your time. Something Ray said over coffee either last night or this morning is that analytic philosophers would be shocked if they read this. They would say 'This isn't the French philosophy we heard about', because he's actually making rational arguments, step by step deductive arguments, which analytic philosophers pride themselves on doing, as opposed to those from the continental tradition. At first the argument about causation using the Cantorian transfinite was less convincing to me than the others in the book. But I've been thinking about this more for the past few weeks, and it's growing on me. So are there other ways to use the transfinite to solve other problems like this, such as the bogeyman of the infinite regress? Could you talk about a transfinite regress instead? I'm not sure how you would do that, but I've been toying with these ideas. You can certainly do it in the other direction: the universe is getting bigger and bigger and bigger. However big the universe is defined there must be a bigger universe, and physics seems inclined to support this lately.

Disagreements? The main disagreement here is obvious as well, which is: causation is the key for me, and for Meillassoux causation disappears. In some ways he leads us to a more chaotic universe than Hume does, because as Meillassoux himself says, Hume really doubts whether I can *know* that there's a causal relationship between things, whereas Meillassoux *knows* that it's absolutely contingent, the way things happen. He absolutely *knows* that there's no causal necessity between things. And that might be a brand new gesture. I don't know anyone else who has done this. He's doubting the Principle of Sufficient Reason while keeping the concept of non-contradiction, and he's thereby doubting necessity. But he actually goes further than this, and he doesn't talk about this much explicitly, but in my view, since he is saying that everything is *absolutely* contingent, what he's really doubting is that there's any relationality at all. Everything's absolutely cut off from everything else, because if one thing could be connected to another or could influence another thing, then he wouldn't have absolute contingency anymore. He would sometimes have relations between things and sometimes not. So it seems to me that absolute contingency entails no relations at all between anything, and this is why I have called Meillassoux a hyper-occasionalist, because he doesn't even have a God to save us from this problem. And unlike Hume, he does believe there's an ancestral world outside of us that exists, and it's totally outside of our minds, and we seem to have no access to that either, because that would require a relationship between me and what's outside of me, and that also seems impossible. So maybe I can know *a priori* that there's an ancestral world, and I may also have these qualities in my mind that are somehow linked in my mind, but – according to my reading of his system – there's really no hope of linking these things. It seems to me that in his system nothing touches anything else at all, not even partially, so in that way we're very close in our positions. The difference is that I try to find some solution so things can relate through the back door somehow, and he doesn't do this. And this leads to several other related problems.

So my first question to Meillassoux is: Does a thing touch its own qualities? He may disagree with my assessment that he's saying that nothing relates to anything else or touches anything else, but if he accepts that reading of his system, the question will come up as to whether a thing can even touch its own qualities. What is the relation of a thing to its own qualities? Within the mind, things do seem to relate, because there are many things in my mind at once, so there already is a kind of relationship. This is the criticism I made of Hume – you're starting with a relation. I see different splotches and colours and shapes around the room, and they are somehow related, because they're all in my mind at once. Also, if it's true, then there would be no relation between my perception of the world and the world itself. So that even if we know through his brilliant argument at the beginning of the book that there must be an ancestral realm outside of knowledge, what's the bridge between those two? How does my knowledge have any correspondence at all with what's out there? Correspondence seems impossible and so does unveiling, on Meillassoux's model. How does my mind relate to the world? And finally, what are the things outside the mind? Because if it's true that there's a problem, for Meillassoux, of linking a thing to its qualities, this means you have nothing but disconnected qualities outside the mind. And that doesn't make any sense to me, because, as I mentioned earlier about Merleau-Ponty, the black is already impregnated with the thing of which it is the blackness. So there are already these bridges in perception, and I would say, then, in causation as well. So, my question or objection to Meillassoux – and again, he might disagree with this reading completely – is that he's dealing only with necessity and contingency. Isn't there a middle ground, and isn't that middle ground a relation or interface? Because when two things relate, when you talk about a relationship, well, that's not absolute contingency, because they are affecting each other, right? And necessity implies almost a lack of separation between them, since it implies a kind of seamless mechanical whole in which an action already contains its effects. What a relation really consists of is two things that are somehow partly autonomous yet still manage to influence each other. And so my question is: Is there any possibility of interface in Meillassoux's system? Can one thing influence another without there being a necessary relationship between them? And finally, my real objection to him is that he hasn't published his system yet, because I'd love to stay up the next three nights and read it! That would be great reading. He says he's got multiple volumes coming, six or seven hundred pages. I would be delighted to read this right now, so please hurry! Alright, now I'll listen to the responses from my fellow panelists.

*

RAY BRASSIER: I take your point absolutely about the unfeasibility of reductionism. I think you're right. There are two problems: inter-theoretic reduction is often intractable, but even intra-theoretic reduction, even within a single theory there are often intractable problems associated with trying to reduce something to something else. So in a way I think that's right, and it's my own fault for over-emphasising this, over-egging the pudding, in my objections to a straightforward ontological univocity. But I do think we can revise the criteria in terms of which we ascribe reality to something. So, I would favour the term 'revisionary materialism' – which, before the term 'eliminative materialism' was canonised, was a plausible variant. In other words, the point is that you're not throwing something out, you're replacing something and amplifying and augmenting what you know and what you understand. This is the important thing. So, for instance, the elimination of gods, goddesses, all sorts of supernatural aspects – that can be understood as a diminishment of the world, but surely that would be kind of a parochial perspective! It's the amplification, it's all the other things we know about that's important. The point is that science has *multiplied* the kinds of things that exist in the world, it hasn't *diminished* them. So it seems to me to be a mistake to think that science and the amplification of our cognitive capacities is about having to give lots of things up and having to eliminate things. Sure, we eliminate things, but only in order to re-describe them as vastly more interesting and complicated things.

The second thing is, I think you're also right that it's unfeasible to claim that there's some kind of ultimate ontological substrate underlying appearances. This is the reason why I think materialism is highly problematic and, as Iain pointed out, it seems to dissolve into some form of alibi, a claim about the primacy of practice or suchlike. Because once physics has eliminated any kind of substantial understanding of materiality – and the whole point about the critique of metaphysics is the destitution of substance, of the idea that substance is the ultimate stuff of the world – materialism doesn't make any sense unless you adopt a materialism of process, of pure productivity, which I accept is entirely viable. In which case I think the problem then becomes one of convincingly explaining the interruptions or discontinuities in the process.

So I would say that there's no limit to realism. It's crucial not to have a parochial definition of realism in terms of available semantic or cognitive categories, because we will invariably end up revising or even abandoning them. The reason why I think epistemology is important is because of history, and because it's impossible to fix a moment in time and say now we really know everything there is. There's always a kind of dynamic and a revisability about the way in which we understand the world. And what's interesting about science is just how much it enriches the categories and the criteria we have for making differences in the world. So it's not a diminishment at all, it's a fantastic enrichment and amplification of our discriminatory capacities. We can make all sorts of differences that it was impossible to make previously. So that's my response, basically.

GH: You defended reductionism less than I thought you would. One of the things I like about talking with you is always the way you force me to think about this problem, because it is a problem. In a sense, it's hypocritical to say that nothing can be reduced to anything else, because what does philosophy do? Philosophy takes a very complicated world and reduces it to four or five structures that explain everything else. I guess all the sciences do this as well. Your point about how science has complicated things is also a Latourian point. He sees modernism as hypocritical. At the same time that it's trying to purify the natural from the cultural, it's also creating a multitude of Frankenstein-like hybrids that are crossing over the gap. The ozone hole is both natural and socially-constructed and narrated at the same time. So things only get more and more complicated. How much reduction actually happens? Often when we 'reduce' we are really just explaining things in terms of a new sort of belief. Chemistry is more complicated in the Periodic Table than it was before, in a sense. They weren't just reducing, were they? Although Mendelev did reduce chemicals to a small number of elements via the Periodic Table, he also pointed to a host of new elements and chemical properties that had not been suspected before. I think that's all I have to say, but I'm sympathetic to the idea that reductionism should not just be thrown out. We have to be able to do a better job of showing how the tooth fairy is less real than a forest.

QUENTIN MEILLASSOUX: I would like to say to Graham that there can't be any contradiction between our positions, and I will try to show why. I try to elaborate a principle, the principle of factuality, which says that only contingency is necessary. Not merely that contingency is necessary, but that *only* contingency is necessary. So, what do I try to do? I try to demonstrate that contingency has properties, fixed properties. And why do I have to demonstrate it? Because contingency is necessary, and a discourse about something necessary must be a demonstration. And if contingency and only contingency is necessary, everything which exists is contingent. So, I can't speak about what exists. I can't speak about what exists, because it is contingent. Now, what can you do with that which is contingent? You can describe it. What I try to demonstrate is that if you want to speak about what exists you can only *describe*, as phenomenology does – phenomenology is a description. If you want to know where I am, where my system is, in relation to your thinking, the connection lies in the fact that you describe things. It is necessary that phenomenology must be description, because, unlike what I do, phenomenology speaks about things which effectively exist. And what I try to do is to show that if you can describe it, it's not for a contingent reason. It's because what exists is just *a fact*. It's a fact that there is relation, that there are really substances, *etc.* And if you want to know how my work relates to what you describe, I would say, maybe it concerns the 'withdrawing substance', because what withdraws from description, for me, is the *fact* that it is. The fact that the thing *is* cannot be described. You can describe *what* it is, *how* it is, relation, *etc.*, but that relation, substance, *etc.*, are facts, and because they are facts you can only describe them. In my language, this is 'ontical' description. Ontical – concerned with what there is. But the *ontological* is concerned with demonstration. The discourse of being is, for me, demonstration, because for me, to be is to be a fact. Why do I say that? Because when you try to speak about being, you have this problem: for me, Heidegger doesn't speak about being. He speaks about modalities of being – conscience, Dasein, *etc.* That there is something, of course, he speaks of it, but it is very difficult to see if he really manages to produce a discourse about it. For me, if you want to have a discourse, an extended discourse, about this very narrow fact that there is something, you must remark that for something to be means the *fact* that it is. The fact, it clearly means to be, and I just speak about this invisible property, this invisible reality of things. Because animals, etc., don't see factuality, we don't see factuality. We *think* it. So you speak about what there is, whereas I speak about this, that it is a fact. There could be another world than ours. So my conception is not to deny the existence of relations but just to affirm their factual existence.

GH: Okay, but the relation between anything I see and what it might be representing? There doesn't seem to be any such relation for you, because what's withdrawing is the factuality rather than the subterranean being of the table, or something like this.

QM: It is not a necessary relation, but it is a relation. I say that laws exist. There are laws. For example, if I'm a Newtonian, I can say there are gravitational laws. I don't deny the existence of laws. I don't deny the stability of laws. Maybe these laws will persist for eternity, I don't know. I just say that it is *possible*, really possible, that laws just stop working, that laws disappear. They are facts, just facts, they are not necessary. It's not that you say that if something is contingent, you say that that it doesn't exist. It's factual, that's all. I fully uphold your right to be a phenomenologist, if you want to speak about things, because you have to describe them.

GH: Right. This is very helpful. I'm seeing your work differently now. There are relations, they are the relations of something contingent. Yes, that makes a lot of sense.

QM: What is strange in my philosophy is that it's an ontology that never speaks about what is but only about what can be. Never about what there is, because this I have no right to speak about.

GH: Wonderful. I need to think a little more. Maybe I was reading too much into this by interpreting that there were no relations between anything at all in your philosophy.

IHG: Actually, that is fascinating, and I think I accept completely the idea that contingency is fact. We can't gainsay that, because if we do we claim access to some positional element of necessity. But I don't think, actually, that it applies wholly to the position that you're [GH] adopting. You want egress from phenomenological treatment to a genuine description of causality, as you were saying, or a genuine account of causality. And you do that not because you don't want merely to *speak* about being. You reformulate the ontological difference, as it were, not in terms of being and beings but ... sorry, how did you put it?

GH: In terms of the subterranean thing and its relation to something else.

IHG: Yeah, in terms of relations. So you really want to speak about causality. Causality must of its nature be responsible for facts, but is it itself a fact? If there is real causality rather than just the laws we might subscribe to concerning causality, then it entails that there's an egress from the phenomenal envelope, the transcendental envelope, if and only if there is such causality. So there are, as it were, ontological commitments or entailments of your position, it seems to me, and so it's not wholly describable in terms of fact. Unless, of course, we have a specifically temporal understanding of facticity, such that factual states, ontic states, do appear and disappear with roughly the speed that they would under the model you explicitly evoked vis-à-vis Arab scholars' versions of occasionalism, where the raw speed of possible replacements, states of affairs, becomes bafflingly unthinkable.

So that was a comment I just wanted to make to pull things together. I do think there's an interesting question there, or a series of questions, actually. Vis-à-vis what you said about bodies, I have a roughly similar point. It's true I do suggest that it's wrong to identify matter with bodies but not that bodies are immaterial. So, at one level, the reason why it must be wrong to identify matter with bodies is that if it were the case that matter was a body, then all different bodies would not be matter, which wouldn't make sense of what a body is. So it must be the case that bodies are matter, but bodies are not all there is to matter, and I think that's roughly, actually, one of the central lessons of the advent of field physics. The dereliction of substance in any corporealist form is made real, is made concrete, with Faraday and so on – the idea of field replacing substance around the 1830s. So you have this replacement of a conception of substance as no longer attaching solely to bodies, but rather being a regional element of *physis*, which is comprised of forces. The question then is not reducing bodies to forces, nor saying bodies are other than matter because forces are genuine matter, but rather how these two elements are in fact elements of a process which is productive. Actually it was incredibly poignant when you said I don't go to geology – I would have, had the time not run out! You pointed out that I hadn't in fact dealt with certain things in the examples I gave of my project – technological objects and geology as a science, actually dealing with the earth and so on. But in fact that's the subject of my next book on ground. So I wanted to suggest a clarification of the relationship between body and *physis*, body and matter – which is why I think Plato's idealist account of what matter is is the best we have in so far as it's an account of matter …

GH: You also mentioned Giordano Bruno as an obvious ally of yours.

IHG: Yes.

GH: I immediately thought of his books when I read yours. But am I not right that, for you, *physis* does not exist in the bodies, except maybe as *expressed* in the bodies – but the action is all at the lower level?

IHG: I don't think one element of it is dispensable. I think maybe there's some work I need to do here, because I think this is a similar question to the question of the relation between productivity and product. Clearly, the relation as I described it earlier, that productivity is unthinkable without product is a dialectical trick at one level. But at another level, productivity really is productivity if and only if there are products. Otherwise, what is it? Is it force? Is there force without resistance?

GH: For you, when fire burns cotton, what's happening? Is the fire burning the cotton or is there some deeper layer at which the causal relationship is unfolding? I thought the latter.

IHG: I'd want to claim that there are innumerable things going on when fire burns cotton, and in the burning of the cotton by the fire.

GH: But it's not a somatic event for you?

IHG: It's a somatic event, a somatic event is one dimension of it, yes.

GH: So you're not actually denying causal relations between bodies, you're just saying that it's paralleled by another relationship at another level?

IHG: Actually, no, I think I *am* denying causal relationships, but only because it's between bodies. And this is not to say that there are no causal relations. It's rather that they go in a variety of directions. If there are causal relationships between bodies – in fact, there must be at one level, there must be, but at another level, it's not by virtue of the bodies that there are causal relationships between them, because there are other things going on as well. So it's the additional element rather than the one or the other. In fact, that was one of the things about your account of occasionalism that I found so useful.

GH: Good, good.

BENJAMIN NOYS: Earlier you made the remark dismissing Marxian materialism as impoverishing. And I just wondered, in relation to the conversation you had with Ray, there seems to be a question of different kinds of reduction …

GH: My idea, which I had vaguely in mind until Bruno Latour said it explicitly about a month ago, is that materialism is a kind of idealism. And that's what I want to say, because when you have materialism, what you're doing is reducing the things of the world to a fairly one-dimensional conception of what they are. Physical bodies taking up space in a measurable fashion. And the funny thing is, Žižek does this and *embraces* it and says the only possible materialism is idealism. The irreality of the world outside of my experience of it. So he actually takes that and celebrates it and Latour condemns it from the other direction. I want to condemn it, too. So I was happy with Iain's answer. I'm an anti-materialist.

ALBERTO TOSCANO: I'd like to just follow up on Ben's point. I was wondering if there was another way of organising your index cards, and it has to do exactly with whether the notion of realism should be understood in terms of – this might be a bit abstruse – but in terms of a reference to the real or a reference to reality. It seems to me that if realism has a reference to 'reality', then there is an implicit totalisation of that notion of reality. And I was struck, for instance, by the fact that, in your talk, in a way that didn't really seem to be thematised, you talked about 'the world', and Iain to some extent or another talked about 'nature'. And

I suppose the question is: Is it necessary for speculative realism to totalise reality, or to posit a grand total object of speculation? There are a number of reasons for asking this. I mean, partly, it's out of the notion that if indeed someone like Ray, for instance, or perhaps Quentin, has an attachment to certain aspects of Badiou's ontology, one of those aspects would be a fairly radical gesture of de-totalisation, the idea that the very notion of a universe might be scientifically useful but is philosophically incoherent, the notion of the All. And it also links partly to the question about politics and Marx and so on, because, in one sense, it only becomes a kind of suppressive gesture to politicise ontology or to talk about politics at all if you think that there is actually a total domain of reality or being; because then obviously if this total domain were overdetermined by one aspect of that domain, then this would be some kind of instrumentalisation of ontology. Because that implies the idea that what speculative realism relates to is *all* of reality, and then obviously if politics comes to overdetermine that entire reality, then that would be illegitimate. Now, if there is no total reality or total universe over which ontology or anything, speculative realism, operates, then it seems there's no sense in which one would need to have a speculative realism or an ontology that encompasses science, *etc.* This also has to do with the question Ray raised, because it's also the issue about the extent to which the demands of science and the demands of ontology overlap. Because it does seem that science is wedded to some extent or another to the notion of a universe. Now, it seems to me that speculative realism need not be – in fact, perhaps *shouldn't* be – wedded to the notion of a totality or of *a* reality or of *a* universe.

So when you said 'the world', does a philosophy of objects, of absolutely individuated, vacuum-packed objects, so to speak, as you put forward – does it depend on some totalisation? Because then that would imply that that totalisation is actually the relation within which all those objects are already included.

GH: Ray and I were discussing this on the Tube on the way in. It seems that I have to be committed to the notion of an infinite regress and also infinite progress to avoid this problem of totalisation. And I do feel that I'm committed to that, and I think science is leading that way more and more all the time, right? Where is the smallest particle? They've never found it. Where is this largest universe? Many physicists doubt it now. And I've been speaking openly in the past few years in defence of the infinite regress and the infinite progress. Maybe I should start calling them transfinite. So, no, I don't actually have a totality of the world. There are just objects as far as you look. I never come to the end of them and say there's a largest object that contains them all, precisely for the reason you mention, because then you'd have a final, present-at-hand – in the Heideggerian sense – present-at-hand totality which was constituted totally of relations and which itself was nothing but relations. And I can't have that, for the same reason that I can't have a smallest particle, because then you'd have a tiniest present-at-hand atom that had no other qualities, because it would have no relational structure at all. So yeah I do seem to be committed, and this upset me a little bit for the first couple of years …! No-one wants to be trapped in the infinite regress, right?

Well, what's inherently illogical about the infinite regress? There seem to be a fewer negative consequences than there are to saying there's got to be a final atom.

Daniel Miller: I want to ask you a bit more about infinity, with reference to your notion that the object has infinite qualities. You spoke of the chair, earlier, as having infinite qualities. There seems to be a problem, because, again, earlier still, you spoke about what the difference would be between a real crown and an imaginary crown, and you suggested that they could be distinguished on the basis of their qualities. The real crown would have different qualities to the imaginary crown. But if an object has an infinite amount of qualities, how can you distinguish it on the basis of those qualities?

GH: Just by appealing to Cantor, that there would be different sizes of infinities. You could say the imaginary crowns have an infinite number of qualities and the real crowns may have more or less qualities than the imaginary ones, but you can still have different sizes of infinities.

DM: Do you make a distinction very cleanly, between imaginary and real infinities, in that case?

GH: No, there's only one kind of infinity. They'd be different infinities in each case but only one kind. What I'm trying to say is, I don't think you can distinguish between imaginary and real crowns on any basis outside of qualities, because the distinction has to be in those qualities themselves. My suspicion is that there have to be different qualities in the cases of the real crowns and the imaginary ones. Existence is not something either imposed or not imposed on the qualities from outside, by God, or by its position in relation to a Kantian subject. In the qualities themselves there has to be a difference between real and imaginary crowns – that's just my suspicion in the last couple of months.

Peter Hallward: Without trying to ask questions I've asked before, I understand your system as far as it works for intentional objects: a chair is not exhausted by your sitting in it, but nevertheless it is a chair as opposed to a hybrid of materials or a commodity or something else, in so far as it can be sat on and have all the other associations that make it a chair and not another kind of object; and it's slightly different, then, from a pile of rocks that we can sit on outside – that alone doesn't make it a chair, right? And we've used it as a chair already today. So as regards the issue of its 'chairness' it seems to me that you have this problem of what it means for this particular object, what it is that objectifies it as a chair or as a table if it's not something to do with a very large number of relationships in that very complicated history of the evolution of something like a chair in the course of history and so on that would explain it. And if you abstract from all those relationships, I don't see what's left of the chair *qua* chair. I can see that you can abstract something. You can probably abstract something that starts to look a lot like a Kantian thing-in-itself, but how would it be a chair? Or if you take something that's less obviously an intentional object, like a cloud or something, and you try, in a rigorous way, to isolate the product from the process, you abstract it, then, from all the processes whereby water vapour condenses at a certain temperature and altitude and so on, what are you left with? In what sense is it really a cloud as opposed to a particular moment that we can isolate in the way precipitation is condensing up there in the sky? In what sense is it a cloud except for someone who *intends* it as a cloud?

GH: Right. You made a very similar objection to 'On Vicarious Causation' before it was a *Collapse* article, which is when I was using shoes as an example, and saying the shoes are the same shoes for me and other people and for ants, and you were asking: Is it really a shoe for ants? And I guess now that I've thought about it for a few months, I think the answer is no, obviously, it's not really a shoe for ants, it's something else, but that doesn't mean there's nothing withdrawing behind my use of it as a shoe. DeLanda makes this point very well on the first page of his new book, which is that, even though we are the ones that create social institutions, this does not mean that our concepts of them exhaust them. So yes, I can be the first person ever to see that pile of rocks as a chair, but couldn't there still be a 'chairness' to it deeper than my use of it? Because I could still keep using it as a chair and still find some leeway to use it as a chair differently from how I'm doing it now. So I think that 'chair-form' that I myself have discovered there is still something deeper than my current use of that 'chair-form'. That's how I would describe it. I don't know if that helps.

ROBIN MACKAY: This very much follows on from Peter's question. I'm very sympathetic to the idea that we have to try to break reality out from its incarceration in our relation to it, our conditioning of it, but it seems to me that physics already does that, but it does it precisely at the expense of the commonsense idea of what an object is. And what puzzles me about your system is that you seem to carry over that commonsense idea of what objects are into this other realm. So, for instance, if there's a billiard ball that hits another billiard ball and it envelopes that other billiard ball in its intentionality – first of all, I can't understand, this is not really an important point, but I can't understand why the intentionality is an object; what is it that makes you call it an object? But secondly, what part of the second billiard ball does the first billiard ball envelop? Only the bit that it hits? The whole thing? How does it know the billiard ball's an object? Does it only envelop half of it, quarter of it? And it seems to me the only way you can answer that is by saying every single piece of the billiard ball envelops every other piece in contact with it, with its intentionality. And so you go down and down, and you're just going to end up with physics again, you're just going to end up with the same ontic explanation of causality that disappointed you in the first place. So, just to go back to Peter's point, it's entirely possible that the ant doesn't know the difference between the shoe and the table that the shoe's on or the piece of grass it's on; I don't understand how these things can be unequivocally named 'objects', in other words, and for me this is the profundity of Lovecraft, why he's a profound realist. Because when you go through the gates, when reality is revealed to you, it's just this complete chaos which you can't objectify. And obviously Lovecraft is Kantian in that respect, but I can't see how your system can get past that problem.

GH: There are three questions there and I'll take the easiest one first: Why is an intention an object? Well, if you look at the usual definitions of objects throughout the history of philosophy, criteria are along the lines of naturalness, indestructibility, irreducibility to anything else, and so on – these are the classical definitions of substance. My definition of an object is simply a unified thing that has a reality that's not exhausted by any approach to it from the outside, and intention clearly has that feature, because what is phenomenology about? It's about retroactively analysing intentions. Even if I analyse what my intention is at the moment, what looks and what is looked at are not the same thing. So what I'm doing when I'm looking at my own intention of the cup is converting my relation to the cup into an object. It can remain mysterious and puzzling and they do long phenomenological analyses, even of these very simple relations. So that's why it's an object.

RM: But when you say you're converting your intention into an object, that's a very Kantian thing to say, isn't it?

GH: I think anytime we intend something, the intention can be converted into an object, yes. But, just as DeLanda says about social institutions: even if we're creating it, that doesn't mean that our creation of it exhausts the reality of the thing. So, yes, in a way my relation to the cup isn't really an object until I convert it into one as a phenomenologist. I can decide, 'Okay, I'm going to analyse my relationship to this', but that doesn't mean that my act of identifying the relation for the first time exhausts it. That's why you have to go on and analyse that intentionality there, because there's more in it than meets the eye. Just by creating kids, you don't know everything about the kids. There's always going to be more to them than you suspected. Causation is productive. I don't think you can ever get from my position to physics, because physics never makes causation into a problem, as far as I can see. The problem of causation in physics is always one of whether causation is deterministic, or whether it's statistical, or how you read quantum theory. There's not really any discussion in physics of what actually happens when one thing influences another.

RM: Isn't that because physics has revealed that that's a false problem?

GH: I don't think it's a false problem. I think it's a *forgotten* problem, by physics. You've got four causes in Aristotle. Where have the four causes gone in physics? Nowhere. You have efficient causation, maybe material causation, they've gotten rid of formal and final. Fine, get rid of final, I'll give you that one! – What about formal causation? Formal causation is where all the action's happening in philosophy, I think. Forms do all the work in Aristotle and elsewhere, and that's what I want to retain. There's no formal causation in physics. My favourite author for dealing with formal causation is Marshall McLuhan, one of the really unrecognised giants of the past one hundred years of the humanities. Fabulous stuff, wrongly written off as a kind of pop TV analyst, really brilliant systematic work about how one medium reverses into another under the right conditions. McCluhan deserves to be the founder of a philosophical school. Again, he's a fan of formal cause. And Francis Bacon before him – another completely misunderstood philosopher – not an empiricist in the way people think. You're not just doing experiments and reducing things to their causes, you're actually finding the forms that are locked up and compressed inside of things. And he even says that efficient causation is ludicrous. I was shocked when I read that. We have this textbook image of Bacon that has nothing to do with the real Bacon. So I would appeal to Bacon and McLuhan, great champions of formal cause, which science does not handle properly.

Presentation by Quentin Meillassoux

I would first of all like to give my thanks to the organisers of this conference. I'm very proud to participate in it, considering the exceptional quality of the contributors. And I am very happy to have this opportunity to express my admiration for the books of Ray Brassier, Graham Harman, and Iain Grant. I think that the very existence of such a philosophical configuration of original conceptual projects is in itself remarkable. I think that we also must have in common, the four speakers, the difficulty of explaining our jobs to our families! But as I said to Graham, I think it is a configuration of what could be called a 'weird realism', four modalities of 'weird realism'. I'd like to discuss here one of the theses of Ray Brassier's beautiful book, *Nihil Unbound*, and try to respond to some of his stimulating objections, supported by the non-philosophy of François Laruelle. Thanks to this discussion, I will expose and mark out the fundamental decisions of *After Finitude*, especially concerning correlationism and the principle of factuality.

As you may know, I have given the name 'correlationism' to the contemporary opponent of any realism. By this term, I wanted to avoid the usual 'parade' of transcendental philosophy and phenomenology against the accusation of idealism – I mean answers such as: 'Kantian criticism is not a subjective idealism since there is a refutation of idealism in the *Critique of Pure Reason*'; or 'phenomenology is not a dogmatic idealism, since intentionality is orientated towards a radical exteriority, and it is not a solipsism since the givenness of the object implies, according to Husserl, the reference to an intersubjective community'. And the same could be said about *Dasein*, which is originarily a 'being-in-the world'. Even though these positions claim not to be subjective idealism, they can't deny, without self-refutation, that the exteriority they elaborate is essentially relative: relative to a consciousness, a language, a *Dasein*, etc. No object, no being, no event, or law which is not always-already correlated to a point of view, to a subjective access – this is the thesis of any correlationism.

By the term 'correlation', I also wanted to exhibit the essential argument of these 'philosophies of access', as Harman calls them; and – I insist on this point – the exceptional *strength* of this argumentation, apparently and desperately implacable. Correlationism rests on an argument as simple as it is powerful, and which can be formulated in the following way: No X without givenness of X, and no theory about X without a positing of X. If you speak about something, you speak about something that is given to you, and posited by you. Consequently, the sentence: 'X is', means: 'X is the correlate of thinking' in a Cartesian sense. That is: X is the correlate of an affection, or a perception, or a conception, or of any subjective act. To be is to be a correlate, a term of a correlation. And in particular, when you claim to think any X, you must posit this X, which cannot then be separated from this special act of positing, of conception. That is why it is impossible to conceive an absolute X, *i.e.,* an X which would be essentially separate from a subject. We can't know what the reality of the object in itself is because we can't distinguish between properties which are supposed to belong to the object and properties belonging to the subjective access to the object.

In my opinion, the *Principles of the Science of Knowledge*, written by Fichte in 1794, is the *chef-d'oeuvre* of such a correlationism. The *Science of Knowledge* is to date the most rigourous expression of the correlationist challenge opposed to any realism. I'd like to begin this talk by remembering the principal aspect of this philosophy, so that we can be conscious of the very nature of this anti-realism at its climax. I won't speak, of course, about the details of this very difficult book, but I shall only recall the heart of its argumentation: the principle of its conceptual production, which appears to me as the most precise form of the obstacle that a contemporary realism has to surmount. I will rely on a recent interpretation of the *Science of Knowledge*, which has completely changed the comprehension of Fichte, at least in France: in 2000 Isabelle Thomas-Fogiel[14] proposed a devastating criticism of the dominant interpretation of Fichte in our country – Philonenko's interpretation – and allowed us at last to read the true *Science of Knowledge*, instead of the extraordinary but also eccentric reconstruction elaborated by Philonenko in 1966.[15]

Briefly: Philonenko claimed that the three first principles of the *Science of Knowledge* – including the famous 'I = I' – were not true principles, but dialectical illusions that Fichte undertook to deconstruct throughout his system. So, in the *Science of Knowledge*, you have three principles, and he deduces all that follows from these three principles? – No, it's not true! According to Philonenko, they were illusions that Fichte deconstructed! Therefore, of course, Philonenko also had to explain that Fichte was a strange

14. I. Thomas-Fogiel, *Critique de la réprésentation: Étude sur Fichte* (Paris: Vrin, 2000).

15. A. Philonenko, *La liberté humaine dans la philosophie de Fichte* (Paris: Vrin, 1966).

guy, since he had said to everyone the exact opposite of what he really meant! The situation in France was as if a famous interpreter had claimed solidly for thirty years that the definitions and axioms of Spinoza's *Ethics* were in fact certain illusions deconstructed by Spinoza, and convinced everybody that Spinoza was just a very weird man to say systematically the exact contrary of what he really thought. Thomas-Fogiel quite simply restores – in my view, indisputably – the immediate truth on this point: the principles of the *Science of Knowledge* are *true* principles; and, thanks to her, French philosophers have at last discovered what everyone else already knew!

How must we read Fichte, consequently? According to Thomas-Fogiel, as a thinker of the pragmatic contradiction: Fichte is a thinker who intends to evaluate every philosopher by his capacity to do what he says and to say what he does. A pragmatic contradiction consists, as you know, in contradicting the content of a sentence by the enunciation of this very sentence. It is not a logical contradiction – such as: 'Peter thinks and Peter does not think' – but a contradiction between the content of a sentence and its performance, its effective formulation. For example: 'I don't think' does not contain a logical contradiction, but consists in a pragmatic contradiction between the content of the proposition and the fact that I think or pronounce it. The fact that I think this proposition is in contradiction with what I say in the proposition. Thomas-Fogiel used this notion, elaborated by Hintikka in relation to Descartes and Austin,[16] to interpret the *Science of Knowledge* as a philosophy

---

16. J. Hintikka, '*Cogito, ergo sum*: Inference or Performance?', *Philosophical Review,* Volume 71, No. 1, Jan. 1962: 3-32, included in *Knowledge and the*

written under the systematic constraint of pragmatic non-contradiction. In particular, the *Science of Knowledge* destroys any attempt at realism by proving it is always and immediately self-contradictory in a pragmatic way. What is a philosopher really doing when he claims to have access to a reality independent of the I? He posits, says Fichte, an X supposed to be independent of any position. In other words, he posits the X as non-posited. He pretends to think what is independent and exterior to any conceptualisation, but in doing so he doesn't say what he effectively does. He says his X is indifferent to thought, but what he does, of course, is simply to conceptualise an X perfectly dependent on his own thinking. Hence, according to Fichte, the pragmatic contradiction between the acts and the thesis of any realist.

But Fichte's very originality, in which he anticipates Hegelian dialectics, is that his contradiction is essentially fruitful. Contradictions produced – notably, by realism – in the *Science of Knowledge* do not lead to the end of the discourse, but to the creation of new concepts able to temporarily neutralise the mortal opposition between content and act. Only temporarily, since such concepts allow one to shift the contradiction again and again but not to abolish it – at least in the sphere of theory, the resolution of the initial contradiction being the privilege of practical reason, not of theoretical reason.

To be more precise, we could say that there is for Fichte a sort of 'double bind' for philosophy itself: it has both to posit the secondariness of thinking relative to

Known (Dordrecht: Reidel, 1974); '*Cogito, ergo sum* as an Inference and a Performance', *Philosophical Review*, Volume 72, No. 4, Oct. 1963: 487-96.

an independent real – otherwise we couldn't explain the passivity of sensation – and at the same time it can't posit such a reality without contradiction. This 'double bind', which is ultimately still what 'realism' means for contemporary philosophy – we need it, but we can't claim it, so we claim *and* deny it – this double bind never oversteps, according to Fichte, the limits of the I, because the active I is the first and absolute principle of his philosophy. But Fichte carries out the most elaborate destruction of any realism through a strategy we could call the 'pragmatico-genetic contradiction'; that is, an exhibition of the way in which the realist is forced to create his own concepts in order to escape, for a while, his ultimately fatal contradiction.

To be a contemporary realist means, in my view, to efficiently challenge the Fichtean fatality of pragmatic contradiction; not exactly to challenge the very thesis of the *Science of Knowledge*, but the mode of refutation which is therein invented, and whose principle is always the same: If you think *X*, then you *think* X. That is what I called the 'circle of correlation', the first argument of every correlationism which claims that realism is necessarily a vicious circle, a denial of its very act. Can a realism pass the test of pragmatic contradiction? That is the question which has governed my own investigations and which I shall examine in relation to the non-philosophy of François Laruelle, on the one hand, and the principle of factuality I set out in *After Finitude*, on the other. But why this comparison with Laruelle?

In his wonderfully radical book, *Nihil Unbound*, Ray Brassier devotes a chapter to *After Finitude*[17] and another

17. *Nihil Unbound*, Chapter 3; also see **Collapse** Vol. II, 15-54.

to Laruelle's non-philosophy.[18] Brassier, who is a first-class reader, tries to show that Laruelle's 'transcendental realism' is a more reliable and rigorous way to root out the philosophy of correlationism than that which I propose. Even if Brassier's reading is generally kind towards *After Finitude*, he points out what he sees as some weaknesses in my argument, and particularly the fact that I speak of an intellectual intuition of facticity. In this expression – 'intellectual intuition' – Brassier suspects a possible absolutisation of meaning, and maybe a remnant of speculative idealism that threatens my will to escape from the circle of correlation. I shall try to respond to this objection in the following way: First, I will show why the non-philosophy of Laruelle, despite its admirable rigour, fails, in my view, to efficiently fight the argument of the correlational circle. And I will demonstrate this point by applying to non-philosophy a Fichtean model of refutation – that is, a refutation based on the pragmatico-genetic contradiction. Then, I'll show that what I called 'intellectual intuition' in *After Finitude* – and what I shall now call, more precisely, 'dianoetic intuition' – is able, unlike non-philosophy, to neutralise correlationism, even in its Fichtean version – that is, even at the high point of its rigour.

The funny thing is that I discovered, after I decided to confront Laruelle with Fichte, that Laruelle himself, in his *Principles of Non-Philosophy*,[19] compared his own reasoning with Fichte's in the *Science of Knowledge*. But Laruelle is a tributary of the outdated commentary of Philonenko; that's why his confrontation is disappointing.

---

18. *Nihil Unbound*, Chapter 5.

19. François Laruelle, *Principes de la non-philosophie* (Paris: PUF, 1996).

Quentin Meillassoux

Let's start with Laruelle's conception of what he calls 'philosophy' – or the 'circle of Decision' – which we could also call the 'circle of objectivity'. Decision – with a big 'D' – is for Laruelle the source of every philosophy in any time. Brassier sums up precisely the meaning of this 'Decision' by recalling the Kantian structure which underlies its conceptualisation. Every philosophy is constituted, according to Laruelle, of three moments: first, an empirical *datum*; second, a *factum* made of *a priori* categories, categories unified by a transcendental (for Kant, transcendental apperception); and finally, we have a return of the *a priori* to the *datum*, that is, a unification of *datum* and *factum*, a moment which, in Kant, corresponds to the transcendental deduction. From this last unification proceeds experience as the transcendent reality produced by philosophy. Those moments we might also call 'circle of philosophical Decision', or 'circle of objectivity'. Brassier contests – and I think he's right to do so – that this triple movement constitutes, for Laruelle, the eternal essence of philosophy. He suggests that what Laruelle calls 'philosophy' can be identified with what I call 'correlationism'. Consequently, Brassier claims that Laruelle, with his non-philosophy, works out a non-correlationism more radical and sure than my own version, burdened as it is by intellectual intuition. Let's see how Laruelle proceeds to extricate himself from the field of philosophy – that is, correlationism, in Brassier's version. I can't of course reproduce all of Laruelle's reasoning, which is complex and evolves from one book to another, but I won't need to do so to explain my objection.

First, I remark that there is a precise reason, different from Brassier's own reason, to refuse the identification of philosophy with the circle of objectivity. Brassier claims it is vain to look for an eternal essence of philosophy, philosophy being constituted by the contingent history of texts. But I think there is another reason, a structural one, to refuse the idea that philosophy should be encapsulated in the circle of objectivity, one that Fichte was probably the first to conceive. This reason is: if you want to think the circle of objectivity – what Fichte calls the representation, the unification of *datum* and *factum* and the *a priori* – you need a point of view outside of this circle. That is, if you want to conceive what a representation is, you need a faculty which can't itself be representative, because there is no representation of representation. You can have a representation – perceptual or imaginative – of a horse or a wall, but you can't have any representation of a representation. If you want to think what a representation is – that is, a unity of *datum* and *a priori* – you need something other than objective knowledge, this being itself constituted by the unity of *datum* and *a priori*. This was Kant's essential failing, according to Fichte: Kant didn't explain how it was possible to write the *Critique of Pure Reason*. He described all knowledge in terms of objectivity – that is, in terms of representation, constituted by the synthesis of categories and space-time – but his own *philosophical* knowledge about objective knowledge, that is, about representation, couldn't be described in the same terms. How was Kant able to elaborate transcendental notions such as matter and form, categories and representation? This operation needed, according to Fichte, another faculty which was almost described by Kant: the faculty of reflection. And this faculty, reflection – contrary to the apparent opinion of Laruelle – is essentially different from objectivity. Reflection is a non-representative, non-objectivating faculty, which is the condition for conceiving objectivity as such. Reflection is what allows Laruelle himself to stand outside the circle of objectivity when he conceives its unity. Laruelle is outside the circle of objectivity when he describes it, because describing it means not being in it anymore. But this is also the case with every philosopher who was able to describe this circle: all of them adopt, consciously or not, the point of view of reflection, but Fichte was the first to consciously and systematically adopt this point of view in order to construct his system.

Consequently, if you want to escape from the circle of correlationism, you must not only escape from the circle of objectivity, but also from the larger circle of reflection, which is outside Laruelle's circle and includes it. Correlationism, as I define it, includes reflection, since reflection is position. When you conceive the circle of objectivity, you are outside this circle, but still in the circle of correlationism, according to me. So if, like Laruelle, you posit something outside the circle of objectivity – in his case the Real outside 'Philosophy' – this Real will still be, according to me, in the circle of correlationism. Because it will be a posited Real: a Real posited by reflection outside of representation. This is exactly what Fichte calls, in his technical vocabulary, the 'independent activity' – that is, to simplify a great deal, the notion of the 'thing in itself', outside representation – Kantian representation – and impossible to conceive through this representation.

Let's demonstrate this point more precisely. Here is my strategy: as I said previously, I propose to apply to Laruelle the Fichtean way of reasoning – not his precise thesis, but the pragmatico-genetic contradiction which constitutes the principle of his argumentation. I am going to reconstruct Laruelle's position in a correlational way, showing how what he calls 'the Real' is nothing but a posited Real, and how the concepts created by non-philosophy just shift this contradiction without being able to abolish it. We shall see clearly, then, why I think that Laruelle doesn't really escape from the circle of correlation.

Let's begin with the Real as described by Laruelle. The Real, he says, is radically indifferent to and independent of the circle of objectivity. The Real precedes thought, but thought, conversely, is always dependent upon the Real, which is essentially unaffected by thought. That is what

Laruelle says, this is the content of his discourse. But – Fichtean question – what does he do? What is the act of his discourse? Laruelle, of course, posits such a Real as independent of any thought. Consequently, he does exactly the contrary of what he says. He says, 'the Real precedes thought – in particular, philosophical thought – and is indifferent to it', but the order of what he does is the opposite of the order of what he says: he begins by thinking, and especially by thinking what philosophical thought is, and then progresses to the Real. The Real is truly a notion of the Real which is dependent on thinking, and which is post-philosophical, elaborated from his notion of philosophy. The real order – or the order of acts, not of content – is manifest in the very name of Laruelle's theory: 'non-philosophy'. Non-philosophy is supposed to think the relation of thinking with a Real which precedes philosophy, but the name 'non-philosophy' can only be constructed from the name 'philosophy' together with a negation. Philosophy precedes non-philosophy in nomination, as in the acts of thinking. Hence, we have the first and manifest pragmatic contradiction between what Laruelle says about the Real and what he does when elaborating this notion.

But of course this contradiction, this pragmatic contradiction, is far too trivial to worry Laruelle, and we can imagine that he could easily respond to it. But how? By producing new concepts. So the contradiction, the pragmatic contradiction, becomes fruitful because it compels the thinker to shift it so that he can avoid a gap which in fact will never be filled in. Laruelle could first demonstrate that our objection proceeds from a series of confusions. The Real is a negation of nothing: it is relative to nothing, according to him, and especially can't be identified with the concept of the Other which presupposes the X whose other it is. The Real, on the contrary, is radically autonomous, without relation to thought. Thought, on the other hand, can distinguish itself from the Real if it ceases to identify itself with philosophy, locked up in the circle of objectivity, to think under the axiom of the Real. Then thought knows itself as determined-in-the-last-instance by the Real, says Laruelle. That is: thought knows itself as relatively, but not radically, autonomous. This means that thought can produce by itself its own concepts, but has to avoid the sufficiency of absolute autonomy proper to philosophy and which is its intrinsic illusion.

We now have a series of new concepts: radical and relative autonomy, sufficiency, determination-in-the-last-instance, etc. But have we then escaped from the correlational circle? Of course not; we have only deduced what is necessary to think a *posited* Real, if we admit that this Real effectively precedes any position. But Laruelle gets this first position just by force, just by a *coup de force*. The Real is *posited* as indifferent to its positing and as non-related to thought. After that, Laruelle reflects on the possibility of his own theory by claiming the relative autonomy of thought; but in fact, it seems, on the contrary, that his thought is able to posit the Real itself and its relation to the Real. That is, to posit that the Real has no relation to thought, and that thought has a relation of relative autonomy to the Real. He also posits all these concepts as essentially non-dialectical, but what he does is of course easy to dialecticise. For the Real is now linked more than ever to his concepts, more dependent on more and more intricate elaborations aiming at the exhibition of its independence. And of course, every thesis added by Laruelle will only make the situation worse. That's why the only solution for Laruelle will be the solution, according to me, of every modern realism against correlationism or idealism: as it seems impossible to escape from this position, from this objection, the only solution is to disqualify what you can't refute. The solution for Laruelle can only be: First, to say that the Real is posited by an axiom – that is, something that can be neither demonstrated nor discussed – and secondly, to introduce a precise concept which will disqualify in advance anyone who contests such an axiom; that is, the concept of 'resistance'. I will end my Fichtean reconstruction of Laruelle with this concept that I propose to examine, considering its genealogy and its strategic importance for any contemporary realism.

To understand the fortune of the concept of resistance, we must be conscious of the main characteristic of the correlational circle, which is that this circle is both monotonous and apparently implacable. It is just the same objection, tedious and irritating: if you posit X, then you *posit* X. Sometimes we encounter this enraging situation: a brilliant, subtle and interesting theory is easily refuted by a well-known and trivial argument, put forward by a stupid opponent. That is often the situation of the post-Kantian realist faced with the correlationist. And this necessarily produces the same psychological reaction on the part of the realist: he will become both tired and furious. The perfect illustration, the primal scene, of this psychological law of modern realism, in my opinion, can be found in a Tintin comic book. In one of his adventures, Tintin's acolyte Captain Haddock tries to unstick a plaster from his finger.

But of course, each time he removes it with another finger, the plaster sticks immediately onto it! And since the process is endless, Haddock quickly loses his temper. The plaster is identical to the 'that is what *you think*' that the correlationist just has to add to any realist thesis one might try to assert. The realist always has to posit more concepts to prove he has accessed pre-conceptual reality. The situation seems desperate: how could you refute that whenever you think something, you *think* something? That's why the realist, conscious that his reasoning is apparently in vain, has generally renounced any attempt to refute the correlationist and has adopted what I call a 'logic of secession' towards him. This secession is a blunt refusal addressed to the correlationist: an 'I won't discuss *with* you anymore, I will rather discuss *about* you'. This is a logic of unbinding, of independence, but this independence is not the originary independence of the Real towards the correlation but that of the realist towards the discussion with the correlationist. This logic of secession, it seems to me, takes two principal forms in modernity.

The first one consists in fleeing voluntarily from the discussion in order to rediscover the richness of the concrete world. Schopenhauer said that solipsism was a fortress impossible to penetrate, but also pointless to attack, since it is empty. Solipsism is a philosophy nobody can refute, but also one that nobody can believe. So let's leave the fortress as it is, and let's explore the world in all its vastness! The first strategy of the realist, similarly, concerns the fortress of correlation: 'If you want to stick your plaster on me, please do, but then leave me alone; I have so many interesting realities to investigate!' This is what I call the 'Rhetoric of the Rich Elsewhere'. The realist disqualifies the correlation-ist argument as uninteresting, producing arid idealities, boring academics, and pathological intellectuals. 'Let's stop discussing, and let's open the windows: let's inhale things and feel the breeze'. This is an attractive and sometimes powerful rhetoric – not in a pejorative but in a Nietzschean sense. A rhetoric of the fruitful concreteness of things, the revenge of descriptions and style on repetitive quibbles. Latour, sometimes, severs all links with correlationism in such a way, and does so with much talent and humour. It must be added, of course, that he also uses other elaborate instruments to fight the circle. But in the case of the 'Rich Elsewhere' rhetoric, it is clear that it is not an argument, but a disqualification of he who argues: the sickly and boring correlationist.

The other method of disqualification used by modern realism is a more fundamental one: it brings out the implicit logic of the 'Rich Elsewhere', which consists in replacing the discussion with the correlationist with an exposition of his motivations. We no longer examine what he says, we examine *why* he says what he says. It is the well-known logic of suspicion that we find in Marx, with the notion of ideology, or in Freud, with precisely the notion of resistance. The realist fights every form of idealism by discovering the hidden reasons behind these discourses – reasons that do not concern the content of philosophies, but the shameful motivations of their supporters: class-interest, libido, *etc.* In this way, the realist explains in advance why his theories must be refused by those who are unable to see the truth for such and such objective reasons. Hence he will neutralise any refutation as an already-described symptom of social or psychological resistance, unconscious resistance which is, according to the realist, often unavoidable. But what is interesting, from my own point of view, is that this well-known strategy of suspicion can be understood as the necessary result of an inability to rationally refute the insipid and implacable argument of the correlationist. And we could say the same about the Nietzschean suspicion of the sickly Kantians of the University. Laruelle inherits these strategies through his own concept of resistance: he says, of course, that his non-philosophy must necessarily excite great resistance from philosophy – he predicts that philosophers will reproach him for a *coup de force*, exactly as I did – and he claims that any refutation he will encounter from the point of view of the circle of Decision is the necessary effect of his theory of the Real upon philosophical sufficiency.

Brassier makes an interesting suggestion regarding Laruelle's theory: he says that one of his major concepts – unilateralisation – is a 'surgical intervention upon the body of transcendental synthesis; severing terms from relations, amputating reciprocity and sharpening one-sidedness'.[20] Unilateralisation is a complex concept in Laruelle that I can't explore now but which is admirably explained by Brassier in his book. It is, generally speaking, the consequence of the thought of the radical autonomy of the Real towards thought. What Brassier says, it seems to me, is that Laruelle introduces into the transcendental circle – constituted by the reciprocal synthesis between categories and intuition – the essential asymmetry of the Real and thought, an asymmetry which disjoins the correlations of critical and idealist philosophies. But my own hypothesis about this power of disjunction is that it proceeds more profoundly from the strategy of secession towards correlationism. The radical autonomy of the Real, its unbinding from thought, is produced by the radical autonomy of the non-philosopher, of Laruelle himself, towards any discussion with the correlationist. Laruelle posits the Real as an axiom, and then he posits his refusal to discuss the correlationist refutation of this axiom with the concept of resistance, which disqualifies any objection without answering to it. It is this very secession with the correlationist which creates in the discourse the effect of the radical autonomy of the Real, and which then produces all the effects of surgical interventions upon transcendental synthesis. The meaning of radical autonomy is Laruelle's secession rather than the severing of the Real.

The concept of resistance is an effect, as we said, of the theory of suspicion. But, in my view, and even if I admire Marx, Nietzsche and Freud, realists should at last start becoming suspicious of this venerable theory of

---

20. *Nihil Unbound*, 147.

suspicion; Because, as I said, it seems to me that we can trace a genealogy of suspicion and its favourite notion, resistance, which discovers at its root an inability to refute, precisely and simply, the unbearable argument of the circle. I refuse suspicion because realism, in my view, must remain a rationalism. The circle argument *is* an argument and must be treated as such. You don't refuse a mathematical demonstration because the mathematicians are supposed to be sickly or full of frustrated libido, you just refuse what you refute! I clearly understood the calamitous consequences of the notion of resistance when I heard an astrologer, answering placidly to a sceptic, that the latter's incredulity was predictable since he was a Scorpio!

What is at stake, consequently, is to build up a realism released from the strategy of suspicion: a realism which doesn't need to *disqualify* the correlationist because it has clearly *refuted* him. I want that easy and implacable refutation to be transferred to the other side, from correlationism to realism; and, conversely, the argument of resistance to become the last possible defence of correlationism itself. But I don't want to refute only to refute and win the discussion. As we shall see, I'm looking for a creative refutation. That is, a refutation which discovers a truth, an absolute truth, inside the circle itself. That's why I propose an access to the Real not grounded on an *axiom*, but on a *demonstrated principle* – the principle of factuality that I'm now going to set out.

The main problem I try to face in *After Finitude* is precisely that of building a materialism – or a realism – able to refute clearly the correlational circle in its simplest form, which is also the form which is the most difficult to fight with: that is, the argument that we never have access to something apart from that access – that the 'in-itself' is unknown since we only know the 'for-us'. Here is my strategy: the weakness of correlationism consists in the duality of its opponents. Correlationism is not, in my definition, an anti-realism but an anti-*absolutism*. Correlationism is the modern way to reject all possible knowledge of an absolute: it is the claim that we are closed up in our representations – whether conscious, linguistic, or historical – with no sure access to an eternal reality independent of our specific point of view. But there are two main forms of the absolute: the realist one, which is a non-thinking reality independent of our access to it, and the idealist one, which is the absolutisation of the correlation itself. Therefore, correlationism must also refute speculative idealism – or any form of vitalism or pan-psychism – if it wants to reject all the modalities of the absolute. But the argument of the circle is useless for this second refutation, because idealism and vitalism consist precisely in claiming that it is the circle itself which is the absolute.

Let's examine briefly the idealist and vitalist arguments. I call 'subjectivist metaphysics' any absolutisation of a determinate human access to the world, and I call 'subjectivist', for brevity, the supporter of any form of subjective metaphysics. Correlation between thought and being has many different forms: the subjectivist claims that some of these relations, or indeed all, are determinations not only of men, but of being itself. He projects into the things themselves a correlation which might be perception, intellection, desire, etc., and makes it the absolute itself. Of course, this process is far more elaborate than I can describe here, especially in Hegel. But the principle of subjectivism is always the same. It consists in refuting realism and correlationism by the following reasoning: Since we cannot conceive a being which would not be constituted by our relation to the world, since we cannot escape from the circle of correlation, the whole of these relations, or an eminent part of this whole, represents the very essence of any reality. According to the subjectivist, it is absurd to suppose, as the correlationist does, that there could be an in-itself different from any human correlation to the world. The subjectivist thus turns the argument of the circle against the correlationist himself: since we can't think any reality independent of human correlations to the world, it means, according to the subjectivist, that the supposition of such a reality existing outside the circle is nonsense. Hence, the absolute is the circle itself, or at least a part of it.

This is why I disagree with Brassier's identification of what I call correlationism with what Laruelle calls 'philosophy'. It seems to me that Laruelle's notion of philosophy as a circle of Decision includes Hegel as well as Kant – idealist speculation with transcendental correlationism. In my view, it is on the contrary essential to distinguish between them since this distinction demonstrates the necessity for correlationism to produce a second argument able to respond to the idealist absolute. This necessity of a second argument is extremely important, since, as we shall see, it will become the flaw of the circle-fortress. This second argument, as I claimed in *After Finitude*, is the argument of facticity, and I must now explain its exact meaning.

I call 'facticity' the lack of reason of any reality; that is, the impossibility of giving an ultimate ground to the existence of any being. We can reach conditional necessity, but never absolute necessity. If definite causes and physical laws are posited, we can claim that a determined effect must follow. But we shall never find a ground to these laws and causes, except eventually other ungrounded causes and laws: there is no ultimate cause, nor ultimate law, that is a cause or a law including the ground of its own existence. But this facticity, this ultimate ungrounding of things, is also proper to thought. The Cartesian *cogito* clearly shows this point: what is necessary in the *cogito* is a conditional necessity: *if* I think, then I must be. But it is not an absolute necessity: it is not necessary *that* I should think. From the inside of the correlation, I have access to my own facticity, and so to the facticity of the world correlated to my subjective access to it. And this because of the lack of an ultimate reason, of a *causa sui*, able to ground my existence.

Facticity so defined is, in my view, the fundamental answer to any absolutisation of the correlation, for if correlation is factual, we can no longer say – as the idealist does – that it is a necessary component of any reality. Of course, an idealist may object that conceiving the non-being of a subjective correlation is a pragmatic contradiction, since the very conception of it proves we exist as a subject – so that we exist, when we speak of non-existence, non-being, we are existing. But we can reply, this time, that we can conceive our facticity even from the inside of the correlational circle, since Fichte himself has proved it. Indeed, Fichte conceived his first principle – I = I, the relation of the I to itself – as essentially ungrounded – in my vocabulary, as essentially factual. Of course, for Fichte, the first principle is not a fact, but an act: the act of conceiving the I. But this act is essentially *free*, according to Fichte – and that means not necessary. We choose whether or not to posit our own subjective reflection, and this choice is not grounded on any necessary cause, since our freedom is radical. But to say this is just to recognise, after Descartes, that our subjectivity cannot reach an absolute necessity but only a conditional one. Even if Fichte speaks abundantly of absolute and unconditional necessity, his necessity is no longer dogmatic and substantial necessity, but a necessity grounded upon a freedom itself ungrounded. There can be no dogmatic proof that the correlation must exist rather than not. Hence this absence of necessity is sufficient to reject the idealist's claim of its absolute necessity.

Correlationism, then, is constituted of two arguments: the circle of correlation against naïve realism – let's use this term for a realism unable to refute the circle; and facticity against speculative idealism, against subjectivism. The idealist, the subjectivist, claims to defeat the correlationist by the absolutisation of the correlation; I believe that we can defeat the correlationist only by the absolutisation of facticity. Let's see why.

The correlationist must claim, against the idealist, that we can conceive the contingency of the correlation, that is: its possible disappearance; for example, with the extinction of humanity. The correlation is contingent: we can conceive the contingency of the correlation. But, in this way, the correlationist must admit that we can positively think of a possibility which is essentially independent of the correlation, since this is precisely the possibility of the non-being of the correlation. We can draw an analogy with death: to think of myself as a mortal, I must admit that death doesn't depend on my own thinking about my death. Otherwise, I would be able to disappear only on one condition: that I was still alive to think of my disappearance and make this event a correlate of my access to it. In other words, I could be dying indefinitely, but I could never pass away, because I would have to exist to make of death a correlate of my own subjective access to it. If facticity can be conceived, if it is a notion that we can effectively conceive – and this must be the case for the correlationist if he wants to *refute* the idealist – then it is a notion we can think as an absolute: the absolute lack of reason of any reality; or, in other words, the effective ability of every determined entity – event, thing, or law of subjectivity – *to appear and disappear* with no reason for its being or non-being. Unreason becomes the attribute of an absolute time able to destroy and create any determined entity – event, thing or law – without any reason for thus creating and destroying.

What I try to show by this thesis concerns the condition of the thinkability of the essential opposition of correlationism: the opposition of the in-itself and the for-us. The thesis of correlationism is that I can't know what the reality would be without me, without us, without thinking, without thought. According to the correlationist, if I remove myself from the world, I can't know the residue. But this reasoning supposes that we have access to an absolute possibility: the possibility that the in-itself could be different from the for-us. And this absolute possibility is grounded in turn on the absolute facticity of the correlation. It is because I can conceive the non-being of the correlation that I can conceive the possibility of an in-itself essentially different from the world as correlated to human subjectivity.

Consequently, I can refute the correlationist refutation of realism, grounded as it is on the accusation of pragmatic contradiction, because *I* discover in correlational reasoning a pragmatic contradiction: the correlationist's fundamental notions – for-us and in-itself – are grounded on an implicit absolutisation: the absolutisation of facticity. Everything can be conceived as contingent, dependent on human tropism – everything except contingency itself. Contingency, and only contingency, is absolutely necessary. Facticity, and only facticity, is not factual, but eternal. Facticity is not a fact, it is not 'one more' fact in the world. I call this necessity of facticity 'factuality'; and the principle which announces factuality, the necessity of facticity, the non-facticity of facticity, I call the 'Principle of Factuality'. Finally, I call *spéculation factuale* speculation which is grounded on the principle of factuality. Through the Principle of Factuality, I can access a speculative realism which clearly refutes, but no longer disqualifies, correlationism. I think an X independent of any thinking, and know it for sure, thanks to the correlationist himself and his fight against the absolute, the idealist absolute. The principle of factuality unveils the ontological truth hidden in the radical skepticism of modern philosophy: to be is to be factual – and *this* is not a fact.

I shall now move on to my last point: intellectual intuition. I used this expression in *After Finitude* to characterise the intellectual access to factuality – that is, the access to facticity as an absolute – and Brassier wrote that such a notion threatens to close me again into the circle of correlation. Intellectual intuition, with its heavy idealist connotation, seems to entail an absolutisation of meaning, hence an absolutisation of thought. It seems to be a dangerous concession made to correlationism. Let's try to respond, to give an answer to this objection.

What did I mean, exactly, by this expression, 'intellectual intuition'? Why did I take the risk of using an idealist expression in order, of course, to subvert its meaning? From now on, I shall use, if you prefer, the oxymoronic term *intuition dianoétique*, 'dianoetic intuition'. I mean by these words, the essential intertwining of a simple intuition and of a discursivity, a demonstration – both being entailed by the access to factuality. Let me explain this point.

Why do I think that Laruelle fails to escape correlationism? It is because he doesn't begin by refuting correlationism but by positing as an axiom, a Real supposed to precede any position. If you begin with the Real, you can't refute the objection of the circle – that is, the Real is a *posited* Real. Laruelle posits the Real as autonomous and deduces from this axiom that thought is contingent for the Real. I believe, on the contrary, that you must begin with correlationism, then show that correlationism must itself posit the facticity of the correlation, and demonstrate in this way that this facticity is absolute contingency. Then, finally, you will accede to an independent Real. Hence, the only way to the Real, according to me, is through a proof, a *demonstration*: a demonstration unveils that facticity is not an *ignorance* of the hidden reasons of all things but a *knowledge* of the absolute contingency of all things. The simple intuition of facticity is transmuted by a *dianoia*, by a demonstration, into an intuition of a radical exteriority. I thought that facticity was the sign of the finitude and ignorance of thought. I thought I had, in facticity, a relation to my own deficient subjectivity. I discover now that what I took for human idiocy was truly an intuition, a radical intuition – that is, a relation to the Great Outside. We have a *nous* unveiled by a *dianoia*, an intuition unveiled by a demonstration. This is why I called it an intellectual intuition: not, of course, because it is an intuition which creates its object, as Kant defined it, but because it is an intuition discovered by reasoning.

I'd like to conclude with a final comparison between the principle of factuality and other philosophies in the twentieth century which tried to access a Real outside the circle of subjectivity, from Heidegger to Derrida. The main difference between these philosophies and *spéculation factuale* is that the latter avoids what I'd like to call the syndrome of a 'Real without realism'. Philosophies of the twentieth century, even when they tried to escape correlationism, generally – not always, but generally – denigrated realism, which was identified with naïve or dogmatic realism. In his book, Brassier excellently presents the significance of these ways of thinking. I quote:

> Thus for much of twentieth-century continental philosophy, from Heidegger and Derrida to Levinas and Adorno, the only conceivable alternative to the Scylla of idealism on the one hand, whether transcendental or absolute, and the Charybdis of realism – which it seems is only ever naïve – on the other, lies in using the resources of conceptualisation against themselves in the hope of glimpsing some transcendent, non-conceptual exteriority.[21]

I think we can say the following: this Real, as a non-conceptual residue of the concept, separates itself from any realism, because it forbids any possibility of a conceptual

---

21. *Nihil Unbound*, 129.

discourse about the Real in itself. We can speak about the Real as the impossibility of any conceptualisation, but we can't conceptualise the Real. There is a disjunction between the Real and *logos*. A realism is, on the contrary, according to me, a *logos* which turns to the Real instead of turning *around* it. But what do I mean by 'turning to the Real' as regards *spéculation factuale*? My thesis is that there are specific conditions of contingency, which I call 'figures'. For example, I try to show that non-contradiction is a condition of contingency, since a contradictory reality couldn't change since it would already be what it is not. The necessity of non-contradiction is for me a consequence of the falsity of the Principle of Sufficient Reason: since nothing has any reason to be and stay what it is, since everything can change without any reason, nothing can be contradictory. That is what I try to demonstrate in *After Finitude*, so that a conceptual discourse about the properties of the Real proves to be possible. We are not condemned to a 'Real without realism'. I refuse this 'Real without realism', because if I don't have a rational procedure to discover specific properties of the Real, those properties threaten to be arbitrarily posited. My own work consists in elaborating this procedure – which I call 'derivation' – grounded on the Principle of Factuality and the conditions of contingency. Producing a procedure of this sort is for me one of the main challenges of a contemporary realism.

To conclude, I would say that what contemporary philosophy lacks is not so much the Real as realism: the Real *with* realism is the true challenge of philosophy, and that's why I think that the title of our day – speculative realism – was perfectly chosen, and is in itself a sort of event.

*

SUHAIL MALIK: If your argument against correlationism is an argument which, as you said, must be a rational argument, and at the same time, the fact upon which your rational argument turns around, is a non-absolutisable fact of the argument for contingency you make, then it seems to me that the fact that's important for your argument is that you can't have absolute reason. So I'm wondering if there's a possible complaint of resurrecting a kind of relativism, because your own reasoning has no absolute reason to it.

QM: I think that the correlationist argument is destructive of the relation to the absolute. If you want to destroy absolutism, you just have to use the correlationist argument. So my strategy is to access the absolute *through* the correlationist argument. The correlationist argument is in fact the demonstration that thinking must think itself as a relation to the absolute. Why? Because as an argument it only works if you suppose that it is possible for it to think its own facticity. But you can't think this facticity without thinking it as an absolute, because if you think that this facticity exists only as a correlate – that the facticity of thinking exists as a correlate of thinking, so thinking itself cannot be factual – facticity disappears. If facticity is a correlate of thought, thought is no longer factual. And if facticity was only thinkable as a correlate of thought, we would be – not just philosophers but everyone – idealist philosophers. We could not even imagine our dying.

Ray has a very interesting reading of Heidegger and being-toward-death. For me, it is not being-toward-death, because death is a correlate of being-in-the-world. Death cannot fight Heidegger because death is a correlate of being-in-the world and *Dasein*. So there is no being-toward-death, because if you want being-toward-death you have to conceive an event able to survive you. You have to conceive a time able to survive you, because if time disappears with you, you don't disappear. To disappear is to disappear in time. This is a demonstration, then. The demonstration of correlationism means the contrary of what it thinks it means, but it is still a demonstration. Now, what is the demonstration, what does it prove? It proves that you can destroy in me the reality of any discourse, as an absolute discourse on absolute reality, using the Rortian tactic of saying that it is contingent: 'Give me the reason why it should be a universal discourse, a universal truth, a universal reality – give me the reason. It's not possible to give a reason.' And I think it's always like that in the history of philosophy. Metaphysics and scepticism – they are always like two enemies fighting against each other, but it is always in scepticism that we discover how to realize metaphysics. Montaigne's scepticism was the key to Descartes' new metaphysics, because it discovered a new way of thinking. I think that contemporary scepticism, the contemporary correlationism, shows us where to look for the absolute. You can pursue contingency, but you can't say that facticity is a fact. If you say facticity is a fact, that even contingency is contingent, what are you saying? The only one who can say that is Hegel. But I think – it's difficult for me to show you – I think that a demonstration is possible.

I think that philosophy can be a discourse constituted by demonstrations if it renounces being a Hegelian demonstration of what there is. But, as I said to Graham, I think that it is possible to strictly demonstrate a certain truth, but this truth being the truth of the radical contingency of things, you absolutely allow for the freedom of all possible phenomenological descriptions and conceptual descriptions of the world. And effectively, I think that speculation can only take the form of this sort of demonstration. Sure, there is no reason to the world, but this absence of reason is not madness. It's not just delirium. You can have reasoning, strict reasoning, supervening on the absence of reason.

DUSTIN MCWHERTER: I want to ask you about something you said earlier. I think, when you were responding to Ray, you said that your project was one of possibility – how is it possible for science to know things about the pre-human world, such as the arche-fossil?[22] But then when you were responding to Graham you mentioned that if everything is factical – if everything is contingent it has to be factical – the only way we can know about *particular* things is through description, like phenomenological description. So my question would be: what would a phenomenological relation to something like the arche-fossil be like? How would that be possible?

QM: In *After Finitude* I try to persuade the reader with what I call 'the problem of the arche-fossil'. The problem of the arche-fossil was for me a way to write in a context

---

22. For 'the problem of the arche-fossil' see **COLLAPSE** Vol. II, 15-54, 83-169.

principally dominated by correlationist philosophy. So I tried to show the correlationist reader – probably a correlationist – that there could be a problem in correlationism. The whole first chapter is saying: maybe there is a problem with this metaphysics … And I just demonstrate the problem like that. Correlationism is just a consequence of Kantian philosophy, and Kantian philosophy is philosophy which pretends to answer the question of how sciences are possible, how physics is possible. Okay, but the problem is that physics describes some reality which precedes the existence of the human and even that of the earth, of any living reality. So, can we explain the meaning of science without the principle of the correlationist philosophy, which says there is no science, no meaning, in affirming that reality could exist without a subjective correlate to that reality? Is the Big Bang just a correlate of a proposition? You might say, 'Ah, your Big Bang is just your correlate'. No, no I assure you it isn't. I'm not that old! There is a problem, there is a little problem here! But, in my view, there is no particular problem in description. You can describe the real fact, but you have to explain how thought is able to speak to a reality which is *not* correlated to thought. That's why my project of realism is to try to respond to the Kantian question of how sciences are possible. It is a transcendental question, but the response, the answer, can't be transcendental. It's always from the inside that I try to defeat the correlationist. It's from the inside – the arche-fossil is a way to challenge the Kantian philosophy from the inside. My problem is a problem of the meaning of the sciences. If sciences have significance, have sense, reality is not merely a correlation of thought – how can that be possible? My project is to derive from a contingency which is absolute, the conditions which would allow me to deduce the absolutisation of mathematical discourse. So it would ground the possibility of sciences to speak about an absolute reality – by which I mean, not a necessary reality, but a reality independent of thought. I mean the physical universe, which is not necessary, but which is independent of thought. There are two senses of 'absolute' here: 'absolute' in the first sense means 'absolutely necessary'. Contingency is absolutely necessary. But in the second sense, 'absolute' is that which is not essentially related to the thing. The physical universe is not necessary, in my view, but *is* absolutely independent of thought. I want to ground the possibility of these two 'absolutes'.

ROBIN MACKAY: Your argument is philosophically positive and constructive, a constructive movement; but on the plane of natural science it seems as if it could be destructive, because you begin with a position where we assume that natural laws are necessary, but we can only assume that *for us*. So, in other words, we have a working system of natural science, but always with a correlationist coefficient added to everything we say. Where we end up is with a situation where you get rid of the correlationist coefficient but instead you have the factical coefficient. So you have the absolute knowledge of contingency – the necessity of contingency – but my question is: can you then replenish this emptiness with natural science? Can you rebuild natural science from that? Because, surely, any scientific statement you make may not be valid tomorrow or in the next minute, so don't you destroy the basis of natural science at the same time as you secure a rational foundation for it?

QM: I say that everything is contingent. So laws, according to me, are contingent. They are not necessary. As Hume said, we are unable to demonstrate any such necessity. I think that irrationality, in fact, is a consequence of believing in the necessity of laws. If you believe that laws are necessary, what are the consequences? 1) You believe that laws are necessary, and 2) You are unable to explain why they are necessary. You are unable to demonstrate the necessity of laws – unless you are Hegel. So you have a mysterious necessity, and if you want to look for God in this mysterious necessity, as the anthropist does, you will find it.

I make a distinction between speculation – what I do – and metaphysics. Metaphysics is dominated by the Principle of Sufficient Reason, and the Principle of Sufficient Reason says that things are necessary. If you think that things are necessary, but you can no longer demonstrate this necessity – unless you are Hegel – then you create a mysterious entity. 'Why are the laws necessary? It's an extremely big mystery'. And this creates a lot of superstition – anthropism, providentialism, etc. 'Oh, we are astonished by the laws, they are incredible. 1) The laws are necessary, 2) They have created man – *there must be a reason*'! No, there is no reason, because they are *not* necessary. That's my response. They are not necessary. 'But how do you know that?' By reason, by my reason. Hume shows that. Hume says just use your reason, faced with the facts. Try and demonstrate that it is necessary – you can't. What does it mean? It means that reason says, 'No, it is not necessary'. And reason has said this very loudly, century after century. It is not necessary. It's just a fact. Reason can't demonstrate that it is necessary

– not because reason is deficient, but because we are mistaken in supposing that it *is* necessary. What makes us believe that these laws are necessary? Our perception, says Hume, our sociality. It's the result of experience, of the fact that laws are stable – stable, not necessary. Stability is not necessity – it's a fact, it's a fact. For example, for an insect I am very stable. If the insect lives for only three days, then I will seem immortal to it. I'm stable, more stable than the insect, but stability does not mean necessity. So, experience says there is stability, and we can say it is not necessity, and who are metaphysicians believing? Reason or perception? Reason or experience? Me, I want to believe reason, and reason says there is no reason. And I don't think this is a destruction of science. Why? Because it is, on the contrary, a rational demonstration that sciences must be empirical. Why can't physicists demonstrate the necessary determination of a law by reason alone? Because these are *facts*, not necessities. We could say, 'Yes, but with your philosophy, laws would disappear in one minute.' But this is probabilistic argumentation. And I try to show this, I try to deconstruct this reasoning, this probabilistic reasoning about the laws. I try to show that in Hume and in Kant you have this sort of reasoning. We believe that if laws were contingent they would change frequently. No, no, no, because we don't have the right to apply probability to the laws, because this would presuppose a totality of cases. But in my view there is no such totality of possibility, because the transfinite of Cantor in mathematics and set theory demonstrated that there is no quantity of all quantities.[23]

---

23. See **COLLAPSE** Vol. II, 55-81.

IHG: I want to ask you about the Principle of Sufficient Reason, which you use exquisitely, I think, and in a properly Leibnizian sense. The Principle of Sufficient Reason asks only that there be a reason for being, not that it be *the* reason, not that there might not be another later – only that there be one. There must be reasoning. And it seems to me that was one of the reasons why you demonstrate, both in your book and in your talk just now, considerable admiration for, and a logical or argumentative indebtedness to, the classical idealists. You have, it seems to me, an homage in your book to Schelling and his critical understanding of Hegel, for example.[24] This is in part a response to what Dustin was saying about saving the sciences, and to go back to the question that Ray raised much earlier in the day which concerns, really, the issue of revisability. We don't need to specify the quantity of sufficient reasons to be given over an infinite time. The Principle of Sufficient Reason merely states that there be *a* reason, not that it be *one* reason. That gets you revisability.

QM: Yes, of course, but I would say, the Principle of Sufficient Reason is able to support a theory of revisability – we can change our reason, etc. But there must be at least one reason. So, you can change a theory, but it is

---

24. *Après la finitude* (AF) overtly seeks to 'renew the thinking of the absolute' (AF 39) in post-Kantian philosophy. For examples of its homage to Schelling, consider Meillassoux's differentiation of subjective from objective, or of transcendental from wild, idealism (AF 35-6); the modal extension of ontology in the form of the '*pouvoir-être*' (AF 73-80) or '*Seynkönnen*'; the asymmetrical and irreversible temporalisation of ancestrality, factuality, and speculation (*passim*). Finally, for Meillassoux as for Schelling, Hegel is the thinker who subjugates difference to identity (AF 95). [– IHG]

not the changing of nature. But what I am trying to do is to claim that nature can change. There is the problem of believing in the necessity of laws, but that's not the problem of believing in the necessity of theories. Nature stays what it is, but theory changes. At the beginning of the twentieth century, Newton perished and Einstein replaced him, but it is not because nature changed in 1905! So, the Principle of Sufficient Reason can extend to, can justify, the evolution of theory, yes. But I want to justify the possible evolution of *nature*.

IHG: So, there needs to be an additional ground.

QM: Without any reason.

IHG: Yes.

PETER HALLWARD: That was a fascinating paper. I'm confused by a very commonsense kind of problem, and I'm sure people have asked you these things many times. But it seems to me that you shuttle between an *ontological* argument that you associate with metaphysics – and particularly the metaphysics of sufficient reason, pre-Kantian metaphysics – and use that to demolish what are essentially *epistemological* arguments that underpin the correlationist post-Kantian position, where, for example, the question of necessity is much more difficult to distinguish from the status of the fact, of the factual. So the question of what is necessary about a certain factual configuration – that we necessarily breathe oxygen, or that gravity has a necessary relation between masses and so on – all those kinds of facts the correlationist says we can *know* as necessary – in other words, as having a rational justification – and so we can have an account of gravity and so on. But the correlationist position is not about the ontological status of things. For the correlationist, it's not that to *be* is to be the correlate of thought. Correlationism is just a bland epistemological argument of what we can *know* about gravity, or about evolution, or those kinds of things. And so I don't see how the correlationist would be affected by your refutation. They would simply say, 'You're telling us that we can *know* things about an absolute reality independent of knowledge', and they would simply ask you, 'Well, tell us what you know about death, or about the Big Bang, and so on, independent of our knowledge of it', and you will be able to tell them nothing. In other words, it would have the status of arguments that justify something like a negative theology: we can reason our way to knowing that there must be something about which we know nothing.

QM: Correlationism – you're right – is not an ontology, strictly speaking. The correlationist – it's true – doesn't say that reality is the correlation. It's the metaphysics of subjectivity that says that. He just says we cannot know anything apart from what we can perceive or conceive, *etc*. That's all. I refuse to say, on the contrary, that I can't say anything about the absolute. If I can deduce from the absence of reason, from contingency, certain aspects of what things in themselves must be like then I am saying something about the absolute. I know for instance that even if we don't exist, whether or not we think, things are non-contradictory. So, my problem is precisely to deduce from facticity some precise, fixed determinations which are able to explain very simple things.

When I look at this bottle, I see qualities which seem to be contingent, but in this bottle there is also something which is not visible, perceptual: its facticity. Its facticity is invisible. Only humans can conceive the facticity of the bottle, because to conceive it means to be able to ask certain questions. And facticity, I believe, is a position which is necessary for correlationism, because correlationism, ultimately, can't answer and doesn't want to answer the question of the ultimate ground. If it could answer it, it wouldn't be correlationism anymore. So facticity is a correlationist thesis. But facticity, for the correlationist, is just our *inability to conceive* the ultimate ground, not the *lack* of an ultimate ground. But what I say is that in conceiving this facticity as just ignorance, you in fact implicitly conceive the capacity of thought to conceive its own end, and thus conceive positively an event which is not dependent on its contingent existence. You – the correlationist – say, 'You cannot say anything about death'. Well, I can't say anything about what it is like to be dead, but I can speak about death as an absolute time which is able to destroy any determined entity, in which respect, the principle of non-contradiction says something about the condition of death. I don't speak of what it is *like* to be dead, of course.

RAY BRASSIER: That was great. It cleared lots of things up. It's just that I wonder if the argument from performative contradiction – the key correlationist argument – is as strong, as irrecusable, as you seem to be suggesting. Because the claim is that to posit something non-posited is a performative contradiction. But the correlationist must claim to know that the difference between the posited real and the non-posited real is already internal to this concept, to this act of positing. So, in other words, how does the correlationist know that there's no difference between the *concept* of an indifferent real and the indifferent real? He accuses the metaphysician of transgressing the bounds of knowledge by insisting that there's a difference between indifferent reality and our *concept* of indifferent reality, but in order to do that the correlationist must know that that difference is itself conceptual. How does the correlationist know that the difference between the concept of indifference and real indifference is itself internal to the concept? Because the act of positing itself presupposes that there's already a relation, and you must know that you exist in order to be positing, and the relation is not self positing. There's always something that seems to kind of escape and precede as a condition of positing. And in order for the correlationist to say, 'Yes, but I've already posited this difference', he must claim that this is already internal to the concept, that it's already internal to thought. In other words, it might be that the argument from performative contradiction used by the correlationist is not as robust and as devastating as they claim it is.

QM: You're asking how the correlationist knows that there is a difference between the X and the posited X?

447

RB: How he knows there is *no* difference – there is a difference but the difference is internal to the act of positing.

QM: In fact, the correlationist says he doesn't know, but he says that metaphysics doesn't know either. He says to the metaphysician, 'How do you know that you are speaking about the X which is essentially the same as the posited X about which you are effectively speaking? How do you know that?'

RB: Okay, but how does he know there isn't a difference?

QM: No, the correlationist doesn't say that he knows that. I will speak for the correlationist … I asked myself a question, a single question. When I was reading Kant, one day I asked myself: for Kant, are we sure that the thing-in-itself is different from the phenomenon? Because we might well think that Kant says: that the thing-in-itself is unknown doesn't mean that the thing-in-itself is different from the phenomenon, it just means that we don't know whether it is the same or not. But the Transcendental Aesthetic, in fact, says we know that the thing-in-itself cannot be the same as the phenomenon. In fact, Kant says three things about the thing-in-itself. He says that the thing-in-itself exists, that the thing-in-itself is thinkable as non-contradictory – that's what the commentators say – but in fact he also says a third thing: that the thing-in-itself is not identical to the space-time phenomenon. He knows that. He knows that by a very interesting argument which says that science can only be about phenomena. So if the thing-in-itself was phenomenal, just empirically known, we couldn't have scientific knowledge of it, because there would be no form, no subjective form which is always the same. For Kant, science is possible because we have the subjective form which is always the same: space, time, and the categories. So if science is possible, it demonstrates that we don't know the thing-in-itself – science demonstrates that we don't have any knowledge of the thing-in-itself. So, for a correlationist, Kant has an argument, a very interesting one – that we know that the thing-in-itself cannot be the same as the posited phenomenon. But I don't even say that, I don't think that. My correlationist is more modest than Kant. He just says that we don't know if the X, the absolute X, is the same as the posited X. Maybe it is the same, maybe, why not? 'But', says the correlationist, 'I don't know if it is the case or not. How could I know? How could I possibly know?' As Hegel said, you cannot surprise the thing from behind to know what it is when we are not there. If we are paranoiac we can install microphones in our house so as to know what people are saying about us when we are not there, but we cannot do that to things. Where are the things? They are not there. We cannot go outside our skin to know what is out there. Maybe the irony would be that this world is in itself exactly as it is for us – wow! In that case philosophers are absolutely useless! Maybe, maybe. Correlationism doesn't say it is impossible, it says it's unknowable.

Notes on Contributors
and Acknowledgements

ARNAUD VILLANI

Philosopher and poet, author of *La guêpe et l'orchidée: Essai sur Gilles Deleuze* (Paris: Belin, 1984) and *Kafka L'ouverture de l'existant* (Paris: Belin, 1999), along with many articles on philosophy, poems and translations of poetry. Co-director, with Robert Sasso, of *La vocabulaire de Gilles Deleuze* (*Cahiers de Noesis* 3, 2003). His most recent books are *Précis de philosophie nue* (Nice: Éditions NU(e), 2005) and *Petites méditations métaphysiques sur la vie et la mort* (Paris: Hermann, forthcoming). He teaches at the Lycée Masséna in Nice.

QUENTIN MEILLASSOUX

A graduate in philosophy from the École Normale Superieur, Quentin Meillassoux wrote his doctoral thesis on *The Divine Inexistence: An Essay on the Virtual God*, and has been teaching philosophy at the ENS since 1997. Author of *Après la finitude: Essai sur la nécessité de la contingence* (Paris: Seuil 2006; English translation *After Finitude*, trans. R. Brassier, London: Continuum, forthcoming 2008).

JOHN SELLARS

Senior Lecturer in Philosophy at the University of the West of England, a Fellow of The London Consortium, and a member of Wolfson College, Oxford. Previously a Junior Research Fellow at Wolfson and a Post-Doctoral Fellow at King's College London. Author of *The Art of Living: The Stoics on the Nature and Function of Philosophy* (Aldershot: Ashgate, 2003) and *Stoicism* (Chesham: Acumen / Berkeley: University of California Press, 2006).

HASWELL & HECKER

Since meeting in Vienna in 1996 Russell Haswell and Florian Hecker have performed together internationally and remixed pioneering artists such as as Voice Crack and Popol Vuh. Having both received Awards in their own right at the Prix Ars Electronica for Digital Music – Haswell with 'Live Salvage 1997 - 2000' and Hecker, 'Sun Pandämonium' – in 2007 they released *Blackest Ever Black: (Electroacoustic UPIC Recordings)*, their first full-length collaborative work together.
http://florianhecker.blogspot.com/; http://haswellstudio.com/

MEHRDAD IRAVANIAN

Mehrdad Iravanian is a leading Middle Eastern architect based in Shiraz, Iran. In 2002 he was awarded the first prize for Urban Landscaping by the prestigious IMM Carrara. He has worked on numerous architectural and urban projects since 1990, including the Quran Gateway, Chamran Park, Garden of Memories and House series. He is currently constructing the *Park of Phenomenology* in Sadra city, Shiraz.

ÉRIC ALLIEZ

Professor at the Centre for Research in Modern European Philosophy at Middlesex University, London. Author of *Capital Times* (trans. G. van den Abbeele, Minneapolis: University of Minnesota Press, 1996), *The Signature of the World: What is Deleuze and Guattari's Philosophy?* (trans. A Toscano, E.R.Albert, London: Continuum, 2004), *De l'impossibilité de la phénoménologie* (Paris: Vrin, 1995), *La Pensée-Matisse* (with Jean-Claude Bonne. Paris: Le Passage, 2005) and *L'oeil-cerveau: Nouvelles histoires de la peinture moderne* (with Jean-Clet Martin. Paris: Vrin, 2007).

452

Notes on Contributors

JEAN-CLAUDE BONNE

Art historian, director of studies at the École des Hautes Études en Sciences Sociales, Paris. Author of *L'Art roman de face et de profil: Le tympan de Conques* (Paris: Le Sycomore, 1984), *Le Sacre royal à l'époque de Saint-Louis* (with Jacques Le Goff. Paris: Gallimard, 2001), and, with Éric Alliez, *La Pensée-Matisse*.

THOMAS DUZER

Studied philosophy and mathematical logic in Paris. Currently working on the non-dialectical passage between Deleuze and Badiou and, in a wider context, on the systematisation of theories of the multiple.
http://www.anaximandrake.fr.

RAY BRASSIER

Research Fellow at the Centre for Research in Modern European Philosophy at Middlesex University, London. Author of *Nihil Unbound: Enlightenment and Extinction* (Basingstoke: Palgrave Macmillan, 2007). Translator of Quentin Meillassoux's *After Finitude* (London: Continuum, forthcoming 2008), Alain Badiou's *Saint Paul* (California: Stanford University Press, 2003) and Editor/Translator of Badiou's *Theoretical Writings* (with Alberto Toscano, London: Continuum 2004).

GRAHAM HARMAN

Professor of philosophy at the American University in Cairo, Egypt, and currently Visiting Associate Professor at the University of Amsterdam. Author of *Tool-Being: Heidegger and the Metaphysics of Objects* (Chicago: Open Court, 2002), *Guerrilla Metaphysics: Phenomenology and the Carpentry of Things* (Chicago: Open Court, 2005), *Heidegger Explained: From Phenomenon to Thing* (Chicago: Open Court, 2007), and *Prince of Networks: Bruno Latour and Metaphysics* (forthcoming).

IAIN HAMILTON GRANT
Senior Lecturer in Philosophy at the University of the West of England. He has written widely on post-Kantian European philosophy and is translator of Lyotard's *Libidinal Economy* and Baudrillard's *Symbolic Exchange and Death* and author of *Philosophies of Nature After Schelling* (London: Continuum, 2006).

*

Translation of 'Mathesis, Science and Philosophy' by Robin Mackay, based on a draft translation by David Reggio published online in draft form by Goldsmiths, University of London in their series 'Working Papers on Cultural History and Contemporary Thought'. With thanks to David Reggio, Thomas Duzer, Christian Kerslake and Knox Peden.

Translation of 'Responses to a Series of Questions' by Robin Mackay, with thanks to Arnaud Villani, and Anne Vignau and Geneviève Bouffartigue of Éditions Belin.

Translation of 'Subtraction and Contraction' and 'I Feel I am a Pure Metaphysician' by Robin Mackay, with thanks to the authors for their help and co-operation.

Translation of 'Matisse-Thought' by Robin Mackay, with the generous assistance of the authors; with thanks also to Kamini Vellodi.

Translation of 'Another World' by Robin Mackay.

Translation of 'In Memoriam' by Matthew Evans and Robin Mackay.

'Speculative Realism' transcribed, edited and introduced by Dustin McWherter, with thanks to the speakers and to Alberto Toscano and Goldsmiths University of London's CSISP.

Accompanying photographs to 'Speculative Realism' by Peter Hallward.

'Computer Deleuze' image (p.4) from a photograph by Marie-Laure de Decker.

Special thanks to Reza Negarestani and Mehrdad Iravanian for technical assistance, to Damian Veal for his meticulous reviewing of the volume, and to Ruth and Donald Mackay for their patience.

Printed in the United States
by Baker & Taylor Publisher Services